THE
RAGMAN'S
SON

KIRK
DOUGLAS

THE

RAGMAN'S SON

AN AUTOBIOGRAPHY

SIMON & SCHUSTER

LONDON • SYDNEY • NEW YORK • TOKYO • TORONTO

First published in Great Britain by
Simon & Schuster Ltd in 1988

Copyright © 1988 by Kirk Douglas

Simon & Schuster Ltd
West Garden Place
Kendal Street
London W2 2AQ

Simon & Schuster of Australia Pty Ltd
Sydney

British Library Cataloguing in Publication Data

Douglas, Kirk
    The ragman's son
    1. American cinema films. Acting.
    Douglas, Kirk – Biographies
    I. Title
    791.43′028′0924
    ISBN 0-671-69959-8

Printed and bound in Great Britain by
Richard Clay Ltd, Bungay, Suffolk

Thanks are due the following publishers for
permission to excerpt certain lines:

"To All the Girls I've Loved Before," by Hal David
& Albert Hammond, © 1975, 1984 April Music, Inc.
& Casa David, 49 East 52 Street, New York, NY 10022.
International Copyright Secured. Made in the U.S.A.
All Rights Reserved. Used by Permission.

"Let Me Live Out My Years," from *Lyric and*
Dramatic Poems by John G. Neihardt. Published by
The University of Nebraska Press.

For my wife, Anne,
who knows Issur better
than I do. . . .

LINDA CIVITELLO worked long and hard in helping me to dig this story out of my guts. Without her encouragement, research, and help in the writing, this baby might never have been born. I wish to express my deep thanks and appreciation to Linda.

CONTENTS

ACKNOWLEDGMENTS

I ALWAYS KNEW that making a movie is a collaborative effort, involving the talents of many people. I assumed that writing my life story needed only one—me. How wrong I was!

I thank my editor, Michael Korda, for his constant prodding; Ursula Obst, for her meticulous criticisms; Mort Janklow and Larry Stein for all their help; Karen McKinnon, my encouraging assistant; and Sonya Seigal, my childhood friend.

I thank them all for teaching me that writing your own life story is still a collaborative effort.

FOREWORD

I STARTED WRITING this book over twenty-five years ago to tell the story of myself and wrote over five thousand pages. Now I find that the story is the search for myself; the telling is the discovery. It's an attempt to delve deep into my past, and more important, into my innards, to put together all the scattered pieces of my life. I will try to place them all in proper perspective to form a mosaic of me, a mosaic that I will dare to look at. I want to evolve a true picture of me, warts and all, that my sons can look at, my wife can look at. Perhaps others will want to see it, too.

The biggest lie is the lie we tell ourselves in the distorted visions we have of ourselves, blocking out some sections, enhancing others. What remains are not the cold facts of a life, but how we perceive them. That's really who we are.

As I plow on the road that I hope will lead to the discovery and fulfillment of myself, I am impatient. I must hurry, for fear that my life will be over before all the pieces of the mosaic are put together and I can step back and look at the finished picture.

THE GOLD BOX

I arrived on this earth in a beautiful gold box delicately carved with fruits and flowers and suspended from heaven by thin silver strands.

My mother was in the kitchen baking bread one sunny winter morning, when she thought she saw something outside. She rubbed the frost from a spot on the window, peered, and saw the beautiful gold box shimmering in the snow. Quickly throwing a shawl around herself, she rushed into the yard, opened the gold box . . . and there I was! A beautiful baby boy! Naked and happy and smiling. She picked me up, very carefully, and holding me close to her bosom to keep me warm, brought me into the house.

And that's how I was born. I know it's true, because my mother told me so.

When I first heard this story, my concern was for the gold box. "But, Ma, what about the box, the gold box with the silver strings? What happened to it?"

"I don't know. When I looked out the window again, it was gone."

"But, Ma, why didn't you grab the box and keep it?"

"Son, when I found you, I was so happy that I couldn't think about anything else."

I was disappointed that my mother had let the beautiful gold box disappear. But I was also very happy, because I was more important to my mother than even a beautiful gold box with silver strings attached to it, going all the way up to the sky. From then on, I always knew that I would be somebody.

But for a very long time, I was nobody.

One

46 EAGLE STREET

"Nobody" meant being the son of illiterate Russian Jewish immigrants in the WASP town of Amsterdam, New York, twenty-eight miles northwest of Albany. It meant living in the East End, the opposite side of town from the rich people on Market Hill. It meant living at 46 Eagle Street, a run-down, two-story, gray clapboard house, the last house at the bottom of a sloping street, next to the factories, the railroad tracks, and the Mohawk River.

My father, Herschel Danielovitch, was born in Moscow around 1884, and fled Russia around 1908 to escape being drafted into the Russian army to fight in the Russo-Japanese War. Those were the days when ignorant peasants like my father, conscripted into the army, had hay tied on one sleeve, and straw on the other, so that they could tell their right hand from their left. My mother, Bryna Sanglel, from a family of Ukrainian farmers, stayed behind and worked in a bakery to earn enough money to come to America two years later. She wanted all her children to be born in this wonderful new land, where she thought the streets were paved with gold—literally.

Ellis Island is a museum now, but between 1892 and 1924 it was the welcoming platform for more than 16 million immigrants coming into this country. Crowded together in steerage, the stink of vomit strong everywhere, they looked in wide-eyed silence at the statue of "Liberty Enlightening the World" on nearby Bedloes Island.

"Give me your tired, your poor, your huddled masses yearning to breathe free." Such lovely, inspiring words, but the immigrants—Poles, Italians, Russian Jews—were herded like animals in pens, rudely treated by functionaries, made to wear cards with their names, or what some clerk guessed were their names, pinned to their clothing. Their papers had to be in order, health exams passed. No matter how rude the reception, they were the lucky ones. Anything was better than where they came from. They passed into this land filled with hope, determination, and a little fear. Only a quarter of a million were sent back. Three thousand of those decided that they would be better off taking their own lives in America than living in the country they had fled.

My mother and father were in the lucky group, happy to escape the pogroms of Russia, where young Cossacks, exhilarated by vodka, considered it a sport to gallop through the ghetto and split open a few Jewish heads. My mother saw one of her brothers get killed on the street in front of her this way.

My father was being trained as a tailor, but his hands were such huge claws that he didn't have the finesse, the delicacy, to hold a needle and maneuver it. So they tied his thumb and forefinger together all day long. It must have been excruciating. It was cold in Russia in the winter, and he had no shoes, only burlap wrapped around his feet. He would hop from one foot to the other, rubbing his foot against his leg.

Somehow, Herschel and Bryna Danielovitch ended up in Amsterdam, New York, and proceeded to have children. In 1910, 1912, and 1914, my sisters Pesha, Kaleh, and Tamara were born. Then me, Issur, in 1916. Then three more girls:

twins Hashka and Siffra in 1918, and finally, Rachel in 1924, when my mother was forty.

"Danielovitch" means "son of Daniel," so I suppose my father's father was named Daniel, but I don't know for sure. Later, we were all called "Demsky," because my father's older brother, Avram, who had preceded him to Amsterdam, was for some unknown reason called "Demsky." So my father became Harry Demsky. (Another brother bought a little shoe repair shop from a man named Greenwald. The name was over the store. A customer walked in and asked, "Do you own this shop?" "Yes." "Now, Mr. Greenwald . . ." For the rest of his life, his name was Greenwald.)

My sisters and I were all born on either the seventh or the fourteenth of the month. One day we were talking about it, remarking on the odds of that happening. We decided to check our birth certificates. We found out that none of us were born on the seventh or the fourteenth. My mother, being illiterate, knew only that we were born in the first or second weeks of the month, which became the seventh and the fourteenth. My birthday, December 9, had always been celebrated on the fourteenth.

I think of my life like a stone thrown into a calm pool. The first ripples are the security of the kitchen. I remember wonderful moments of tranquillity in the kitchen, always a refuge and a haven for me: my three older sisters at school, the three younger ones asleep, or not born yet. Nobody but Ma and me. How peaceful, content, how cozy. Sometimes in the quiet kitchen, the sunlight would dance on the wall in rhythm to my mother's rapid movements as she kneaded the challah, bread for the Sabbath.

"What's that on the wall, Ma?"

"The angels making bread."

I believed what my mother told me. When it thundered, the angels were bowling. When it snowed, the angels were sweeping off the porch of heaven.

I was happy in the kitchen, with the wood-burning stove. It was quiet. No one there but Ma and me and the angels.

Eventually, I had to leave the kitchen. There were moments of adventure in the early morning, when I ran all the way down to the front gate, with just a little shirt on, bare-assed. My mother would come running after me and scoop me up and bring me back in. I felt adventurous, wicked, daring.

I remember my first day at school, that first real trip away from home. I stumbled not far from the house and fell into a mud puddle. I had to go back, bawling, change my clothes, and start off for school again. Dangers lurk ahead when one leaves home! I think of this when I remember my son Peter saying, "I don't want to go to nursery school, Daddy! I want to stay home. I want to stay home!" Yes, he wants to stay home where everything is secure and comfortable. And yet, all of life is pushing kids away from home, enabling them to stand on their own feet. But part of every person doesn't want to go out. Part of every person wants to stay home. Part of every person doesn't want to go into the mainstream of life, and is content perhaps, as I was, to just spend one's life in the comfort of the kitchen.

The first day at school, my older sisters took me to the kindergarten a block away at the Fourth Ward School, which we all called "Fort Wart." They left me at the door, and the teacher took my hand. I remember peering around the corner as my sisters, who seemed so much bigger, went upstairs to the higher grades. I was pulled back into the room with the younger children, away from my sisters, away from my mother.

I had to make the transition from the broken Yiddish/English my parents spoke at home to the English spoken at school. The teacher asked me once where my report card was, and I told her I had left it in the *almer*—the pantry. I knew no other word for this. But I didn't think of it as a failing on my part. I ran home. "You know what, Ma? The teacher is so stupid, she doesn't even know what an *almer* is!" I had probably left the report card there because my parents hadn't signed it. My mother could only make an "X." Years later, I taught her to write her name. She practiced the letters and very painstakingly wrote out her name—Bryna.

When I went to school I was no longer Issur Danielovitch. By now, everyone in town knew us as "Demsky." My father was Harry. My mother went from Bryna to Bertha. My sisters all had American names, too: Pesha was Betty, Kaleh became Kay, Tamara was Marion. The twins were now Ida and Fritzi. Rachel became Ruth. My new name was Isadore, which I have always hated, even though they tried to console me by telling me it meant "Isis adorer"—worshipper of Isis. The nickname was worse: Izzy.

And so it was that little Issur Danielovitch, with his quietness and shyness and dreaminess, his passivity and sensitivity and belief in angels, was left behind, while Izzy Demsky, who was learning how to be tough, went out to face the world in Amsterdam.

Amsterdam, with a little over 31,000 people, was one of the leading industrial cities in the world. Its three huge carpet mills, including Sanford and Mohawk, led the United States in carpet production, rolling out over 12 million yards each year. Its knitting mills made it the greatest producer of mesh underwear in the country, and second in the overall manufacture of knitted goods. It boasted the largest pearl button factory ever built. Every year, nine factories turned out 1.75 million brooms, more than anywhere else in the world, while two silk mills produced 100,000 pairs of gloves. Not one of the thousands of people engaged in any of these enterprises was Jewish. Jews were barred from working in the mills.

So my father, who had been a horse trader in Russia, got himself a horse and a small wagon, and became a ragman, buying old rags, pieces of metal, and junk for pennies, nickels, and dimes. Collecting the things that people had thrown away was an awful way to make a living. Even on Eagle Street, in the poorest section of town, where all the families were struggling, the ragman was on the lowest rung on the ladder. And I was the ragman's son.

Pa was rarely home. He would leave early in the morning to get a shave or a haircut or both. He was always well groomed, but never shaved himself. Then he would go to either Carmel's or DiCaprio's Diner on East Main Street, about a block from the house, for breakfast. Carmel was a very small, nervous Italian man. My father would order a nickel cup of coffee, drink half, and then say, "Carmel, this coffee is too hot. Could you put some more cream in it?" Carmel would put cream into it and refill it and my father would get half a cup of coffee for nothing. The next day my father would say, "Carmel, it's too cold. Could you put some more hot coffee in?" After a while, Carmel was walking around behind the counter muttering to himself and shaking, "Too hot, too cold, too hot, too cold." Finally, one day my father complained about the coffee being too cold. Carmel poured it out of his cup and into a little pot, and warmed it up. My father got mad, and went to DiCaprio's Diner next door. Eventually he'd get into some trouble at DiCaprio's, go back to Carmel's, and start the whole cycle over again.

My father went out every day with his horse and wagon, from street to street yelling, "Rags! Any rags!" He would usually be back by early afternoon. He never worked a full day. Many times, as I was walking home from school, I'd see him riding along on his wagon filled with junk and rags. I'd race ahead, jump up on the back of the wagon, and climb over the junk to sit alongside him. I remember once thinking that this embarrassed him, but I wanted so much to let him know that I wasn't ashamed of him. I wanted so much to let him know how much I loved him.

Then I'd help my father stuff the rags into burlap bags. I'd jab four holes in the top of the bag, lace a woman's discarded stocking through the holes, knot it, and add it to the pile of bags. I got to be quite good at stuffing ragbags; I don't think I'd have any trouble doing it today. The metal—copper, zinc, lead, brass—was all chopped up and separated and piled up in the yard, to be sold later. Our yard was always full of junk.

My father was a big drinker, spent most of his time in saloons, much of it in fights. Once he got into a brawl with seven men. He tossed one through a window, jumped over the bar, and brained a few more with bottles. Laid them all out. In court, the judge looked at the crowd accusing my father of giving them black eyes, broken noses, bruised ribs, and threw the case out: he didn't believe that one man could beat up so many people. There were other stories about my father that raised him to the level of legend: that he popped metal bottlecaps and crushed shot glasses with his teeth; that he would go from saloon to saloon with an iron bar, betting for drinks that he could bend it with his bare hands, and doing it; that nobody could beat him at arm wrestling. He was probably the toughest, strongest Jew in our town, the *bulvan*. There were other Jewish peddlers, but none of them dared to go up on Cork Hill, the Irish section. Pa did. Ma warned me not to be like him.

Pa always managed to find alcohol, even during Prohibition. Many of his friends were Italians who made wine or Ukrainians who made grain alcohol. When these sources were tapped out, he took alcohol wherever he could find it. During one of the holiday services in the synagogue, the rabbis reached for the bottle of wine. Empty. They all knew it could be only one man. My father was sitting in the first row. They said, "Harry, did you drink the wine?" "What are you talking about?" But they could smell it on him. They were going to throw him out of the synagogue, but a friend of my father's, Stan Rimkunas, a Lithuanian auto mechanic who lived up the street, got him a lawyer. The lawyer said that my father wasn't in trouble, the synagogue was in trouble for having alcohol where people could get at it. Now the synagogue was in danger of being closed. The rabbis took my father aside and gave him fifty dollars to drop the charges, which he did. When the lawyer found out, he said, "I hope you got three or four hundred dollars out of this, because it's a good charge." My father was very upset that he had sold out so cheaply. "Oy! Oy! Three, four hundred dollars I coulda gotten. I only took fifty. You shoulda pounded in my head how much it was worth. Oy!"

My poor father! Poor Harry! Why was he a ragman? He had a tremendous personality, could hypnotize people with his dramatic storytelling. Wherever he went, he made an impact. Ragman or not, they all knew him. He would have made a wonderful actor. He was like a character in some of the movies I would later make.

I loved my father but I hated him, too. He was a ragman who drove a horse and wagon and couldn't read or write. But to me he was big. He was strong. He was a man. I didn't know what I was. But I wanted to be accepted by him, to be given a pat on the back. I would walk past the saloon at night, its curtains raised high on the tall windows so that no young boy could peer over them. I'd hear my father's voice in there, in that roaring accent, regaling his drunken cronies with some story about things that had happened in Russia; I'd hear them all burst into laughter. It was the world of men. No women were allowed, and I wasn't allowed either. I kept waiting for my father to take me by the hand into the world of men.

Once he gave me just a taste of it, a tease. One hot summer day, Pa took me by the hand and led me into a saloon. I can see it so clearly, the streaks of brilliant sunlight streaming through the window and then the black shadows in contrast . . . just like the movie sets that I would later play in. No one was there but the bartender. My father bought me a glass of loganberry. Nectar of the gods! I was in the world of men for a brief moment, even though the men had not yet arrived. But I was in their habitat. Later on, I would be in those settings often with Burt Lancaster or John Wayne. It always made me smile, because it seemed to me that we were all still children pretending to be in the world of men.

Walking down East Main Street on his way home, Issur wanted to fly. He wanted to defy gravity and exceed the bounds of the earth. He started to run, faster and faster. Maybe if he gained enough momentum he would rise above the earth and soar toward the clouds. Then he could look down on the people of Amsterdam. He would be completely detached from his environment. Years later, Issur would attain the same detachment by flying off into the souls of other characters, like Vincent van Gogh painting swirling strokes in the blinding sunlight of Arles.

Issur lay on a grassy bank, his hand trailing in the water, looking up at the sky with big white clouds going by, hardly breathing. To do nothing, alone, unseen, was so restful. He was happy to be away from the turmoil of that house at 46 Eagle Street with six sisters and a mother—all women. So often he found himself gasping, engulfed. All those women: Issur didn't know who he was or even who he was supposed to be. Oh, how he needed his father's approval! But his father was away on mysterious male doings, as usual. Issur hated his father—and loved him.

My father was not exactly a good provider, and food was always a problem in our house. Often, we had nothing to eat. I have a vivid picture of our little icebox: the pan underneath to catch the dripping water was usually dry—no money to buy ice. But it didn't matter, because usually there wasn't anything in it to keep cold. Nothing, except in a dark corner, a small can of Mazola Oil, the smallest can you could buy. We were hungry.

I remember my mother so often begging my father, "Hershe, Hershe, the kids need something to eat." He would shrug and say, *"Hob nit,"* a Yiddish abbreviation of "Have not. Haven't got it." Once, when my mother was pleading, he threw fifty cents down on the table. We all clamored about what we should buy. "Let's buy some milk!" "Eggs!" "No, let's get . . ." My father yelled, "I can't stand it! I'll just take the fifty cents and get out of here!" Finally, he left the house and the fifty cents. We bought Cornflakes and milk and stuffed ourselves. I thought about what had happened. "Ma, what did Pa mean? If he took the fifty cents, what would have happened to us?" My mother just smiled enigmatically.

I stole food. I reached under a neighbor's chicken for the warm egg, cracked it open, swallowed it raw in secret. I crept down the steps into the cool, dark cellar where my mother stored the dill pickles she made, lifted up the rock weighing down the wooden lid, dipped my hand into the barrel, fished around in the brine, and pulled out a pickle. Ah, the pleasure of biting into it, crisp and hard and delicious. The price of a tomato from the garden of the Italians next door was an ass full of buckshot, so I swiped fruits and vegetables from the stand in front of a store. One day a man saw me and gave me a long lecture about taking things that didn't belong to me. That shook me up. I never did it again.

I worked, earning money at whatever a child could do: I ran errands, bought candy and soda pop for the workers at the mill next to our house. This was long before vending machines. They lowered long strings with money at the end, I tied a bottle of soda pop to the string, they hauled it up. With the money I got, we could enjoy the luxury of milk and Cornflakes.

Gradually, I expanded my business. I got a wagon, bought my candy and soda pop wholesale, and dragged my wagon around and sold my merchandise through the windows of the mills. My sisters helped me with this, especially the twins, Ida and Fritzi. We lived so close to the mills that sometimes the men would come and tap on the bedroom window and ask when we were going to get their candy. I did pretty well, always contributed two-thirds of what I made to the house, and saved one-third for my escape—college.

Then someone from the mills got the idea of renting out carts to someone inside the mills. They wouldn't let me in anymore. I tried to compete with them from the outside, but they kept chasing me away. That was my first contact with big business.

So I thought I was lucky when I found a few coins in a kitchen cabinet. I ran up the street and bought an ice cream cone—one for me, and one for every kid who came into the store, until the money was all gone. My father kicked the shit out of me.

Sometimes my mother sent my sister Kay and me to Meisel's kosher butcher shop. We would sit and wait while he took care of other customers. After all, we bought the least. Usually it was one pound of meat, at the most two. "Two pounds of meat, and lots of bones, please." Oh yes, lots of bones, those precious things from which my mother could make some soup for us, and stretch that pound or two of meat to feed the entire family. This was the source of nourishment for all of us, this little bundle of meat.

As we left the store, Kay and I would play a terrible game of "Who's going to pick up the meat?" First, there would be an argument about who was going to carry the meat. I insisted that she carry it, she insisted that I carry it. The package of meat would drop to the sidewalk and we'd both walk away. It was a game of nerves: who was going to break first and go back and pick up the meat? The meat, lying there on the sidewalk on the corner, might be scooped up by a dog, or a child, or someone passing by. We'd walk along, each waiting for the other to break. I ran back to pick up the meat more often than Kay.

It was my attempt, even at that young age, to try to assert what I suppose is male chauvinism. My father was rarely around to help me, and here I was trying to assert myself over all my sisters by making Kay pick up the meat. I wanted to feel like a man: I could go out and get the meat, but the woman should carry it. A man is supposed to be strong, to be active, he must do things. He must provide and protect the womenfolk. What a lot of shit that is. All the movements now are encouraging women to be stronger. I'd like to be in a movement for men to be weaker. The right to be weak, the right to be passive, the right to do nothing. Why do men always have to be strong? We're not, and we know it. Why do we force ourselves to play those roles and why do men and women force those roles on each other?

My older sister Marion and I were good friends and used to stroll through town with our arms around each other. One day, we had a picnic. We took a couple of slices of bread with a little butter on them, a quart bottle of water, and went to a grove at the edge of the city. There we sat down with our feast of bread and water. Two girls came along, hitchhiking. They had milk and cake. When they noticed what we were eating, they gave us part of their food. What excitement it was for us! They seemed so wealthy. They were just two girls who had very little money, but to us they were like the rich princesses in fairy tales. Milk and cake!

One Thanksgiving, we applied to the Salvation Army for food. They came to our house to give the food to "Harry Denton." They had gotten my father's first name, but the last name of the family that rented the upstairs. We both claimed the food. They got it.

On our street was every conceivable nationality, a little League of Nations: Italian, Polish, Irish, Russian, German, British, Lithuanian, and probably many others. They had names like Stosh, Ginga, and Yabo. That was *after* they were Americanized. None of us went very far from home; usually we played in the street. Sometimes, we would beg or steal potatoes from home, build a fire in the gutter, and roast them.

Once, after I had my own children, I reprimanded my young son Eric. "Why can't you do simple things like we did?"

"Oh sure," he said, "I'd like to do that. And I'd like to hear you explaining to the Beverly Hills police when they see the fire that I'm roasting potatoes in in the gutter."

Times change.

We had games to initiate a newcomer to the street. One was called "Let 'er Fly." We would tell him to stay on one side of the street, alone. We would all be across from him. He was to turn his back to us, count to ten, then turn and face us, and yell, "Let 'er fly!" While he was counting we picked up all the debris we could find. When he turned and faced us and yelled, "Let 'er fly!"—we did.

Another game was more sophisticated. The new boy in the neighborhood would lean against the fire hydrant, count to ten, and yell "Church on fire!" We all helped put it out by pissing on him.

I always liked "Wolfie," real name Wilfred Churchett. He was three or four years older than I, with a gentleness about him that was soothing after the rough gang on my street. I often sat on his front stoop playing a game of baseball that he had created. It was a cutout, a piece of cardboard, with different sections marked "Base on balls," "Sacrifice bunt,"

"Two-base hit," "Trickle to pitcher," "Outfield error," etc. Then he would put in an arrow and spin it around. Since there were seven kids in our house and my mother and father made nine, he would make the whole Demsky family a baseball team and get each one up to bat and spin around and see what happened. I was delighted when my mother got up to bat and hit a home run.

When I was about eight, they were building another mill near my house. A huge, deep trench was dug for the foundation. A pipe broke, filling it with water. One Saturday, wearing my best clothes—a little suit—I tried to walk across the trench on a pole, slipped, and fell in. The other kids ran away, frightened. The water was well over my head. I was drowning. Suddenly there was Wolfie, who couldn't even swim, rushing toward me. He pulled me out. He brought me home crying and soaking wet. My father started to beat him up, thinking that Wolfie had pushed me in. When he found out that I had just fallen, my father beat me up instead.

Wolfie was such a nice, gentle person. I never forgot him. He was amazed that I sent him money regularly for many years. If he hadn't pulled me out of that ditch, I would have been just the little eight-year-old boy of a large family that died years and years ago. Wolfie died in 1986. I'll miss him.

Sometimes my father sold fruits and vegetables in baskets. I liked this better, but he didn't do it often. He might have a wagon load of potatoes, and I can hear his voice now yelling, "Yeaaa, 'Tatoes! 'Tatoes!" Once he had a pile of new baskets stacked against the wall of the house in the back. I was alone. Matches in hand, I went around burning up little scraps of paper in the yard. One ignited the baskets. They erupted into flames; the whole side of the house started burning. I ran up the street to my Uncle Morris's where my father was, screaming that the house was on fire. He leaped on the wagon and went hurtling down to the house. By the time he got there, the neighbors had put out the flames. I got the worst shellacking I had received in a long time. My father collected some insurance money on the house, but never did anything about fixing the burned boards.

I have always suspected that this was not an accident on my part, but subconscious arson. I really wanted to destroy the whole house. There was an awful lot of rage churning around inside me, rage that I was afraid to reveal because there was so much more of it, and so much stronger, in my father. My mother was always saying, "Don't be like your father. Be a good boy, be a good boy." That made me angry! What should I be like? My mother? My sisters?

When they took me out of my older sister's bed, they put me on a hard sofa alone in the parlor. I was frightened. I missed not being next to the warm body of Betty, of having her read to me from *The Bobbsey Twins* or the Frank Merriwell stories. Everybody had somebody to sleep with: my mother and father together, three of my sisters in one bedroom, three in the other. Everybody but me, all alone in the parlor.

Alone except for the hoboes, gaunt and dirty, rootless and nameless, who rolled off the trains at night and looked in the parlor window. They frightened me.

Issur lay awake in the dark, eyes straining up toward the ceiling. He worried about the gas. Issur knew people had been killed by escaping gas fumes. He had seen them being carried away.

Were all the gas jets off? Issur got up from the hard sofa and tiptoed into the kitchen. He checked the two gas knobs on the small range. He did it carefully, so that his damp fingers would not let the gas escape and seep into the rooms where Ma and Pa were sleeping, or the rooms where his sisters slept.

Quietly, Issur placed a chair under the gas light in the middle of the room, climbed up. He was ever so careful to check the spigot and make sure it was completely off. And he had to be careful not to knock the light and break the gas mantle, the delicate core. If it was broken, there would be no light. And the gas mantle cost fifteen cents!

Satisfied that all the gas jets were turned off completely, Issur would go back to the sofa. Sometimes he got up again, terrified that there was one jet he had left partially open. Every night, he repeated the ritual.

Maybe one night Issur would OPEN all the jets and let the gas silently slip into the house and kill all of them.

It was cold in upstate New York in the winter. We used a thrifty, age-old peasant method of insulation. We had a fenced-off section in the backyard next to the barn where my father kept Bill, the horse that pulled his wagon. All year long, we threw the horse manure in there and let it pile up. In the fall, I helped my father build a low wooden wall around the base of the house. We filled this with the collected horse manure, and it helped to insulate the house during the winter.

Often, on winter evenings, I would lean on the fence in front of the house, chin resting on top. It was nice to get away from all the hubbub inside. I would look at the mounds of snow in the gutters, dark blue in the light coming from the mill windows. Leaning there, my face stiff with cold, I would dream. When I grew up, where would I be? What would I be? I would dream about far-off places and wonder what people were doing at that precise moment, people that I might meet later on in life. The piercing scream of the mill whistle cut through my reveries. Six o'clock. I watched white steam from the whistle shoot up into the darkness. I thought it was the steam from all the factories that made white clouds in the sky; the dark rain clouds were caused by black smoke from the smokestacks. The workers came pouring out of the mill and hurried home. I went inside, my dreams ended.

Christmas was not a holiday we celebrated. Nevertheless, we resented that Santa Claus never came to our house. Until one Christmas Day, we woke up and there were stockings filled with fruits and nuts and candy—and *toys!* And best of all, Pa was there. We all demanded in a chorus, "What happened?" He told us, very dramatically, that when he had come home the night before, he heard a whirring and a whirling and he looked up and there was a sled with reindeer racing through the sky and it came and landed on the roof of our house. He told us that a big, fat man with rosy cheeks and a white beard and a red suit came down the chimney and said, "Hullo! Danielovitch?" My father answered, "Yes!" and Santa Claus left all these things. I remember how we all sat, our eyes wide as we listened to my father telling us about the one Christmas that Santa didn't forget us. Those nuts and candy and apples . . . nothing had ever seemed so delicious.

That is a rare memory of my father. It hurts. If he could be like that once, why couldn't he do it more often?

I found a mongrel dog I named Tiger, part Doberman and part hound. He was my friend, big and powerful and male. I loved him very much, and he loved me. I'll never forget when I used to come home from school. Way down the street, I could see his head by the gate, looking for me. As soon as he saw me, he'd race like mad up the street and knock me down and lick my face while I laughed. He was a wonderful protector. When I played games, if any of the other boys yelled at me or made threatening gestures, Tiger was there, growling, ready to spring to my aid.

During the winter, I would hitch him to my "sled"—a trash-can lid, or some barrel staves. Tiger was so powerful, he would pull me along, much to the envy of the other boys. I loved that dog. And then one day someone said, "I think your dog got run over." I couldn't believe it. I ran up the street and sure enough, Tiger was lying in the gutter, blood coming out of his mouth. Dead. I was completely indifferent, numb at the loss of my best friend. I felt nothing, shed no tears. Thirty years later, on a psychiatrist's couch, I recounted the story and burst out sobbing.

In the spring, we emptied out the frozen manure insulation, which no longer had a smell, and used it for fertilizer around the house, especially for a large white lilac bush in the front yard. Everyone else on Eagle Street had purple lilac bushes; we had the only white one. It was the one thing of beauty we had, and I was proud of it.

Bill was a great horse, big and white. When you unhitched

him from the wagon, he walked right into the barn. My father never tied him up. I would feed Bill hay and oats, struggling with both hands to lift his pail of water, which my father did so easily with just a few fingers.

Sometimes, when my father came home, he would stop by O'Shaughnessey's Saloon, on the corner of Eagle Street. He would jump off the wagon and give Bill a slap on the rump. Bill would trot down to the end of the street, pulling the wagon, turn up our driveway into the yard, and just stand there and wait patiently until my father was through and could come back to unhitch him and unload the wagon.

On hot summer nights, Bill would go for a walk. He would just walk out of the barn. But he wouldn't go up the road. He would walk on the sidewalk—clip-clop—at a very leisurely pace, halfway up the street. People became accustomed to seeing Bill on the sidewalk. Then he would turn around and stroll back to the barn.

In the winter, my father didn't work very much, so Bill just stayed in the barn, except for the times he would walk over to the mill yard next door, race around, roll in the snow, and come back.

One night the barn caught fire. I didn't do it! My father tried to get Bill out of his stall, but Bill was petrified and wouldn't move. Pail after pail of water was useless. My father came out of the barn, coughing from the smoke, and alone. Bill was engulfed in flames. We heard the crackle of burning horseflesh, but I can't remember hearing any sound from Bill.

When the Fire Department finally arrived and put out the fire, it was all over. Bill, the white horse, lay stiff and charred black.

One night I was playing tag when I fell and split my head open. I was bleeding and crying. The other kids picked me up and were carrying me home. I looked up and saw my father walking home on the other side of the street. I was so glad to see Pa. He looked over at me, and said, "That's what you get for going out and playing." I would have given anything if he had come over to me, leaned down, and said, "Son, how do you feel? Are you all right?" But he wasn't capable of that.

On one of the rare occasions when my father ate with us, we were all sitting around the table, drinking tea in a glass, Russian style. Pa held the glass of hot tea in his hand, bit off a hunk of sugar and slurped the tea through the sugar. He sat there, sullen, so big, so strong, so quiet, ignoring us all. The more I looked at him, the weaker I felt, until I was sure I would die if I didn't do something. Suddenly, I found myself taking a spoon and filling it with hot tea from my glass, David facing Goliath. My sisters were all looking at me, holding their breath. I took the spoon carefully in my hand, and I flicked it across the table, right into my father's face. He let out a roar like a lion, reached across the table and grabbed me, just lifted me up and flung me through a door into the next room. I landed on a bed. I like to think that he was aware that the bed was there when he threw me. All my family, including my mother, were petrified.

I was triumphant. I had risked death and I had come out alive. I always look back at that as one of the most important moments of my life. If I hadn't done that, it seems to me that I would have drowned, perhaps in that mass of women I was living with. I know that flicking that teaspoon of tea in his face made me feel different from my sisters—a man. He couldn't ignore me. At that moment, he knew I was alive. I have never done anything as brave in any movie.

I remember Friday nights very well. That was the Sabbath. Friday during the day, my mother worked harder than usual, putting everything in order, cleaning up the house, kneading and shaping the loaves of sweet egg challah, decorating the top with clasped hands sculpted from the dough, and painting it all with a shiny egg varnish. She made chicken soup with egg noodles rolled out and cut by hand and left to dry on clean sheets on the beds. Sometimes there was fish, a large carp flapping in the bathtub until my mother cooked it. Being an Orthodox Jew and keeping kosher is a tremendous amount of work for a woman. Meat had to be killed a certain way and the blood drained out of it. You had to keep two sets of dishes, one for meat products, and one for dairy, just for daily use. There were a third and fourth set used for nothing but Passover.

On Friday night, my mother would light the candles. I remember those four candle holders. Two of them were quite tinny, but the other two were very solid-looking, and very old, and were handed down from my mother's mother and who knows how many people before that. Then we would walk to the Orthodox synagogue nearby on Grove and Liberty streets. I remember watching all the old Jewish men with big beards praying and singing ancient Hebrew songs. I always had the feeling that God must be a really old, old man, with a big beard, because they all seemed to be in such close touch with him, and he seemed so far away to me.

The Sabbath was the only time Ma was not in constant motion—washing, ironing, cooking, cleaning. Saturdays, she sat in a rocking chair with her Hebrew Bible, the only thing she could read, even though she couldn't understand the words. On her face was a wonderful serene smile.

Do you realize how much time you spend praying if you are an Orthodox Jew? Every morning I tied phylacteries, amulets containing scriptural passages, to my forehead and left forearm, and prayed for at least fifteen to twenty minutes. And that was if I raced through it. Every day after regular school, fighting my way back and forth to Hebrew School through the gangs—another hour and a half. Every Friday night at the synagogue to welcome in the Sabbath. Back to the synagogue Saturday morning for another three hours. Sunday morning—Sunday school. All this for the reward, at thirteen, of becoming Bar Mitzvah.

But what was sometimes a chore for me must have been heaven for Ma—to be able to sit quietly and pray, out in the open, without having Cossacks gallop by and club you to death. But as much as they enjoyed their religious freedom in America, Jews like my mother would never think of forcing it on other people. That was what had been done to them in Russia. That's something I don't understand, even today

—people pushing to get prayer in the public schools. If these people are so religious, why don't they say their prayers at home in the morning with their families, and let the schools teach what they're supposed to?

The Bible stories frightened me. Jehovah seemed such a cruel old man. I was afraid of him and didn't like him. A thought, needless to say, that I shared with no one. The picture from my Sunday school book is vivid in my mind. Abraham grasps his son Isaac in one arm; in the other he has a raised knife. He is remonstrating with the angel, who is trying to stop him from fulfilling God's commandment— "Sacrifice your son Isaac as a burnt offering to me." Isaac's eyes are open wide with fear. That little kid looked a lot like me. God had to come and help the angel and reassure Abraham that he was only testing him.

Now, is that any way for a God to act? Don't you think he's taking advantage of his position? Don't you think he's cruel? Would my father use the knife that he cut holes in ragbags with to slit my throat if God asked him? It scared the hell out of me!

I also didn't like the way God treated Moses, who had a speech impediment and had to have his brother Aaron speak for him. And yet God insisted that Moses deliver the Jews from the bondage of slavery in Egypt into the land of milk and honey—Canaan, Israel. It took Moses forty years of wandering. He went to the mountaintop and saw the face of God when he received the two stone tablets with the ten commandments. When he came down to deliver them to the people, they were worshipping a golden calf. In a rage, he smashed the tablets. I always admired that anger in Moses. It made him human. Then he had to go back up the mountain to get another set of commandments. And what was his reward? To be told that he would not be able to enter the Promised Land. Why? Because he had seen the face of God. It's pretty hard to like someone who behaves that way!

It's tough enough to be a Jew, but it was very tough in Amsterdam. There were constant reminders. No Jews worked in the carpet mills. No Jews worked on the local newspaper. No Jewish boys delivered the newspaper. Kids on every street corner beat you up. Why? Who taught them that? Their parents! After school each day, I'd have to walk about twelve blocks to Hebrew school. I had to run the gauntlet, because every other street had a gang and they would always be waiting to catch the Jew boy. There was a Lark Street gang, the John Street gang, the Kline Street gang. They would throw things, so I had to try to go around the street. Sometimes they would catch me and beat me up. I'll never forget the first time that I was beaten up by a bunch of kids who kept punching me, yelling, "You killed Jesus Christ!" I ran home, my nose streaming blood. "Ma, what did they do that for? They said I killed Jesus Christ. I don't even know who he is!" What a terrible way of life. I resented it, but had to accept it because that's the way it was. And I remember my mother quietly saying to me, "As a Jew, you will always have to be twice as good to get ahead in life."

There were very few Jews in the town of Amsterdam. There was no threat from them. I think that on Eagle Street there were only two Jewish families, including ours. But still, there was a tremendous hatred of Jews.

The kids weren't to blame. What do parents say when they're around the dinner table with their young children? What remarks do they make about "those kikes," or "those spics," or "those wops"? So often, later on, I'd be talking to people I thought wouldn't be that way, only to hear them say things like, "He tried to Jew me down." They learned it from their parents.

And their churches. It was not until 1965 that the Roman Catholic Church declared that Jews could not collectively be blamed for the death of Jesus, and decided to actually admit the fact that Jesus was Jewish. This was about the same time they decided that Galileo might have had a point when he said that the planets revolved around the sun, not the earth, and reconsidered their excommunication of him three centuries earlier.

But what about the local newspaper, the *Amsterdam Evening Recorder?* My friends had jobs delivering papers for them, but I couldn't get a route. It took me a long time to realize why. So I had to take a job delivering the Schenectady paper, which was much harder. Almost everybody in Amsterdam got the *Recorder*, so you went up one street and down the other delivering the papers, and that was your route. But almost nobody took the Schenectady paper, so I had to cover half the town.

All Jews are lonely. I think we all have hidden scars. I think all Jews go through a period of hating being a Jew. I did. There was a time when, if someone asked, "Are you a Jew?" I would gulp and say, "I'm half Jew." I would vary the blame—sometimes it was my father who was a Jew, sometimes my mother, but not both. Being half a Jew did not seem quite as bad as being a whole Jew. How sad.

I think the strongest anti-Semitism sometimes exists among Jews. To this day a German Jew often hates Russian or Polish Jews. There are German-Jewish clubs around this country that did not allow Russian or Polish Jews when they first started. Some have relented a little, but not all. I'm sure that when Hitler started, many German Jews didn't mind what he did to other Jews. They didn't expect him to turn on them. Isn't it ridiculous? But if anti-Semitism can exist among Jews, why shouldn't it exist among others?

When I was twelve, I used to chant the Friday evening services at shul. *"L'chu Nerauany, L'adonai, Nariyah, Yshur, Mishenu."* Before I was even Bar Mitzvah, the people in my synagogue wanted to send me to school to become a rabbi. This was considered a great opportunity for a poor Jewish boy. But how could I tell those fine Jewish people that I didn't want to become a rabbi, I wanted to be an actor.

I have always wanted to be an actor, I believe from the first time I recited a poem in kindergarten about the Red Robin of Spring. They applauded. I liked that sound. I still do.

In second grade, I played the shoemaker in "The Shoemaker and the Elves." It was quite an event. Children from all different schools came to East Main Street School for an evening festival. My mother sewed a little black apron for my costume. My father seemed to have no interest in any of the things any of his children did. But without my knowing it, he came in and watched the play from the back of the auditorium. I had no idea that my father was there; I never expected him to come. But he was there and he saw the show. And after it was over, he bought me an ice cream cone. He didn't say much, but he bought me an ice cream cone. That memory is so vivid. That was the man who had played Santa Claus, years ago. No award I have ever received has meant more to me than that ice cream cone.

One summer, when I was eleven or twelve, I hitchhiked to Schenectady, fifteen miles away. It was my first long trip, my first adventure away from Amsterdam. I finally arrived in the metropolis of Schenectady. How large it was! The streets were so wide! And Proctor's movie theater was so much bigger than anything in our town. There was something frightening about being off in another world. I hurried back. And yet I longed for the ripples in the stream of my life to widen and widen. Would I ever really leave my hometown?

I loved the circus, the carnival, that strange world of people and animals that arrived in town overnight, changing a quiet, deserted field into a world of exciting lights and noise. I loved watching the hucksters urging people to try their luck knocking down dolls with three balls. The dolls were heavily fringed with yarn, allowing the balls to go whizzing through.

I was frightened, but fascinated by the freaks. Once I got into a fight with one of the carnival boys. The boy bloodied my nose, while the other members of his carnival family urged him on. I felt very alone. No one was encouraging me. I didn't want to fight; I wanted to join the carnival boy and become part of his family.

But the carnival always moved on, gone in the middle of the night, just as it had come. I would walk over the deserted, quiet fields of debris that they left behind. Where did they go? Where are they now?

When I was twelve, I had my tonsils taken out. It was not in a hospital but in a doctor's office. He did it all himself, with no nurse. My mother went with me, but I didn't want her to be in the room when he was cutting out my tonsils. The doctor administered the anesthesia, and I remember going to sleep. While I was under, I had a vivid dream. In it, there were two of me, Izzy and Issur. Izzy was laughing hysterically with contempt at Issur, who was frightened, tiny. Issur's nose was running and he tried to hide. He didn't like to be laughed at, but Izzy found him out: "I see you there, hiding behind the garbage pail. Come on out, come on."

"Please leave me alone. I don't want to come out."

But Izzy just kept taunting Issur and laughing hysterically.

When I came to, I saw my mother there. I felt dizzy. The doctor had left the room. I felt I was going to faint and I asked her to leave me alone. "Go away, Ma. Please leave me alone."

As I was losing consciousness, I heard her calling for the doctor.

I remember that incident very well. Little Issur has never left me. He is always somewhere within me, often out of sight, but never too far away. Sometimes I catch glimpses of him scurrying around. He wears a little shirt and his ass is bare. His face is dirty and smudged by tears. That's Issur, and he hasn't changed. Often, I tried to kill him, but he never dies. I hate him—and yet sometimes I love him, because he has never deserted me.

Thirteen is the age of Bar Mitzvah, when a Jewish boy becomes a man. I recited the Hebrew words, gave a speech in Yiddish. I got a few gold pieces as presents. Those, added to what I'd saved working, amounted to $313, a fortune in those days. My father asked to borrow it from me. He wanted to buy up a lot of metal, because the prices were so cheap, and then sell it at a killing. This was his big chance. My mother pleaded with me not to give it to him. She knew I was saving it for college. But there was nothing that could have prevented me from giving it to him. I was proud of it.

The time came for my father to negotiate with scrap-metal dealers to sell all the metal he had collected. Copper was selling for around twenty-four cents a pound. Unfortunately, it was 1929, and the bottom dropped out of the scrap-metal market about the same time it dropped out of the entire United States economy. A week later they said, "It's twenty cents a pound." My father was yelling, "What do you mean? You were paying twenty-four!" A few days passed, and it was eighteen cents, then sixteen, fourteen, twelve, eight, four cents a pound. My father finally had to sell the metal for about two cents a pound. That was what the Depression meant to me, that prices came tumbling down and my father lost my savings. Our scale of living wasn't much different before, during, or after.

My older sisters wanted to better our living conditions. Betty, now twenty, had left school in the ninth grade to work, and had been the major support of the family. We were all working now, had changed the gaslights to electricity, gotten a telephone. We all chipped in and got Ma some teeth. My mother had been toothless as long as any of us could remember. It was a shock to see her with her new teeth. Kay ran out of the house crying, "That's not Ma!" but the house was still just a dilapidated house next to the mills, and my sisters were going on dates now and wanted something better.

Bitter arguments developed in the kitchen at 46 Eagle Street. My father didn't want to move. As I look back, it seems to me that he was hanging on to some last shred of dignity. Poor Pa, the head of the household, with six daughters, his wife, and one son.

I never, never heard my father call my mother by her name, Bryna. Instead, he said, "Hey you!" or "Tell the missus," or "Where's the mama?" I rarely remember him having a conversation with my mother, let alone any of the rest of us. And yet, they slept in the same bed—when he was home. And, with seven kids, they must have had some kind of communication.

Often, when he was home, he would pace back and forth in the kitchen. Back and forth, endlessly. He would stop at the window, peer out into the yard. And then, back and forth, the muscles in his jaw twitching.

I never took my eyes off of him. He didn't seem to know I was there. What was he thinking? About early days in Russia when he was a *balegale,* a taxi driver with a horse-drawn sled? Or maybe of his early dreams: America, the land of opportunity, the land of plenty. Did he consider himself a failure who could not provide for all those mouths?

And now, they were threatening to move away, to a different street, a better house. What should he do? If only Pa had said, "Stay with me, son." But Pa said nothing. He stormed out of the house, to O'Shaughnessey's or Boggi's saloon, a world where men drank and forgot their problems. And he left me in a world of women.

I left Pa at 46 Eagle Street, pacing the kitchen, and went off with my six sisters and my mother. And I felt as if I had been circumcised again and a little more of my cock had been cut off. From that day on, until I left Amsterdam, I was gasping for breath.

As we left the house, my last thought was: it's fall. Who will help Pa put the horse manure around the house?

Two

HIGH SCHOOL

"You are certainly not college material," my French teacher told me. That made me feel terrible. Maybe she was peeved that I was the pet of another teacher—tall, patrician Mrs. Louise Livingston, a graduate of Mount Holyoke College, member of the Daughters of the American Revolution, head of the English Department, a widow with a son five years older than I. She changed my life. She introduced me to the world of poetry—Byron, Keats, Shelley. She became my confessor and listened to the dreams I didn't dare tell anyone else. I would have been run out of the East End if I had ever admitted to liking poetry or said out loud, "I want to be a great actor."

"To be a great actor," Mrs. Livingston said, "you have to be a great person. You must be educated. You must be trained." Because of her, I sent away for college and drama school catalogues and saved every penny so I could get there.

Most students, including me, were afraid of Mrs. Livingston. I met her when another teacher sent me to her for disciplining because I had failed to turn in a book report on *David Copperfield*. I read the book, but didn't do the report. She questioned me thoroughly, was impressed with how much I understood and retained. But she marked me down for being late with the report.

Mrs. Livingston was cool and detached when she walked into the classroom. She never raised her well-modulated voice. Emotion crept in only when she read poetry:

> *God knows 'twere better*
> *To be buried deep*
> *In silk and scented dawn,*
> *Where love throbs out*
> *In blissful sleep.*
> *Pulse nigh to pulse*
> *And breath to breath.*

I used to get a funny feeling when she read those lines, and I looked at her in reverence. I composed my first poem and recited it in class with great feeling:

THE DISCARDED SHIP
by Izzy Demsky

> *Above me have flown many flags*
> *But now my sails are torn to rags*
> *My bows are white from swirling foam*
> *As o'er the many seas I roam.*
> *But now there's nothing left for me*
> *I live in days that used to be.*

Mrs. Livingston thought I was wonderful. She encouraged me and kept me after school. I liked that. I was late for work, but I liked being with her. We sat at her desk next to the window, looking out over the beautiful autumn landscape, in that light that precedes dusk. What a sparkle came into her eyes as she read poem after poem with me sitting by her side. "Oh, I'm in love with the janitor's boy/And the janitor's boy loves me."

Her hand reached under the desk and clutched my hand close to her thigh. The colors of the autumn leaves raced around in my head. I hoped she couldn't hear my heart beating. It was so loud. And my hand touching her thigh was so sweaty. I hoped it didn't rub off on her thin silk dress. I tried to draw it away, slowly, but she held it more tightly, as she went on in a reverie: "And he's going to build me a green isle/A green isle in the sea."

I left, late for work, and as I ran down the school steps littered with leaves, I looked back. She was standing at the window watching me. Wow! I must be the janitor's boy!

I couldn't wait for her to walk into class. Each day, using the words of Keats, Byron, Shelley, we spoke to each other. I can hear her now:

> *Beauty is truth, truth beauty—that is*
> *All ye know on earth,*
> *And all ye need to know.*

She would call on me to read, and I did, with a little too much emotion.

> *For thou wast that all to me, love,*
> *For which my soul did pine—*
> *A green isle in the sea, love,*
> *A fountain and a shrine,*
> *All wreathed with fairy fruit and flowers*
> *And all the flowers were mine.*

She asked me to come by and help her with some English papers one evening. She lived in what I thought then was a spacious room on the top floor at 34 Pearl Street, a three-story home that had been converted into a boardinghouse. She shared the bathroom down the hall with several other schoolteachers who lived there.

That first night, I was sitting on the bed—she kissed me.

My lips felt so hot, I thought they would burst into flames. She held me and wanted to do more, but I was too frightened, just a fumbling schoolboy of fourteen. I kept saying, "No, no, no." I had never had sex. Oh, I knew about masturbation. That was easy, alone in a dark room with your fantasies. But this was real. So much white skin, and such a large, dark, bushy spot. So mysterious. My heart pounding hard, I ran out of the room before I had pierced any mysteries. It wasn't very late. The streets were quiet, and under the harvest moon, I never stopped running until I reached home.

I was angry with myself. Why hadn't I done it? I wanted to. Why was I afraid? All the words of the great poets didn't help. I was sure she would never invite me back again.

But she did, many times, and our relationship endured through high school, college, New York, and Hollywood, even though we saw each other less and less and the letters became fewer as we grew older and I traveled to different countries making movies. I helped take care of her until she died. I was her "janitor's boy," and she left me a book of poetry that she had written and published, each page a different moment during the years of our friendship and love.

One of my best friends in high school was Pete Riccio. He was a handsome Italian boy. He didn't live far from me, with his mother and eight younger brothers and sisters. He would often joke: "Of course, you come from a small family of seven kids, so you don't know the problems of a large family." Pete was about five years older than I. He had quit school after junior high, when his father had died, and had gone to work for five years in the carpet mills, ten hours a day, thirty-five cents an hour. When he came back to finish school, we were in the same grade.

His mother was a wonderful woman. Often, I had delicious dinners of chicken cacciatore and spaghetti at their house. I've liked pasta ever since. Pete would come to our house and share our dinner, usually eggs scrambled with water.

Pete and I were together often. On warm evenings, we

would spend hours and hours talking and talking. When other kids were out playing around, we'd go to a park, sit on a bench, and talk. We would exchange dreams. I was going to be a great Broadway stage actor and he was going to become the governor of the state of New York. Neither of us attained our dreams.

I had another friend in high school, a girl named Sonya. She was very bright, and pretty, wore no makeup. I would walk to her house in the evening sometimes, munch on apples, and talk and talk. We have remained friends through the years, writing back and forth. Sonya has kept track of me better than I have of myself; her scrapbooks and memory and energy proved to be an enormous help when I set out to rediscover my past by writing this book.

Issur would walk along the railroad tracks at five-thirty every morning to meet the train from New York that dropped off newspapers and magazines. New York City. It was one hundred and eighty miles away. It might as well have been on another planet, but Issur was more fascinated by the trains that didn't stop in Amsterdam, like the famous Twentieth Century. Sometimes, when the wind blew in the right direction, Issur would be hypnotized watching them hurtling silently toward him. Not a sound. And then they raced past in a ROAR while Issur got a quick glimpse of sparkling white tablecloths, black waiters, gleaming silverware. Then the thundering roar dissolved back into silence. How Issur longed to be on that train, speeding to some far-off destination. Where were they rushing?

Maybe California. Issur's Uncle Morris had gone to California. When Issur asked, "Where's California?" he pointed west, where the sun was setting, golden behind pink-streaked clouds. "What a beautiful place," Issur thought. "Will I ever get to California?"

We loaded the out-of-town and foreign newspapers and magazines into a truck, and delivered them to stores around town. I was home at seven o'clock, ate a little breakfast,

walked two miles to school. Once, I caught my mother looking at me pensively, sorry for me. "You work so hard." I
didn't think I was working so hard; it was a job that I had to
do. I've felt that way throughout my lifetime. Much later in
my life, when I was making a movie, my driver was looking
at me sort of funny. "Could I ask you a question, Mr. Douglas?" I said, "Sure." He said, "I just want to know, why does
a rich man like you work so hard?" I thought, what a strange
question, how odd that he would equate working hard only
with making money, not with liking your work. Of course,
delivering papers wasn't a job that I particularly wanted to
do. But I needed money to escape to college.

And I wanted to play a musical instrument. I bought a very
cheap banjo on the installment plan. For fifty cents a lesson,
I learned to play the banjo—not very well. I missed some
payments and wasn't home when they came for the little
money I still owed. They bullied my sister Kay, threatened
to put me in jail, so she handed the banjo over. I was desolate
when I found out.

My junior year, I won the Sanford Prize-Speaking Contest
with a very dramatic recitation about a dying soldier. It was
called "Across the Border." They gave me a gold medal. I
had been afraid that I might not win, since my sister Marion
had won two years before. At the time, I was working at
Goldmeer's Wholesale Grocery Company. That Saturday,
Mr. Goldmeer decided that it would be nice for me to recite
my winning oration for all the employees. We all crowded
into his office next to the roaring Chuctanunda Creek. I
started. The phone rang. Mr. Goldmeer motioned me to continue as one of his salesmen answered it. I was dramatically
depicting this dying soldier's last thoughts on the battlefield.
The salesman was saying, "Yes, two hundred pounds of
sugar, three cases of beets . . . " It almost made me hate winning that gold medal.

One of my classmates took me to his house for lunch, and
we had hot cross buns. I had never seen them before. I ran
home. "Ma, these people eat cake! They eat cake with their
meat!" Ma didn't believe me.

I didn't tell Ma when I ate one of the many wonderful foods forbidden to Orthodox Jews—bacon. I was fourteen. It was one of the most terrifying experiences of my life. I expected Old Jehovah with a long beard to strike me dead. But nothing happened. So I kept eating. I guess from that time, I began to move away from religious observance.

I've been married twice, each time to a shiksa, a non-Jew. My children were brought up to choose their own religion. But once every year, on Yom Kippur, the Day of Atonement, I revert to my upbringing. That's the big day. That's when it's written in the Big Book—and sealed—who shall live and who shall die, who by fire and who by water. I may not be in the synagogue as a good Jew should, but on that day I know deep down in my guts that I'm related to slaves who escaped bondage in Egypt, and that the people who are now trying to turn Israel into a land flowing with milk and honey are my brethren. I hear the lament of "Kol Nidre," even if I'm riding a horse side by side with Burt Lancaster, and I hear the shofar blowing in the middle of a love scene with Faye Dunaway. And I fast. Yes, I'm a Jew. And that feeling lasts me the rest of the year until the next Yom Kippur.

A most wonderful event took place my senior year. Katharine Cornell, first lady of the Broadway stage, was going on an unprecedented tour of the country with one of her biggest successes, *The Barretts of Wimpole Street*. They were going to play in Albany, and I was saving up to go! I was in heaven at the thought of this combination of great theater and the poetry of Robert and Elizabeth Barrett Browning. Mrs. Schuyler, the drama teacher, organized our class trip. It was my first real play, and it was perfect. I never suspected that some day I would not only know Katharine Cornell, but work with her.

Sometimes during lunch hour we danced in the gymnasium, but I had never been to a school dance in the evening because I didn't have the clothes or the money. I was a pretty good dancer, especially with a step called the glide and dip. But senior year, I decided to save up and go to the Senior Prom. It was a big event to me, my first prom.

There was a girl, Ann Brown. She was pretty and always wore nice clean dresses. She lived on Market Hill, the rich part of town. I danced with her sometimes during lunch hour. I felt she liked me. I invited her to go with me. She said yes! I was ecstatic, counted my pennies to make sure I had enough for the ticket and a nice corsage. I was going to press my suit very carefully.

The next day I came to school very happy. I saw her, my date for the prom, and waved. She didn't wave back. That's strange, I thought. I guess she didn't see me. During lunch hour when people were dancing, I couldn't quite seem to get her attention. I didn't understand. I ran up to her and she turned away. Finally, I trapped her in the corridor.

"What's wrong?"

She started to stutter, then finally said, "I can't go to the prom with you."

My heart sank. I was bewildered. She had seemed so happy about it the day before. "Why?"

She wouldn't answer. I insisted. "Why? Have I done something?"

"No." Long pause. "My father won't let me."

I said, "I'm sure the prom won't be very late. I'll get you home whenever he'd like."

"No, no," she said. "It's not that."

"Well what *is* it?"

"Because you're a Jew and your father's a ragman!" She ran away.

I just stood there with my mouth open. Certainly it was not new to me to be persecuted for being a Jew. But somehow I didn't associate it with this nice, freshly scrubbed American girl with her well-pressed dresses. I couldn't believe it. I knew that she came from a wealthy family and her father was a college graduate. I had always thought that people who hated Jews were like my immigrant neighbors who had come from a tough background with no education.

The night of the prom arrived. I had already told many people that I was going, and I was expected to go, because I was on the dance committee. But I didn't go. I began retreating into my shell. So often, I had to build a protective shell around me. Usually, it took the form of daydreams or fantasies. Issur couldn't deal with the pain. Sometimes, when it was really bad, Izzy couldn't, either.

I was always looking for some form of escape, even if it was only in my dreams. Every night, before going to bed, I tried to think of a happy thought, like a dog that has hidden a bone. If I had a pleasant thought during the day, I would tuck it away with the reminder, "Oh yes, I must think of that tonight." For many nights, I had been using my dreams about going to the Senior Prom. Now, that hope was gone.

The Wilbur H. Lynch High School graduation exercises for the 322 members of the Class of 1934 were held at 10:00 A.M. on June 27, in the Rialto Theater, a movie house. Years later, many of my films would be shown there. Pete Riccio was class president and I was treasurer. My mother was there, and all my sisters. I don't know where Pa was. But Ma was proud as they called off my name for Best Acting Prize and Best Speech at Commencement. I also won a prize for my essay, "The Play's the Thing," in which I wrote: "Art can only be obtained through hunger—hunger for beauty or harmony or truth or justice." Idealistic, but I still believe it.

Immediately after the graduation exercises, I rushed off to my new job as a janitor across the river at the Fifth Ward School. I needed that job, and was lucky to get it in the middle of the Depression, at twenty-one dollars a week. I was a good janitor. But within a week I was fired. I couldn't believe it. Louise Livingston told me that Wilbur H. Lynch himself had me fired. I couldn't believe that, either. He was such a distinguished man, an educated man, Superintendent of Schools. The high school was named after him. I had never done anything to him. I didn't even know him. Why?

I was very anxious to find a good-paying summer job, and decided to try the resort hotels in upstate New York. Louise invited me to spend the weekend at her house on Lake George and apply for jobs in the area. I walked and hitched, hitched and walked from hotel to hotel, turned down for any kind of a job. I passed through Saratoga, which was just getting ready for the height of its season, hotels crowded with wealthy people. No jobs at any of them.

It got later and later, and I had no place to stay. I had to spend the night somewhere, and I didn't have any money to waste on a hotel room. Someone had mentioned a ranger with a house in the woods. It was night now. I found my way through the woods by moonlight, walked up the steps to the cabin, knocked on the door. It opened. The barrel of a .45 was in my nose. At the other end was the inebriated ranger, growling, "What the hell do you want?" I politely explained that I was looking for a place to sleep. His response was, "Get out of here or I'll blow your head off!" I took him at his word, exited his porch precipitously, and spent an uncomfortable, petrified night under a tree.

The next day was more rejection after rejection. Busboy, bellhop, waiter. Nobody wanted to hire Izzy Demsky. I thought about this as I walked and hitched some more. By the time I came to a tiny little hotel called the Orchard House, I swallowed hard and introduced myself as "Don Dempsey." I got the job.

The Orchard House was "restricted"—no Jews. There were a few families, but it catered mostly to young Gentile ladies who had accumulated enough money during the year to come for a two-week vacation at Lake George hoping to find romance. The woman who ran the hotel was attractive and liked me. She confided in me often that there was something about Jews she could not stand; she could spot them in a minute, no matter what their name was or what they looked like. There was a smell about them.

I was a bellhop, the only one there. I was pretty busy. Invariably, my last call before going off duty at night would be to deliver ice to one of the guests in her room—a guest who had not found romance along the shores of Lake George and was willing to find it behind a closed door with a bellboy.

As the end of the season approached, the lady proprietor grew more interested in me. I had tried to maintain my distance. The night before the hotel closed, my lady boss was

more attentive than ever. She suggested that we have a farewell drink in her room. I was certainly aware of the season
finale she was planning as I climbed the stairs to her room.
She talked about my coming back the next summer. I
thought of all the things she had said this summer: "Hitler is
right, the Jews should all be destroyed," "No Jew will ever
set foot in this hotel." After a few drinks, we were in bed
together. Strange how hate can be such an aphrodisiac. My
hate grew into a tremendous erection and I thrust it inside
of her. She was wet and ready, extremely passionate,
moaned and groaned. I made certain that over all of these
sounds she could hear me very clearly when I said into her
ear, "THAT IS A CIRCUMCISED JEWISH COCK INSIDE
YOU. DO YOU THINK YOU'LL GET CONTAMINATED?
MAYBE EVEN DIE? I AM A JEW. YOU ARE BEING
FUCKED BY A JEW!" I exploded inside her. She said nothing, just breathed heavily and lay there as I left the room.

The next morning I hitchhiked back to Amsterdam. On the
way, I stopped off to see Louise Livingston at her cottage.
What a wonderful surprise it would be! I walked for miles
around the lake and then down the path that led to her
house. As I went to knock on the door I looked, and there
inside I saw my dear friend Wilbur H. Lynch, that highly
respected man who had fired me from my janitor job. Now I
understood why. He walked across the room in his underwear, followed by my dearly beloved in a bathrobe. I walked
away and hitchhiked back to Amsterdam. I never told her.

It was September; kids headed for college. Pete Riccio left
for St. Lawrence University. I didn't have enough money to
get to college. College seemed like such a magic word to me.
It was the key: escape from Amsterdam, six sisters, my
mother. It could be an escape from my father, who didn't
seem to want to see me. Yes, and even an escape from
Louise. As I grew cooler, she became fiercely jealous, sometimes coming to where I worked, her eyes flashing with
anger as she questioned where I had been, or what I had
done, or with whom, in a low, fierce voice so that she
couldn't be overheard.

I needed money. My sister Betty got me a job at the M. Lurie Department Store in Men's Ready-to-Wear. What a desperate year. I lived most of it in fantasy. I had one suit and a light topcoat. Each night I pressed the pants by placing a damp cloth over the creases and steaming them with a hot iron. I walked back and forth from home to the department store, my topcoat neatly folded over one arm. I walked very erect. I don't know who I was pretending to be. Anybody but me. How the time dragged. I would try not to look at the clock for as long as I could. Then I looked: four o'clock. Two more hours before closing. Would six o'clock never come!

I began to steal, small sums. If someone bought something for $2.98 and gave me three dollars, I made out the slip for $1.98 and let a dollar fall to the floor and picked it up later. I was frightened. I had never stolen money before. I caught one of the men in the store eyeing me suspiciously after one of my transactions. I never did it again.

During that year I played John Barrymore in a little-theater production of *The Royal Family*. I saw how the rest of my life would be, stuck in Amsterdam. In years, I might become the manager of the Men's Department of M. Lurie and Co. I would be active in the little-theater group. I might even become a member of the golf club—the one that let Jews in.

One of the wholesale grocery outfits had offered me a big job taking over their publicity. They promised that in a short time, I might make as much as a hundred dollars a week. That seemed a fantastic amount. I dreamed of riding around in a beautiful car, with girls, wearing nice clothes. I often wonder now what it was within me, even at that young age, that made me say no, that kept me from getting trapped. Somehow my dream of being an actor must have been more alive than I realized.

Somehow time did pass, a whole year of walking up and down in my neatly pressed pants, still carrying that light tan topcoat, until another September rolled around. People were going back to college again. Pete Riccio was returning to St.

Lawrence University for his sophomore year and he urged me to go with him.

How could I? All my savings amounted to $163.00, much less than I had had at my Bar Mitzvah, when I had loaned my father $313.00.

"Take a chance," he said.

I grabbed all my school records, the prizes I had won, and tucked my $163.00 deep in my pocket. Pete and I started hitchhiking to St. Lawrence University in Canton, New York, about two hundred miles away, up near the Canadian border.

My sisters encouraged me, proud that I was going to take the chance. They could have taken the opposite viewpoint. I was now the only man in the household. We got nothing from Pa. They could have insisted that I stay home and continue to help support the household. They couldn't help me, but they let me go. Thank you Betty, Kay, Marion, Ida, Fritzi, and Ruth.

Ma had tears in her eyes when I left. She didn't know then that I was never coming back—oh, for a few days to visit, but never to stay. She kissed me good-bye, and said something softly in Yiddish that startled me: "A boy is a boy, but a girl is *drek* (shit)."

Pa had remained alone at 46 Eagle Street. I found him sitting at the kitchen table, rubbing garlic on a slice of pumpernickel, eating it with a piece of herring. He was dry-eyed and said almost nothing when I went to say good-bye. He gave me a rough kiss on the mouth and grumbled something that sounded like "good luck." I left him in the kitchen.

Pete and I didn't make it all the way to Canton, New York, that first day. We begged a room at a house near the road. The next day, our last ride was on a truckload of fertilizer. We crouched on top of the flapping canvas, our heads bowed against the whipping wind as we sped away from Amsterdam, toward the unknown—college—with that strong odor that I knew so well.

What about Issur? Leave him behind! I started to feel sorry

for him, but I pushed away all compassion. I had to cut him off. I had to run away. Don't you understand? I don't want to go back there. I don't ever want to go back there again. I want to keep going. I want to find my "green isle in the sea."

Horseshit had always played an important part in my life, and I arrived at college reeking of it.

Three

BIG MAN ON CAMPUS

The truck slowed down and drove into the little town of Canton, New York, the home of St. Lawrence University. Pete and I slid off and yelled "Thanks!" to the driver, who was already on his way. I looked around. Across the street, on the corner, was a coffee shop and ice cream parlor—the Sugar Bowl. I saw tall young fellows with pretty girls. Some of the men were wearing sparkling white sweaters with a big scarlet "L" in the middle. Pete explained to me that they were Letter men, who had earned their letter at some sport. They seemed so confident as they strutted down the street, hand in hand with their girlfriends, into the Sugar Bowl.

As Pete and I walked in the opposite direction, toward the campus, I wondered if I would ever get to wear a white sweater with a scarlet "L." It all seemed so far away. And we had arrived a few days late. The freshman class had already had an orientation program to instruct them in the rules and regulations of this mysterious world of the university, the world that was going to set me free. I was, literally, disoriented.

My first sight of St. Lawrence University was impressive. Large green lawns were covered in varicolored leaves. The steeple of Gunnison Chapel pierced the sky. Pete pointed out other beautiful buildings: the library, the chemistry building; in the distance, the dormitory. We were going to the administration building to talk to the dean, to see if I could get in. I watched the lucky students, who already knew for sure that they were enrolled, as they walked along leisurely, comfortable in this place. I was frightened. It was a new experience.

Dean Hewlitt had a lined face and steel-gray hair. He peered at me from over his glasses. Laid out on his desk were all my transcripts and credentials that had been brought in to him by the secretary. My records were good. I had won lots of prizes, and my grades were high.

He looked up at me, and in a gruff voice said, "So, you want to go to college."

"Yes, sir," I answered.

"How much money do you have?"

"A hundred and sixty-three dollars."

His eyes widened as he studied me. His nose wrinkled as he caught a whiff of the horse manure. He looked at me for a long time. I felt uncomfortable. It was very quiet. Then, in that gruff voice, he said, "All right. We'll take a chance on you. We'll work out a college loan. My secretary will show you where to go to register."

I was a college man!

The first few days, I was permitted to live in the dormitory until I could find some cheaper place to live and get a job. With that income, added to my loan, I would be able to go to college. I had slept alone on the couch for so long that I was uncomfortable sharing a room, even with Pete. It was strange to be living in a room with another person.

That first afternoon, Pete went off to visit friends. I stayed in the room alone, just lying on the bed, thinking how quickly everything had happened, how quickly the circle of my life had widened, how far away I was from the kitchen at

46 Eagle Street. It was five o'clock in the autumn afternoon; the chimes from the college chapel started playing. A melancholy song. I later learned it was the alma mater. I couldn't push away my thoughts of Amsterdam; I lay there, overcome by waves of sadness and nostalgia. Why was I homesick for a place that I had wanted so desperately to leave? Why wasn't I happy? Instead, tears came to my eyes. I was frightened. I hoped that I could live up to the high standards of college students.

I heard a loud voice in the hallway. "Fuck off, you asshole!" I was startled. I couldn't believe that could be coming from a college student. I thought that when you came to college, you were very serious and very dignified. I had thought about smoking a pipe. My sister Kay bought me one to make up for the banjo. You discussed lofty, philosophical subjects: literature, poetry. I thought of college as a repository of the noblest literature. I heard an answering voice: "Up yours, prick!" Wow. This was worse than the language used by the gangs that had waited to beat me up when I came back home from Hebrew School.

The deep homesickness stayed with me a long time. It perplexed me, because as long as I could remember, I had wanted to escape the prison of my hometown, to escape the last house down on Eagle Street, to escape my family, to rush away and find my identity. Now I had escaped, but I felt like a man who has been in prison for so long that when the gate finally opens and he walks out into freedom, all he can do is walk back into his cell.

Hunger hounded me. Sometimes in the evening, I'd make the rounds of dormitory rooms, ostensibly to visit other students, but actually looking for goodies their families might have sent them. One fellow received a bushel of nuts; he was amazed at how many I ate. Another might get some fruit, and I would eat apples.

I devised a system of getting food at lunch. I would saunter into the cafeteria and sit at one of the tables, waiting for students to come over after they had gone through the line.

Each one gave me something off his tray—a few string beans, a potato, some turnips. For a while, I managed to eke out a meal this way.

News of my procedure reached the woman in charge of the cafeteria, a tall, thin spinster. One day at lunch, while I was sitting there eating what I had gleaned from my friends, she came barging toward me, yelling. The clatter of spoons and forks and cups stopped. In the silence she towered over me. "HOW DARE YOU COME IN HERE AND SCROUNGE FOOD THAT DOESN'T BELONG TO YOU!" She pointed to the door. "YOU GET OUT OF HERE! AND DON'T YOU EVER LET ME SEE YOU COME BACK AGAIN!" Everyone stared at me. Shame-facedly, my eyes downcast, I slunk out.

I wanted to belong. Around the campus were the fraternity and sorority houses, very imposing buildings, each with a distinct personality. Tri Delta was the rich, pretty girls. Another house was the good students. Alpha Tau Omega was the jock house. They all had secret meetings and hand-shakes, and special social events, dances and parties, to which they invited each other. They were a group, a family. They belonged.

During hazing, a freshman had to do whatever any upper-classman told him. Pete would get me to recite poetry or scenes from Shakespeare, which I could do for hours. This impressed the fraternity brothers; I was invited to dinner at ATO during Rushing. One of the upperclassmen was going to pick me up at six o'clock and escort me to the fraternity house, where I would have dinner with all the members and get to know them better. I was very proud and excited, took a shower and scrubbed myself, borrowed a few things to wear, and sat in my room and waited as the rest of the students in the freshman dorm went off to other fraternity houses, or went downstairs to the dining room.

I sat and waited for a long time. It got very quiet. Nobody was on the floor. Nobody came. And nobody called. I could hear the students starting to come back from dinner down-stairs, and still no one came.

I went to bed that night with no dinner, not that unusual for me, but completely perplexed. I later learned that they had thought I was Polish. When they found out I was Jewish, they just dropped me. No one even made an attempt to call to say that something had come up, maybe we'd make it some other time—to lie, even. They just ignored me, said nothing. They never made any reference to it.

That rejection hurt. I had assumed that a university was above anti-Semitism. Not at all, I learned painfully. I should have remembered Ann Brown's father. University groups were deeply instilled with all the training they had received at the dining table at home. The constant cry would be, "It's not us, it's the national charter."

Freshman year was very difficult. Adjusting, surviving. I had had absolutely no idea of what college life would be like. Someone suggested that I apply for a scholarship. I had no idea what a scholarship was. But I was granted one. Still the dormitory was much too expensive. I moved into a house with two of the janitors. Dean Hewlitt had promised me a job. How ironic that my first job, at twenty-five cents an hour, was as a janitor. Back to being the janitor's boy, pushing the wide broom down the long hallways and dreaming of other things, wondering what Louise Livingston was thinking, wondering if she was dreaming about her janitor's boy. It seems to me that most of my time at college was spent sweeping hallways.

I felt a desperate need to express myself physically. In Amsterdam, I had never had a chance to go out for sports, because I was always working. I had been a cheerleader, and resented it. I didn't want to cheer the exploits of others —I wanted to be the one doing the exploits. I wanted to risk danger. I needed to *do* something.

So even though I had a rough schedule and worked to support myself, I went out for one of the major sports at St. Lawrence—wrestling. It was the one sport in which we could compete with much larger schools—Syracuse, Cornell, Columbia, Rutgers, Princeton—and even defeat them. Now SLU excels at hockey, a sport that was in its infancy when I was there.

I was very good at wrestling. It was easy for me to make the freshman team based on my ability, but difficult based on the amount of time it took to practice. I usually wrestled in the 145-pound class. One night, a bunch of big fellows started to hassle me. One very big fellow, about six foot three, on the football team, kept taunting me. "So you're a wrestler, huh?"

"Yeah."

"O.K. I'll wrestle you." He kept pushing me.

I said, "What is it with you?" Finally, it irritated me so much that I felt almost the way I had when I threw the spoonful of tea in my father's face. I was being threatened. I had to risk disaster. I said, "All right." Word spread, and a group of students followed us into the attic of the dorm where the mats for wrestling workouts were.

He was much bigger than I; if he ever got ahold of me, I'd be a goner. My only chance was to get in a position of advantage immediately. There was a big smirk on his face as he lumbered toward me. I made a feint to his head, dropped to my knees, and spun around, grabbing his leg and pulling him up, knocking him to the mat. I quickly put a scissors around his body and rode him, on his back. He was very powerful, but when he bucked, I hung on to him, my legs wrapped around him. When he rolled, I rolled with him, squeezing his stomach with my legs. Then he was lying flat out. He started to get up, with me still clinging to his back. I waited until he was on his knees with both arms straight. With all my strength, I thrust my palms against his elbows. He collapsed. His face smashed into the mat, his nose ran blood. He became furious, howling and trying to shake me off. I wouldn't let go. He bucked and flailed; I squeezed and squeezed. Finally the pressure on his stomach made him throw up. That ended the match. I had won. People looked at me with more respect. Especially the fellow I had defeated. We became friends after that, but we never had any more wrestling matches.

Paul Wolf was a tall, burly, but gentle fellow from Rochester, New York, the son of a Reform rabbi who had died some time before. We were quite friendly. I say "quite friendly," but there were always limits to my friendships, parameters that I imposed. I never had many friends. I was always alone, somehow always outside of the circle, and yet desperately wanting so much to be a part of it. I never allowed anyone to get too close to the soft, vulnerable core of me that was Issur.

Paul asked me if I wanted to join Phi Psi, where he had house privileges. It always amused me, this thing called "house privileges," which permitted you to pay dues, pay to eat at the fraternity, and attend their social functions. But you were not permitted to go to the sacrosanct meetings and know the secret handshake. Participate at the meetings? No, no, no. No Jew was allowed to do that. But when fraternities needed money, they granted house privileges to Jews. I said "Fuck you" to house privileges.

Paul came to me with an idea one day. "Why don't we form our own fraternity?"

I laughed. "Why should we form a Jewish fraternity? To keep out the Gentiles? That would make us just as bad as they are, and we would be doing something for spite. Hell, no! I don't want any Jewish fraternity."

He didn't understand. "Then why aren't you a member of the nonfraternity group?"

There was something rather pathetic about everybody wanting to belong to some group. I don't mean that I was so strong and independent that I had no need of a group. As a matter of fact, I did. Just as, later, when I was an independent actor in Hollywood and everybody else belonged to a studio, I was lonely. I envied them as they bitched about being tied down to a studio, yet every day they had a place to go, somewhere to study and take their lessons and be looked after. But I also saw the ridiculousness of the situation: if you won't take me as a member, I'll form my own club. So I remained a man who didn't belong to a fraternity, wouldn't accept house privileges, didn't want to form a Jewish fraternity, and certainly didn't want to belong to the non-fraternity group. But I still liked Paul, and I think he was rather unhappy about the compromise he made of accepting house privileges.

The girls' dormitory was a safe distance from the men's and had very rigid, restricted hours as to when the boys could come over to pick up their dates. All the girls had to be back by ten o'clock. How different from colleges of today. I thought of that when I was helping my son Eric get settled in his dormitory room at Claremont College, and found that directly across the hall from him was a girl. I was dumbfounded. I hadn't realized that things had changed to that extent.

In the little town of Canton there was also another school, an agricultural college which was much less expensive and had much less rigid standards of conduct. Most of those students boarded in homes around the campus. Very often, the St. Lawrence boys would have a St. Lawrence girlfriend that they had to bring back at ten o'clock, and then they would have an Aggie girl that they could date after ten.

I had an Aggie girlfriend named Liz, a tall, buxom, well-built girl that I used to see quite often. I remember one double date that first fall. A friend of mine had a dilapidated old car, and after ten o'clock, we picked up our Aggie girls and went for a beer. Not far from St. Lawrence was an old flooded quarry. It was a wonderful swimming hole. We went there and swam in the moonlight. Then we had blankets and we separated and I took my Aggie girl up on the side of the mountain. We made love under the stars and cuddled together and stayed there until it started to get light and we had to rush to get home. I remember that evening, wonderful, warm, and pleasant. I felt so comfortable, so cozy. I've always wanted to let Liz know how much that evening meant to me.

I met a girl at St. Lawrence, Isabella Phelps. A lovely girl, with a peaches-and-cream complexion and beautiful titian hair. She was very quiet, with a sweet smile, and carried herself very erect. She seemed unattainable, like the girls on

Market Hill in Amsterdam. She sat in front of me in German class. I would stare at the back of her beautiful head of red hair while the German instructor went on, *"Ich bin, du bis, er ist,"* and I would whisper to myself, *"Ich liebe dich, ich liebe dich."* For a long time, I didn't dare risk rejection. Then, while sitting behind her, I wrote a poem:

> *How oft have I behind thee sat*
> *In awe and watched thy titian hair*
> *Resplendent in the rays*
> *Of morning's golden light,*
> *Which danced about thy head*
> *For joy, a gorgeous sight!*
> *Each ray thus shaped*
> *A sparkling diadem*
> *Of jewels to crown*
> *You Queen of Beauty over all.*
> *Then happily you turned and looked at me*
> *And changed my humble state to ecstasy.*

I slipped her the poem and studied her while she read it. Nothing revealed how she felt. WASPs have such mechanisms for masking their feelings. My wife always tells me I'm the worst actor she knows. My repertoire does not include poker face. Anyone can tell immediately what I'm thinking or feeling. This extends to my voice: she tells me I'm a bust when I try to lie on the telephone.

But something touched Isabel. Soon after that we became very close. We spent a lot of time together, but there continued to be something enigmatic about her. I never quite knew what she was thinking. But Isabel—they called her "Izzy," and they called me "Izzy," so it was Izzy and Izzy—was a lovely girl. She was a great solace many times during our college life, and I was grateful for the affection that she had for me. Sometimes I want to call all the girls in my life who have given me affection, even more than sex, girls that I've held close to me, and thank them. But I always knew that Isabel would not be a permanent part of my life. There was always a part of me that was reaching outward, away from Amsterdam, away from college, to the world beyond.

I became friends with a very correct, slim, gentlemanly economics professor with a slight southern accent, who always sprang to his feet when either a man or a woman entered the room. I never took any courses from him, but we would talk in his room in the dorm, very often about music. I remember his pointing out to me that one of the greatest pieces of music is the second movement of Schubert's Unfinished Symphony. I enjoyed listening to music and learning.

Every summer he took a trip. The previous summer, he had taken a college student to Europe. How I wished it had been me. I wanted so much to travel. He promised to take me on a trip to Mexico the next summer, and he did.

It was a fantastic trip. We drove across the United States to Mexico. Everywhere was new and strange to me, mind-boggling. I was surprised at the heat and humidity in Washington, D.C. Just driving around the city was exciting, seeing the Washington Monument and the Lincoln Memorial and the Capitol for the first time—sights that thrill me even today. As we drove through the South, I was overjoyed the first time I saw a field of cotton. I made the professor stop. I had to rush out and look at the cotton fields, pick pieces of cotton and think of all those songs: "I'm Alabamy Bound," "Mammy," "Ol' Man River," and "Carry Me Back to Old Virginny." I was excited about everything.

As we drove along a high bank, he said, "That's the Mississippi River."

"STOP THE CAR!" I rushed up the bank, holding my breath, to see the mighty Mississippi that bisected the United States. I was disappointed to see a rather calm, narrow river. The Mississippi is very wide in some places, but I happened to pick a spot where it wasn't so mighty.

Then the most exciting thing of all: leaving the country, near Laredo, Texas, and entering into Mexico. I had a Spanish phrase book, and when we were in Monterrey, not quite sure of the road to Mexico City, I said, "No, no, leave it to me." I spotted a man, quickly thumbed through the book, and said to him, "*Donde está el camino a Mexico?*" He looked at me and in perfect English said, "You go straight ahead, then make a left." I was chagrined that it was so obvious to him that I was an American, but on second thought I considered the possibility that if he had answered me in Spanish, I wouldn't have known what he was saying. But I had communicated in a foreign language in a foreign country!

We finally arrived in Mexico City, very tired, and went to our hotel. Usually we had a room with twin beds. Here we had one large bed. He said, "Let's rest for a while." We lay down in bed. Then he turned to me and said, "Let's cuddle."

I leaped out of the bed. I didn't know how to handle the situation. Homosexuality was something quite new to me, some vague thing that I had only heard about. Maybe I should have laughed or joked my way out of it, but I was incensed. And this poor, timid man became terribly upset. There was a pall over the rest of the trip.

From Mexico City we went to Taxco, a beautiful little town on a mountainside, where the stars were low and there was guitar music. I went to a bar alone, and spent a wonderful evening with an American girl I met there. Then I went back to the room that I was sharing with the economics professor. With twin beds. By then, everything he did annoyed me. If he opened a door for me, I said, "Will you stop treating me like a woman? I don't need you opening doors for me!" He would stiffen and be upset, and that in turn upset me. The whole last part of the trip was unpleasant. Yet I was grateful to him for the wonderful experience of my first trip outside of America.

Sophomore year, I tried out for the varsity wrestling team. The competition in my weight class was the only student in the entire university on a wrestling scholarship. He came from a high school where wrestling was a big sport and he was considered a champion wrestler. I beat him. The coach was flabbergasted. I beat him out of sheer desperation. He was wrestling for a place on the varsity team. I was wrestling for my life. When I got into a position of advantage, I held onto him with every sinew, every muscle. He couldn't shake me loose. I wrestled on the varsity team from the first match. He immediately tried out in the 155-pound division, and won. I was shocked at what I had done. How dare I defeat the only man who had a scholarship for wrestling? I never beat him again.

Wally Thompson, six feet four, Indian-looking, was a friend of mine at college. I'll never forget how impressed I was when I learned (he never told me) that he had gotten into a fight because someone had insulted me. Some typical "dirty Jew" remark, and he had stuck up for me and fought. I never discussed it with him, but I was always touched. Wally ran the cafeteria; he was sort of the maître d'. He was a wonderful person, and years later, after I left college, there were very few people from those days that I would think about or want to see. But Wally was one of them. I always wanted to see him, but I was wrapped up in the constant hectic activity of my own life. He never wrote to me, either. Was it because he thought I had attained some sort of success that he didn't want to infringe on? I don't know. Then one day I got a letter from his daughter telling me that Wally had died. I felt very bad that I had never made the effort to write him and thank him, to let him know how grateful I was for the friendship he gave me at a time that I needed it so badly.

I had another friend at college, briefly. Bob Irwin was much older than the other students, a talented sculptor. He was friendly, interested in boxing, did odd jobs, like me—a paper route, shoveling snow off sidewalks. I liked his sculptures, and enjoyed talking to him, but he had a violent temper. He offered to buy me a milkshake one day. I declined, because he didn't have much money either, and I figured going Dutch would be better. He insisted with such vehemence that I backed off and let him buy. He left school a little while later. A few weeks after that, peaceful little Canton was swarming with detectives and FBI men looking for Robert Irwin in the biggest manhunt since the Lindbergh baby kidnapping. Three people had been murdered on Easter Sunday, 1937, in New York City. An artist's model and her mother had been strangled; their boarder was stabbed with a sculpting tool similar to an ice pick. Irwin was finally captured, tried, and sent to the state hospital for the criminally insane at Dannemora. I felt sorry for him, a talented artist at the mercy of incomprehensible forces. When I played Van Gogh, I thought of Bob Irwin.

I needed work the summer after my sophomore year. Paul Wolf suggested Rochester, his home town. I could live at his house, and work as the gardener. This started out well enough, but his mother and I didn't get along, so I decided to look elsewhere in Rochester for work.

It was difficult, in the Depression. I went to many places. I finally found a job in a steel mill that made steel drums and barrels. The manager was a nice man. "You sure you want to work here? Because this is what happens." He held up his hand. Two of his fingers were missing—a common occurrence in steel mills, which had rather dilapidated machinery and, I'm sure, nowhere near the safety devices that exist now. But I was desperate for the job and he gave it to me.

Every morning, we were issued gloves for handling the sheets of steel and rolls of steel wire. I watched, fascinated, as the workers put their gloves into the cutting machines and chopped off the empty, flopping glove fingers that corresponded to the missing fingers on their hands. It seemed to me that every other man had at least one or two fingers missing. That gave me an eerie feeling. I was determined to be very careful about keeping my hands away from the sharp cutting edges in the machines.

The work was very difficult and for the first week or so I was exhausted when I got home to my little cubbyhole in a rooming house near the factory. But I enjoyed the physical labor and while I was there I met a friend of Paul's, a cute girl named Peggy. She had a very happy disposition and an infectious laugh, was always ready with a joke. "Sunny" would best describe Peggy. She was tiny, no more than five feet two, with a bosom almost too large for her body. Her family was well-off and had a very nice home. Very often I was invited to dinner and had a wonderful meal. Food. Food.

How else can you keep alive unless you keep stuffing your-self with food?

We had only half an hour for lunch at the mill, and we'd usually eat sitting on the steps outside by the street. Often, Peggy would drive up in a big Cadillac, wearing a clean, starched dress, and bring me thick sandwiches wrapped in waxed paper. The other workers would eye me suspiciously as I went across the street, grimy from working in the mill, to partake of my luncheon with this lovely girl. It was always strange to me that the workers said very little. They still accepted me. But they never knew—was I the boss's son, or what? At first I was embarrassed and discouraged Peggy from coming. But the temptation of those beautiful sand-wiches with mayonnaise was too much, so I let her come almost every day.

I was the youngest one there. In general, they were a nice enough bunch of fellows. One had tattoos of flags and eagles and whatnot all over his body. I was fascinated by tattoos and am to this day. I've always thought about getting one, don't know why I never have. If I live long enough, I might still do it.

One day, the fellow caught me staring at him. "You like tattoos, huh? Come here. I'll show you a tattoo."

I followed him into the men's room. He dropped his pants and showed me his bottom. I was dumbfounded to see, very artistically done, a wildcat pursuing a rat that was just enter-ing the man's anus. I couldn't take my eyes off it. I asked him how it had been done.

He said, "In the Navy, drunk one night." He pulled his pants back up. "The wife nearly killed me. She wants me to have it taken off, but, Jesus, that's too much trouble."

From then on, whenever I looked at that man, I thought of him going through life with a cat chasing a rat up his asshole.

Peggy and I spent almost every evening together. The summer was coming to a close and I was going back to col-lege. We talked about my plans. She knew that I wanted to go to New York and enter a dramatic school and study acting. One night, after we'd made love in a secluded spot in a park in Rochester, she turned to me and said, "Why don't we get married?"

I was startled by her proposal. I said, "Married? I can't think of marriage. I have all I can do to try to struggle through to my next meal."

"But why would you have to struggle?"

"What do you mean?"

"My parents will help us. We could go to New York. They would give us a nice apartment."

"I couldn't do that. I don't want a handout."

"Don't think of it as a handout. Think of it as an investment in your career. You would have a comfortable apartment. Let me take care of you," she said. "All I want to do is take care of you and make sure that there are no holes in your socks, make sure that you have enough to eat, and make sure that I can cuddle you when you need my affection."

She presented her case most attractively and made me pause and really think about it. I was taken aback and said, "Let me think about it."

She didn't press it. She just said, "Think about it. But why shouldn't you be comfortable while you work for what you want?"

I thought, "She's right. Why not?" Up to that point, my life had been just a day-to-day struggle for the basics—food, clothes, an education, a job. The more I thought about Peggy's offer, the more attractive it became. She was a sexy girl. I thought, "My God! I'm a lucky guy! This is the answer to everything!" I was completely in agreement with all the arguments that she advanced for why we should get married. But I thought, "I don't know love. I like her, but I don't think I'm in love with her."

I look back and wonder what made me realize that we shouldn't get married. Decisions like that have been the most crucial and vital in my life, because they came at a time where the temptation was so great, and my knowledge about myself and life so limited. But there was always an instinct for artistic survival within me that made me realize that if I accepted the offer, I was doomed. I would be lost.

I politely declined her invitation. But I was always grateful for the wonderful summer that she gave me, and for the proposal that she made to me out of, I think, real, deep affection. Many times later I wondered if I had made the right decision.

On the way back to school, Issur stopped off in Amsterdam. Ma and the girls had moved to Schenectady, but Pa still lived at 46 Eagle Street—alone. Issur walked past the spot in the backyard where Ma had found him in the gold box, and entered the kitchen. The house was more dilapidated than ever, cats everywhere to keep down the rat population that nested in the junk and rags that Pa, a packrat himself, hoarded on the second floor.

Pa was sitting at the table, rubbing garlic on a heel of pumpernickel. With the bread, Pa was eating some herring. He said "Hullo" in a gruff voice and kept on eating. When he was through, he wiped his mouth on the sleeve of his torn jacket and said, "Come on." Pa and Issur walked up the street to Rimkunas's Garage. Stan Rimkunas took them in his car, and they went pub-crawling. Issur was thrilled. When they walked into a bar, Pa would announce, "Hey, this is my boy. He goes to college." And they'd have a drink together. Several drinks. Boilermakers. Issur tried to keep up with Pa, to compress into one evening all the time he had wanted to spend with him. Issur went from feeling elated into feeling drunk and sick. Rimkunas and Pa drove him back to Schenectady. At Ma's house, Pa dragged Issur to the front door, propped him up, rang the bell, and left. Ma opened the door to see them drive off. Issur staggered into the bathroom. Ma cursed Pa in Yiddish while Issur vomited and smiled: he and Pa had been out together.

Back at college, I made another crucial decision—not to take any more courses in education. I had been advised to get a teaching credential so that I would have "something to fall back on." But I didn't want to have something to fall back on. I didn't want a trap to fall into if getting an acting job was difficult. I was one course—one *easy* course—away from the credential. I didn't take it. I totally cut off that avenue, deliberately boxed myself in.

My junior year I was selected as one of the candidates for president of the student body, even though I knew that unaffiliated with any fraternity or other group, I had no chance of winning. But I had some things to say, and I said them to the assembled student body.

My girlfriend Isabel and I were dancing to a record player in her sorority house when I was told that I had been elected president. I thought it was a joke. I was almost numb. A very peculiar situation. When I accepted the gavel as president, I stood at the podium, looked out across the student body—and had no idea who had voted for me. For the first time in its history, a student not connected with any fraternity was elected president of the student body at St. Lawrence University. And he was Jewish.

The alumni were furious, threatening to withhold contributions. "What's happening to SLU? A Jew boy president of the student body!"

Obviously, I had many non-Jewish friends at SLU. One was a recent graduate, now an associate professor. Fred was very bright, interested in drama. We had many talks. One night while we were having a beer, he looked at me strangely. Suddenly, he curled his lip and said, "How awful to be a Jew." I looked at his cadaverous face, sunken cheeks, misshapen nose. I howled. I became hysterical with laughter. I was the BMOC—president of the student body, president of the Mummers Club, president of the German Club; tapped for Kixioc, the senior men's honor society; had a varsity letter, my big red "L," for wrestling. My girlfriend was the campus beauty. I had at my disposal a car that belonged to a Spanish teacher with whom I had developed a liaison, even though I had never taken a course in Spanish. She lived in a house right behind one of the fraternity houses. At night, I would sneak in quietly. She would leave the door unlocked; I groped in the dark until I felt her outstretched arm grab me and pull me into bed. But Fred, an unattractive man who couldn't get a girlfriend, found something in me to make him feel superior.

I took off for my summer job. Every year, I would stop in for a brief visit with my mother and sisters. My mother would look at me with sad eyes and wonder why I didn't work somewhere nearby so she could see me. I couldn't give her a very good answer, but somehow, I think she knew. My father, when I could find him, had very little to say. Louise and I were still friends; she encouraged me and was proud of my successes.

Wrestling in carnivals was my earliest dramatic training. One of the other SLU wrestlers, a hulk named "Pinky" Plumadore, was the "Masked Marvel," huge and intimidating. The barker on the platform outside the tent would tease and taunt the audience, challenging anyone to dare to go five minutes with the Masked Marvel. I was the ordinary Joe in the audience who would challenge him. At the right moment, I would leap up amidst a burst of applause from the spectators, led by Pete Riccio. Tickets were sold as I went in and changed into a pair of trunks. Pinky and I came out again, wrapped in blankets, and squared off, looking ready to kill each other. More tickets were sold. And then the wrestling match. Five minutes of drama, comedy, grunting, and slamming, at the end of which I was declared the winner. The crowd went wild. Pinky was enraged, screamed for a rematch. The tent was cleared out, we got a rest, more tickets were sold. In the wrestling match, Act II ("The Fight to the Death"), Pinky played dirtier, our looks at each other were more murderous, the wrestling more spectacular. I won again—ten dollars and a lot of bruises.

I moved on to the Tamarack Playhouse, on Lake Pleasant, New York, in the Adirondack Mountains. But as far as I was concerned, it was another planet. And I was lucky enough to get a job as a stagehand. At last, I was working with a professional acting company. The Playhouse had been built by Malcolm Atterbury, heir to a railroad fortune. He and his wife Ellen played most of the leads. Every day was exciting, intoxicating—even pounding nails. Everybody chipped in, even a fellow who had started out in the steel town of Gary, Indiana, as Mladen Sekulovich, but who now called himself Karl Malden.

Even then, you could see how talented Karl was. It later pleased me that when my son Michael did his first TV series, "The Streets of San Francisco," he worked with Karl. I said, "Michael, you're going to learn a lot. You're never going to be able to keep up with the pace that Karl will set." That was true; those years of working set up a work pattern that's very often difficult for young actors to maintain. And Michael admits that he learned an awful lot working with Karl Malden.

Most of the people at Tamarack came from the Goodman School of Theater near Chicago. The ingenue was sexy, and a bitch. Her boyfriend played smaller roles or worked backstage with scenery, but most of the time he had to drive a truck. It made him bitter, because he wanted to be an actor, and he had talent. The ingenue found me attractive. We had sex many times. She would sneak away from her boyfriend. I felt a little guilty about it and was always surprised how easily she handled it.

After I had had a taste of being on a stage, even playing minor roles, putting together props and building sets, eating with actors, having the ingenue fall in love with me, I was more desperate than ever to leave SLU.

My senior year was a strange experience. When I returned to campus that fall, as president of the student body, I was given a double room all to myself in the men's dormitory, the only one with a private phone. And I was undefeated wrestling champion.

Roy Clarkson, the wresting coach, liked his athletes to be completely dedicated to the sport they were engaged in, and to him. He taught football and wrestling and was obeyed as a slave obeys a master. I had divided loyalties. My main interest was acting and I was always in the school plays. Very often, rehearsal time conflicted with workout time, so I'd miss one or the other. Clarkson would yell at me when I missed a workout, because he had hopes that I might try out for the Olympic wrestling team. "Goddamn it! What do you want to be—an actor or a wrestler?" I had to laugh. I had never wanted to be a wrestler. Wrestling was just something that I needed emotionally, and a way to get that sparkling white sweater with the crimson "L." I wanted to be an actor.

I wanted to attend a drama school in New York. I had heard that the American Academy of Dramatic Arts was the best. It was the oldest one in the world; even the Royal Academy of Dramatic Arts had been patterned after it. I had to try to get into a drama school and find a way to live while I attended. Thoughts of Peggy drifted back. Had I made a mistake? I could have a comfortable apartment, money to pay my tuition. Instead, I had nothing.

I saved up enough to go to New York City for a few days. I wrote letters in advance for appointments at drama schools. First, I visited the American Academy of Dramatic Arts and gave several readings in the hope of getting a scholarship. I was told that my reading was very good, and that I showed promise. They would love to have me attend their school, but they didn't give scholarships. I was deeply disappointed; I had my heart set on the Academy. But I was determined to go to drama school, and gave readings until I found one that would grant me a scholarship. At the same time, I was inquiring about how I could live in New York and what I could do to eat. Someone told me that the Henry Street Settlement House and the Greenwich House might be able to help me.

I had an interview at the Greenwich House, and got a job putting on plays and skits with the immigrant children in the neighborhood. In return, I would get a room and two meals a day, breakfast and dinner.

I began to hate being president of the student body at St. Lawrence. It was draining my energy, because a large group opposed me. They were always writing editorials in the college paper unfairly attacking me. I have never sought the presidency of anything since. I am content to work on a committee, to be a troubleshooter. Whatever ego trip drove me to become president of this or chairman of that went out of me at St. Lawrence and left me forever. My wife is the president of my own company. I wasn't sorry to be leaving St. Lawrence University. I never felt the gung-ho college spirit that others did. Everybody else was feeling nostalgic, and looking forward to reunions. For me it was all over. I had warm feelings about big, tall Wally Thompson with his prominent nose. Before I left for New York, he gave me his overcoat. It came down to my ankles. Moments like that touch me when I remember them. Paul Wolf, who helped me get a job in Rochester and introduced me to Peggy, was killed on the beaches of Anzio, a nice boy who died young. And there was lovely, lovely Isabel, with her enigmatic smile, never asking for anything. I think she missed me. I think she knew I was going out of her life. I hope she's happily married now. She was a nice part of my college life. But I had to get away.

Now, I look back at St. Lawrence with much more warmth, with much more appreciation for what I got out of my four years there, in making the transition that Louise Livingston wanted me to make, from janitor's boy to actor. If I had tried to go directly from Amsterdam to New York, the jump would have been too great.

My last year is very hazy. I can't even remember graduation day. An old program tells me that it was the 77th Annual Commencement, on June 12, 1939. I think the speaker was Mayor La Guardia, but I don't remember. I already had one foot firmly planted outside of SLU. Once I left, I didn't come back until years later, when they gave me an honorary doctorate degree. I never stop to savor a victory. When victory is inevitable, I've already left. A subconscious part of me does the mopping up, while the rest of me, like Patton, is already off flanking something else.

I was vaguely aware that something was afoot in the world that summer. Hitler was on the move, taking over Czechoslovakia and Austria. But all my thoughts were of the theater, drama school, getting a job, Greenwich Village. New York was the next big ripple in my life, and I couldn't wait to get there. I grabbed that diploma the way a runner in a relay race grabs a baton, and I ran for my life.

Four

NEW YORK, NEW YORK

I went back to the Tamarack Playhouse the summer after graduation. Every day, we all played the game of deciding what name would lead me to fame and fortune. "Norman Dems" was considered. I wanted a last name that started with "D," that wasn't Danielovitch or Demsky. Somebody suggested "Douglas." I liked it. The first name took longer. Finally, someone suggested "Kirk." It sounded right. I liked the crisp "k" sound. I didn't realize what a Scottish name I was taking.

It was exciting, seeing my new name on the program—"Kirk Douglas." I was a professional actor! My new life was beginning. When I left Amsterdam to go to college, I left Issur behind and Izzy took over. (Little did I know that Issur was with me all the time.) Now Izzy, who had done so much and won so many honors at SLU, was killed in the Tamarack Playhouse, and Kirk Douglas took over.

I think it's because I went from Issur to Izzy to Kirk that names have never meant anything to me. I've always confused the names of my four sons. I'll be calling one of them

Peter, and suddenly he'll say, "Dad, remember me? I'm Michael." It has finally got to the point where they don't even correct me, because they know who I mean, even if I call one of them "Kirk."

I had already arranged to work at the Greenwich Settlement House, but I arrived in New York about three days early, because I had nowhere else to go. I didn't want to go to Amsterdam, where my father was, or Schenectady, where the rest of my family was. And I no longer wanted to see Louise Livingston. I felt guilty, as if I had used her. On the other hand, I always tend to underrate what I give as a person; I put no premium on my contribution, and don't consider that I probably gave at least as much as I got. Perhaps we had used each other. In any case, I came to New York three days ahead of time and took a room, a compact little cubicle, at a place called the Mills Hotel. I paid a dollar a night.

The first thing I did was to go to a lawyer to officially change my name to Kirk Douglas. That was important to me; it took away some of the chicanery involved in having a different name. It was a surprisingly simple process: the lawyer made a petition, we went to court and gave the reasons I wanted my name changed, and I was legally Kirk Douglas, the name that I have carried for the rest of my life.

Now that I had a WASP name, I was introduced to another level of anti-Semitism. I'd find myself in a group of people who didn't know I was Jewish, listening to them say the things that are accepted in large sectors of the non-Jewish population, the things that in their nightmares Jews speculate non-Jews say, and that I found out, they do.

Until my job started, I had absolutely nothing to do. The three days seemed to drag on endlessly. I didn't know a single soul in New York. I was terribly lonely. I would walk around, wander into a clothing store, and talk to a sales clerk about the stripes on a shirt just to have someone to talk to. I walked around Times Square, all over Manhattan. I would look up at the immense, Art Deco Chrysler Building, and the Empire State Building—at that time, the tallest building in

New York. Everybody seemed to be hustling to a direct destination and I meandered.

Finally the day arrived—I went down to Greenwich Village to take on my chores. They installed me in a little attic room on the third floor of a house at 20 Jones Street, a narrow street congested with tenements, not far from the Greenwich House. Greenwich Village was very colorful, the place of struggling artists, with a wonderful mixture of older American and newer foreign-born elements. Passing by the lovely homes of very rich people around Washington Square, the children of immigrants came to the Greenwich House, which, like similar settlement houses, was founded originally to help the tremendous rush of immigrants adjust to the new world. People who have been helped by such places include Sam Levene, Alan King, Sammy Cahn, Burt Lancaster. This one was very accessible, easy to reach by subway. In those days the subway service was fast and safe, the pride of New York.

The Greenwich House had a little auditorium with a stage on the ground floor, a gymnasium, and workshops underneath. On the second floor was a long pleasant dining room where a simple breakfast—cereals, juice, coffee, and so forth —would be put out on the table in the morning. The evening meal was very congenial because we all dined together. Mrs. Simkovich, from a New England WASP family, ran the Greenwich House. She sat at one end of the long table, and Dr. Simkovich, a Columbia University Russian professor with a thick accent, sat at the other. The rest of the people around the table were social workers who were studying and working and living at the Greenwich House. An anthropologist named Bill Henderson was the most important one. They told me about him when I first arrived, but he had not come in yet; he was on his way back from Los Angeles—his second trip across the United States riding freight trains for his study of hoboes.

I remember the first time I saw Bill, a stocky Scotsman, striding down Jones Street. He wore a cap. His hard, creased face was totally encrusted with grime. He looked like a different person after he got cleaned up. He had a great sense of humor, and I liked him immediately. His room was opposite mine, and we became close friends. Some of the most pleasant moments of my early period in New York were spent with Bill Henderson.

Money was scarce for all of us, but occasionally Bill and I would go out and have a beer, and he would teach me Scottish songs like "I Belong to Glasgow," his home town. He kidded me that with a name like Kirk Douglas, I had to know some Scottish songs. I joked with him about some day singing that song in Scotland. Years later, I agreed to do a benefit in Edinburgh to raise money for the Olympic games. The Queen of England was going to be there. There was no rehearsal; I rushed in just before the performance, with no idea what I would do. "Just make something up," the public relations people said. Suddenly, I thought of my friend Bill Henderson, who had been killed in Alaska in World War II, and what he had taught me about the traditional rivalry between the cities of Edinburgh and Glasgow. I made my whole talk about him. Then, *a cappella*, I sang the song that Bill had taught me more than forty-five years earlier. It made me sad, because I loved Bill, and we had had many wonderful experiences together.

I was disappointed at not being able to go to the American Academy of Dramatic Arts (the tuition was five hundred unaffordable dollars) but immediately enrolled in another school that had accepted me and granted me a scholarship. I had attended classes there for three days when the American Academy notified me that they would give me a scholarship. I was embarrassed at leaving, but they were very gracious about it.

At that time, the American Academy of Dramatic Arts was located in the Carnegie Hall building at Fifty-seventh Street and Seventh Avenue. It was easy to take the express subway from Greenwich Village to Columbus Circle, and walk to Carnegie Hall. The entrance to the classrooms was next to the main entrance to the Hall, and I liked to sneak in and look down at the stage and listen to someone playing the piano or practicing for a singing recital—the only concerts I could afford. Next door was the famous Russian Tea Room, where the food of Russian aristocrats was served, and where I could never afford to eat. Now, the restaurant is very popular with show people.

During the first year of the two-year course, we had classes for half a day in pantomime, voice, makeup, costuming, dramatic analysis, fencing, etc. The second year, we worked on plays and then had dress rehearsals in the little theater down in the basement with the feared and famous Dr. Charles Jehlinger ("Jelly" behind his back) who had been the mentor of so many famous actors of stage and screen.

I was a little older than most of the other students. Many of them had not gone to college. I had graduated from college, and had also had professional experience—summer stock at the Tamarack Playhouse. Also, being male was an advantage. In those days, men were at a premium in drama schools, because there were so few of them. In my first year, I was the darling of the directors. They usually gave me leading roles. I began to think that I was hot stuff.

Life went along happily until Thanksgiving Day. I awoke and found that not only was the Greenwich House closed, so that no meals were being served, but that I had only a quarter in my pocket. No one was around. Most people were away, gone home for the holiday. I wasn't sure what to do. Then I remembered the Salvation Army, down in the Bowery. It was far from the Greenwich House, but I walked all the way to the Bowery, found the Salvation Army, and lined up with a lot of stumblebums to get my chit for a free Thanksgiving dinner. After I got my chit, I waited in another line to get my dinner. My stomach was rumbling as I watched people coming away from the counter with what looked and smelled to me like a delicious meal—pieces of turkey with a lot of mashed potatoes in a brown sauce. I suppose now it would be called slop. When I finally got to the counter, starving, I was abruptly told that they had run out of dinners. No more dinners. There I was with a little piece of paper in my hand and no meal. I walked all the way back to the deserted

Greenwich House, feeling lonely and sorry for myself. I used the quarter to buy something to eat to get me through that day. I ate a lot at breakfast the next morning.

The voice training and improvisation class at the Academy was conducted by Mr. D'Angelo. In one class, our assignment was to pretend that we were an owl.

> *There was an old owl lived in an oak,*
> *The more he heard, the less he spoke.*
> *The less he spoke, the more he heard.*
> *O if men were all like that wise bird.*

I thought a lot about it, and I came to class prepared to be a wise old owl. The professor went around the room asking each student to perform his interpretation of an owl. My friend Paul Wilson was sitting next to me. It was Paul's turn. He walked to the center of the room, squatted down, and became an owl. Mr. D'Angelo's eyes widened. He looked around the room and shushed everyone. Then he turned to Paul. He talked to him as one might talk to an owl, and said, "Hoooow oooold are you, oooowl?" Paul, who really looked amazingly like an owl, sort of ruffled his feathers, and in an old owl voice said, "Veeeerrry old." D'Angelo looked around the room. His lips muttered the words "genius, genius," and he carried on a conversation with this old owl. I was eager for my turn next, to do my version of an old owl. But Mr. D'Angelo was so swept away by the artistry of Paul's interpretation that he stopped the class. Then he arranged for the school to get together so that Paul could give his characterization of an old owl. All the members of the first year class got together, and again, D'Angelo talked to Paul as an old owl. Paul had never displayed such talents before, and had never had so much attention showered on him. Now he was basking in the glory of creating a masterpiece. I, on the other hand, was seething inside: perhaps I had a better owl to portray. But I was never given the opportunity. To this day, I resent that Mr. D'Angelo never gave me a chance to be an owl. From Paul's portrayal, which so swept Mr. D'Angelo away, we went on to other things. He never did say, "Mr. Douglas, I would like to see your interpretation of an owl." I think I would have given a masterly impersonation of an owl. But that's something lost to the world.

At the Academy, I fell in love. Oh how I fell in love! She was tall, slim, with ebony hair and ivory skin, beautiful blue eyes, and an Irish turned-up nose. Her name was Peggy Diggins, and she was Miss New York. The vote must have been unanimous. She was quiet and soft-spoken with a cool, slightly mocking look. She dressed very well, because even though she was a student at the Academy, she also made enough money modeling to take good care of herself. I was so smitten that I could hardly speak in her presence. I don't remember how we first met, what she said, or what I said. All I know is that I was shocked to find that she returned my affection. What I felt toward Peggy Diggins wasn't love. It was madness. I felt so vulnerable, cared so much about how she would look at me, what she would say. From time to time, we were permitted to bring a guest to dinner at the Greenwich House. I'll never forget the first time I brought Peggy. I was so proud, the way everyone looked at her, and stared at her. Behind his thick glasses, Dr. Simkovich's eyes went around in circles. He looked at me, and in his heavy accent said, "Ach, my provider." He insisted that she sit beside him, and he held her hand. Mrs. Simkovich didn't seem to be bothered at all by this demonstration of affection, or by Dr. Simkovich's constantly asking me when Peggy was coming back to dinner. I brought her several times, because it was one of the few ways that I could entertain her. I had no money. Very often, Peggy would take me to lunch or to a movie.

Burgess Meredith, one of the young stars of Broadway and Hollywood, asked Peggy to a formal dinner dance. She asked me if it was all right. I said, "Why, certainly, whatever is best for you." But oh, how my heart sank. The night she was at that dinner dance, I lay in bed up in the garret. I couldn't go out with Bill; I wanted to be alone. He was out with his girlfriend, and I was quietly suffering, thinking of my beautiful Peggy dancing with a Broadway star. What could I possibly have to offer her.

Then, around midnight, as in a fairy tale, I heard delicate footsteps on the creaky staircase. They sounded very familiar. And sure enough, the door, which had no lock, opened. There she stood in her beautiful evening gown, like Cinderella back from the ball. I just looked up at her. She undid the fastenings, let the gown drop, and quickly took off all her clothes and got in bed beside me. Tears of joy bubbled out of my eyes—to think that in the midst of all that wonderful glitter, she preferred to escape and run to be with me. My feeling for her was overpowering and I insisted that we get married. She agreed. As we lay together I couldn't believe that I, little Issur, had this beautiful creature in my arms who wanted to marry me.

I had heard that the easiest place to get married was Newark. I cajoled Bill Henderson into coming along as a witness, and off we went to get married. We answered some question incorrectly and weren't able to get a license. We went back to New York, determined to do it right next time.

Suddenly, Peggy was offered a Hollywood contract with a group of girls called the Navy Blue Sextet, billed as the six most beautiful girls in the world. My heart sank again. I couldn't believe that she would be leaving me. Hollywood seemed so far away. I was frightened that I would lose her, even though she assured me that I never would. The night before she left, I was miserable, but tried to hide it. After all, this was a great break for her.

The next day, she was gone. I dragged myself up to my little room and lay on the bed like a zombie. I heard a plane flying overhead around noon, the time of her flight. I imagined Peggy on that plane, flying away from me. The sound of the plane faded away. I was heartbroken.

The misery continued. She didn't write, she didn't call. I would have written to her, but I didn't know where. Night after night, I would just lie in bed, wide awake, completely convinced that I would die. I calmly accepted the fact that I would die—one couldn't go on without sleeping, just staring all night into a ceiling, enduring such misery. I was prepared to die. That summer, my third at the Tamarack Playhouse, is a blur of pain and thoughts of Peggy. I did my work some- how, but at night I would lie awake and think of her.

When I returned to New York in the fall, I had no place to stay. My job at the settlement house was over. Bill Hender- son was still working there, but they didn't think they were getting enough value out of me and my little playlets to merit a room and two meals a day. Paul (the owl) Wilson invited me to stay at his home until I found a place of my own. Paul's father was a well-known doctor, and he had a magnificent home on the East Side. I had my own bedroom; in the morn- ing the butler came in to raise the curtains and bring me breakfast. I liked it. I could have stayed for the rest of the year. But after about two weeks, I sensed that Mrs. Wilson was a little perturbed at the prospect of this drama student becoming a perennial boarder.

I met up with Peyton Price, a graduate of the Academy who was working there as an associate teacher, but primarily in charge of the technical side backstage. He had a small apartment in Greenwich Village with bunk beds. He let me use the upper bunk for about two months, until I finally got a job and could afford to move out. When I tried to pay him back, he said something to me that I've never forgotten and that affected a lot of what I did later in life. He said, "You don't owe me anything. I've been helped by others, and I pass it on to you. Now you owe it to someone else." Many times, when I've had the chance to help someone, I've thought of it as paying back a debt to Peyton. And they, in turn, owe it to someone else. What a beautiful philosophy! It could increase in geometrical progression, like a chain letter. We might even end up in a world with people actually being nice to one another.

I had to get a job to survive. And that's where Bill Van Sleet helped me tremendously. Bill was the most handsome man at the school, and a model. To me, he never looked like a student actor. He looked more like a businessman just leav- ing the office: he wore a hat and topcoat, and always had a newspaper tucked under his arm when he went to take the subway. He was very correct, with a wonderful sense of humor. A nice fellow. In addition to going to drama school and modeling, he also worked as a waiter to support his mother and sister, with whom he lived in Greenwich Village. His father was dead. Bill told me that his father had wanted to be cremated and have his ashes spread near where they used to live, upstate. He and his sister took the ashes to scatter them in the fields to fulfill their father's wishes. It was a windy day, and the wind blew the ashes back at them, into their eyes. The two of them became hysterical, laughing and saying, "Daddy's in my eye." I liked them, and very often Bill would have me over to share their modest dinner. He'd come back from waiting on tables with his pockets full of tips. I ate at their house several times. Bill was very good to me.

He took me to Schrafft's, at Broadway and Eighty-sixth Street, introduced me to the manager, and I had a job. Schrafft's doesn't exist anymore, but it was a chain of restaurants that had a very popular soda fountain and a restaurant that served light food—sandwiches and steaks and hamburgers, potatoes, coffee, milk shakes—that kind of thing. You worked mostly on tips. A lot of the waiters were aspiring actors. John Forsythe worked there for a while. So did John Hargreaves. Working at night gave you time to go to school, and later on, to look for an acting job, during the day. So I was very lucky, thanks to Bill, to get the job as a waiter at night.

I got a room on the West Side for three dollars a week. It was so tiny that when you opened the door halfway, it banged into the bed. That made it difficult to invite a girl in. You could say, "Let's go up and sit and talk," but when you opened the door and it banged into the bed, your intentions became rather obvious.

And then I got a call from Peggy Diggins. I thought she was in Hollywood. No, she was in New York on some publicity junket. She apologized: she'd meant to call, and she'd meant to write, but she'd been working so hard. She wanted to see me. I was ready to come right over. No, she couldn't do that, she had interviews and picture sessions, but why didn't I come over tomorrow morning, around eleven? She was at the Waldorf. To me, the Waldorf-Astoria seemed like the moon. I had heard of it, I had even walked by it. But who would go into the Waldorf-Astoria? The next morning, at eleven o'clock, I was there. I called her room from the lobby. In a sleepy voice, she asked me to come up. And there she was, still in bed, in a magnificent bedroom in a luxurious suite. Then I looked at her. She hadn't taken off her makeup, and the mascara around her beautiful eyes was smeared. Pain started to gnaw at my stomach. It hadn't even occurred to her to try to make herself presentable for me. I was tortured wondering what had happened the night before that she couldn't have cleaned her face before she went to bed. Hollywood had done this to her, and it made me hate Hollywood. She told me that she was sleepy and didn't have much time, she had such a busy schedule, but when she was through . . .

As I listened, I knew she was going out of my life. "How are things?" she asked, and handed me some money. Part of me wanted to fling it back at her. Why didn't I? Because another part of me looked and saw that it was fifty dollars. Fifty dollars. That would buy a lot of meals. I took the money. Like a little pimp, like a nothing. That act has always haunted me. I didn't have the strength to refuse. My love for her died that morning in that room in the Waldorf-Astoria as I stood looking at her smudged face. It died, but it left a terrible scar. From that moment, I was always frightened of falling in love, because to fall in love meant to become vulnerable, weak, enslaved, helpless. I was determined not to let it happen again.

I never saw Peggy Diggins again, but I always tried to get news of her. She had a bit part in a Warner Brothers B-movie called *Lady Gangster*. For a while she was a WAC. Then she married a rich doctor. And then I heard that she was killed at an early age in an automobile accident.

But sometimes at night, when I wanted a pleasant thought

to chew on before I went to sleep, I would hear footsteps coming up the stairs, and see her framed in the doorway, that tall figure with her hair tumbling down, the dress that came off her naked shoulders, cinched into her narrow little waist, and then flared out to her ankles. I could hear the rustle of her dress as it left her body. It was pleasant to think of before going to sleep.

I had made it into my senior year at the American Academy of Dramatic Arts, one of approximately 80 students out of the original 168 who had survived the weeding-out process of examination plays at the end of the junior year. I looked foward to my second year, because that was when we were ushered into the presence of Charles Jehlinger. Charles Jehlinger, the great director, the great teacher of acting who had taught Spencer Tracy and Rosalind Russell and Katharine Hepburn and Sam Levene, and who would later teach Jason Robards and Jennifer Jones and Anne Bancroft and Grace Kelly and so many others. He was almost eighty years old, slightly deaf, a little gray-haired man about five feet two with black eyebrows and piercing eyes that looked out at you from behind thick glasses. Everyone was intimidated by him.

You worked on a play with one of the directors in the school and then the dress rehearsals were conducted in the little theater in the basement of Carnegie Hall with "Jelly." We worked for several weeks on the first play, *Bachelor Born*. I had the lead, a Mr. Chips-type old man. The director was a woman who thought I was just marvelous. I couldn't wait to impress the great Jehlinger. Finally, it came time to go down into the little theater to present our play. We were all backstage, all nervous. The play started. I waited as it went on for a while, then I made my entrance. From the back of the dark auditorium, I heard a deep voice yell, "GO BACK!" It jolted me, but I turned around, took a deep breath, and made my entrance again to the same command, "GO BACK!" I began to perspire. I made my entrance again. "I DIDN'T SAY FASTER. GO BACK!" My hands started to get wet. I made my entrance again. "I DIDN'T SAY

SLOWER. GO BACK!" And again. And again. Seventeen times. Each time, I was met with the same command, growing in intensity, from the back of the theater: "GO BACK!" By now, I was rather dizzy. I didn't know what to do. Suddenly this little man came racing down the aisle and up the steps to the stage, waving a script in his hand and yelling, "DOUG-LAS!"

"Yes, Mr. Jehlinger."

He opened the script, held it under my nose. "Show me where it says 'Mr. Douglas' in the script."

"No, Mr. Jehlinger, it doesn't say 'Mr. Douglas' in the script."

He got very close to me and peered up at me with those eyes piercing through me, and said, "Then I don't want to see Mr. Douglas on the stage." Then he proceeded to tear me to shreds. He said he didn't know why I was wasting my time and my money going to the Academy when I obviously had no interest in being an artist. Why did I waste everybody's time if I was not going to work, if I was just going to do crummy imitations like this without doing my homework. He called me a cheap stock actor. I crumbled.

As I left the stage, dazed and totally shattered, I saw the ingenue, Diana Dill, sitting on a trunk in the wings, sobbing. I said, "What's the matter with *you?*"

She said, "Oh, God, this is just terrible! This whole thing! He's such a mean son of a bitch!"

I was touched by her sympathy. We went out for apple pie and milk, and she sort of snuffled herself together. I was devastated. My world was at an end. Jehlinger had proven to me that I was not meant to be an actor. I was destroyed. Diana was solicitous. I cried as we walked in Central Park. I told her about all the years that I had spent wanting to be an actor, from the time I recited the poem about the red robin of spring, the grade school plays, junior high and high school plays, all the college plays and all the studying and summer stock, only to find that acting was not my profession. I said, "I feel so awful about this. My sisters sacrificed so much so that I could go to college, and now I find out, after all this time, that I don't have what it takes. I always thought that I had talent, but I don't. I'll probably have to go back to Amsterdam and sell shoes."

She said, "You know what Jelly's doing, don't you?"

I said, "Obviously, I have no talent. What's the point of my staying on here? I've got to think of another line of work."

She said, "No. He's testing you. He's mad as hell because you didn't do your homework. He wants to know if you're open to work with, that you haven't got a resistance. He does this all the time—he tries to break people down."

A ray of hope. Maybe she was right. I was very grateful for the comfort Diana gave me, and felt a little more hopeful. We kissed for a while. I knew I had to give acting one more try. The next day I went down to the little theater. Jelly said, "Oh, you're back, young man, are you?"

I said, "Yes."

"You interested in working now?"

"Yes, Mr. Jehlinger," very humbly.

That dress rehearsal under Jelly's direction took three days. We never did get through more than an act and a half. All of the delays were caused by criticisms directed at me. I would start to do a very dramatic scene and a voice from the back of the theater would yell, "Nya nya nya nya nya! Why is that boy making those hideous sounds?" I would stop for a moment and start again.

I was going through the most miserable period of my life, but I was determined not to leave. By now word had gotten around the school about what was happening, and other students came in to watch. Many of them were delighted to see the arrogant Douglas, such a star the first year, always playing the lead, get this beating from Jehlinger. They would sit quietly, muffling their laughter, while Jehlinger crucified me. At one point, when he started to yell at me as I was in the middle of a scene, I just lost all control. He came up to the stage, yelling, "Nya nya nya nya nya. What's the matter, boy? Got a pain in your tummy?" Without realizing what I was doing, I picked up a chair. I wanted to smash it right down across his head. He just looked up at me and said calmly, "If striking an old man will make you a better actor, go right ahead, son."

Jelly was notorious for driving students mad with frustration. There was a rumor at the Academy about a student who had thrown a table at him from the stage and knocked him flat on his back. It hadn't fazed Jelly; he went right on criticizing, prone. Rumor had it that that anonymous, probably untalented, student had left the Academy and was never seen or heard from again, just disappeared into oblivion. Years later, I found out it was Edward G. Robinson, and that his only regret was that he hadn't killed Jelly.

Jelly worked in different ways with different students. He was very gentle and sweet with Diana, and offered to lend her money to buy galoshes once when she came in with her shoes wet, because he felt that actors had to look after their health.

Diana was a very attractive, charming girl, very well liked. I always thought she had a crush on Bill Van Sleet. But Diana and I saw each other for a while, casually; she felt that I had quite a reputation with the ladies, and kept her distance. It was an attraction of total opposites. She was from an old established family in Bermuda, where her father was the attorney general. As far as I was concerned, she had been born with a silver spoon in her mouth. I used to call her "Miss-Everything-Is-Lovely-Dill." We were intrigued by each other's backgrounds, and learned from each other how the other half lived. We had very long conversations, sitting on the wall up by Riverside Drive.

In 1940, there was a lot to discuss. There was a war going on in Europe. Refugees were beginning to come into the United States—the lucky ones, who escaped the concentration camps. The Schrafft's where I worked became a hangout for a lot of them, and I heard them all speaking in German. But what I resented, especially as a Jew, was that so many of them were so richly clad, with expensive furs and jewelry. At a time when the world was shaken by this horrible war and at a time when the United States was at the brink of entering the war, these rich German Jews sat in Schrafft's flaunting their wealth, and I was embarrassed.

It is strange to me how little I remember about the war that was taking place in Europe. I would hear about the blitzing of London, the wonderful brave English who were withstanding the assaults of Hitler's regime. I read about Hitler and his speeches. I heard about the lightning warfare in what became the Iron Curtain countries. I heard, but not in defined terms, about the war against the Jews. But the war itself seemed a long way away. And when you're young, in your early twenties, you read about it, but you're more concerned with getting the job that's going to make you a star on Broadway.

After Peggy Diggins, there was no special girl for quite a long time. There were lots of girls, but nobody special. I went out occasionally with Betty Bacall, who later became Lauren Bacall. She was a junior at the Academy, not more than fifteen or sixteen years old. I was a senior, and had been in summer stock, so Betty looked up to me, and I think had kind of a schoolgirl crush. She lived near the Schrafft's where I worked, and she would come over, usually alone, sit at one of my tables and nurse a cup of coffee for an hour. We usually tried to keep the tables moving, because we worked for tips. Betty would sit there, pretending to sip her coffee, and watch me. One evening when I presented her with her bill, she said, "I don't have the money," with that throaty laugh. I was rather annoyed. But she always had that tremendous personality, and you couldn't stay mad for long.

Betty used to make fun of the long overcoat I wore, the one that Wally Thompson had given to me. I was still wearing it, and it still came down to my ankles. When she realized that I couldn't afford to buy a coat, she talked an uncle of hers out of an overcoat that was closer to my size, and gave it to me. I was always touched by that act. And how did I repay her? One warm spring evening on a rooftop in Greenwich Village, I tried to seduce her. Unsuccessfully. As far as I'm concerned, Lauren Bacall can do no wrong.

Somehow I got through my second year at the Academy.

Jehlinger was never as cruel to me as he had been in the first play. Occasionally he even complimented me. I realized what he was working toward, and he helped me tremendously. He was working against a certain glibness that I had, a quick facility, a lack of depth. And that's what he kept harping on. Jelly taught me how to build a character. I finally figured out what he wanted: for me not to make an entrance, but to be going from one room to another with an intention, to know why I was going from one room to another. Jelly would make you find things out for yourself. He wouldn't say what he wanted, but let you go on and on and on until, just as you thought you were going crazy, you finally figured out that what he wanted was truthful behavior. The worst thing he could say was "amateur," and that shrunk you right into the ground. After a scolding from Jelly, you were never unprofessional again.

Every so often during that second year, I would hit a moment in a play that even I knew was very good, something unusual that an actor occasionally hits. It's as if there are two brains in your head, two different personalities, and one is watching the other. The one that's playing the role is completely in the part, with all the warmth and feeling, while the other is watching and guiding it. In a peculiar way, it reminded me of when I had my tonsils out and in my nightmare there were two of me, and one was looking at little Issur behind the ash can.

I've talked with other actors about this. I remember once talking with Laurence Olivier, who told me that this is very often true for him. There's a part that's controlling you, even though in acting one always says, "Don't direct yourself." What we mean by that is, you don't want the audience to see you saying to yourself, "Now I'll sit down. Now I'll take out a cigarette." The part of you that's in control of the whole situation must be way back. That's also the part of you that, no matter how dramatic the scene is, must continue to function. For example, when I was playing Vincent van Gogh in *Lust for Life*, in the scene where I cut off my ear, I had to look into the mirror. In order to get it in the camera, I had to appear as if I were looking in the mirror. The camera looked into the mirror and got the reflection. I couldn't see myself in the mirror, but had to pretend that I did. And then I had to hit exact marks in order to get the light on my face the right way. So, you can be playing someone who's lost all control of his senses, but there's got to be a part of you that's guiding the whole thing. And it sometimes happens that suddenly, while you're doing it, even the part of you that's detached and in control knows that it's good. It's a wonderful feeling. And I must say, it hasn't happened to me often enough. But when you do hit those moments in acting, it's very gratifying.

Working at Schrafft's was pleasant. When a customer didn't finish a sandwich, you'd stuff it in your mouth as you brought it back into the kitchen, so you'd get something extra to eat. The waiters were a nice bunch. Often, after we were through working, around midnight, and our pockets were filled with tips, we'd stop somewhere and have a couple of beers. I remember one night, a rather warm evening for spring. I was feeling a little giddy. We started to walk back through Central Park to Columbus Circle to get the subway. I looked up at the skyline of Central Park South and pointed to the Hampshire House, which symbolized great elegance to me. I said, "You see that? One of these days, fellas, I'm going to be somebody, and I'm coming back to this town, and I'm going to take a suite on the twenty-fifth floor of the Hampshire House, and I'm going to look down and see you guys here in the park." We all laughed.

I was graduated from the American Academy of Dramatic Arts in June of 1941. I had worked my way through four years of college and two years of drama school, all to prepare myself to become an actor on the stage. In the last year at the Academy, agents would come to see the plays. I was disappointed that not one agent asked to sign me, and six agents asked to sign Bill Van Sleet. I suppose the agents always thought in terms of "this would be a fellow who would make a hit movie." And, as I've found so often later in life, the agents were wrong. Bill, with his six agents, never worked

on Broadway and never worked in movies. He was a wonderful guy who continued to make a good living as a model.
But no agents seemed to see any quality in me. Diana Dill
was the only one of our class who was offered a job acting—
a one-year Hollywood contract. I was furious. Another
woman about to be ruined like Peggy Diggins. I dashed off
a twelve-page letter telling her that she should absolutely
not go to Hollywood, that it was a terrible, artificial place,
and that if she had any guts at all, she would stay in New
York and try to get work on the stage. I didn't hear from her,
but I heard about her: she had gone to Hollywood.

I made the rounds in New York, trying to get an agent. I
remember one agent in a crummy office, with broken-down
sofas. He consented to an appointment. I could do a scene
with one of the girls from our class. We worked out a dramatic scene, came at the appointed time. We waited a long
time in the very run-down outer office, and finally were admitted to his slightly less run-down inner office. We sat on
two chairs in front of a battered desk across from the stereo-
typical fat, cigar-chomping agent. "Go ahead." We started
performing our scene. The telephone rang. We stopped. He
said, "No, no, go ahead." We continued our scene while he
talked on the phone. Occasionally he'd look up at us, then
turn away and concentrate on what he was saying on the
telephone. It was painful, like that Saturday morning at
Goldmeer's warehouse, the roaring Chuctanunda Creek in
the background, the telephone ringing, and the salesman
taking orders for groceries, while I was reciting my Sanford
Gold Medal prize-winning oration.

That is the pathetic side of our profession: the rejections.
They're so shattering, so devastating. The hurt of it never
leaves you. The pain is always there: those moments when
you think you've got the part; the constant calling back, the
false reassurance that you'll get it. Then you don't. It's so
humiliating. I discouraged all four of my sons from ever
going into this profession. Obviously, they didn't listen to
me. But my feeling is, there's only one way to go into this
profession, and that is, there's nothing else you can do; you

have to do it. The best thing an actor can do is try to stop others from becoming actors. You have to overcome almost insurmountable obstacles to achieve success. Ruth Gordon attended the American Academy for one year, and was told to go home and forget about acting, because she didn't show any promise. A few months later, she made her Broadway debut. But if you don't have that drive, and if you don't have that tough skin to protect you from those rejections . . . Most people don't. Rejection is just something that you endure. It doesn't leave even if you become a star. Then you get rejected on a different level. There's a part that you want to do, and some other star gets it. The definition of an actor—someone who loves rejection.

The great John Barrymore, in the twilight of his career, was playing in *My Dear Children*. His drunken escapades offstage filled the newspapers with scandals. He had become a self-parody. But I wanted to see him perform. I bought a half-price student ticket and sat up in the balcony, tingling with anticipation.

I was surprised at how short Barrymore was. But as the play continued, he became a giant, a great actor whose talents could soar at a whim. Playing opposite him was Joan Barry, his new young wife. In the middle of a dramatic scene, a heckler started giving her a bad time. Barrymore stopped, walked down to the footlights, raised that famous eyebrow, and stared the heckler down. "Shut up, you drunken S.O.B.! Or come up on this stage!"

The man stared, open-mouthed.

Barrymore finished him off. "You're goddamn quiet now. Keep it that way!" Barrymore casually picked up the line, the scene, the emotion, right where he had left them. I was in awe.

But I didn't have an agent, and I didn't have a job. I went back to summer stock. The Nuangola Playhouse was a little summer theater in Nuangola, Pennsylvania, run by Royal Stout and his wife, an elderly couple, old-time actors; she still played many roles. It was an unusually long season for summer stock—almost eighteen weeks. When the actors complained to Royal Stout about the small salary (twenty-five dollars a week) he said, "Listen, summer stock is just to keep the wrinkles out of an actor's stomach." I started out doing work around the stage and playing bit parts, and was always begging them to give me a chance to play a leading role. Finally, I got one in *Broadway*, and I made a good impression.

From then on I played leading roles. We would rehearse for a week, and play the show for a week. It didn't take me long to realize what a difficult chore it was to be playing a leading role in one play every night while rehearsing a leading role for another play every day. I laugh now as I look back at it. I was so greedy, so anxious to play leading roles, but after three or four leading roles in a row, I was exhausted. It was all you could do to just learn the lines before you were suddenly starting the next play. Every Monday morning they handed out "sides"—printed pages that gave you the last line of the speech before yours and then your speech. I would wait to see what I was going to get and despair when they handed me a big, thick manuscript—a very large role. After only a few weeks, I was begging them again—this time to let me play a smaller part, just so I could get some rest.

Back in New York that fall, I worked at Schrafft's at night and during the day made the rounds. I would get doughnuts and orange juice at Nedick's for ten or fifteen cents, and go into Walgreen's Drug Store on Broadway and Forty-fourth, the actors' hangout, and spend another ten cents on a copy of *Actor's Cue*, a sheet published by Leo Shull, which gave tips to aspiring actors, listing what plays were coming up, and where to go for interviews.

Once, on my rounds I went to the Katharine Cornell–Guthrie McClintic office in Radio City. That was the acme of theater: Katharine Cornell Productions, Guthrie McClintic Productions. On one of my trips there, Stanley Gilkey, McClintic's assistant, sent me down to the Booth Theatre, where they were doing tryouts for a Grace George–C. Aubrey Smith show called *Spring Again*. Guthrie McClintic was producing and directing. I waited around for a while, and then came my turn. They handed me a piece of paper with about four lines on it. "Learn this to the tune of 'Yankee Doodle.'" So I was offstage, quickly looking through the lines, humming to myself, "Yankee Doodle came to town, a-riding on a pony." Then, finally, after about an hour, they called me on. The stage manager told me to make an entrance through the front door and sing the telegram to the tune of "Yankee Doodle." I came in, sang as loudly as I could, and was shocked to find that I had the part, the role of singing-telegram boy. I was actually going to be in a play on Broadway! I was going to be paid to do something that I would have been delighted to do for nothing. I was on Broadway!

During rehearsals, I was never far from Guthrie McClintic. I did everything I could for him. If he needed something, I immediately got it for him: a match, cigarette, milk shake, coffee. The second day, they made me the assistant stage manager. I did everything I could for the stage manager, too. It got to the point where, if either of them wanted anything, all they had to say was "Kirk!" and I was right there. I was also given the job of understudying four of the other parts, and by the time we went on the road for five one-night tryouts in New England (Northampton, Massachusetts; Bridgeport, Connecticut, etc.) I had become the stage manager. As far as I was concerned, there wasn't enough for me to do. I was now the stage manager, understudying four roles, singing the telegram onstage, and I also directed the understudy rehearsals. And I worked in the office.

I was the first student in my class at the Academy to get a job on the Broadway stage. On opening night, Lauren Bacall was there with her mother. I was pleased, but surprised. After the show, I was in the dressing room that I shared with four or five other actors, three flights up at the top of a circular iron staircase. In the midst of the excitement of opening night and all the friends of Grace George and C. Aubrey Smith and the other people backstage, I heard a voice yelling up the staircase, "DOUGLAS!" I recognized that voice; I'd heard it often enough. My heart started to pound as I raced down the steps, thinking, "Boy, I'm going to get it again." As I came down, out of breath, to ground level, there he was. "Yes, Mr. Jehlinger." He again peered up at me with those piercing eyes and said, "You're on the right track, son. Keep it that way." That was one of the happiest moments of my life.

Grace George and C. Aubrey Smith were both charming, delightful people, real professionals of the old school. The curtain opened with Grace George sitting on a sofa, and every night, perhaps ten minutes before the curtain went up, she would be in place, sitting on the sofa as if she lived there, ready, all set, waiting. She would talk to me for about five minutes before the curtain went up. And usually she would ask me for half a cup of Coca-Cola. It tickled me. The drink of Coca-Cola gave her a lift, like a shot. Sometimes she hummed "Bewitched, Bothered, and Bewildered." She loved those words. She was always there, always on time. And I was always nearby. I looked forward to it. I treasured those moments with her.

Then it was Thanksgiving. I was invited to Guthrie McClintic and Katharine Cornell's house at 23 Beekman Place for Thanksgiving dinner. It was beautiful, with French windows that opened onto a garden terrace overlooking the East River, and memorabilia on the walls. The two lower floors were for living and dining. Katharine Cornell had the third floor to herself, and Guthrie McClintic had the fourth to himself. The fifth floor was taken by their friend Gertrude Macy. I was ecstatic! There was champagne. There was caviar. There was Tallulah Bankhead looking at me and saying in that deep voice of hers, "Don't look at me like that, young man." Two years earlier, I had been down on the Bowery and couldn't even get a meal from the Salvation Army. Now here I was in the lap of luxury. And I remembered my mother's words: "America is a wonderful land."

Suddenly—Pearl Harbor—the shock that the Japanese had come all the way across the Pacific and dropped bombs on Pearl Harbor, blown our men to bits, destroyed our Navy. All the other attacks had been far away, against other countries, other people. Now they were attacking *us*. There was fear of more attacks. People fled their homes along the beach. California was blacked out.

Actors were forming units, doing *This Is the Army;* Moss Hart and others were writing plays. I was asked to join a unit. I was young and strong and healthy. I didn't want to become a member of some acting group. I felt a wave of patriotism, and a wave of Jewishness about what was happening in Europe with Hitler. We had no exact picture of the atrocities. But we knew enough. Hitler wanted to take over the world, eradicate the Jews—*"Deutschland über Alles."* I wanted to fight, to drop bombs on them.

I applied for the Air Force. I failed the psychological tests —I evaluated all my options too carefully. "To fly a plane, we need someone young, who makes a quick decision and acts." The Air Force considered me too old, too mature and rational at the ripe old age of twenty-five.

In the meantime, I was very flattered that Guthrie McClintic was taking a personal interest in me. That fall, he was going to direct Katharine Cornell and an all-star cast in *The Three Sisters*. There were parts for two young Russian soldiers. He told me that I could play one. I was excited.

While we were still doing *Spring Again*, McClintic invited me over early one evening, before the theater. We were alone in his house. He talked to me about Katharine Cornell, told me wonderful stories about the theater. Finally, I said, "I think I ought to get over to the theater." McClintic kept talking. I said, "Uh, it's getting late. I'm the stage manager. I have to go." Then his hands started to wander. Frightened, I bolted for the door, raced to the theater. For the first time while I was stage manager, the half-hour call had already been given when I arrived. "I was late because I was having a meeting with Mr. McClintic." There were titters from the older members of the cast. I was embarrassed.

It came time for the summer road tour of *Spring Again*. That first day, the whole cast, including many new faces, was assembled in the theater waiting for McClintic to show up and begin the rehearsal he had called. The telephone rang

—McClintic. He would be over later, told me to go ahead and start the rehearsal because I knew how the play was done. I did this for about forty-five minutes when McClintic suddenly appeared. He had been backstage for half an hour. Pleased with what he had heard and seen, he said, "Continue, Kirk. You take care of it." From then on, I directed the rehearsals.

McClintic was now putting together the cast of *The Three Sisters*, and I was going to play one of the young Russian soldiers. Then he told me that he had been thinking it over, and had decided that I wasn't quite right for either part. This shattered me—if ever there was a part I could play, it was a young Russian soldier. Maybe my rejection of Guthrie that night in his home did it, because two other actors—one of them rather effeminate—played the Russian soldiers.

McClintic gave me the choice of playing the juvenile lead in the road tour of *Spring Again,* or working on *The Three Sisters* as the second assistant director—not the assistant director, but a *second* assistant—and playing a walk-on where I carried a samovar behind Edmund Gwenn and said nothing. He threw in the role of an offstage echo.

Our lives are filled with decisions. Here I was, twenty-five years old. Should I travel to different towns all over the country, playing the juvenile lead, a role that I wanted so badly? Jayne Meadows was the ingenue; maybe a little romance might develop on the road. Or should I work with this all-star cast—Katharine Cornell, Ruth Gordon, Edmund Gwenn, Judith Anderson, Dennis King, and Alexander Knox? I'm proud of myself for deciding that it would be better for me to stay in New York and be close to this talented group of people, even if it meant that every night I had to stand offstage and watch two young actors handsomely dressed as Russian soldiers playing the parts that I wanted.

The Three Sisters opened at the Ethel Barrymore Theatre on December 21, 1942, and ran for 122 performances. Every night I'd be backstage, and when the young Russian soldier (the part that I coveted) was going off to war, he would look out across the forests and cry, "YO HO!" in farewell to the trees. My job, as his echo, was to call back, "Yo ho-o."

Humiliating! I was bitter. But I did everything I could with the walk-on samovar role. I got all made up, put on a beautiful Russian uniform. One of the pictures in *Time* magazine was of me in the center with the samovar, in my white tunic, looking very important, surrounded by Katharine Cornell and Judith Anderson and Ruth Gordon and all the others. When we did the scene, I was supposed to follow Edmund Gwenn onto the stage, but I would wait a beat and then sweep on behind him, flourishing the samovar. The audience always expected me to say something, to be someone important. But that was my entire role. An aspiring actor is so anxious to make an impression that it doesn't occur to him that he is distorting a scene.

Katharine Cornell was a gracious, charming woman. She dealt with this problem of my entrance in a diplomatic way. I think anybody else would have just kicked me in the ass and said, "Look, don't come sweeping on." But she suggested that I try a little bit of makeup to look more like a Russian peasant. So they put unattractive, dopey peasant makeup on me, and got me to just follow on behind Edmund Gwenn.

Every night I was thrilled to stand on the sidelines and watch these great actors perform. Judith Anderson was sweet and affectionate. Garson Kanin was backstage sometimes, courting Ruth Gordon. She was very aloof, as if unaware of anyone else's existence. But what an actress! I never tired of watching her brilliant performance, especially her scene in the third act. To be associated with all those great artists and Chekhov's *The Three Sisters* was worth dopey peasant makeup.

I still wanted to fight for my country, but I didn't know where to go after my rejection by the Air Force. I was told that the Navy was the most difficult branch of the service to get into, so I applied for the Navy. Again, I was shocked by the results of one of the tests: my eyesight was not quite good enough. It was just on the borderline. I bought a book called *Sight Without Glasses.* I read it and did the exercises for a month. Then I passed the eye examination and joined the Navy.

My notions of war came from poetry. There were cynical poems, like:

> *Does it matter? losing your legs? . . .*
> *For people will always be kind.*
> *And you need not show that you mind*
> *When the others come in after hunting*
> *To gobble their muffins and eggs.*

There had been a man on our street in Amsterdam who had difficulty with his speech, and someone said that he had been gassed during the war. But that was all mixed in with my mother's singing me to sleep with "It's a long way to Tipperary" in her broken accent. In school, war was always romantic: "I have a rendezvous with death/At some disputed barricade . . . " That ended with, "When Spring trips north again this year/And I to my pledged word am true/I shall not fail that rendezvous." It was glorious and romantic.

That was what I was feeling when I headed off to South Bend, Indiana, to train as a naval officer at Notre Dame Midshipman School.

Five

ENSIGN DOUGLAS

The Army turned out new officers in three months—
"Ninety-Day Wonders." The Navy took 120 days, and nobody called us wonders. I was surprised at how difficult
Notre Dame Midshipman School was. A lot of cheating went
on. If there was any way to get information on tests in advance, few people hesitated to avail themselves of it. And
still, many flunked out. I had to work like hell just to pass. I
had been out of college for four years, and learning so many
subjects that didn't interest me—navigation and gunnery
and damage control—was difficult. I was particularly bad at
aircraft identification. An airplane silhouette was flashed on
a screen, and we were supposed to identify it immediately
—friendly, enemy, what kind. The first time, the plane was
shown for one second. I could identify most of the planes,
but by the time it got down to half a second, I was lost
completely. We were supposed to be able to identify them
at one-tenth of a second. Everyone else in the class seemed
to be able to do it. I thought, "My God, if I'm ever in command of a ship and they have to depend on me to identify

aircraft, we're in trouble." I couldn't tell a Messerschmitt from a Mercedes.

We did everything on the double: run to classes, to drill, to mess hall, to our quarters. We lived six to a room. I hated it. I'd lie awake at night, just to feel that I had some time to myself.

But it's all vague, because I've pushed away everything connected with World War II. Even people who know me well would be surprised to learn that I was a Communications Officer in antisubmarine warfare during World War II. I never talk about it. I don't know what happened to my uniform or whatever medals I got for being in the Atlantic or the Pacific or wherever. They're all packed away somewhere. There's only one picture of me from that time, in shorts, sitting on the railing of a ship, with a rifle in my hand. War is such a stupid waste of time, young people on a ship looking for other young people and trying to blow them up.

While I was at Notre Dame Midshipman School, I read that Katharine Cornell's production of *The Three Sisters* was coming to Chicago, not too far away. On a weekend leave, I went to see them, full of anticipation. My cut-rate hotel was about thirty blocks from the luxurious Ambassador East where they were staying and where we were going to have lunch. It was a sunny day, even though it was winter, so I walked, wearing my uniform and a thin black raincoat. I didn't know that there is less correlation between sunshine and air temperature in the Windy City than anywhere else in the world. I can't remember ever being as cold as I was that day. Each breath was like inhaling clusters of needles. I thought I would die. But I made it. And there, sitting at the first table in the Pump Room at the Ambassador East, was Katharine Cornell, the first lady of the theater. I was proud as I made my entrance in my naval uniform. They all looked at me with admiration, as if our country had nothing to fear with men like me to protect it.

Some time after that, I happened to see the cover of *Life* magazine. "Hey, I know that girl!" I said. "The hell you do!" my roommates responded. There, wearing a checked blouse and carrying a parasol, was Diana Dill. I hadn't heard from her in the two years since I'd sent her that letter and she'd gone off to Hollywood. "Yeah, I know her. And you know what else? I'm going to marry her." They didn't believe me. I wrote a letter to Diana, care of *Life*. A while later, I got a response—favorable. The letter had been forwarded to the John Robert Powers Modeling Agency, then to Diana. Hollywood had turned out to be just as terrible for her as I had predicted, and she was now back in New York, modeling during the day, and working as a nurse's aide at Bellevue at night. I suggested we get together next time I was in New York. She agreed.

After the four months at Notre Dame, I came back to New York wearing my new uniform with the single stripe of the ensign on the sleeve. I immediately looked up Diana. She was in Bermuda. That was unfair—unpatriotic! I was on my way to the wars, possibly to be killed, and she wasn't in New York.

Everyone else I knew was away. I spent a miserable leave, lonely in my ensign's uniform. I went back to Amsterdam and Albany to visit my family. They had mixed feelings about seeing me in uniform. After all, my father had left Russia to escape serving in the army. Before I knew it, I had to report to Miami to take courses in antisubmarine warfare.

We lived comfortably in Miami. The other sailors there told me it could go on for a while: after you took the courses, you hung around, sometimes a year, before being assigned to a ship. This was all right with me, because I had met a very attractive divorcée with a lovely apartment and a Cadillac. I was all set to spend a terrific year.

Within two weeks of finishing the course, I was ordered to New Orleans for further instruction and for commissioning of a ship, although men who had been in Miami for months were still there. Before reporting to New Orleans I got two weeks' leave. I got in touch with Diana and went to New York.

We met in midtown, had lunch and talked. She had done a lot of reading in Hollywood to keep herself sane in be-

tween posing for cheesecake photos with battleships and life
preservers—fairly humiliating after having spent two years
studying Sophocles and Shakespeare. I had tickets for a matinee of a play called *Kiss and Tell,* then we went out to
dinner at the Penthouse Club on Central Park South. I said,
"You might not know it, but you're going to be my wife."
She seemed willing to entertain this notion—after the war
was over.

Wartime—everything so intense. Here I was, going off to
antisubmarine warfare. We had so little time, and were together constantly. Diana often rode in Central Park, and
asked me if I'd like to go. We went to the stables on Central
Park South. I wanted to impress Diana, so I said something
I'd heard somewhere: "I'd like a good piece of horseflesh."
They brought out a giant, snorting, stomping stallion. They
gave Diana a very docile horse, and off we went into the
park. Diana, who had ridden all her life, was in the lead, and
couldn't see me struggling with the monster I was riding.
When we got up near the reservoir, she said, "If there are no
cops around, we can really let it out and go like a bat out of
hell right around the reservoir. It's marvelous." She spurred
her horse and it galloped off. I spurred my horse and it threw
me. Then he galloped off, stirrups flapping. Somewhere on
the path, a woman screamed. I got up and brushed myself
off and waited. Diana finally rode up, leading my horse. It
really pissed me off that she had taken care of the horse
before she had come to see how I was. She claimed that she
knew that I would stay put, so she caught the horse first. She
held him while I climbed back on. By now, the demon steed
knew who was in charge and kept turning opposite any direction I tried to lead him. I was literally riding around in
circles. Now that she looked, Diana could see that I was
having a problem, and swapped horses with me. Back at the
stable, they bawled the hell out of me. "Get off! What are
you doing riding a ladies' horse?" It was the final humilia-
tion. Diana just howled with laughter.

We also saw lots of plays. Or at least, the second acts of
lots of plays. We became adept at mingling with the crowds

returning after intermission. And then, all too soon, I had to report to New Orleans, and Diana went to Arizona on a modeling job. We were calling and writing every day, back and forth, back and forth, trying to grab every moment before I shipped out. Finally, we decided, "This is crazy. Why don't we just do it?" If we were married, Diana could meet me wherever we went on our shakedown cruise, and maybe follow me around as a navy wife. So Diana took the train straight to New Orleans from Arizona, and we were married the next day, November 2, 1943, by the navy chaplain. We were both very nervous on the ferry to the Naval Chapel on Algiers Island—"Not too late to back out," "Really, it's O.K. to back out," "No, no, I'm fine." It was a magical ceremony, with young officers in dress uniform holding their swords up to form an arch as we walked underneath. The reception was held in the studio of a sculptor named Angela Gregory, with a candlelit path leading to the door.

We were also married by a rabbi, who made us sign an agreement that our children would be raised as Jews, which I assured Diana I would not adhere to. Our feeling was that if we had children, we wouldn't raise them one way or another. I thought it was silly of the rabbi not to marry us unless we had signed a contract that was totally unenforceable and nobody's business but ours.

We spent a very romantic month in New Orleans, living in the most enchanting setting, in one of the Pontalba buildings, two famous buildings with that wonderful New Orleans steel grillwork. We lived on the top floor, a little attic overlooking St. Louis Cathedral and Jackson Square. There were no clocks in the apartment, and all the windows were about a foot and a half off the floor, so if you wanted to know the time on the clock on St. Louis Cathedral, you had to lie flat on your stomach and look out the window. We ate our fill of oysters and Creole and Cajun food. Every morning I would take the ferry out to the Algiers Naval Station, where we were preparing the commissioning of our ship.

Finally the day came for the departure of our ship, the PC (for Patrol Craft) 1139. It was about 175 feet long. We had a crew of seventy-two, and five officers, of which I, at twenty-six, was probably the oldest. It was an all-green crew. Two noncommissioned officers had been to sea before; the skipper had been to sea once. The rest of the officers, including me, and most of the crew had never been to sea. I was the proud new Communications Officer, and also the Officer of the Deck, which enabled me to carry a firearm on my side. Our ship was tied alongside a dock with other vessels in front and behind as our wives and sweethearts, including my new bride, gathered on the dock to wave us off. A small brass band played, the chaplain blessed the ship, the new young captain gave orders: "Right rudder forward! Left rudder back!" The stern of the ship bounced against the dock. Sailors ran over with little bumpers to try to protect it. Then the bow started to bounce toward the dock, and they ran to the other side with the little bumpers. Then we backed up too far and rammed into the ship behind us. It partially sank. We swerved again to one side and ripped a life raft off the ship in front of us as we finally pulled away from the dock. Everyone watching us was embarrassed. Except Diana, who was doubled up with laughter, tears rolling down her cheeks, as the skipper's wife glared at her.

We sailed peacefully down the Mississippi, en route to Miami to pick up some radar gear before joining the war. I was being very gung ho, terribly official, and had my communications group, the four sailors under me, come into the wardroom so I could explain to them how I intended to run the department. As I was talking, the movement of the ship altered. It started to go up. And down. And up. And down. And I began to get a queasy feeling in my stomach. I ignored it for as long as I could and continued explaining codes. But the queasy feeling kept mounting, mounting, and suddenly I bolted out of the wardroom, ran to the side of the ship and threw up. I was the first one on the ship to be seasick. We had not yet entered the Gulf of Mexico.

I could see my team suppressing their grins as I came back looking green and still trying to carry on with my instructions. The rest of the shakedown cruise from New Orleans to

Miami was disastrous. The waters were rough. I felt miserable most of the time. If you've never been seasick, you don't know what it is. You want to die. You actually entertain the notion of throwing yourself into the sea and ending it all. But, since I was an officer, seasickness was no excuse; I still had to perform my duties. Having command of the ship lessened the seasickness; my fear of the responsibility of being in charge was so tremendous that seasickness paled in comparison.

One day, when I was Officer of the Deck and the seas were not too rough, I decided to call a drill, and sounded the alarm for general quarters. Everybody rushed to their positions.

The skipper came running up, wild-eyed and breathless. "What have you got?"

"Oh, nothing. I just thought I'd have a drill."

"You dumb son of a bitch! Don't you ever do that to me again! Don't you ever have a drill without letting me know!"

It hadn't occurred to me that he might be concerned; the war still didn't seem very real. It was a little bit like a movie. I'd seen drills in the movies, with men running around, strapping on their helmets, getting into gun positions. Exciting stuff on a dull day. But I never did it again.

I was glad when we finally got to Miami in early December. I felt a little better when I saw Diana, who had taken the train from New Orleans, standing at the dock. But when we started to walk toward the Miami Beach apartment she had found us, I felt sick again. The land was too firm—land sickness. I was in my naval uniform, and as we walked (she walked, I weaved) down the street, another naval officer approached us.

Diana looked at him. "Dick! Dick Goddard! How *are* you?" she said, and gave him a big hug. She said, "God, it's so good to see you!" Then she turned and said, "Dick, I want you to meet my husband . . . uh . . . uh . . . "

I said, "Kirk."

She said, "Oh, yes, of course. Kirk." And then drew another blank.

"And Douglas is the last name, dear," I said. She was a little embarrassed.

We were scheduled to stay in Miami for two weeks, shaking down the ship. Diana and I were thinking that it would be nice if we could make it to Christmas before I had to ship out. We not only made it to Christmas, we made it through New Year's, and we almost made it to Diana's birthday, January 22, because each time my ship went out, we bashed into something else and had to go back into drydock. The first thing we scratched was a Russian destroyer. We went out drinking with the Russian sailors, and we taught each other some words. A Russian would point at the road and say, "*Droga.*" I would say, "Road." "Drink beer"—"*Piet peva.*" We got along fine.

After almost a month and a half in Miami, we finally got our radar gear and got out of drydock. Diana went back to live with her sister, who had a house in the country in New Jersey. I headed for Cristobal, on the Atlantic side of the Panama Canal. We were going to go through the Panama Canal and into the South Pacific. Again, the trip toward Cristobal was very rough; I was constantly uncomfortable. When any messages came in, they had to call me, because all messages were coded. That was another part of my job that I detested. Since I was the Communications Officer, all messages that came in were usually sent to me for decoding, in spite of the fact that every officer was supposed to learn decoding. One, a strip code, made me particularly miserable. All the letters in the alphabet were on narrow strips and you had to keep pulling them into different positions until you found a message which read horizontally. Doing this while you were feeling queasy on a swaying ship did not help.

Two sailors were always getting into fights. One was an Italian who spoke with an accent. The other younger sailor would tease him. They started to get into a fight once while I had the watch. I didn't know what to do to stop them and I made the stupid error of pulling out my gun and saying, "Stop that right now or I'll shoot." The Italian said, "Go ahead. Shoot! Shoot!" So there I was with my loaded gun pointed at him, and him taunting me to go ahead and shoot. I had to back down. I felt like a dummy. I learned a very valuable less then that I applied later, when I was doing movies: if you're playing a real tough guy, don't ever pull your gun unless you intend to use it.

We arrived in Cristobal to pick up supplies before going on to the Galapagos Islands for maneuvers with a submarine. The water had been so rough, it felt as if we had made an incredibly lengthy voyage. It was wonderful to be on land. We got cleaned up, put on our wrinkled uniforms, and took a taxi to the Officers Club to enjoy a little luxury. And there certainly was plenty of luxury there. Cristobal was cushy: uniforms neatly pressed and cleaned, a beautiful Officers Club overlooking the Atlantic Ocean, very attractive WACs, officers buzzing around on Vespas and jeeps. They were a breed apart and did not mingle with us. We really felt out of it, lost, lonely, little boys. We were all so young, just kids getting ready to go off to war. The more we drank, the more jealous we became.

A few drinks later, we came out and saw a Vespa parked in front. I looked at the skipper, he looked at me, we got on the Vespa and drove off. We rode down to the dock, and up the gangplank, aboard the ship. Evidently, the crew was feeling the same. One group saw a boat with an outboard motor. Our liberty boat was just an overgrown rowboat; it took four men to row ashore. They stole the outboard motor. Another group was even more enterprising. They somehow appropriated a whole barrel of beer. I remember seeing them stealthily coming up the gangplank to store the beer in one of the refrigerators. None of us officers said a word.

The next morning we went through the Panama Canal to Panama City. Then we fastened the outboard motor to the liberty boat and rang the liberty bell. We were really Big Navy now, with our own makeshift power launch. We were taking sailors back and forth to Panama when a regular launch loaded with naval officers approached to ask if we knew anything about a missing Vespa, a keg of beer, and an outboard motor. We tried to play dumb, but as they said the word "motor," we could hear the "put-put-put" of the outboard as the liberty boat returned. We all pretended ignorance, but they issued a warning and we had to return our new acquisition. We pleaded ignorance about the Vespa and the beer, too. A search party went over the ship, but by that time the men had dismantled the Vespa and stowed it away. The beer was also stashed somewhere. The search party departed, content to have recovered one item. We were sorry to see the outboard motor go, because for one glorious half hour, we really were Big Navy.

We had a twenty-four-hour layover in Panama. A few of the officers and I went into town, walked around, and were directed to a club just outside the city. It was elegant, with a large bar, nice tables, waiters, music. There were beautiful women in lovely gowns, and couples sitting and drinking. We were all rather naive, and assumed we were in a Panamanian nightclub. Great stupidity on our part, when you consider that the name of the place was Maison d'Amour. As I stood at the bar with the captain, having a drink, I saw a beautiful young Panamanian woman in a low-cut dress across the room, and wondered how I could get to know her. She saw me looking at her and smiled. I smiled back. She undulated over to me and whispered in my ear, "Suckee fuckee?" I was startled. Perhaps I hadn't heard correctly. "What?" She leaned closer and said, "You like suckee fuckee?" This time she punctuated it by dipping her tongue deep into my ear. Even I got the message then. It wasn't exactly a subtle proposition, but the next thing we knew, we were all upstairs watching some interesting exhibitions that the madam put on for us. Soon we all responded in the affirmative to the young ladies' questions, and went back to our ship feeling much better.

Sex is a temporary cure for loneliness, a way to hang on to someone, be close to someone, even for a short time. We were young people in a frightening situation. We had gone through all this training that we had never thought of before; suddenly we found ourselves lonely, and reached out to cover up our fears.

We left Panama reluctantly, and somewhat mystified; we had always heard that duty on one of these small PC boats was a breeze, because wherever you went, you were left there for months at a time. But it seemed that no sooner had we arrived somewhere, than we already had orders sending us off somewhere else. We left to rendezvous with a submarine off the Galapagos Islands, to engage in war games. We practiced tracking each other and doing imitation attacks. The submarine would start twenty miles away. As we approached each other, we were supposed to determine where the submarine was, the path it was taking, and block out a course of how we would drop explosives; there was a way to determine whether we were successful or whether we had failed.

I was bad at aircraft identification, worse at periscope sighting. Often in our maneuvers, I would be on the bridge, responsible for sighting the submarine. But it was always one of the crew who was the first to yell out, "Periscope sighting 045!" I would look intently in that direction, trying to see a periscope cutting through the water, and see nothing. In a low voice, I would ask him, "Where? Where?"

The sailor would look at me in amazement and say, "Over there, sir, at 045."

I would look again, and ask again, "Where? Where?"

"RIGHT THERE, SIR!" And a huge submarine, like a mammoth gray whale, would break water and surface in front of us. This lack in my perception embarrassed me. The crew was beginning to notice, too.

But I liked this part of military service. It was fun, like playacting. At night, we anchored off a tiny deserted island and sometimes rowed ashore and looked around at the beauties of an island that seemed to be totally uninhabited, with its amazing mixture of animal life. One night, as we were anchored offshore after a day of war games, the officers were all in the wardroom talking when suddenly there was a knock on the door. The door opened partway, and a tattooed arm thrust a big pitcher of ice-cold beer into the room. We looked at each other, took the pitcher, and the door closed immediately. We never asked any questions. The mysterious tattooed arm appeared several times every evening, until the big keg of contraband beer was gone.

We were now ready to go to war. Our mission was to escort a cargo ship to Hawaii. We began active duty in an ignominious fashion, being towed by the cargo ship, because, even though we were escorting them, we could not carry enough fuel to make it all the way to Hawaii. It was a good conservation measure, but it was humiliating to be a young war officer on a warship being hauled on a towline by a cargo vessel. The crew of the cargo ship looked at us contemptuously. Their vessel was twice the size of ours, and I'm sure they didn't have much faith in our ability to protect them under any conditions. From Hawaii, we were to continue on toward the smaller islands in the direction of Japan to search for Japanese submarines.

We sailed toward Hawaii for several peaceful days. I liked the waters in the Pacific—much calmer than the Atlantic. I particularly liked the watch from four until eight in the morning. It was lovely to be alone in the quiet dark, to hear the splash of flying fish, see dawn spreading over the ocean.

One day during drills, the bored men on the antiaircraft guns used the gulls skimming around the ship for target practice. I watched as the men fired at the swift, graceful birds. All of a sudden there was an explosion. The flight of one was arrested completely; a few feathers floated slowly down to the ocean. I wanted to cry at the death of the beautiful bird, but I couldn't in front of the crew. They were busy cheering their kill, their great victory over beauty and life. I kept thinking about what would happen if those bullets hit a human being, how he would be extinguished, completely. It wasn't playacting and fun anymore. It was too real.

After we were out for several days and had conserved enough fuel, we released ourselves from the towline and became the escort vessel for the cargo ship, using our sonar to search for Japanese submarines. All day long on the bridge, you'd hear the echoing of the underwater sound waves: "ping ping ping." When contact was made, the "ping" would bounce back, and you would hear "ping-*ping*, ping-*ping*." I was familiar with this system, having played an echo myself. Sometimes the echo would bounce back off a school of fish, but you learned to detect the difference. The closer you got to the object under the water, the closer together the echoes would come: "ping*ping*, ping*ping*, ping-*ping*." That would cause a lot of excitement on the bridge as we plotted, judging by the echoes, the distance and the speed and the position of where the supposed Japanese submarine was heading.

One day, sure enough, the steady "ping, ping, ping" changed to "ping*ping*, ping*ping*." We were excited, and a little nervous, certain that we had hit upon an enemy submarine. The cargo ship receded, its crew watching us through binoculars as we plotted our attack. At the point where we had positioned the Japanese submarine, we released our mousetrap attacks. This was a series of little bombs on a rack in the forward part of the ship. The bombs shot off into the water, and we were elated to hear an explosion, because they exploded only on contact. Now we were really excited. I felt like I was in a B-movie. It didn't seem real. I had that exciting feeling of the unreality of it, mixed with the feeling of, "Do we really want to blow up this ship with young Japanese sailors inside?" I couldn't help thinking of it all in dramatic terms. I heard myself muttering. "This is it, chaps!" Everyone went to his post. I was the gunnery officer, astern. The captain cut back the engines and went slowly toward the site of the explosion. I heard his order over the earphones: "Release depth charge marker." This was a green slick on the water to let us know where to drop the depth charges, bombs that looked like ash cans filled with dynamite. I relayed this message to the nervous sailor on the stern of the ship in as military a style as I could. Suddenly, there was a huge explosion. The ship raised up

out of the water. People went flying everywhere. I was
thrown against the bulkhead, my stomach smashed into the
equipment alongside of it. I found myself doubled up on the
deck. Torpedo! Torpedo! There was confusion everywhere.
But it didn't take us long to realize that we hadn't been
struck by an enemy torpedo—we had blown up our own
ship. Instead of a depth charge *marker,* the nervous sailor
had released a depth *charge.* It wrecked our steering gear.
We tried to reconstruct our position to make our attack, but
that was the end of our engagement with the enemy. We
never saw the submarine. A great controversy arose. Should
we report the sinking of a Japanese submarine to Washington? Could you get a Purple Heart if the wounds were self-
inflicted? We settled for reporting a possible hit, and then
tried to fix our gear.

One of the sailors developed acute appendicitis, and I had
to radio Washington for instructions, although I was doubled
up in agony. I had hit the side of the iron carrier for the
depth charges and had tremendous bruises on my stomach.
We were told to reverse course and headed for Manzanilla,
Mexico, leaving the cargo vessel to proceed on its own. They
were relieved, now that the most dangerous ship in the Pacific was out of their vicinity.

There were no Japanese airplanes en route to Manzanilla,
but our own planes were more dangerous. At night, from the
air, the outline of our vessel looked very much like the silhouette of a submarine. Very often we would hear the drone
of an American plane in the darkness overhead, and suddenly hear the sound of the motors change as the plane
started to dive toward our ship. We quickly signaled to indi-
cate that we were friendly. The signals changed each day,
and we would frantically flash lights toward the diving
plane, hoping that the young pilot from Kansas City or wherever, out to get a big one, would see the lights and know that
we were a friendly vessel. We always held our breath as the
plane dived toward our ship, and then at the last minute
swerved. I wondered if these pilots were just having a little

fun to relieve the monotony of their patrols. Still, I prayed that they had done better at ship identification than I had done at airplane identification.

Manzanilla—beautiful, enormous cliffs rising out of the sea. We carried the sailor to a small naval hospital. On our twenty-four-hour layover, I ate and drank everything in sight. When we proceeded up the coast to San Diego, I began to feel lousy. And my bruises were really bothering me. I tried to ignore it.

The first day in San Diego, most of the other officers and men had shore leave. I was the Officer of the Deck, with just a skeleton crew. There was nothing to do, and one of the crewmen asked if he could take a ride on our stolen Vespa. The Vespa was a wonderful addition to our ship. I used it the most, since I was the Communications Officer. As soon as we pulled in somewhere, I hopped on the Vespa and went to headquarters to get the new codes. Since we were securely tied to the dock, I gave him permission to ride the Vespa. He hopped on like a happy kid and sped around the dock. As he approached the ship, he couldn't find the brakes. I watched as Vespa and sailor flew gracefully off the dock and into the harbor. After about half a minute, he came to the top, yelling, "I rode 'er to the bottom!" I failed to see the humor in losing our only means of onshore transportation. We finally succeeded in bringing it back up. Getting all the salt water out of it was an arduous process, but soon it was back in running order.

I, however, was not. I became deathly ill, with severe cramps and a high fever. They took me to the San Diego Naval Hospital. The ship went off to war again without me. I was given all kinds of tests. In addition to my internal injuries, I had amoebic dysentery.

Months of mail finally caught up with me, the first letter from my wife since leaving Miami: . . . *and when the baby arrives* . . . " The *baby!* What baby? I almost fell out of bed. Diana, in New Jersey, got a shocked phone call from me. She wanted to leave her job at the Squibb chemical company testing a new drug, penicillin, and join me right away, but it looked as if I'd be rejoining a ship very soon. I told her not to bother coming.

Then I found out that I was going to be in San Diego for some time. Diana got on a train and came to be with me. I was in the hospital for a few weeks, and then became an ambulatory patient. We had an apartment, we'd go to the Hotel del Coronado and lie on the beach, and then to the Officers Club at night. The only thing I had to do was check in at the hospital every day. Not a bad life. One morning, I woke up with the world's worst hangover. I groaned, "Honey, I'm too sick to go to the hospital today." We didn't know how long I would have to keep doing this, or when I would have to ship out again, so Diana left; she wanted to have the baby back in New Jersey, where her sister was.

In June of 1944, after I had been an inpatient and an outpatient at the naval hospital for several months, it was determined that the amoebic dysentery could recur. I was given an honorable discharge. I took my three months' duty and severance pay, and left for Los Angeles, to take a plane for the East Coast.

Betty Bacall, now Lauren Bacall, was in Hollywood to be in a movie, *To Have and Have Not*. We had dinner at Frascati's restaurant on Wilshire Boulevard. Betty brought the script with her. She was excited. She turned to a page, and said, "Now here, I go to the door and I turn to look at Bogart, and I say, 'If you want anything, just whistle. You know how to whistle, don't you, Steve? You just put your lips together and blow.' " When I heard Betty say that, I told her, "I don't see how you can miss." I thought the role was perfect for her. So did the moviegoing public. And so did Humphrey Bogart.

The next day I left for the East Coast to join my wife and offspring-to-be, and to see if I could get work as a civilian.

Six

Civilian

Diana met me in New York. We took a train to New Brunswick, New Jersey, and Diana drove to her sister's house, where we would be staying temporarily. We were driving down a road in the country alongside a high, massive stone wall that stretched for miles. "This is the beginning of my sister's place," Diana said. I laughed at her joke. We came to the main entrance of this estate, gate houses flanking an enormous stone archway. We turned into the driveway and went up a winding road through the woods. I looked at her, wondering, but said nothing. As we rounded a curve, I saw a house that was just perfect. "Is this your sister's house?"

"No, it's the gardener's cottage."

Cottage?

"My sister is living there now. Her husband is living over there, in the chauffeur's cottage. They're getting a divorce. Until then, we can stay in the main house."

Main house? We continued up the winding road to a big plateau overlooking the Raritan River. In front of us was a gigantic, sprawling English castle with turrets and a slate roof. I was dumbfounded. As we drove into the cobblestone courtyard, Diana said. "We'll live in the west wing." We walked through a big, heavy door in one of the towers, up a circular stone staircase, and down a long corridor lined with art objects and suits of armor, with many empty rooms off it. At the end of the corridor was a beautiful suite. That's where we spent several months.

Diana's sister Ruth had been married to Seward Johnson of the Johnson & Johnson family, which had a large factory on the other side of the river in New Brunswick. He was a multi-multi-millionaire. In 1987, the name of Seward Johnson covered the front pages of New York papers for weeks— a battle over his will. His recent Polish bride, who had started as his chambermaid, wanted all of it—almost a billion dollars. The children contested it. Little did I know that these three nice girls and one boy that I saw every day would become involved in such an imbroglio.

Ruth was very gracious. She helped us enormously and enabled us to save some money by allowing us to live there. Diana had not been trying to make a joke when she told me that her sister had a house in the country. That was just her matter-of-fact way of expressing things. She had never said it was a little white house with a picket fence; I interpreted it that way. Using the castle as a base, I went into New York every day to try to get a job. I wore my white uniform, hoping it might help. Guthrie McClintic and Katharine Cornell were in Europe, bringing *The Barretts of Wimpole Street* to GIs at the front; no job for me there.

I went out on an interview with Mae West, who was looking to do a show with six men. When I arrived at her apartment, a mincing little man ushered me into a dimly lit living room, asked me to sit down, and disappeared. For quite a while, I just sat there alone. Finally I heard a swishing sound, and Mae West, fifty-two years old, wearing too much makeup, entered the room in a long black negligee that swept the floor behind her. In front, very low décolletage, and white bosoms squished together almost up to her chin. She looked me up and down, asked me a few questions, and when she spoke, sounded like a parody of herself. Then she took off again. The little man—I guess he was her secretary —minced in and told me that I was dismissed. I never heard from her. Evidently, I wasn't her type of man.

Again, I made the rounds of casting offices and radio programs. Of course, before television, radio was the big thing. I envied many of the radio actors, especially the clique that played in most of the series. They made a lot of money doing easy work; in radio you didn't have to learn a part, you just read it. Many of them worked all day long, going from one program to another, stopping only to have lunch at "21" or Sardi's or other places that I couldn't afford. Years later, when I came back to play the lead in a radio show with Bette Davis, they were still there, in the supporting roles on my program.

It was a mixed blessing to get a sustaining role in a radio serial. On the plus side, you had a steady income and a good salary. The other side was that it was difficult to leave the serial if you got a role in a play. Leaving the sure thing of a radio job for a play was a big risk, because you didn't get paid during play rehearsals. You rehearsed for three or four weeks at no salary, then went on the road doing try-outs, usually in Washington, Boston, or New Haven, at half salary. Then you came into New York at full salary, but if the two leading papers, the *New York Times* and the *Herald Tribune*, didn't like the play, forget it. You closed the next night.

But I was lucky. *Kiss and Tell*, a simple, frothy comedy, had been running on Broadway for over a year. It was the play I had taken Diana to see when I was on leave. Richard Widmark, who played the part of the army lieutenant, was leaving to go into another play, and I got a call to try out. I read for the part and was shocked to find that they gave it to me. I was always shocked when I got a part. It was a delight to be working in the theater in a regular role.

Diana's parents arrived from Bermuda for a visit. Her mother was a spry, delightful, birdlike character, always chirping happily. Diana predicted that I would not get along at all with her father, the tall, gruff attorney general of Bermuda. He was formidable, conservative, and scared the hell out of everybody. We got along very well—a surprise and a vast relief to Diana.

Every night after the curtain went down on *Kiss and Tell*, I would rush for the subway to Penn Station. A train to New Brunswick, then a taxi from the station up the winding roadway to the courtyard of our castle. By the time I got home, it was usually around one o'clock. I would enter the door of this huge black castle and in the dark, walk quietly up the winding staircase and down the long corridor leading to our suite. There would be Diana, sound asleep, feeling completely safe. I never mentioned it to her, but I thought that I would be troubled sleeping alone in a deserted sixty-room castle high on a hill with woods all around.

Coming home after the theater one night, I found Diana wide awake and packed: it was time to take her to the hospital. Husbands were not allowed to participate in births then, and it looked as though it was going to be a while, so they sent me home. I got a little sleep, then got up, rushed to the hospital to find that Diana was still waiting, went to the train station, took the train into New York, and did a radio show all morning. When I called the hospital, I found out that my son had been born at 10:30 A.M. on September 25, 1944. I did the matinee of *Kiss and Tell*, rushed to Penn Station to get a train to New Brunswick, got to the hospital about 6:00 P.M., saw Diana and our son, then rushed back to the station just in time to catch the train to New York for the evening performance of *Kiss and Tell*.

Diana wanted our son to be named after me: Kirk Douglas, Junior. I have never liked the idea of junior. It is a diminutive, makes a person an offshoot of someone else, less of himself. He would always be stuck with that junior, and never become a senior. In the Orthodox Jewish religion, you never name someone after a living family member. When I look at the great success that my son has now, I shudder to think how awful it would be for him to be Kirk Douglas,

Junior. I resisted having him named that, and we compromised by making Michael's middle name just the initial "K" —Michael K. Douglas.

The first nights home with Michael were traumatic. If he cried, we were petrified. If he didn't cry, we were afraid that he was dead. So it went, back and forth, until things finally calmed down and we could all get some sleep.

I was very happy with my wife and my son and was beginning to make some money acting. I didn't want to impose on my sister-in-law's hospitality any longer, so when Michael was about three weeks old, we moved. We left on a dreary fall day. As I looked back at the castle, I thought, Boy, I'd hate to have to build a wall around *that* and fill it with horse manure.

Our apartment on West Eleventh Street in Greenwich Village, not far from the Greenwich House where I had stayed as a student, had high ceilings and big, long windows with window boxes. A balcony in the back overlooked a garden. It had a living room with a fireplace, a bedroom with a fireplace, a tiny dining room, a little room off the bedroom, which we used as Michael's room, and a kitchen and bath. It cost ninety dollars a month. Ruth had some beautiful antiques, and told us to take anything we wanted. The furniture went perfectly in our Village apartment.

It was quite a shock to my family that I married a shiksa, a non-Jew. Orthodox Jews looked with horror upon, and very often disowned, a son or daughter who married out of the faith. I was always grateful that my mother (and father, for that matter) accepted Diana gracefully and never said anything to me about marrying a woman who was not Jewish. This was a great gesture, for my mother especially, who was brought up in the strictest Orthodox traditions, and yet had within her enough love not to interfere with what I wanted to do.

One weekend she came, with her angelic smile, to visit us. It was Friday night, and we had also invited Barbara Van Sleet, who lived nearby. I asked Diana to have four candles on the table for prayers. We sat down, and my mother had a *sidder,* a prayer book, which she tentatively pushed toward me, hoping that I would read the service. When you said prayers, your head had to be covered. A yarmulke was traditional. But I had no yarmulke. And I never wore hats. I looked around for something to cover my head, and said to Diana, "There's got to be a hat around somewhere. Anything to cover my head. One of yours." She handed me something, and I put it on. Diana and Barbara tried very hard not to laugh at me in Diana's delicate lace Dutch cap with little wings on the sides. My mother just looked at me adoringly as I pushed back the prayer book and recited, by heart, the entire Friday evening kiddish. Finally, when I was through with the prayers, Diana and Barbara exploded in laughter. Ma never understood what was funny.

While I was working in *Kiss and Tell,* I would still go out on auditions, hoping to get a role in a play where I could create the part. A Hungarian writer, Laci Bus-fekete, and his wife, had written a play called *Star in the Window* together with a young writer who showed much talent, Sidney Sheldon. I tried out for it. I started to read. They said, "That's enough. Thank you." I left depressed. I was setting new speed records for rejection. An hour later, they called to tell me I had the part. Years later, Sidney Sheldon told me that the minute I walked in, they knew I was the guy. I immediately gave my notice to the *Kiss and Tell* company. They were annoyed; I hadn't been in the show very long. But I was anxious to get my career started. After a few weeks out on the road, *Star in the Window* opened in New York. And it closed three days later.

George Abbott was directing a new play and asked me if I could sing. I said, "Gee, I don't think so." He said, "Why don't you try out anyway?" That afternoon, I went to a theater and in the audience were Leonard Bernstein and Betty Comden and Adolph Green and Signe Hasso and George Abbott. I came out onstage.

They said, "What are you going to sing?"

It had never occurred to me to come with a song prepared. "I don't know." I thought for a moment, remembered a song that I had learned from the janitors I lived with my freshman year and sang once in a minstrel show at St. Lawrence University. I said to the piano player, "I know a song called 'I'm Red Hot Henry Brown.'"

He said, "I don't."

"That's all right, I'll sing it anyway." It had also never occurred to me that I should be accompanied by a piano. When I auditioned for the singing Western Union boy, they said, "If you can't sing well, sing loudly." Loudly, I sang this corny, old-time musical number: "I'm red hot Henry Brown/ The hottest man in town." When it was over they all applauded, and George Abbott told me I had the part of Gaby. The play was *On the Town*.

I was excited. A musical! Sing, dance, make people laugh to music by Leonard Bernstein, choreography by Jerome Robbins, with a book by Betty Comden and Adolph Green . . .

Then I learned what it means to have a psychosomatic illness. As we worked on the songs, I got more and more frightened and my voice got smaller and smaller. Finally, I developed laryngitis and could not speak at all. By that time, Diana and I were beginning to have our differences, and, naturally, we argued. I had been told not to talk, to rest my voice, so I kept a huge roll of shelf paper handy. When Diana said something, I'd go, "Ummmmmmmmmm," and rip off a sheet to scribble an answer. The producers waited and waited, and I still had laryngitis. As opening night—December 29, 1944—approached, they started to worry. Finally, after several weeks, they gave the part to John Battles, and my voice came back. That was a big disappointment to me. I felt like a coward. I had had the chance. I wanted so much to be in a musical. Gene Kelly played my role when *On the Town* was made into a movie.

I went up for a part in a play called *Truckline Cafe*. I didn't get it. Bitter, I went to see the play, watched another actor play my role. I loved the first two acts—he was terrible. He mumbled, you couldn't hear what he was saying. I congratulated myself on how much better I would have been. Suddenly, in the third act, he erupted, electrifying the audience. I thought, "My God, he's good!" and looked in the program for his name: Marlon Brando.

I went to the *Kiss and Tell* company and was surprised when they took me back in the same role. I was restless to create a role, and still went out on auditions. Walking down the street one day, I bumped into a very depressed Karl Malden. After sixteen flops in a row, he was ready to leave acting and go home to Gary, Indiana. I didn't feel so bad then. At least I had steady work.

I wasn't in *Kiss and Tell* very long when I left again—once more to replace Richard Widmark—in *Trio*, a play about a lesbian teacher trying to seduce a young student. I played the student's lover. I worked nonstop for three days to learn the part, and went on the third night. Everything went well . . . until we came to the climactic scene in the third act, where I discover my girlfriend in the lesbian's apartment. I flung the door open and flew into the room. The audience burst out laughing. I could barely finish the performance.

That night, lying in bed with Diana, I couldn't sleep. "They laughed at me," I kept saying. "They laughed at me." I dreaded the next night's performance. But the solution came to me in my dressing room. I realized that the night before, all my tensions had erupted as I banged onto the stage, and it became funny. This time, when the climactic moment came, I slowly walked into the room and very calmly looked at the two of them. There was an intake of breath from the audience, and complete silence. Unfortunately, the subject matter of the play was too daring for the times, and we were closed down on moral grounds.

In June of 1945, I went into a play called *The Wind Is Ninety*, written by Ralph Nelson, who later became a movie director (*Lilies of the Field, Soldier in the Rain, Charly*, etc.) I have often wondered why he gave up writing, because he displayed such a tremendous talent for it. *The Wind Is Ninety* was one of the ghost themes that were so popular in plays and movies around the end of World War II. I played the Unknown Soldier of World War I, who was leading Wendell Corey, a World War II fighter pilot who had been killed, back to his home. We were invisible to the other characters onstage as we watched his family receive the news of his death. I had a very hard time with Corey. His character was supposed to look to me for support. Instead, Wendell played the role ignoring me, as if I weren't even on the same stage with him. Occasionally, he glanced at me over his shoulder. I felt like a puppy dog following him around. When I tried to discuss it with him, he yelled and cursed at me. The director didn't want to get involved. On the road for tryouts, Wendell cold-shouldered and upstaged me so thoroughly that I felt truly invisible. The critics didn't notice me, either. Wendell got great reviews. He was happy. I was miserable.

Opening night in New York, the solution came to me. I would play the role within my own world, with an air of mystery. Instead of dialogues with Wendell's character not listening, I would have soliloquies, and pull the audience to me. When the reviews came out, there was a picture—my picture, and underneath, the caption, "Nothing short of superb." That night, lying in bed with Diana, I couldn't sleep. "What do they mean, 'Nothing short of'? If they think I'm superb, why don't they just come right out and say so!"

As unpleasant as Wendell was to my face, he was even more unpleasant behind my back. People passed on to me some of the things this minister's son said about me, like "That dirty Jew." We came to Hollywood about the same time and did one movie, I Walk Alone, together, but didn't have many scenes with each other. Wendell became increasingly reactionary and a drunk. When he died in 1968, his wife, Alice, called me, crying. "Would you please give the eulogy at Wendell's funeral?"

I tried to be tactful. "Don't you think someone else would be better?"

"No, no. You're the one. You both started together in New York."

Because she was a sweet, pathetic woman, I agreed.

After a couple of months with The Wind Is Ninety, I went into rehearsals for a David Merrick production called Rain-

check for Joe, in which I had to play the saxophone. I practiced at home, driving Diana and Michael, who was almost a year old, crazy. Diana and I were having problems. We had gotten married, like so many other young people during the war, in a rush of fear and urgency, afraid that I would be killed, wanting to hold each other for whatever little time we might have. It all happened so quickly, and we had dated such a short time that when we actually settled down to the everyday business of living, we found that we really didn't know each other very well. Diana had, and still has, a wonderful sense of humor and is very easygoing; she has none of my tensions or insecurities or drive, although she is a talented actress. About that time, Diana's father died, so she decided to take Michael to Bermuda for a visit. *Raincheck for Joe* was supposed to open for ten days of tryouts in Detroit at the end of September. (This romantic comedy about a saxophone-playing boxer who was mistakenly called to heaven before his time had been done in 1941 as a movie called *Here Comes Mr. Jordan,* with Robert Montgomery, and was remade in 1978 as *Heaven Can Wait,* with Warren Beatty.) But we didn't have a completion bond, and we never started.

Without my knowledge, Lauren Bacall had been doing kind deeds for me. Earlier, she had told Hal Wallis about me, and he had called me about doing a role in *The Strange Love of Martha Ivers,* a movie that he was producing. It starred Barbara Stanwyck, very hot after her recent work in *Double Indemnity.* I had turned him down then, because I was doing what I wanted—working in theater. Movies were the farthest thing from my mind. I had never even considered being a movie actor. My image of a movie actor was someone tall and gorgeous, and I had never thought I fit the bill. My ambition was always to become a great actor in the theater. But now I didn't have a role in the theater, and I was a married man with a family. Wallis's offer was beginning to look better. But still . . . I walked the streets of Greenwich Village, thinking. Very early one quiet Sunday morning, I saw another solitary soul doing the same thing. She was dressed all in black, walking slowly. There was something familiar about the slope of her shoulders, her gray hair with a little wave in it. As she approached, I realized it was Eleanor Roosevelt. President Franklin D. Roosevelt had been dead for only a short while. I thought about what full, courageous lives they had both led. My life was still ahead of me. I was a strong, healthy young man with a great opportunity. I called Hal Wallis. He said, "Come on out." I would give Hollywood a try, just for a little while, and then work on the stage again. Diana and Michael could come to Los Angeles directly from Bermuda.

David Merrick walked me down to Grand Central Station. "Who's handling your deal with Hal Wallis?"

"I don't know. Any suggestions?"

"Charlie Feldman, the head of Famous Artists, can be a good agent—if he works for you. Or a son of a bitch. I'll call him."

I boarded the Twentieth Century—the crack New York-to-Chicago train that Issur had watched roar by Amsterdam so many times, a blur of white linen and black waiters. Now Amsterdam was a blur as Kirk Douglas roared by on his way to Hollywood.

Seven

HOLLYWOOD

The heat that blasted my lungs as I stepped off the train in Los Angeles in 1945 came straight from hell. Back East, September signaled the beginning of fall, of chill and frost. I was surprised that it could be this hot anywhere so late in the year. So this was Hollywood, built on the San Andreas fault. Earthquakes, mudslides, forest fires, floods. The dream of millions.

I was surprised to find a man at the station looking for me. Michael Pearman was from Famous Artists Agency. David Merrick had arranged it. Perhaps he felt guilty that I had left *The Wind Is Ninety* to do his play.

Michael Pearman took me to a tiny hotel room he had found for me, no mean feat in Los Angeles at the end of World War II. I had a place to stay, an agent, and a job. I felt pretty good, and was looking forward to playing a tough guy in *The Strange Love of Martha Ivers*. Then I got a shock. The role had been given to Van Heflin, who had just returned from the war. Instead, they wanted me for Barbara Stanwyck's weak drunkard husband. The part wasn't as good, but as long as I had it . . . Another shock—I *didn't* have it. I had to make a screen test against four other actors, all of whom, like me, had stage experience, but had not yet made a movie—John Lund, Montgomery Clift, Richard Widmark, and Wendell Corey.

I was nervous. I was a stage actor, used to dealing with people, not technicians and equipment. A camera can be a really frightening thing. I had a six-page scene to do. We kept rehearsing until finally the director, Lewis Milestone, said, "Now, do you feel ready to shoot it?" I took a deep breath and said, "Yes." He said, "Go home. I already shot it." What a wonderful, painless way to do a screen test! I was grateful to him.

I sweated, literally, for a few days. Finally the phone call came—I had the part. To celebrate, one of my agents, Milt Grossman, got me invited to a large, lavish party given by Atwater Kent. It was black tie. I had to rent an outfit. Milt also fixed me up with a very pretty, sexy German girl who had come to Hollywood, like so many others, hoping to become a movie star and succeeding only in working at Saks. I went to her apartment to pick her up. She took one look at my car, and suggested we go in hers instead. She did have a nicer car, so I left mine there.

We drove to Kent's huge mansion, up the circular driveway. Valets were hopping, opening doors and parking cars. The house was enormous, palatial, with an orchestra playing and tables overloaded with shrimp and lobster and caviar. Where were these parties when I was starving in New York! People were laughing and having a good time. Everybody seemed to know everybody else. Even the girl I was with knew several people. I didn't know anyone and I was rather shy. But I was enjoying it, especially when I looked up and, my God, there was Jimmy Stewart! Then, a man with his back to me turned around—Henry Fonda! All happy and laughing. I just took it all in, a kid from Amsterdam, New York, gawking at the stars I had seen on the silver screen.

It grew late; the party began to dwindle. I asked my date if she wanted to go home. She said, "Yeah, sure." Just then,

Henry Fonda's wife motioned to her. The two women moved away a bit and chatted. I watched, wondering what they were giggling about. Frances Fonda was a high-strung woman, always laughing nervously. Five years later, Henry asked for a divorce. She had a breakdown, spent months in sanatoriums, and just when she seemed to be recovering, on her forty-second birthday slashed her throat with a razor blade.

My date came back. I said, "Shall we go?" She replied, "Just a minute, I'm going to the ladies' room." So she went into the ladies' room while I waited. I watched Henry Fonda and Jimmy Stewart, who had come alone, talking with Frances Fonda. They were all laughing. I thought how nice it would be to be a part of it. Maybe some day I would be. Quite a few minutes went by. There was a general exodus. Everyone was leaving, and I was still waiting for my date to come out of the ladies' room. I became concerned; perhaps she was ill. I asked one of the waitresses to please see if everything was all right. She obligingly checked and came out with puzzling news: "The ladies' room is empty."

The musicians were packing their instruments, and the clean-up crew was moving in. I didn't know what to do. I was really perplexed. Then one of the waiters came up to me and said, "Are you waiting for that blond girl you were with?"

"Yes."

"Oh, she left a half-hour ago with Jimmy Stewart and Henry Fonda. They went out the back door."

I couldn't believe it. My date had taken the proverbial powder. I still waited, thinking she would appear with some explanation, until people began to look at me oddly. There was nothing to do but leave, so I walked out of the mansion. By that time, hers was the only car there; the attendants were annoyed. I got into the car. I didn't even know enough to tip the valet. I realized my omission as he slammed the door. I kept thinking that there had to be some reason. Perhaps she was ill and they had taken her home quickly. I drove back to her apartment, rang the bell. I saw no lights, and rang quite a few times. Finally, through my thick skull, I realized that Frances Fonda had probably said, "Why don't you dump this nobody and join us for a drink? We've got Jimmy Stewart with us—he's got no girl." Of course, this little German girl, who I realized later was quite a gal around town, jumped at the opportunity. Anything to be with a star. My evening of celebration had turned into a humiliating experience. Welcome to Hollywood.

The Strange Love of Martha Ivers started shooting. The first day, the company sent a limousine to pick me up. Star treatment on my first picture! I was more impressed when I got in and sat down next to Van Heflin. Wow! They must really think I'm something. I was deflated when we got to the studio—picket lines everywhere, people waving clubs, yelling, and pounding on the car. A strike. The only way to get onto the lot was in a limousine guarded by studio police.

I was young, scared, trying to look older than I was. I didn't know what it was all about, this new world of moviemaking, having to hit marks for the camera, to repeat actions exactly the same way every time so that they would match other shots. Everyone had told me how nice Barbara Stanwyck was, so I was looking forward to working with her in this hostile environment. The crew adored her. They called her "Missy," and when she came on the set she went around hugging them, asking about their wives and children by name. She was a professional, she was there, always prepared, an excellent actress. But she was indifferent to me. Crew members need and want attention, but who needs help more than somebody working on his first picture? Several weeks later she noticed me. I could see it happening, like the lens of a camera turning into focus. She looked at me, made eye contact for the first time. She said, "Hey, you're pretty good." I said, "Too late, Miss Stanwyck." I don't think she knew what I meant. But after that she was nice to me, and we became friends.

I always remember that first picture, and whenever I am in a movie I try to help anyone who is new. I will make mistakes deliberately, to help the nervous newcomer feel more relaxed. I'll flub a line or something, because I know what it's like to be so anxious to be good.

After my experience with Barbara, I was really worried, because everybody had said, "Watch out for Van Heflin." But he turned out to be very helpful to me. I played a weakling, and I always worked on the theory that when you play a weak character, find a moment when he's strong, and if you're playing a strong character, find a moment when he's weak. I had a moment when I was at the desk—I stood up, grabbed Van Heflin by the shirt, and stared him in the eye. He was amazed at this sudden moment of strength, and it confused him. We shot it, and the director said, "Very good." Van Heflin said, "Let's do it again." The next time I grabbed him, he just looked down contemptuously at my hand. How smart of him—he took away the strength. Nothing wrong with that. As an actor, it was the right thing to do.

I was supposed to smoke a cigarette in the movie, something I'd never done before in my life. Much more difficult than I ever imagined, like seasickness. One day Hal Wallis visited the set, surprised to find I wasn't there. Where was I? In my dressing room, turning green and throwing up. Wallis got mad; I was holding up the production. "For God's sake, get him out of there and let's get moving!" So I pulled my green body and my queasy stomach together and kept working.

Unfortunately, once I did learn to smoke, I couldn't stop. I escalated to two packs a day very quickly, and stayed that way for about ten years. When I decided to stop, I adopted the method that my father had used when he quit. He would carry a cigarette in his shirt pocket, and every time he felt like smoking, he would pull out the cigarette and confront it: "Who stronger? You? Me?" Always, the answer was the same: "I stronger." Back the cigarette would go, until the next craving. It worked for him, and it worked for me.

As we continued shooting through October, the strike situation deteriorated. It had begun in March, when the set decorators' union started to negotiate a new contract with the studios. All of a sudden, the International Alliance of

Theatrical and Stage Employees, IATSE, claimed that they should represent the set decorators. To keep control of their own union, the set decorators walked out.

Now the set decorators, joined by sympathetic unions—blacksmiths, carpenters, cartoonists, electricians, plumbers, painters, metal workers, story analysts plus machinists from Lockheed and thousands of students from the University of Southern California and UCLA—picketed studios en masse, in defiance of a court order. Warner Brothers was shut down. When scabs attempted to cross the picket lines, their cars were overturned. Thousands of people fought in the middle of Barham Boulevard with knives, clubs, battery cables, brass knuckles, chains, and saps. Two hundred police were called in, and subdued the crowds with fire hoses and tear-gas.

After Warner Brothers, Universal was shut down, then RKO. Then Paramount, where we were shooting. We continued to shoot, but it meant that we were locked in at the studio—if we went out, we couldn't get back in. The director, Lewis Milestone, was in favor of the strikers, and went across the street to Oblath's restaurant, where a lot of strike supporters discussed it over coffee. For a while, the picture was directed by Byron Haskin. I felt guilty. What was I supposed to do? Stanwyck was working. It was difficult for a newcomer to sort out all the issues. I kept asking what position our union, the Screen Actors Guild, was taking. They were wishy-washy about it. Finally, the president of the Screen Actors Guild, George Murphy, declared that actors didn't have to cross picket lines where there was danger of violence—a lot of latitude. Everyone was afraid that now Hollywood would come to a total standstill. The violence grew worse; four hundred people were arrested outside Paramount. I was afraid that for me Hollywood would end before I began.

In the middle of all of this, Diana arrived in Los Angeles on the train with her mother and Michael, who had just spent his first birthday in Bermuda. I was living at the studio, couldn't even get a message to them. Diana thought my agents might know where they were supposed to stay. Right after the war, you couldn't get an apartment, a hotel room, a motel room, or a boardinghouse in Los Angeles. She called Famous Artists. They said they'd never heard of me. Milt Grossman was on vacation. She finally got through to him at home. He explained about the strike, told her that I had found us a place to live, but that we couldn't get into it for a few days. That didn't ease Diana's immediate problem. For several hideous moments, she thought they might have to sleep in the station. But Milt came to the rescue. The Grossmans put them all up.

It was a couple of days before I could sneak out of the studio to see Diana. They ran a limousine out in the dead of night, when even the most die-hard pickets were gone. I had a couple of hours with her and a chance to look at Michael sleeping, but I had to rush back before four o'clock in the morning, when the picketing resumed. Finally, the strike ended, and I was able to go home at the end of the day, to our apartment on South Bedford, for which I had traded our New York apartment. Diana's mother stayed with us for about a month. She was very sweet and funny, this proper English lady, trying to take an interest in our profession, reading *Daily Variety* religiously.

To make up to them for all the inconvenience they had endured, I took them to the best restaurant in town—Romanoff's. I'd never been there, but everybody knew it was the place to go. We had a reservation for eight o'clock. The restaurant was crowded. The maître d' told us it would be "just a minute," and asked us to wait in the bar. We sat, had a drink, watched celebrities milling about. Diana's mother didn't recognize any of them anyway, so my attempts to impress her that way were useless. Almost a half hour passed. I was getting a little impatient. Diana was throwing covert glances at me. I went to the headwaiter to remind him that we had a reservation for eight o'clock; it was now eight-thirty. "Oh yes, yes," he said, "just a minute." I went back, had another drink, waited another fifteen minutes, watched people coming in and being immediately escorted to their tables. I was getting restless. I went again to the headwaiter. "It's almost quarter to nine." "Oh yes, yes, just one minute." Another ten went by. Now my Russian blood was beginning to boil. I went back to him, and he started to give me the same line. I grabbed him by the shirt. "Look. I made a reservation for eight o'clock. You accepted it. It is almost nine o'clock. I want a table. And I want it NOW." By that point we were touching noses. A minute later, Diana, her mother, and I were sitting at a table.

I can understand if a place says they don't know me, don't want my reservation, my business. But they accepted the reservation, assumed that I would just sit there and wait, until they had a loose table to squeeze me in. To this day, when I come into a chic, crowded restaurant, and I'm immediately escorted to my table, I feel a little guilty when I see people standing around at the bar.

The Strange Love of Martha Ivers wrapped. I was eager to get on another project. Diana had been to Hollywood before and knew it didn't happen that way. She'd had a bitter taste of the system of making actors sit around and wait. Now she watched me. How would I deal with it? I asked my agents what they had for me.

"You have to give us a little time."

"I'll give you three weeks, and then I'm going to look for a play."

"You can't do that."

"Oh yes I can."

I still hadn't met Charlie Feldman, the head of my agency. He certainly hadn't handled my deal with Hal Wallis. That was too small. Charlie was friendly with all the heads of the studios—Jack Warner, Harry Cohn of Columbia, Darryl Zanuck of Fox, and the rest. I wanted to talk to Charlie and see if he could help me get a picture at one of the studios. I made a date to see him at four in the afternoon. (Charlie never came to the office until after lunch.) I sat outside his office and waited. People went in and came out and I sat there. It was like Romanoff's. Some time after five, the secretary, with no embarrassment, told me that he would be too busy to see me that day. Another appointment was made which followed the same pattern. This happened four or five times.

While I was waiting to see Feldman, I met Sam Norton, one of the lawyers at the agency. Talking in the hall one day, we discovered that we had both been wrestlers in college. He made a move toward me, and the next thing we knew, we were grappling. I pinned him on his back in the hallway. Other agents poked their heads out, astounded. Sam asked me to come into his office. I was glad to have somewhere to sit out of the line of traffic going in and out of Feldman's office. I would wait in Sam's office until I was told that Mr. Feldman was too busy to see me. I was very grateful to Sam, and we became good friends.

Finally they brought me in to see Feldman. He bawled me out. "Who the hell do you think you are? We're doing the best we can. When you become something, then you can complain." *He* was mad at *me* because I had been sitting out there for hours—days—waiting to see the man who was supposed to be my agent, and who was getting a commission from a picture that he hadn't even gotten for me. Welcome to the agency.

The three weeks were up. They hadn't gotten a picture for me. I had no work and no income. I called my agent in New York. "I'm available for a play." He got me one, and I went back to New York at the beginning of 1946.

Diana and Michael stayed in Los Angeles, waiting for escrow to close on a little Swiss-chalet-style house with a two-story living room and a separate guest house that we had found on Vado Place, in Laurel Canyon. In the meantime, we'd lost the apartment. Housing was still incredibly tight in Los Angeles. So while I was bouncing around from Philadelphia to Boston to New Haven, Diana and Michael bounced around from motel to motel.

Woman Bites Dog, by Sam and Bella Spewak, was funny and, I thought, well written. We rehearsed for thee or four weeks. Elaine Stritch, very talented, was one of the leads. We went out on the road, and they fired her. I didn't understand why. I liked her, and told her so. "Elaine, you're going to be a star some day." But they replaced her with Mercedes McCambridge. We were out on the road two or three weeks, opened in New York and closed within a week. I certainly hadn't had any success on Broadway. The only run of any kind I had was when I replaced Richard Widmark in *Kiss and Tell*. I went back to Los Angeles.

I did a lot of work on that house on Vado Place. I cut down trees and bushes, lugged wheelbarrows full of cement up a steep incline to make a little patio in the back. I have always worked on my homes. Of course, as my fortunes improved, the houses became larger and more luxurious. But I always find something to do—cut down brush, clean up after the dogs. I am amazed at how many gardeners will not clean up after a dog. To this day, I roam around with a pooper scooper cleaning up whatever Banshee's left in the garden in Beverly Hills, or the house in Palm Springs. Issur is still just an unskilled peasant laborer, like his father.

I bought my first work of art, a big poster by Toulouse-Lautrec of Aristide Bruant, the singer and nightclub entertainer of the time, wearing a black cape with a crimson scarf wrapped around his neck, his head in a black sombrero, tilted in an arrogant pose. That lithograph cost me five hundred dollars, which I thought was an exorbitant price. A friend helped me, and we framed it ourselves and hung it over the fireplace in the living room. I still have that lithograph; it hangs on the wall of my library.

It continued to be a strange adjustment, being married. For that short time when we had lived romantically in New Orleans, it was paradise. It takes so long to grow up. It takes so long to learn about life. It's an endless process. As I look back, I realize I wasn't equipped to be a husband. Coming out of the Navy, my wife pregnant, I was saddled with the double burden of fulfilling my ambitions to become an actor and making enough money to support my wife and child.

Out of the Past was a picture I did on loan-out for RKO with Robert Mitchum. I don't remember much about him, except that his stories about being a hobo kept changing every time he told them. What I do remember was devastatingly beautiful Jane Greer. Whenever I could, I spent time with her. Beautiful Jane could also be very funny. I loved hearing her stories of her brief marriage to Rudy Vallee at the age of seventeen, and how he insisted that she wear black panties, black net stockings, and black shoes with heels so high she teetered.

I went back to work for Hal Wallis in another movie, *I Walk Alone*, co-starring with another young actor, Burt Lancaster. Burt came from Hell's Kitchen, a tough West Side neighborhood, in New York. His first film had been Mark Hellinger's *The Killers*. He did an outstanding job, and Wallis bought his contract. We played friends who turned into enemies. Burt and I got along then just as we do now: we argued, we fought, we talked, we made up. Somehow, everything worked. Lizabeth Scott played the girl we were both involved with in the movie. In real life, she was involved with Hal Wallis. This was a problem. Very often, she'd be in his office for a long time, emerge teary-eyed, and be difficult to work with for the rest of the day.

I have always been known as an actor who speaks his piece. I hated the idea once given by a director: "Shut up. Just learn your lines, cues, and business." I always remembered Jelly, at the Academy, saying, "And idiot can learn lines, cues, and business." I certainly didn't want to be an idiot. So when I work on a movie, I like to think up some ideas. I remember how Hal Wallis's eyes widened in shock when I told him that the ending to *I Walk Alone* was dull. The police come into the restaurant, take me away, Burt kisses Liz, end of picture. It needed an extra dramatic beat. I suggested that as the police lead me out of the restaurant, I appeal to sentimentality: "Do you mind if I have one farewell drink?" The good-hearted Irish cop acquiesces. I go behind the bar, pour a drink, open a drawer with a gun in it. I paused dramatically as Wallis's eyes got bigger at the audacity of an actor suggesting how a script should be rewritten. I said, "I shoot the cop, then rush back with the gun to deal with Burt. We have a dramatic confrontation in which I am subdued and led away. The picture ends with Burt and

Liz safe and happy." Wallis hated an actor voicing his opin-
ions and interfering with a script. But when you see the
movie, the scene is exactly as I suggested. This was the beginning of my reputation for being difficult.

My deal with Wallis was one picture a year for five years,
but after *I Walk Alone*, he wanted me to sign a regular seven-
year term contract. Those were the days when everyone was
dying to be under contract because it was safe, it was guaranteed income. But to me it was like slavery.

We were with my agent, discussing this in Wallis's office,
when a pain like a tight vise gripped my chest. I couldn't
breathe. I slumped to the floor, clutching my chest and gasping. They yelled for help. A trainer came running in and
massaged me. I felt a little better until I heard him say, "A
few minutes more and he would have been dead." I thought,
"My God! I'm only thirty years old, and now I'll have to take
it easy the rest of my life. You've got to be strong, Kirk, you'll
really have to accept it." They picked me up, very carefully
helped me walk out. They took me to the doctor, who
checked me thoroughly. He looked puzzled. I was thinking,
"Oh boy, it's really bad. I'm sorry for being such a shit all
my life."

He said, "What did you do yesterday?"

"I felt wonderful. I was chopping down trees around my
house."

He said, "It was a hot day."

"Oh, yeah. It was hot."

"Were you sweating?"

"Of course."

"Did you drink anything cold?"

"A lot of cold lemonade."

"I'll tell you something," he said. "Your heart's in perfect
condition. What happened is, you contracted a cold in your
chest muscles, and sometimes it's like a delayed reaction,
the next day those muscles might suddenly just contract.
That's what gave you the impression that you were having a
heart attack."

Great! Now I could get back to being a shit again!

Wallis was annoyed that this had interrupted our negotiations. He said. "You don't sign a term contract, I'm going to drop you."

By then, I knew I would live. "O.K. Drop me."

And he did.

Diana was pregnant again. We celebrated her twenty-third birthday at the home of our friends Walter and Mickey Seltzer. Walt had been Hal Wallis's publicity man. We had a wonderful time, lobster and champagne, and didn't leave until around two-thirty in the morning. Pregnant Diana was having trouble getting to sleep, and about three-thirty or four, said, "Boy, that lobster and champagne is not sitting well at all." I mumbled something comforting like, "Go to sleep." Diana nudged me. "I think this is it." I couldn't believe it—she wasn't due for two or three weeks.

I was driving carefully and soberly down Laurel Canyon to Cedars of Lebanon Hospital. Suddenly, Diana started to whistle. "Why do you keep whistling?" I asked, slowing for the stoplight.

"Go right through the stoplight, just keep going."

I said, "What's with you?" Maybe she had had too much to drink, and was still feeling it. When I drove in front of the hospital, she started to bolt out of the car. I tried to calm her down. "Wait until I get to the parking lot, and then we'll go in together."

"No, let me out here!" and out she went.

I didn't understand the rush; Michael hadn't shown up for almost eleven hours after I had taken her to the hospital. I parked the car and walked in and they showed me to a waiting room. I sat down, picked up *Daily Variety*, and had just opened it when the doctor poked his head in the door and said, "Mr. Douglas?"

I said, "Oh, has she had the spinal already?"

"She's had the *baby* already. You're the father of a baby boy." *What?!* So *that's* why she was whistling!

Diana told me later that she was afraid the baby was going to be born in the car. She came flying into the hospital, coat thrown over her nightgown, her long dark hair in pigtails like a teenager's. They waved the usual forms at her. Her protest, "I have no time to sign! This baby's going to be born any minute!" was met with the standard soothing reply, "Now, now, you always think that with the first baby, dear." Just as she was saying, "It's not my first baby, it's my second!" her water broke. They got her on a gurney, rushed her upstairs—no time for anesthetic—and into the delivery room.

Joel was born at quarter to six. At six Diana called Mickey Seltzer, our hostess of the evening before (or rather, of mere hours earlier) and said, "Hi, Mick! Guess what I just did!" Mickey blurted, "My God! That's impossible! We just said goodnight to you!"

After Joel was born, we got a live-in nanny. She and the kids lived in the guest house, connected to the main house by an intercom. Things were getting more difficult between Diana and me. We have very different temperaments. Once I said to her, "You know something? You're always happy unless something comes along to make you unhappy. I'm always unhappy unless something comes along to make me happy. And then I'm not sure that I'm happy." I was very restless, very driven, and Diana was frustrated that she could not make me happy.

I was playing roles I didn't like in pictures I didn't like. In *The Walls of Jericho*, I was Cornel Wilde's best friend on screen, and Linda Darnell's special friend off screen. Linda looked like a Mata Hari, but was really just a charming girl from Dallas bewildered by Hollywood. She rose fast and faded faster. After three divorces, Linda burned to death in a fire in her secretary's house. She was forty-two.

I played another role I didn't like—a writer opposite Laraine Day in *My Dear Secretary*. I enjoyed working with Laraine. She was going with Leo Durocher and introduced me to him at the old Brooklyn Dodgers' Ebbets Field. I heard my name pronounced in real Brooklynese for the first time. One of the fans, who had just seen *I Walk Alone*, yelled "Hey, Koik! How's Boit?" From that day on, I have always called him "Boit"; if I write him a note, I sign it "Koik."

After that, I did *A Letter to Three Wives.* Joe Mankiewicz, who had a great sense of humor, was the director. In one scene I had to be sleeping in bed, and Joe said to me, "Kirk, now look. While we're preparing the setup, I want you to try to fall asleep. Lie in bed, close your eyes, and really try to fall asleep. I want that feeling of someone sleeping, not just pretending." So I dutifully obeyed, lay down and concentrated on clouds and sheep and things. Finally, I drifted off. I awoke with a start to total silence. I opened one eye, looked around—no one. Joe had gotten me to fall asleep just before lunch, then had everyone tiptoe off the set, leaving me sound asleep in a big, deserted studio.

I played an English professor. Ann Sothern played my wife. We rehearsed the relationship offstage. I think Diana knew more than she let on. She went up to Santa Barbara to do *The Hasty Heart.*

Then I found myself in a real dilemma: I was offered two movies at once. One was a class-A MGM project called *The Great Sinner* starring Ava Gardner, Gregory Peck, and Ethel Barrymore. The other was a small independent picture put together by young unknowns. The director was Mark Robson; the producer was Stanley Kramer. The script by Carl Foreman was based on a Ring Lardner short story—*Champion.*

"Stanley Kramer's nobody," they told me. "He used to be an errand boy at one of the studios."

"So what? I used to be a waiter." But I wasn't sure what to do.

While I was thinking it over, Diana and I made a trip to Bermuda, to visit her family. Diana was the youngest of six. Besides her mother, she had three brothers there, and her sisters Ruth and Fanny. This kind of family was very foreign to me. They were the Dills of Bermuda, highly respected landowners. Her brothers became important lawyers; one was later knighted. Diana took me to see a piece of property on the ocean that they had given her, and I immediately said, "You ought to build a little house on it. Then you could rent the house out and have a source of income." I suddenly saw the disapproving eyes of her family turned upon me as the pragmatism of her Jewish husband came through in suggesting such a commercial enterprise. But they were all a delightful family of different personalities, and I enjoyed them.

Walking along the beach, I decided to take the risk and do *Champion*. I have never felt any need to project a certain image as an actor. I like a role that is stimulating, challenging, interesting to play. That's why I am often attracted to characters that aren't likable. Midge Kelly in *Champion* was probably one of the first antiheroes. I had been playing weak characters, and here was a chance at a really physical role. My agents were pleading with me to be in *The Great Sinner*. They thought I was stupid to turn down a sure $50,000 in a big-budget studio picture for what they considered a terrible role and only $15,000 (deferred, yet!) in an idependent shoestring production. Finally, with dire warnings about my career and my future, they gave up on me, writing me off as just another crazy New York actor who didn't know what he was doing.

Decisions have to be based on your gut instinct. My gut instinct told me to do *Champion*. Then I had to convince Kramer and Foreman that I could play Midge Kelly. They had reservations about me. They'd seen my performance as the weak district attorney in *The Strange Love of Martha Ivers,* and as the sensitive schoolteacher in *A Letter to Three Wives.* Now, although they were trying to be delicate about it, they were wondering whether I could play a boxer. I finally realized what they wanted. I thought, This is what the starlets do. I took off my jacket and shirt, bared my chest and flexed my muscles. They nodded approvingly, satisfied that I could play a boxer. I was probably the only *man* in Hollywood who's had to strip to get a part.

I didn't want to use a body double, so I worked out. I already knew how to skip rope from my wrestling days in college. Mushy Callahan, the ex-welterweight champ, taught me how to punch the speed bag and the hard bag. We developed a boxing style suitable for my character: always moving forward, no matter how many times or how hard I got hit.

Even when I got smashed in the face, I kept moving in. I was relentless.

Many of the boxers I fought in the picture were real-life ex-pugs. Most were city, country, or state champions. One day, when we were doing a scene training in the gym, a friend of mine visited the set. I said, "Watch this. Just keep looking at all those fighters." I yelled out, "Hey, Champ!" Almost all of them turned around.

To make a movie punch look real, yet not have anyone get hurt, it takes two people: one to miss the punch when it's thrown, the other to react as if he's been hit. It's very difficult for a real boxer to pretend he's hitting someone; he's trained to hit, not to miss. One of the boxers playing a bit part, a fighter from New Jersey who had very, very sharp punches, really intimidated me. I was always a little nervous about him. In one of the scenes we did together, I bounced off the ropes and he was supposed to catch me with an uppercut. He did—knocked me out. The camera was running. That scene is in the movie, and it looks great. But I don't recommend that you get knocked out to make a scene look realistic.

Making *Champion* was a delightful experience. We all sat around at my house at Vado Place eating sandwiches and working on the script. Everybody made suggestions. That's the way I like to make a film.

My co-star was Marilyn Maxwell, who later sang with Bob Hope for many years. She died of a heart attack before she was fifty. There was a scene in *Champion* where Marilyn finds out I'm dropping her for another girl. She's furious, and threatens to expose me for the heel I really am. In the original script, I grab her by the hair and push her face up against the mirror and tell her that I'll destroy her. It bothered me. To do this to a girl seemed *over*doing it. During a rehearsal, Marilyn happened to grab the inside of my arm, by my elbow. I pulled my arm up and caught her fingers, and she winced. I apologized. Then I thought, Yeah, that's what it should be. In the final version, when she berates me and grabs me, I mash her fingers in the crook of my arm. Then I very tenderly stroke them and say, "No, you're not going to do that. You're going to be a very good girl." Then, very softly. "Because if you're not, I'll put you in the hospital for a long time." And Marilyn just looks at me. Then I walk through the door, taking off my tie as I get ready for my date with the other girl. At the bedroom door, I turn to her and say, very simply, "Don't be here when I get back." I learned so much from that scene—how implied violence can sometimes be much more effective than violence itself. It became a powerful moment in the picture.

Just how powerful was not apparent to me until one day in 1987, when Shirley MacLaine came up to me, laughing, and grabbed my hand. "You know, Kirk, you're responsible for my becoming an actress."

"Really?"

"Yes. When Warren and I saw *Champion*, we used to come home and play that scene between you and Marilyn Maxwell. Warren and I played that scene a lot."

I said, "What part did you play?"

She laughed.

Moments of inspiration come from peculiar sources. An actor has to be open and receptive, and allow things to happen. It's the way a writer writes a character. Suddenly, as he's typing away, the character goes off in a different direction from the one he had intended. In the same way, you can't get too set with a character you're going to play. You've got to be flexible before the mold is set and allow the character himself to dictate to you how he wants to be played.

An example of this comes at the very end of *Champion*, when Midge has a brain seizure in his locker room, and goes out of his mind, babbling about things that happened earlier in his life. He smashes the locker with his fist—his means of livelihood, his means of expressing himself—then he looks helplessly at his broken fingers. When it came time to play that scene, I remembered that not long before, Joel had hurt his finger and it was bleeding. He looked at it in wonderment, then turned to me, showed me his finger, and said, "Daddy? Daddy?" very pathetically. I just re-created that moment—I smashed my hand on the locker, looked at my crushed fingers, held them up to my trainer, Tommy, and very pathetically, like a child, said, "Tommy? Tommy?" And then died.

Diana read lines with me and rehearsed with me. She admired me for being such a hard worker ("You're the hardest worker I've ever known in my life,") and it helped her, because she was inclined to be a little less conscientious. But I would go after a role and milk it dry, and my compulsiveness used to get to her. I would wake up at night thinking about the movie, and wake Diana up, saying, "Let's go over it again." She'd say, "You've got it. You've got the best out of it, and now you're running it into the ground." But I couldn't leave it alone. I would push her until she said, "For Christ's sake! I was up last night going over this thing!"

I had just signed Warren Cowan to handle public relations for me. He and his wife, Ronnie, were having a birthday party for Diana. I was supposed to be back from the studio in time to take her, but I was late, "rehearsing" with Marilyn Maxwell. Diana may have had her suspicions. When I got home, there was a note stuck in the door. I'VE GONE TO THE COWANS. YOU CAN GO TO HELL. I chose to go to the Cowans', entered on my knees. Diana was standing talking to somebody, and they turned around.

There I was, on my knees. "I'm not worthy of you. Anyone can see I'm not worthy of you."

She was furious. "Oh, shut up!"

I followed her around on my knees, saying, "She's a saint. Just look at her, she's a saint."

She started laughing in spite of herself and turned to me. "Why do you always make me laugh, just when I'm ready to punch you right in the nose?"

I think separation was on both our minds. Diana suggested that we go to Lake Arrowhead without the kids, and just try to have fun. But it was difficult for me to do nothing. I felt I should be working, or looking for work, or doing something. Diana said, "I'm going to play tennis, I'm going to play golf, and I'm going to go sailing. Join me. Or don't. If you want to sit in the room and sulk, go ahead. But I'm going to have fun." I was impatient and unhappy. Diana said, "It's ridiculous to live this way. For the first time, we have a little money, but it's not making you happy. It's just making you miserable. I don't know why." I didn't know why either. Then she said, "You know something? Unless you get some psychiatric help, we're going to separate."

"You brought it up," I said. "I didn't."

Diana said, "O.K. I'll remember that."

Once when Diana and I were having an intense argument in the kitchen, we saw Michael, who was about six, walking toward us. We stopped immediately, before he entered, but he burst out crying. He could feel the tension. That was when we realized that staying together for the sake of the children wouldn't work. Diana and the children stayed in our beautiful little house. I moved out. For the first time in years, I was alone. I was restless, unhappy, reaching out in every direction. I thought I wanted to be alone, live on a mountaintop. I rented a little guest house at the top of Mulholland. I couldn't stay there one night. I was gasping. I moved down to Westwood village, where there were people around.

This was, of course, a very difficult time for both Diana and me. We were trying to handle it as well as we could. The pressures of Hollywood were enormous. It was very hard to keep any sense of perspective or sanity. Or privacy, with Louella Parsons and Hedda Hopper and Sheilah Graham— the gossip columnists—calling up all the time. They bullied and terrorized people—the ones they liked. The ones they didn't like, they destroyed in a line. Vultures, they pounced on any kind of garbage. In one column, Sheilah Graham wrote that our "alleged" separation was just a publicity gimmick. This infuriated me. I broke my usual silence and called her up. "You cunt! How dare you print that! This is our life. We have two children. And you make it as if we're playing a game." I didn't care. Who were they?

Reporters from newspapers and fan magazines called Diana and me, sometimes in the middle of the night. They always pretended sympathy—"We want to tell your side of it, blah blah blah." Diana and I always responded in the same way: "There is no side to this. We are separated. We have two children that we both love very much, and we're trying to work things out."

Looking back, I often wonder if things might have been different if we had stayed in New York and worked in the theater, or at least, if we had moved out of Hollywood, to a nearby town. I think the divorce probably would have happened eventually, but it was accelerated by Hollywood, which brings out the worst, not the best, in people. Hollywood people want to be associated with success. If someone is going downhill, they want to keep away from him. A terrible insecurity pervades the place. Hollywood is like a crowded, fast-moving streetcar, with talented young actors and actresses jumping on, constantly pushing other people back. As people get shoved out of their seats, they try to hang on to the straps, while a wave of new talent constantly pushes them back, pushes them back, until the pressure becomes too intense and they jump off. To maintain your equilibrium in Hollywood is a monumental task.

People change when they come to Hollywood. It was difficult to cope with forty years ago, and it's still difficult. This is the town where Cliff Robertson exposed David Begelman as a forger and thief, with the net result that Begelman got a standing ovation at a Hollywood restaurant, while Robertson was blacklisted for four years. On the bad days, you think of what Tallulah Bankhead said: "Who do I have to fuck to get out of this business?"

I think a lot of writers, directors, and actors save themselves now by not living here. Many move to Santa Barbara. I was at an elegant party recently with my son Michael in Santa Barbara, where he has a house. John Travolta was there, and I asked him where he lived. "Santa Barbara," he said. "I can't take Hollywood. That's a place for lawyers and agents." Travolta had a shattering experience. His first two pictures were blockblusters, his third, a flop. He was annihilated.

It's hard to make friends in Hollywood. It's a cruel, un-happy town, and success is even more difficult to handle than failure. You look around and you see what's happened to Marilyn Monroe, John Belushi, James Dean, Freddie Prinz, Bobby Darin, and so many others.

So I was glad when Lex Barker, another young actor, in-vited me to join the Westwood Tennis Club, where he was a member. He took me over, showed me around. Then he said, "It's too bad we can't have a club out here like we have back East. There are too many Jews here, so we have to let a few in." Ironically, he had just finished filming *Crossfire,* one of the first Hollywood movies to deal with anti-Semitism. It didn't seem to have made an impression on him. I said, "Yes, Lex, of course, I understand. But then, being Jewish myself, I have a different point of view." He turned pink.

The Los Angeles Country Club was the biggest and richest country club in the city, with a history of barring not only Jews and blacks, but also anybody from the motion picture industry. How about that? Not only race prejudice, but in-dustry prejudice. Joe Drown, owner of the Bel Air Hotel, told me one day with a wry smile that the club wouldn't let him in.

I said, "But, Joe, you don't fit any of those categories."

"Ah, but I'm a bad risk—I might *marry* someone in show business."

Every once in a while they bend the rules and give guest privileges to Jews. This allows them to hang on to their tax-exempt status. They granted me a guest card for one day and I brought Carl Rowan, the black journalist, and Bob Hope. The club members were very polite. Randolph Scott who loved to play golf and who had a house next to the course, for years could only look at that beautiful golf course, though occasionally he was allowed to play there as a guest. He was a good player. Finally, they broke the line and took him in. So you see, prejudice is declining—if you're a WASP actor, live to be eighty but shoot in the seventies and promise not to make any more movies, you too might get to be a member of the Los Angeles Country Club.

So many of our presidents have campaigned vowing to represent all the people—all faiths, all colors. They're elected, they serve the country, representing all faiths. What happens to them when they come out of office? The great General Eisenhower immediately joined the El Dorado Club in Palm Springs—no blacks, no Jews. Gerald Ford immediately joined Thunderbird in Palm Springs, then considered violently anti-Semitic. When President Reagan leaves office, will he become a member of the Los Angeles Country Club? Such hypocrisy. How can someone go through the drama and turmoil of occupying the highest office in the land, representing all people, and not have anything rub off on him? You begin to wonder what was in their minds while they were president. No one seems to criticize it, everyone accepts it, and life goes on. Gentleman's agreement.

Diana did a play, *Major Barbara.* She was wonderful in it, and it opened up some possibilities for her. I said to her, "You really are a stage actress. You should be doing something on Broadway."

She argued, "I can't just go off and leave you with the kids."

I said, "For once in your life do something totally selfish. Just have the guts to be totally selfish. Say, 'O.K., I'm going to try it.' We've got a very good nanny. I'll be home with them, too. We can all move into the house while you're away. Just give it a try."

"You're right. I'm going."

So she went back to New York. After she'd been there for a couple of months with nothing definite, I called to ask if she was coming back for Thanksgiving. She said that she had been thinking about the separation, about her legal rights, and had been talking to a lawyer, and she was now convinced that it was divorce time. "We've got to talk face to face," I said, and she agreed.

Diana came back to California at Thanksgiving, and we talked—of our romantic wedding under the crossed sabers, living in the Pontalba buildings in New Orleans, eating doughnuts and coffee, then living in the deserted castle up on top of the hill. There were a lot of sweet, sweet moments in our shared life. But now it was obvious to both of us that it was over. Why do people get divorced? Why do people get married? What went wrong? I was desperate for answers.

Maybe Diana was right—I ought to find out more about myself. I decided to go to a psychiatrist. I had been unfaithful; Diana knew it. It was too easy—the constant temptation of a beautiful girl, a dressing room, close contact. Sometimes it became irresistible, even if it meant nothing.

I assumed that the psychiatrist and I would discuss any problems I had in a week and a half, and that would be the end of it. After all, at that time I still believed that I had had a very happy childhood—although we were poor, we were a big happy family. But when Kirk Douglas lay down on the couch in the psychiatrist's office, he suddenly felt like Issur sleeping alone in the parlor. He was shocked to find out that he really had had a miserable childhood. He started to cry. It was painful trying to face Issur, little Issur still hiding behind that garbage can. I was still too frightened to look at him directly. I needed to mourn the things that I hadn't had the strength to mourn, to accept the tragedies of my childhood, like the death of my dog Tiger. All those years of Issur's buried hatred and resentment erupted, flowed out like lava. Most of it was directed against a nameless "they,"— "they" who seem to control things. You'd better be good in pictures, because if "they" don't like you, you haven't got a chance. In my head "they" were people in Amsterdam who were so patronizing and condescending. "Oh yes, the poor Demskys. Wonderful family, and very nice. It seems a shame." Of course, "they" said that only as long as the Demskys were down and "they" could feel secure and strong, knowing that others were weak. Now so many people in Amsterdam claim to have helped us out, given us food, had us over for a meal. If all those people had actually done what they claim, we would have eaten six meals a day and lived like kings.

Five years later, I stopped going to the psychiatrist. I

learned: (1) Everyone has problems, some greater, some lesser. It's just that some people handle them better than others. (2) You never graduate from analysis. (3) My doctor was more screwed up than I was.

It would have been easier—almost—if Diana and I had been divorced because I had fallen madly in love with the "other woman," or Diana had found the "other man." But I hadn't. And she hadn't. There was no other one for either of us.

I told Diana that we had to get her a good lawyer. She said she had one—Arnold Crakower, who was married to Kathleen Winsor, the author of *Forever Amber*. I figured he was probably some schlockmeister and told her I'd have him checked out. Was I surprised! "Listen, Little Red Riding Hood, how did you manage to get the best divorce lawyer in New York?" She said, "I what? I didn't know that!" It turned out that Crakower had handled Kathleen Winsor's divorce from Artie Shaw, and she was the only one of Shaw's seven wives ever to receive any alimony. My lawyer, whom I had gotten at the suggestion of my friend Sam Norton, was Jerry Rosenthal, his partner, who had represented Artie Shaw in that divorce. The lawyers *hated* each other. They didn't know what to do with us. I was saying, "Give Diana whatever she wants, anything she needs." Diana was saying. "But the poor boy, he's worked so hard to make his way up here. We can't stick him now that he's finally making some money. It just isn't right." Our divorce was friendly, but our lawyers almost got into a fist fight in the office while Diana and I sat there gaping.

Diana sued for divorce in February of 1949. There wasn't any such thing as no-fault divorce then. You had to have one party in the wrong, you had to have a specific reason, and you had to have witnesses, which made it much more unpleasant. Mental cruelty was the most innocuous accusation possible; we went for that.

Diana went to court with Ronnie Cowan and a cooked-up story about the party where I'd shown up late and followed her around on my knees. Ronnie loved being on the stand. She testified, with embellishments. "Poor Diana came to the party, you see. Nobody knew where Kirk was, and she was scarlet."

The judge said, "Scarlet?"

She said, "Yes. Scarlet with embarrassment, Your Honor."

Diana started to get nervous giggles, but stopped herself. Television and press were out in full force, and she could visualize the headlines: MRS. DOUGLAS DIVORCED AMID GALES OF LAUGHTER. She rushed home afterward. We had a beer together and watched our divorce on the evening news as we critiqued the coverage. We laughed, but it wasn't funny.

My marriage, Hollywood, and the world were coming apart at the seams. Everyone in Hollywood was a nervous wreck over the blacklist business. The red scare had been growing for the last two years. In a fit of postwar hysteria spearheaded by Senator Joseph "Tailgunner Joe" McCarthy from Wisconsin, the House Un-American Activities Committee (HUAC) was conducting hearings to ferret out subversives in the United States. McCarthy claimed that we were all in danger from Communists lurking around every corner and behind every lamppost. Hollywood was conspicuous; we could do the most damage to the country by spreading propaganda, and they would make an example of us. Already, many people wondered why their telephones had stopped ringing, why there was no work, no parties, why they couldn't reach their agents—people like Edward G. Robinson, John Garfield, Larry Parks. You didn't have to be formally accused of anything—innuendo in the press could ruin you. Nobody knew who would be next.

Champion was released in July of 1949. I've always had a lousy sense of direction, then and now. It was the night of the preview. I was driving myself. They gave me the address, and of course, I couldn't find the theater. When I finally got there, Stanley Kramer was pacing up and down out in front, under a marquee that said: SNEAK PREVIEW. He was annoyed at me. Everybody was already inside; the picture had started. I was nervous. I wasn't sure how the audience was reacting. When the movie was over, everybody came out and filled out cards. A lot of the agents were there to see this fiasco, because they had all been against my doing *Champion*. Most of Famous Artists Agency was there, shaking their heads. I interpreted it as "Jesus, what a lousy picture!" I later found out they were shaking their heads in amazement—"Wow! What a picture!" Then we went into an office and looked through the cards—all glorious. The first inkling that we might have a success.

Diana moved back to New York, to an apartment on the West Side, with the two boys. Why do the children always go with the mother? I remember my feelings when we left my father. A lot of that is changing now, but it never occurred to any of us then that my sons might live with me, or even that they might *want* to live with me. I would fly back every chance I got, and they would spend summer vacations, and often Christmas and Easter, with me. Diana and I worked it out. And according to our agreement, the children were brought up outside of any religion.

Although it was incredibly hard for both of us, we faced up to it and called it quits when we were still both young enough to have full lives ahead. Also, we got out before things got too bitter. We left with respect for each other. I liked Diana very much, and still do. People are amazed that we are still friends. I think that lots of times I am unfairly given credit for Michael's talents, as if he had only my genes. Diana is a talented actress, and Michael has inherited from both of us. My wife and I see Diana and her husband, Bill Darrid, often, talk on the phone, have dinner, get together with them and the kids. We've had them at our house in Palm Springs, and have a pleasant relationship with them. I've worked professionally with Diana and with Bill, a very talented guy. I'm very fond of him, and can never thank him enough for being such a wonderful surrogate father to Michael and Joel.

Now I was alone, unhappy in the one role I never wanted to play: bachelor. I went out of town for the weekend, miserable and self-pitying, and returned the same way. I was so unhappy, deep down inside of me.

And then I saw him—Issur. He wasn't peeping around a garbage can. He was standing up, looking at Kirk. Kirk hated Issur. Whenever Kirk got weak, Issur would get stronger. Now, he looked at Kirk and shook his head.

"What's the matter with you?" Kirk demanded.

"Nothing. What's the matter with you? I feel sorry for you," said Issur in a low, calm voice that irritated Kirk more.

"I don't need your sympathy," Kirk said, raising his voice. "Get back behind your garbage can."

Issur spoke in the same calm voice. "But I could help you."

"I don't want your help!" Kirk yelled, almost losing control.

"You need help from someone."

Kirk didn't answer.

Issur continued. "What did it get you, playing around with those girls?"

Kirk clenched his teeth and kept driving. On the sidewalk, he saw long lines of people. As usual, the whole world was out there having a good time without him. He clutched the wheel. His voice quivered with anger. "What's wrong with fucking beautiful women?" He looked out the window and followed the line around a corner. He only saw more line.

"What's wrong is that it didn't make you happy."

At a red light, Kirk tried not to listen, and wondered where the long line of people was going.

"You lost Diana. You lost Michael. You lost Joel."

Kirk tried to fight back the tears as he watched the line turning a corner.

"Where are you now? Nowhere. What are you now? Nobody."

The tears could not be held back, were spilling down Kirk's cheeks. Then he saw it. The line ended under a marquee:

KIRK DOUGLAS
CHAMPION

Kirk exploded. "Nobody, huh? Fuck you, Issur! Kirk is a STAR!"

Eight

STAR

Champion was a success, a surprise hit. Charlie Feldman called me himself to tell me so. How novel, my agent calling me. Was I free for dinner that night? Was I free? If I wasn't, I would be. "I'll take care of the reservations at Romanoff's," he said. I was glad of that, given my relationship with the headwaiter. And there I was, sitting at a choice table with Charlie Feldman, listening as he oozed charm and talked easily on many subjects. Prince Romanoff himself came over to speak to us in his Oxford accent, a little man standing very erect, immaculately dressed, hands clasped in front of him, bulbous nose overhanging a tiny mustache. I was impressed —a real prince; there was an oil painting of him in royal robes behind the bar. He sat down and told us of an invitation he had received to a charity event. He had asked to see the guest list; he wouldn't even consider going unless all the right people would be there. The limousine came to get him, took him to the event, then home to his hotel suite, where he found that he had been locked out for being two weeks in arrears with the rent. I laughed at the story, mystified. Later, Charlie explained that Prince Romanoff was royalty from Brooklyn. But he was always a very charming conversationalist. What I liked best about him was his sense of humor. He loved to tell stories about himself.

After dinner, Charlie casually suggested, "Let's stop by Warners."

"Yeah, sure." I wondered what could be going on at the studio at that hour. Then it hit me: he didn't mean the studio. He meant the house. Jack Warner's very own personal home.

Soon, we were going up a winding driveway off Angelo Drive. Another castle on top of a hill. This one had the horseshit piled high *inside*. A butler opened the door and ushered us into a sumptuous library. He offered us a drink and informed us that Mr. Warner and his guests were just finishing dinner. Judging by the cars out in front, there were many people there. Voices began to waft in from the next room, women's voices: *"Champion?* What's that?" "Boxing?" "I hate fight pictures!" "Kirk what?" "Who's he?" Obviously, after dinner, they were going to screen *Champion*.

I looked around. On the wall were two paintings by Dali. One was a portrait of Ann Warner, Jack's wife, which I found haunting. There was a tragic look on her face. The background was the pillars of the house, but they were all decaying. It was a picture of tragedy in the midst of decay. Opposite was a picture of Jack Warner, completely slick— pomaded hair, shiny face, phony smile, red carnation in his buttonhole. Shallow, flat. I wondered if they understood what Dali had done in these two paintings. They were tremendous paintings. What happened to them?

The butler escorted us into the large, comfortable screening room. I sat by myself and watched Charlie Feldman circulate among the guests, very much at ease. He came to me with a medium-sized man with black, slick hair and a pencil-thin mustache, the man in the Dali painting. Charlie, my new pal, placed an arm around my shoulder. "Kirk, meet Mr. Jack Warner."

As I mumbled something, Jack Warner struck up a boxing pose and said, "Well, kid, let's see if you're as good as they say."

I felt very uncomfortable. Everyone ignored me when I got there. But after the picture, they all looked at me as if I had just arrived. Charlie was suddenly my agent, discussing a deal with Jack Warner. The women ogled me, as if they were looking right through my clothes.

I received a long, flattering telegram from Joan Crawford, about my "magnificent performance." I was impressed, called to thank her. The next thing I knew we had a date for dinner. I was going to go out with Joan Crawford! I was thrilled at the thought of meeting such a famous star—a legend—someone I had watched in movies and had fantasies about when I was growing up. I went to her home to pick her up. She had the evening's itinerary precisely arranged: where we would dine, at what time, the route to the restaurant. She had probably already decided what I would eat, too.

Claustrophobia began to set in. Joan Crawford all by herself was equivalent to six sisters and my mother. I had to assert myself. "No, we're not going to that restaurant." She looked at me, astonished. I said, "No, we're going to"—I pulled a name out of a hat—"Don the Beachcomber." She sulked a bit, not accustomed to having her orders countermanded.

At dinner, she was glamorous and very attentive, her eyes, as the French say, *clignotants comme un hibou*—flickering like an owl's. We went back to her house. We never got past the foyer. The door closed and she slipped out of her dress. She had a beautiful, trim body. There we were on the rug. In the middle of our lovemaking, she murmured, "You're so clean. It's wonderful that you shaved your armpits when you made *Champion*." A real conversation stopper. I didn't even understand what she meant. I have very light hair. But I don't shave under my arms. A strange comment to make; a stranger time to make it. The breath with which she uttered it blew away all my fantasies about Miss Crawford.

Afterward, we got dressed. She took me upstairs and proudly showed me the two children—how they were strapped so tightly into their beds, how she diapered them so efficiently. It was so professional, clinical, lacking in warmth, like the sex we had just had. I got out fast.

Charlie Feldman called me the next day. Twice in a row! Could I come to the office? Could I! As Charlie's secretary ushered me in immediately, I saw a young actor sitting in a chair, waiting. Does it go on forever? Charlie was in a good mood. "I made a deal for you with Jack Warner—eight pictures, one a year, no options. You won't have to wait around each year to see whether they want you for a picture."

"I don't know."

"You don't know?! I know! You should be ecstatic!"

"I don't want to be tied up to a studio for eight years."

"This is a great deal! No options and only one picture a year. You'll be able to do whatever else you want."

"It's still a trap. They can tie me up with that one picture until I don't have time for anything else. I don't want to do it."

Charlie was furious.

The studios were corrupt. They took advantage of actors and writers and directors. All their deals were unfair. The agents you paid to represent you were very cozy with the studios. When I first came to Hollywood, a standard seven-year contract, with all the options on the studio's side, was almost like slavery. Olivia de Havilland finally sued Warner Brothers, claiming the contract was unconstitutional, indentured servitude. She won. It helped, but the studios were still very powerful. I was reluctant to commit to the deal; Charlie kept pressuring me. I told him I'd think about it while I went back East to do some promotional work for *Champion*.

Television was just beginning, and the movie studio system didn't know how to deal with it. They could very easily have gone along with it, and they would have controlled television. What's television without film?—just electrical impulses going out into the air. An edict came down from

Jack Warner. "Nobody's going on television." Why shouldn't I? How could they stop me? Marilyn Maxwell and I were among the first movie actors to be on television. We did a scene from *Champion* to help sell the picture, like a live commercial.

I got on the red-eye to New York. Why wasn't I happy? They told me I'd made a hit picture. To fulfill one of my dreams, I went to a suite on the twenty-fifth floor of the Hampshire House. An entourage of bellboys brought my bags in. I paid them and hustled them out. Alone, I walked to the window and looked down on the park. It was winter. Kids were sledding, tobogganing on trash-can lids. They all seemed happy. Everybody was happy but me. I had been happier years ago, a waiter walking across the park at night with my friends, pockets full of tips, belly full of beer, looking up at the Hampshire House and imagining how wonderful it would be there. Nothing tasted good to me. Later in life, I told my son, "Michael, if something good happens to you, stop. Enjoy it. Savor it." That has never been an easy thing for me to do.

I went to see Diana and Michael and Joel. They were living in a modest apartment on West Eighty-fourth. I promised myself that they would have a better place as soon as I made more money. I walked in and kissed Diana on the cheek. Michael started to cry. Thirty-five years later, he told me it bewildered him. He thought Mommy and Daddy were angry at each other. Michael made me realize how much tension must have existed between Diana and me and how much he was aware of it. I tried to be cheerful and pleasant, but it was awkward. I wanted so much to create with Michael and Joel the relationship I had missed with my father. The boys were enrolled at Allan Stevenson private school. I was interested in their work, bawled them out if they were not doing well. I wanted them to know I cared. Still, there was a wall between us. Maybe they felt that I had abandoned them. We never discussed it. It's hard to be a father.

I thought about Pa in Amsterdam, alone. Ma was living in

Albany with Betty, the other sisters nearby. They had all gotten out of Amsterdam, but not very far—twenty-eight miles. Like Pa, I was alone now, too. I had a dream of buying him a ranch with beautiful horses. Pa loved horses, had a real feeling for them. In Amsterdam, people would bring horses to him, and he would open the horse's mouth, check the teeth, tell the age.

In my fantasy, Pa would walk around in the clean air under blue skies and argue with the cowboys. They would think he was a pain in the ass, but what could they do about it? I owned the ranch. I could go there and live with Pa from time to time. I had to see Pa.

I got to Amsterdam in the early afternoon. We drove by the Rialto Theater, where my high school graduation had been held. *Champion* was playing.

At my suggestion, Pa no longer lived alone. I paid for him to move to rooms in the 4th Ward Hotel, over Boggi's saloon at the corner of East Main and Lark Street—four blocks from our old house, midway between Eagle Street and DiCaprio's diner.

It took a minute for my eyes to adjust to the dimness of Boggi's and find him sitting at the bar. He was drinking his usual boilermaker, a shot of raw whiskey followed by a swallow of beer. The bartender recognized me and with great solicitude walked away, leaving me with my father.

"Hi, Pa."

"Hullo." He got up, kissed me on the mouth, Russian style. I was shocked to find I was taller than he. He always seemed such a huge man.

"How are you, Pa?"

A grunt.

I studied my father's face. He seemed a lot older. His mustache was gone. So was one of his front teeth, those teeth that he had never brushed ("brushing made teeth loose," he always said), those teeth that could take the cap off a bottle or chew glass. He used to gnash his teeth, grind them together and make a terrible sound. As I looked at him, I thought I'd hate to put those teeth to that test now. He still had all his hair, but it was completely gray. And he needed a shave, which was unlike him.

I never saw my father shave himself. We were poor, but he went to a barber to get shaved. Years later, I was in New York, at the barber's. I thought, My God, I'm a rich man. "Give me a shave." It was luxurious; I liked it. I can afford it. But that was the only time I did it.

After a long pause, "I made a new movie, Pa."

"Yeah?"

"*Champion.*"

"Yeah."

Another long pause. "Did you see it, Pa?"

"Yeah."

"Did you like it?"

"Yeah."

That was a pretty long conversation with Pa. He ordered another boilermaker. I gave him some money and left. I got in my waiting limousine, told the driver to take me to Albany.

Years later, I was told that my father went to see *Champion* with one of his drinking buddies. When I was being slaughtered by my opponent in the ring, my father covered his face with both hands. At the end of the fight, when I was finally winning, Pa got up and yelled in broken English, "Issur, give it to him! Issur, give it to him!"

If only Pa could have said, "Issur, give it to him," when I was a kid. Pa covered his eyes when Kirk Douglas was bleeding makeup in a movie. But when Issur was being carried home, head bleeding for real, Pa was on the other side of the street, grumbling, "That's what you get for playing." He should have covered his eyes *then*. Years later, many people told me how Pa would brag about me. But it was too late to get that pat on the back when Pa was dead.

I was determined to give my kids that pat on the back. But often, what we give our kids is what *we* need. It doesn't work. I took Eric to the steam room once when we were in Palm Springs. Kids were not allowed, but I wanted Eric in the world of men. I needed that, but maybe it wasn't what Eric needed.

My reception in Albany was quite different. All my sisters were at Betty's, all talking at once, hugging me and kissing me. Their husbands joined in. Ma sat in the chair of honor, beaming as she held my hand.

The table was overflowing with borscht, gefülte fish, white fish, lox, bagels, cakes, drinks. All the things Pa would have liked. I looked at my mother. She raised seven children, cleaned the house, fed us all, made do with a small amount of food. Why was my perception of her that she was weak? I can see her on the Sabbath, sitting calmly in the rocking chair. I always assumed that my father was the strong one, but maybe my mother was stronger. Maybe? She was. Beware of women—sometimes they seem weak, but they're really strong.

I was inundated by a wave of affection from seven women. I tried to look happy and laugh. All the time, I felt weaker and weaker, like Pa. I began to hyperventilate. It was all too much, overpowering. Why wasn't Pa there? With him, I might feel stronger.

As long as my mother was alive, I made an effort. At least once a year I would take my mother, all my sisters, and their husbands and children to a restaurant for a big dinner. One time, to liven up the proceedings, I devised a ceremony based on the Oscars. I awarded "B.I.L.L.Y.s"—"Brothers-in-Law"—for meritorious service in being married to my sisters and fortitude in putting up with them. I had a certificate done in calligraphy, and made what I thought was an amusing presentation. It was a joke. To my surprise, everyone's eyes filled with tears, especially the recipients'. I couldn't tell them it was supposed to be funny. Why didn't they laugh? It became a serious ceremony that I performed every year until my mother died.

Back in Los Angeles, I paced up and down the living room of the nearly empty house on Vado Place. Diana had taken most of the furniture, the pieces that her sister Ruth had given us from the castle in New Jersey. She left Aristide

Bruant hanging over the fireplace, still sneering at me. I continued to pace. I reminded myself of my father. I didn't belong anywhere. I didn't belong to my old family. I didn't belong to my new family. I wanted to belong somewhere. I called Charlie Feldman and took the Warners deal. Besides, they were dangling two projects in front of me that I really wanted to do.

The first was *Young Man with a Horn,* about jazz trumpeter Bix Beiderbecke. It was based on a book by Dorothy Baker, who had written *Trio.* I loved doing the movie, working with Harry James. I even learned to play some songs on the trumpet. It's a damned difficult instrument, much harder than the banjo. You can't make a sound out of a trumpet just by blowing in it. You have to develop what they call an embouchure. I've still got it. It's quite a strain on the facial muscles.

Although the movie was quite successful, I thought some things in it could have been more authentic. When Bix leaves the Paul Whiteman band, he goes to a smart little club with elegantly dressed patrons and a maître d' in a tuxedo. It's the same kind of place he'd just left, only smaller. I thought that was a big mistake. Bix was like Larry Bird—the one white guy with rhythm. He would have gone up to Harlem and played with the blacks after hours. I argued with Curtiz about that. I lost. Also, I would have changed the ending, made it real—Bix died. They had to have a good ending, so he's playing his trumpet while Doris Day smiles. In the book, the Doris Day character was a black girl. But you couldn't do that then.

My old friend Betty Bacall was in the movie with me. She had one line that I've always remembered: "I'm just an intellectual mountain goat, leaping from crag to crag." How can anybody say that line? This was the first time we worked together—two kids from New York, co-starring in a movie, and she was married to the great Humphrey Bogart. Lauren invited me to the Westside Golf Course, across from Warner Brothers, for lunch. It was a club well known for its anti-Semitic membership policy. I couldn't help rubbing it in.

"Do they know you're Jewish, Betty? Why would your husband belong to a club that doesn't allow Jews, Betty?" Betty, who has an answer for everything, had nothing to say to that.

I drifted around, met lots of girls, I knew men who had sex with a different girl every night. I never understood it. I understood it less after I did it for a while. It wasn't satisfying; like Chinese food—an hour later, you're hungry. I always needed to have an emotional relationship, warm human contact. After about two months, I began to wonder, What am I doing? Masturbation has more meaning. At least you develop a better relationship with your fantasies.

I went out with Rita Hayworth for a short time. The papers made a lot of it because it was Rita's first date after her divorce from Aly Khan. Rita was beautiful, but very simple, unsophisticated. She used to say, "Men go to bed with Gilda, but they wake up with me." I felt something deep within her that I couldn't help—loneliness, sadness—something that would pull me down; I had to get away. Years later, I saw a picture of Rita in the newspaper. She had Alzheimer's disease. I couldn't look at it, turned the page quickly. The public insists on its fantasies of Hollywood. Marilyn Monroe, on the screen, is the sexiest woman in the world. In real life, she was blah. And always late.

I dated Patricia Neal briefly. Patricia was elegant, intelligent, beautiful. I liked her a lot. She liked me. But she was madly in love with Gary Cooper. They had just finished filming *The Fountainhead* together, and were having a passionate love affair. Cooper almost left his wife. I think Pat reached out to me to try to break the hold that Cooper had over her. But she couldn't. Sometimes when we grew affectionate, she cried. She felt unfaithful to Cooper. I felt sorry for her. We attended the premiere of *The Fountainhead* together. Poor Patricia. She couldn't go with Gary. But I always liked her, and still do. Patricia judged every man by her father. She told me that Gary Cooper reminded her of him. When Patricia married Roald Dahl, I had never met him. But I knew what he would look like: very tall, very slim. When I met Dahl, he was very tall, very slim. He looked like Gary Cooper without hair. I am sure her father looked like that, too. I never worked with Cooper, but I met him several times at dinner parties. He never had much to say. Roald Dahl always had a lot to say.

I made an amazing discovery: I am very often attracted to women who have a slight overbite. My wife Anne has an overbite. So does Diana. She lost the lead in *My Darling Clementine* to Linda Darnell because Darryl Zanuck said, "I don't like your teeth."

Gene Tierney had a beautiful overbite. How charming she was. I adored her. We exchanged gifts. It was a wonderful relationship. But she had some strange habits. She insisted, like a mischievous girl, that when I came to see her at night, I did not ring the doorbell. She would leave the window to her bedroom open, and I would climb in. She wasn't married, she wasn't living with anyone, but if that was the way she liked it, it was fine with me. That window wasn't too high for me to climb through. Maybe it was an aphrodisiac. I didn't question it. Mine was not to question why; mine was just to get through that window.

We had a lovely time until one day I said to her, "Gene, isn't it wonderful that we get along so well together. I don't want to get married, you don't want to get married." Brother, don't ever tell a woman that you don't want to get married. That was the end of it. I didn't know what happened. We would talk to each other, but that was the end of our romance.

Then she went into a picture with Spencer Tracy, *Plymouth Adventure,* and told me that she would be marrying him. This all happened so quickly, I didn't believe it. She showed me a saccharine letter that he had written, telling her that he wanted to arrange things so that they could go off together.

"Gene, I don't believe it," I said. "First, Spencer's married. He'll never get divorced. Second, he has a very intense relationship with Katharine Hepburn, and he'll never give it up."

I don't know what was in Spencer Tracy's head. But I

learned that women like to have hope. They may not want to marry the guy they're going with, but they like to feel that something could happen. I made the mistake of being blunt about not wanting to get married, and here was another man writing a flattering letter telling her what she wanted to hear.

Years later, Gene spent some time in a sanitarium. She left there apparently "cured." Of what? She had lost all of her sparkle, all her charm. I think that idiosyncrasies aren't bad. Some Chinese keep a little rash on their body because it feels so good to scratch. Some things shouldn't be cured. Having your suitor climb through the window to spend an evening with you is nothing that needs psychiatric help. Unfortunately, Gene suffered from severe depressions that necessitated hospitalization.

The second picture I did at Warners was a disappointment —to me, to the critics, and to the public. That was a shame, because *The Glass Menagerie* is a beautiful play, and we had a terrific cast. Jane Wyman, fresh from winning an Academy Award for *Johnny Belinda* and a divorce from Ronald Reagan, was Amanda, the crippled girl who lives in her fantasies. Gertrude Lawrence played the mother. Arthur Kennedy, the wonderful actor who had played my brother in *Champion*, played Jane Wyman's brother. I elected to play the smaller role of the Gentleman Caller. Unfortunately, the movie wasn't directed well, and Gertrude Lawrence's vanity had to be appeased. She insisted on a flashback where she was young and glamorous, so no one would think she was the old lady that she actually was. The elements didn't mesh; the movie just didn't come off. Recently, a much better version was made, directed by Paul Newman and starring his wife, Joanne Woodward, in a wonderful performance.

Driving home from the studio one night, I stopped behind a car at a red light. The door of the car in front of me opened, and a pretty little girl wearing a suede jacket hopped out and ran up to me. "Oh, Mr. Douglas, would you please sign my jacket?" As I obliged, the woman who was driving got out and introduced her. "This is my daughter. She's in movies, too. Her name is Natalie Wood." That was the first time I met Natalie. I saw her many times afterward, before she died in that cruel accident.

I went with Evelyn Keyes while she was in the process of getting a divorce from John Huston. We enjoyed being together. For a month, we had a wonderful relationship—warm, cozy, sexy. In the morning, we'd linger over breakfast and talk. Her apartment was filled with beautiful paintings and pre-Columbian pieces. I remember a powerful Tamayo on the wall, of a dog, almost a skeleton, its bones exposed, howling at the moon. She told me that Huston wanted the works of art back. I said, "Why should you give them back? You were married to him, you've got to have something to protect yourself." I don't think that John ever realized that I advised her not to give them back. Oh, I'm good at giving advice to other people.

She was working at Columbia. It's alleged she had a relationship with Harry Cohn. I don't know. I do know that she invited me to have lunch with her at the studio one day when she was shooting. I walked into Columbia, went to the front desk, and said that I was there to see Evelyn Keyes.

"Just a minute."

I waited quite a while. Finally, the guard came back and said, "You're not allowed to come into the studio."

"What do you mean, I'm not allowed to come into the studio? I'm Kirk Douglas. I have an invitation from Evelyn Keyes. There must be some mistake."

"I'm sorry, but those are my orders."

"Who gave those orders?"

Shamefacedly, the guard admitted, "Mr. Cohn."

I was flabbergasted. Just that morning, I had received an invitation to his New Year's Eve party. I stomped out, yelling, "Fuck Harry Cohn! And tell him not to expect me at his goddam New Year's Eve party, either!"

My relationship with Evelyn ended soon after that. I don't know why. I was there one night, left early, and never went back. Years later, she joked about it: "What happened? You just disappeared."

I was at loose ends again. A couple of months later, I was frightened. I went to see my analyst, managed to tell him that the night before I had been impotent. He smiled. "You tell me that you had sex twenty-nine nights in a row with different girls. On the thirtieth, you say you're impotent. You know, even God rested after six days."

That was the end of my impotence.

I was at the Brown Derby one Thursday. My date was one of my agents, Mortie Guterman, a nice guy, and a great lover of boats. He kept asking me to go fishing. I was fishing for something, but I didn't know what. While he was talking, I saw a blonde in the next booth—beautiful face, beautiful body. I started a conversation with her, invited her to come with me to Catalina on Mortie's boat. I picked her up the next day, drove down to Balboa, where we would stay overnight, and leave the next morning for Catalina. When we got to the motel, I couldn't wait. Before we unpacked our bags, with Mortie in the living room, we were in bed.

Afterward, all the attraction I'd felt before the sex was gone. I thought, My God, I've got to be with her the whole weekend. I can't. All I could think of was that saying: "After sex, a woman should turn into a pinochle table with three other guys." I really became panicky. I was desperate.

Suddenly, the phone rang. It was the hotel desk. "Is everything satisfactory?"

"What?" I said. "I have to go back? You mean now? But I just got here! Well, all right I'll do the best I can."

I hung up, yelled for Mortie. I started babbling. "Mortie, will you be O.K.? You go to Catalina, and I'll take the car."

Mortie caught on, and went along with it. I never stopped talking. The next thing I knew, I had my bag in the car. My last view was of the two of them in the doorway (I hope Mortie had a good time) as I headed back to Los Angeles.

In the car, I thought, What the hell am I doing? I really felt like an asshole. What was the matter with me? Why couldn't I be like a normal person and take an attractive girl for a weekend? There were no demands. Why couldn't I have just gone on the boat, relaxed in the sun? Maybe the next day, I would have found her attractive again. I kept driving to Los Angeles.

I knew that I was afraid of falling in love. It's such a frightening, painful process. It's annihilating. You're weak, vulnerable. Breaking up is worse. Perhaps the perfect love is one that has a short beginning and a quick ending, like the affair I had in Taxco. I was walking alone in that romantic city where the stars were so low at night, bougainvillea draped the walls of the old buildings, and no cars were allowed on the winding, cobblestone streets that climbed up the town. Soft Spanish melodies on steel guitars came floating out of a little cantina. I walked in. And just as in a Humphrey Bogart movie, sitting at a table was a most beautiful girl. I looked at her, she looked at me. I sat at the bar for a drink. Finally we got together. We talked to each other and about each other. We were in love. We spent two wonderful days and nights together and then she had to leave, back to somewhere in the Midwest. We made all kinds of plans to write to each other, and I never heard from her again. That was perfection. It lasted just long enough to bring out wonderful fantasies, but not to incur any wounds.

Back in Los Angeles, I didn't know what the hell to do . So I kept going. I drove to Palm Springs. It was late. The Racquet Club was the hot spot then, but it was full, so I took a room next door at the Bonne Aire. I was exhausted from driving all over the state—from the ocean to the city to the desert—trying to figure out what the hell was the matter with me. I hoped that everything would make sense the next day, in the clear desert air. I needed a rest. I would swear off women.

Nine

OBSESSION

Palm Springs, mecca of the movie stars. At that time, just a sleepy village. I had breakfast the next morning and walked outside. It was one of those unbelievable days that are ordinary in Palm Springs: warm and sunny, even though the surrounding mountains are topped by snow. I went through the fence to the Racquet Club, which had been started by Charles Farrell and Ralph Bellamy as an informal little private club where movie people could come to play tennis and spend the weekend. Everybody wanted to get into the club. You were sure to see a lot of stars—Clark Gable, Spencer Tracy. Errol Flynn might be there. The Racquet Club was what made Palm Springs.

A lot of people were out in the beautiful morning air playing tennis. I felt good. I knew I was on the right track. I just needed a break from running after women.

The Racquet Club was almost empty. I moved on toward the circular bar. Lew Wasserman's wife, Edie, sat there, talking to one of the most beautiful girls I've ever seen—black hair framing creamy white skin, dark eyes, and dark red lipstick. She had the look of a little girl playing grown-up, with a serious expression that suddenly broke into a childish grin. Her ankles and wrists were tiny, her bosom slightly over-developed for her small frame. She was stunning. I looked at her, and it was instantaneous. Edie introduced me to this gorgeous creature, whose name was Irene Wrightsman. When Irene spoke, I saw that she had a slight overbite. I was gone. She had come for the weekend with Oleg Cassini, Gene Tierney's debonair playboy ex-husband. Irene forgot about him. I forgot about my plan of celibacy. For two days, we hardly left the room.

Back in Los Angeles, Irene invited me to dinner. She was living with her mother, who was divorced from Charles B. Wrightsman, an extremely wealthy oilman from Oklahoma who was then living in Palm Beach, Florida, with his new wife. Irene and her mother lived in a large house, left over from the divorce. At dinner, her mother drank more than she ate. After dinner, Irene and I went to the library. A fire was burning in the fireplace. I had a drink, she had two. Then she got up, locked the door, and took off all her clothes. We started to make love on the floor. I was nervous; her mother couldn't be far away. Sure enough, there was a pounding on the door. Her mother, speech slurred, yelled, "I know what you're doing in there! Now you come out of there!" I stopped for a second, whispered to Irene, "It's your mother." Irene hung on to me, and said, "Fuck her. Or better yet, fuck me."

Soon after that, Irene moved in with me, on Vado Place. I was surprised, and enormously pleased, to discover that she was an unusually good cook, but I was terrified by the sexual hold she had on me. I went to Albuquerque, New Mexico, to do *Ace in the Hole* for Billy Wilder. Irene came with me. I was working, and she seemed to be happy. We had an apartment; she'd cook me a meal if I wanted. She was fun to be with. She had a drinking problem, but she kept herself under control, just sipping Dubonnet.

Errol Flynn was shooting a picture in Albuquerque at the same time. He invited Irene and me to dine with him and Pat Wymore. I was flattered. I was a young star; he was a legend. He selected the most elegant restaurant, ordered the most expensive wines, and was extremely charming. I was quite impressed, and a little gaga, envious of his poise, his great savoir faire. At the end of the meal, when the check arrived, he graciously handed it to me and said, "Kirk, I wouldn't deprive you of the honor of being the host of the evening." And I, with my mouth open, just paid it. Nevertheless, I admired him. He had flair. Some people didn't consider him much of an actor, but I did. I think he had great personal style that you don't see anymore. There are very few actors who could carry off Robin Hood the way he did.

Errol had been a close buddy of Freddy McEvoy, who had been married to Irene when she was very young. Errol and Freddy were the great cocksmen of the town, very well known. Freddy never had much money. When he married Irene, he may have thought he was going to get some of Wrightsman's money. He didn't.

Irene told me about a game Freddy would play when she stayed overnight with him and his friends. In the morning, he would have her go out the back door, run around the house and come in the front, pretending that she had just arrived. She later found out they all knew about it and used to laugh at her. I thought that was cruel. I felt sorry for her, and I disliked him, although I never met him. He was an unscrupulous adventurer, and I'm sure very attractive. They had a child. Freddy married another woman and kept the child. While I was with Irene, I never saw or met the child. Later, Freddy was on a rented yacht with his wife, and there was talk of smuggling—arms or dope or something to make money. There was a mutiny, and he drowned at sea.

I enjoyed working with Billy Wilder. He's a brilliant director, a brilliant writer, and a great raconteur. He was always saying amazing things. Joking, he would very often hit the truth. One of his jokes was about the casting of *The Defiant Ones*, a movie in which a black man and a white man (eventually played by Sidney Poitier and Tony Curtis) were handcuffed together. Billy said, "First they went to Marlon Brando and asked him to be in the movie. Marlon said, 'Yes,

I'll be in it, but I want to play the black man.' Then they went to Robert Mitchum, and Mitchum said, 'Hell, I'm not going to be in any picture with no nigger.' So then they went to Kirk Douglas and asked him to be in the picture, and Douglas said, 'Yes, I'll be in it. But I want to play both parts.' "

I thought the character I played in *Ace in the Hole* was too rough. "Billy, don't you think I should come on a little softer, a little more charming to make him sympathetic, make the audience care about him?" But he said, "Give it both knees. Right from the beginning." I did.

There's a scene in *Ace in the Hole* where I grab Jan Sterling's little fur stole and twist it around her neck, enraged at how badly she's treating her husband. I'm really mad at myself, because I'm treating him worse, keeping him down a mine shaft just to get a story. Before we did the scene, I said to her, "Jan, if I'm choking you too much, let me know." I was choking her, saying my lines. Suddenly I looked—she was blue. I let go. She just dropped to the ground. I lifted her up, slapped her face, got her some water.

"Jan, are you all right."

She was gasping.

"God, Jan, if I was squeezing you too hard, why didn't you tell me?"

She croaked, "I couldn't. You were choking me."

I think *Ace in the Hole* is one of Billy Wilder's best pictures. It was a hit in the rest of the world, but it wasn't doing well in the United States, so they changed the title to *The Big Carnival*. I think the reason it wasn't successful here was the newspapers. There was almost no television then. The unfavorable reviews of this movie about an unscrupulous newspaper reporter—based on a true incident, the Floyd Collins case, where a reporter actually kept a man down in a mine—were written by newspaper reporters. Critics love to criticize, but they don't like being criticized. Also, Billy Wilder was saying to the general public, Mr. and Mrs. Average, "This is you, the people who stop and stare at accidents." It's become an underground classic, playing at revival theaters. And it's popped up again, with people glued to their TV's for fifty-eight hours in October 1987, to see if eighteen-month-old Baby Jessica McClure was going to be rescued alive from a dry well in Midland, Texas. As my character said, "A tragedy is not a thousand Chinese drowned in a flood, but one person stuck down in a hole in the ground."

I did only the one movie with Billy Wilder, although he did ask me to play the lead in *Stalag 17*. I'd seen the play, and thought it had lots of weaknesses. I didn't realize what Billy would do with the movie. Bill Holden played the part and won an Oscar. I was dumb.

After the picture was finished shooting, Irene and I went to visit her father. He was one of the richest men in the country, and one of the meanest. My father never gave me a pat on the back, but what her father was doing to her was criminal. He was cruel and selfish, and demanded that his two beautiful daughters be ornamental and obedient. If they did exactly as he said, he would buy them Balenciaga gowns, the most extravagant clothes. If they did not please him, he would just cut them off without a cent. So he kept them in a constant state of turmoil. There was never any consistency in love or affection from him. His ex-wife, Irene's mother, reminded me of the character Birdie in *The Little Foxes*. When I looked at her, I thought of that pathetic scene where Birdie says, "People say I have a headache. I never had a headache in my life. I drink. All by myself in my room." Irene's mother eventually drank herself to death. Irene's sister, Charlene, later committed suicide. She was a sweet girl, married to Ghighi Cassini, Oleg's brother, who wrote a column under the name of Cholly Knickerbocker. It hurt me when I heard about it, because whenever I'd seen her, she was smiling and very pleasant. She seemed to be quite different from Irene—much more stable and self-assured.

We flew to Miami. Wrightsman, a red-faced WASP, picked us up and flew us to Palm Beach in his private plane. The minute we arrived, he ordered us to hurry up and get dressed, because we were meeting the Duke and Duchess of Windsor for cocktails. Wrightsman was supercilious and domineering, treating me the way he treated Irene. I resented it. I couldn't resist saying, "I'm exhausted from the trip, if you don't mind, I'll just stay here." I didn't go; I let them have the cocktail party without me. And frankly, I was very much interested in meeting the Duke and Duchess of Windsor.

Irene always became physically ill when she arrived at her father's home. She had to take to her bed. While Irene was in bed, I played tennis with Wrightsman and a couple of pros he had hired. It was a pretty one-sided doubles game: the pro on his side of the net and the pro on mine both made sure that the ball hit Wrightsman's racket.

One day, Wrightsman called me in and said, "My daughter's mentally sick, you know." I was shocked to hear him talk that way. Of course, Irene had her problems, not the least of which was him. But she was obviously a helpless child. He said, "I don't want you to even consider marrying my daughter."

I looked at that WASP, who, I knew, was thinking, "My God! How awful if my daughter married a Jew. And an actor, too." I said, "C.B." (he allowed only his friends to call him "C.B."), "I am not going to marry your daughter. But a time will come when you'll wish I had."

I don't know what made me make such a prophetic statement, but I never had more sympathy for Irene than at that moment. I forgave her for lots of things that happened after that, because I had met her father. She was ill all the time we were at his house. When we left, she recovered.

I hated the next Warner Brothers picture I worked on, *Along the Great Divide*. I did it just to get my one picture a year obligation out of the way, so I wouldn't be tied up. We shot it in the Mojave Desert and in the High Sierra country around Lone Pine, California, that director Raoul Walsh liked so much. It was desolate, isolated, the Sierra rising more than 14,000 feet on one side; the Panamint Mountains and then Death Valley on the other side. During World War II, the U.S. government constructed a detention camp for Japanese-American citizens near there—Manzanar.

Walsh was a brutal man with a patch over one eye. He had lost the eye one night in Utah in a car driven off-road by a drunk Mormon. A huge jackrabbit, spooked by the headlights, had jumped through the windshield.

Critics talk about how Raoul Walsh movies have such great pace. They have great pace because he was always in a hurry to finish them. After he called "Roll 'em!" to the cameraman, he would turn away and roll one of his own—a cigarette. He didn't watch the scene. He would take out paper, pour in tobacco, roll, lick, and light it. Then he'd say, "O.K. Cut."

Once, as he was puffing away on his homemade cigarette, the script girl came running up, "Mr. Walsh, they left out half a page of dialogue!"

He just squinted at her with his one eye. "Did it make sense?" Obviously, he hadn't been listening, either.

She said, "It made sense, but . . ."

"O.K. Next shot." It was that quality that gave his pictures a lot of tempo.

Walsh loved violence. I was disgusted one day to see him get excited almost to the point of orgasm while watching a dangerous stunt in which a stunt man almost got killed. I could see his sexual glee, watching the stunt man almost get kicked in the head as he ran through a stable full of kicking horses.

Animals were abused on that set. In one scene, a trek across the desert, a horse dies from exhaustion. They gave that poor horse injections. It was drugged, wobbling, and we were trying to hold it up. It didn't die, but it was all doped up. They were much looser then with animals. That kind of thing would not be allowed today. The Screen Actors Guild now has a clause in its standard contract that actors will not work on sets where animals are being abused. It was awful. I hated the whole picture.

Along the Great Divide was my first western. My only other experience riding had been with Diana in Central Park when I got thrown. But I learned to ride, and later on to do tricks. Although I love horses, I never rode for pleasure, but I learned to give the impression of being a good rider: I sat up straight in the saddle, and whatever the horse did, I acted as if that was exactly what I wanted him to do. If the horse was bouncing around, I was never concerned. The more the horse bounced around, the more nonchalant I became. That gives you a feeling of power, and you look like you have control. People began to think I was a great rider. They'd say, "Kirk, you must ride all the time."

I'd say, "Only when they pay me."

I had a gun in *Along the Great Divide,* and I learned about safety precautions. In one scene, I'm knocked unconscious. I fall to the ground, my gun beside me near my head. Walter Brennan picks it up and shoots it. It was loaded with blanks.

I said, "Why should the gun be loaded with anything? We're going to move the camera again before it's fired."

Walter Brennan said, "What are you, afraid?"

"Yeah. I am. Suppose when you grab it, it goes off. It's right by my face and eyes."

He said, "Listen, kid. I've been making westerns for years."

Well, stupid me, I let it go. We shot the scene. Exactly what I was afraid of—he reached down to pick up the gun, accidentally pulled the trigger. It went off right next to my face. Fortunately, the blank didn't hit me; it went into the dirt near my head. Walter was embarrassed. I was mad, and I learned not to back down where safety was concerned.

Sometimes people think that a blank is not dangerous. But a blank fired at close range has a lot of power. Audie Murphy, the most decorated hero of World War II, was a vicious guy. One of his favorite tricks was to stick an empty revolver up against your chest. At the same time, he'd pull the trigger of a gun loaded with blanks hidden behind his back. The pressure of the gun against your chest combined with the noise of the blank firing gave you the feeling that you'd been shot. This is a joke? Then there was the tragedy of John Eric Hexum, who put a gun with a blank to his head, pulled the trigger, and accidentally killed himself.

In *Detective Story,* the next picture I did, director Willy Wyler wanted Joe Wiseman to shoot me at close range with a gun loaded with blanks. Joe Wiseman was a very excitable New York actor doing his first movie. He played a prisoner sitting in detective headquarters. I was a detective. When I walk by, he grabs the gun from my holster and shoots me.

I said, "Willy, hold it right there. You want Joe Wiseman to pull the gun out and shoot me at close range?"

He said, "Yeah. What difference does it make? It's a blank."

I had to laugh. Willy must have forgotten the westerns he'd made in the old days. But my experience was still fresh. I said, "Willy, that's dangerous."

He laughed.

This annoyed me. I had them put up a piece of cheesecloth at twice the distance Joe would be when he shot me. Then I had them fire the blank gun. A couple of hundred holes were in the cheesecloth. I said to Willy, "How would my face look if that hit me?"

Willy, undaunted, said, "But he's not going to shoot you in the face. He'll shoot you in the chest, and we'll give you some protection."

"Oh," says I, "Joe is an expert marksman who can quickly pull the gun, point it, and miss my face? Do you know the difference between the angle of the gun hitting me in the chest and in my face? Fractional! I won't do it."

The great Willy Wyler had to reblock the scene. Joe shot me from across the room as I walked toward him, trying to talk him into giving me back the gun. It's very effective, and nobody got hurt. This incident added to my reputation as a difficult actor. I didn't care. It added to my life.

At first I had misgivings about doing *Detective Story*. I had seen the play in New York with Ralph Bellamy starring. It had problems. The vignettes and characters were wonderful, but the main character had to lug the story line. I knew I was going to be working with most of the New York cast— Joseph Wiseman, Lee Grant, Michael Strong—who had all been doing it for a couple of years. I had what I thought was a brilliant idea. "Willy, why don't you get the cast, and we'll do it as a play. Then you can watch the whole thing." He sloughed it off. I did it anyway. I put the play together at the Sombrero Playhouse in Phoenix, Arizona. We performed it for a week. Willy Wyler came to see it several times. He then had the script rewritten to conform more with the play.

After doing the play, I still felt I needed more preparation. I went to New York for a few weeks to work with the detectives at the Forty-seventh Street Precinct. This also gave me a chance to spend some time with Michael and Joel, and to ease off the tension with Irene.

I spent days at the detective headquarters, observing and eventually participating. One day, they brought in a little black fellow who was caught stealing, and asked me to fingerprint him. As I was putting his fingers in the ink and rolling them around the paper, he kept studying me.

"Ain't you Kirk Douglas?"

I looked at him scornfully. "If I was him, would I be doing this?" And I finished booking him.

That evening, I had dinner at Sardi's restaurant with Barry Sullivan. Sitting across from us was a beautiful girl with dark hair and large eyes. I couldn't resist looking at her during the meal. Several times, our eyes connected and locked. We didn't know who she was.

She was sitting there with other people, looking at me as we left. I went back to the Hampshire House to make it an early evening.

I was awakened by a knocking on the door. Drowsily, I got out of bed and opened it. In the dim light stood the girl from Sardi's, saying nothing.

"Come in," I said in a low voice, and led her across the room without turning on any lights. I got back in bed. I motioned to the side of the bed, "Sit down." I was beginning to wake up. She sat.

"He's got a gun," she said.

That opened my eyes wider and I looked at her.

It was not the girl in Sardi's.

It was Ava Gardner!

She and Sinatra were having a mad romance, and I knew

they were staying at my hotel in Mannie Sachs's apartment. They must have had one of their usual explosions and she rushed out. It was about two o'clock in the morning. She didn't know where to go and ended up at my door.

I had dated Ava a few times, years before. I found her a wonderful country girl who was cursed by being too beautiful. I admired the relationship she had with her sister. I remember the natural way she had of talking to young Michael and Joel.

She was quite upset and we chatted for about ten minutes. She calmed down.

"Ava, come on, Frank has got to be very worried about you."

She sighed, and got up. I walked her to the door, kissed her on the cheek, and she left. No mention was ever made of her nocturnal visit.

I went back to bed, closed my eyes, and heard Issur chuckling.

"Sardi girl! You can't resist opening your door to a beautiful woman, can you?"

I didn't answer, and went to sleep.

Wyler was a strange director: he never directed you. He'd just say, "Do it again," until he got what he wanted. He had a reputation for doing many takes and spending a long time, but we shot *Detective Story* in five weeks, on a sound stage in Los Angeles. The last day, Willy was anxiously looking at his watch, because he had to catch a plane to go skiing.

I assumed that Irene had lots of friends, and was active during the day while I was at the studio. It annoyed me that almost every day when I came home, she was taking a shower or getting dressed. "You know when I'm coming home. Why can't you be ready?" I couldn't understand why she was never ready.

Later, my secretary told me that every day after I left for work, Irene sat in a chair in her bathrobe, smoking cigarette after cigarette and staring into space like a zombie the entire day. She came to life when she heard my car coming up the drive. Then she'd rush upstairs and jump in the shower. When I heard this, it made me sad. It was almost as if she didn't exist when I wasn't there. She needed someone else to give her life. That is too big a burden for any human to carry.

As I look back, I realize that somehow I was attracted to women who were neurotic. But Irene also had a childish vulnerability that was appealing. She was a child-woman, but tragic. There was about her the same quality that I saw in the Dali portrait of Ann Warner surrounded by decayed and rotting wealth. That tragic aspect of Irene touched me.

My relationship with Irene had gone on for about two years. She began to drink a lot. Drunk, she begged me to marry her, said she couldn't live without me. I was frightened to death of marrying Irene. I had an erotic attachment to her, but I knew that if we got married, she would destroy me. I made it very clear that although my attraction for her was still intense, I didn't intend to marry her. I kept telling her that we had to try to live apart for a while. Finally, I forced the issue, and she moved out to an apartment that I found for her. I thought I was strong in making such a wonderful, honest move. But she was rudderless when we broke up, reaching out in every direction. She would call me, and we would go through those terrible games that people play with each other in the lingering death throes of a relationship.

Stanley Kubrick told me a story about a girl he loved. He had a big fight with her, and goddamnit! He felt macho. The hell with it! He'd had enough! That was it! He packed his bag and slammed the door. He went out. As he started walking, that bag got heavier and heavier and heavier and he couldn't carry it. He had to go back. I felt that way. I was more entrapped than I realized.

Trapped by Irene, and trapped by Warner Brothers. I went to see Charlie Feldman. "I want out of my contract."

"What are you talking about? It's a wonderful deal. You don't want to get out. Besides, they won't let you."

"Oh yes they will."

"And why would they do that?"

"Because I'll do the next picture for nothing."

He looked at me. "You mean that?"

"Yes!"

"You'll really do the next picture for nothing?"

"That's right. The next picture they want me for, I'll do for nothing, and then I'm out of Warners."

I had made the greedy studio an offer they couldn't resist. They put me in *The Big Trees*, a remake of a picture they'd done years earlier. They saved even more money by using footage from the previous picture. It was a bad movie.

On location in Oregon, I was in agony over Irene, barely able to function. It was worse than when Peggy Diggins had left. I hadn't felt guilty about Peggy. Irene had been pretty much under control when she was with me. But now I heard that she was going crazy, drunk all the time, at wild parties with anyone—men, women. I felt that I had pushed her into a desperate situation. I think I was just as sick as she was, still obsessed with her. I wanted the separation. I had it. I was miserable. Why was I suffering? I began to think that *I* couldn't live without *her*. I asked her to join me in Oregon. She came.

I asked her to marry me. Yeah, sure, she was ready to get married. But she was different now; the damage had been done. She was wooden, dead inside. We had agreed to be married, but both of us knew it would never happen. She went back to Los Angeles.

Finally, *The Big Trees* was over. I felt happy flying back from location, calm and detached. Until we passed the half-way point. Then I was overcome by melancholia. I knew that something strange was going on. What did I expect? That unstable, neurotic Irene would be cleaning the kitchen, waiting for me? The sudden mood swing—high, then depression—clued me in. My insides knew clearly that disaster was waiting.

It was late. I drove to Irene's apartment, let myself in with my key. She was fast asleep in bed—with a man. This was the woman I was going to marry. I needed to see her with someone else to know what I had known all along: our plans to get married were a charade. Irene was a desperate woman, couldn't help herself. It was hard for her to be alone, even for a night. I was numb. Then I saw that the man was Sydney Chaplin, Charlie Chaplin's son. How strange. I used to play tennis with him. He used to come with me often when I visited Irene; the three of us had dinner together. He was my friend, but couldn't he see that he was taking advantage of this sick girl?

As I stood there looking at the two of them, they woke up, startled to see me. I left. Irene called me incessantly at the studio, trying to explain an inexplicable situation.

Irene eventually married someone else. She thought she had the solution—a house in the country with a white picket fence. That didn't last very long. Then she married some foreigner with a title, and lived in Switzerland. The marriage was unhappy; she graduated from alcohol to dope. Years later, I called her when I was in New York alone, took her to the theater. This beautiful girl had become ravaged; she looked like a cadaver. After the theater, I took her back to her father's apartment at the Hotel Pierre. I felt sorry for her, tried to get closer to her. I put my arm around her. She was stiff, a foreign object in my arms. We talked. She was strange, very strange. Suddenly she said, "I'm going to die." She wasn't being dramatic. It gave me the chills. I thought of lines from *Macbeth*: "I am in blood stepp'd in so far that, should I wade no more,/Returning were as tedious as go o'er." Soon after that, she died.

Recently, I read in *Time* magazine that Charles B. Wrightsman had just died at the age of ninety. I thought he had died years ago. The obituary said "philanthropist and polo player." Polo player! He owned the ponies and paid all the expenses, so they fed him a shot at the goal once in a while.

Maybe he had good qualities that I knew nothing about. But two beautiful young girls and their mother commit suicide, directly or indirectly, and he lives to be ninety. What is God doing? How is God running the shop?

Ten

AFTERMATH

Jackson Hole, Wyoming, is one of the most beautiful places on earth—the Teton Peaks look like movie cutouts of mountains, soaring toward the sky, the Snake River twists its way through the countryside. *The Big Sky* was the first picture I did under my new freedom from Warner Brothers. Howard Hawks was the talented director. We lived in "Anderson Camps," very comfortable tents with wood floors. I had a tent with two rooms. There was a big recreation tent, and a big dining tent. The food was terrific. In the morning, you could have anything you wanted—pancakes, eggs and bacon, sausage, steaks.

Hawks worked at his own leisurely pace. He would start shooting in the morning, and if he was a little unhappy with a scene, he'd think nothing of dismissing the whole company. He'd tell them to go off and have a cup of coffee, then he'd sit down with a yellow legal pad and a pencil and say, "Well, now, let's see, Kirk. Suppose you said . . . " And we'd work out a whole scene that we would shoot that afternoon. Nowadays, with the tremendous emphasis on costs, you couldn't do that, nor is it my concept of how a movie should be made. The actual shooting of the movie should take the least amount of time. The preparation should take more time; post-production even more.

Ray Stark, who was my agent then, came to visit me and brought his son Peter and my son Michael. Michael slept in my tent, in the other room. I kept thinking that we should both sleep in the same room. I wanted to be close, but Michael always had a reserve about him, and I didn't know how to break through it. Perhaps he felt the same about me. Ray took the boys fishing at the Snake River. When I got some time off, we visited Yellowstone National Park. We saw bears, wild animals that seemed so tame. And we saw signs: DON'T FEED THE BEARS. We were driving down the road, on our way to see Old Faithful. A big bear came up to the car. He reached in the window and grabbed the windbreaker in my hand and tugged at it. I tugged back. He tugged his way, I tugged my way. He started to growl. I said, "You can have it!" He grabbed the jacket and off he went into the woods, the only bear with a windbreaker. This little interlude with the bear disrupted our schedule, and when we got to Old Faithful, it was just petering out. I was sad when Ray took Michael and Peter back.

In the picture was a beautiful half Cherokee Indian. She'd been a top model, but had never acted before. She was perfect for her part—an Indian girl. We'd go walking in the woods, skinny-dipping. She'd lie naked on the river bank, look at me with big beautiful eyes, and in a soft voice with just a hint of a southern drawl, ask me to beat her with my belt. I thought it was a joke. She pleaded. I had never run into a masochist before. She really wanted to be beaten. I hit her with my belt. She just stared at me. "You're holding back." It was not easy for me to really hit her. But she *liked* it. I didn't understand it. It was almost as if she wanted to be punished for something. I hit her. There was never any expression of pain on her part. Or mine. We were both numb. When it was over, I was shocked, not at her request but at my ability to comply. I hadn't known this was within me.

I was sick when I came back from Jackson Hole—had a killer cold and a stabbing cough. I had one day of shooting left—swimming in a stream that they had created on the stage. I didn't want to do it. I told Hawks and Eddie Lasker, the producer, that I had a cold.

They laughed. "So you've got a cold now. You don't have to worry about getting one later."

All day, I swam with my clothes on and wind machines blowing. I'd come up chattering into the cold air-conditioning (the temperature had to be kept down so the lights wouldn't get too hot), get blasted with wind, and stand soaking wet with a blanket wrapped around me until we shot it again. I bitched. I got more of a reputation for being a difficult actor. And I got pneumonia. I went to the hospital, and ended up in a room that Eddie Lasker had donated. I was lying there for weeks. But he never came to see me. Howard Hawks never came to see me. I heard that Eddie was telling people: "Isn't it funny that Kirk's in the room I donated?"

I came out of the hospital weak and frightened. I've been strong all my life, but I was weak for several months. I couldn't even make a fist. If I'd had the strength, I would have cried.

Sometimes Marlene Dietrich, whom I had met through Billy Wilder, would come over, cook soup, cuddle me. Affectionate sex. But that was less important than the mothering, the closeness. Marlene is an unusual person. She seemed to love you much more if you were not well. When you became strong and healthy, she loved you less.

When I was feeling better, I was offered a part that Clark Gable had turned down. I read the script and thought it was wonderful. Vincente Minnelli was directing, John Houseman producing *The Bad and the Beautiful* for MGM. I was the "bad" movie mogul. When they announced that Lana Turner was the "beautiful," the papers were filled with "When these two get together . . ." I was ready for it. But she was going with Fernando Lamas, who was terribly jealous. He was always around. Nothing happened. I liked Lana, and I thought she did one of her best pieces of acting in that picture.

Francis X. Bushman, who had been a big star—he had been Messala to Ramon Navarro's Ben Hur in the 1927 silent version—played a small part in *The Bad and the Beautiful* and gave me an insight to the behavior of real movie moguls.

"Mr. Bushman, I'm a great admirer of yours," I told him.

He said, "This is the first time I've worked at MGM in twenty-five years."

I was surprised. "Really? Why?"

"I was doing a play once, and Louis B. Mayer came backstage to see me. I was taking off my makeup, and he had to wait a couple of minutes. He ran off in a huff and said, 'That man will never work in my studio again.' And I never did."

The moguls of that period were a very strange breed. I've seen that aspect of power, of ruthlessness, of selfishness displayed by Jack Warner, Darryl Zanuck, Louis B.Mayer—and let's not forget Harry Cohn.

I was never very good at "playing the game." I never sought out any of the moguls, never tried to become friends with the influential agents. I always suspected collusion, which I think exists even more now between agents and heads of studios. Have you noticed how many agents become heads of studios?

I received my second Academy Award nomination (*Champion* had been my first) for *The Bad and the Beautiful*. That surprised me. I thought I'd get one for *The Big Carnival*. I thought I'd get one for *Detective Story*. I didn't think I'd get one for *The Bad and the Beautiful*. It was a good show, but the nomination surprised me. Again, I didn't win.

If, as people say, Oscar is a popularity contest, I was never a popular fellow. I'm always amazed when I hear that someone thinks of me as a son of a bitch. After *Champion* came out, Hedda Hopper said, "Now that you've got a big hit, you've become a real son of a bitch." I said, "You're wrong, Hedda. I was always a son of a bitch. You just never noticed before." What amazes me even more is that when somebody says, "You're so difficult to work with, you're so tough," ninety percent of the time, it's somebody I never worked with, who claimed they heard it from somebody else. I don't think Howard Hawks and Billy Wilder and Lewis Milestone and Joe Mankiewicz and Elia Kazan thought that. I think a lot of untalented sons of bitches think I'm a talented son of a bitch.

Sidney Franklin, a producer, came to me to ask me to play the part of a trapeze artist in one segment of *The Story of Three Loves*, a three-part movie. This was before Burt did his movie, *Trapeze*. I love the circus, admire trapeze artists. And here I had the opportunity to work with professionals. That was part of the fun of making movies. I said, "But I thought Ricardo Montalban was training for the role."

"No, no. He's not right for it."

"Let me think about it." I went to Ricardo Montalban. I knew that he had been working every day on a trapeze. If there was a way for him to keep the part, I was all for it. I said, "Ricardo, I'm embarrassed. They've come to me to play the role that you're working on." He was very nice about it. "They're not happy with me. The hell with it. You go ahead, Kirk." I got his permission. I couldn't have done it without saying something to him.

My co-star was Pier Angeli (her real name was Anna Maria Pierangeli), a nineteen-year-old Italian girl who looked much younger. She had huge dark eyes, and a refreshing innocence. She was virginal, with a beautiful body and an infectious laugh. I became completely enamored of her, this child that I could mold into the image that I wanted, like Pygmalion. She had been a hit two years earlier playing a fourteen-year-old, in a movie in Italy called *Domani è Troppo Tardi (Tomorrow Is Too Late)*. She had a twin sister, Maria Luisa, who was called Marisa, and a baby sister named Patrizia. Pier talked about her dead father all the time, but her very strong, domineering stage mother ran her. Pier needed her mother's permission for everything. She never went on a date unchaperoned.

I went to their house for dinner. Vittorio de Sica was strolling through the garden, arm in arm with Marisa. He was much older than she, but very attractive. They looked like something out of the eighteenth century. I kidded him, with the few Italian words Pier had taught me. He responded with the English sentences Pier had taught him: "When I was in the airplane, I looked down. A magical vision."

The film's director, Gottfried Reinhardt, wanted me to learn just enough so that he could get a shot of me standing up on the platform ready to leap out. It was frightening at the beginning. You worked with a harness to hold you up. The real danger was how you fell into the net. It would save you, but if you fell wrong, you could easily break a leg or an arm or your neck. When I missed and was able to adjust to falling flat into the net, I lost all fear of falling. From then on, I enjoyed it very much. And I was good at it. Within a month I was swinging on the trapeze, making a crossover to the catcher, being swung back, turning around in midair, catching the bar that was hurled to me by one of the girls, and then swinging back up to the platform. I could do a bird's nest—swing by my calves, body arched up—and cross to the catcher. Reinhardt was dumbfounded. The trainer was most impressed that I learned so easily. He told me that I had learned in a month what took some people a year. He had me already joining the circus. I know now that I could have been a trapeze artist and loved it.

I was surprised at how gutsy Pier was. I was completely bowled over by her. I fell in love with her as she was swinging on a trapeze. She was like a child, giggling, laughing. I thought of her as an angelic creature. Why not? Our romance started thirty feet above the earth. Later, we did scenes fifty feet above, which is much higher than they go in the circus. I was intoxicated by the trapeze, by the altitude, and by Pier. By the time the picture was finished, we had made a commitment to be engaged.

Pier went to Europe. I wanted to get away, too. Sam Norton advised me that it would be a terrific tax break for me if I could stay out of the country for eighteen months. Stanley Kramer wanted me to do *The Juggler* in Israel. I lined up two more pictures in Europe—*Act of Love*, adapted by Irwin Shaw from the novel *The Girl on the Via Flaminia*, by Alfred Hayes, which Anatole Litvak was going to direct in Paris; and *Ulysses* afterward in Italy. The producers of *Ulysses* were a couple of relative unknowns just starting in the motion picture industry—Dino De Laurentiis and Carlo Ponti. I sent my friend Willy Schorr ahead to Italy to work on my behalf setting up the production of *Ulysses*. I'd never been to Europe. I was looking forward to it. Best of all, I would have a chance to spend some time with Pier in Rome.

First I went to New York to visit Michael and Joel. I was making quite a bit of money, wanted them all to have a better place to live than their modest apartment on Eighty-fourth Street. I had found a beautiful brownstone on the East Side. I wanted to buy it and put it in the kids' names. I felt good that I was going to give this gift of a beautiful home to them. The nanny took Michael and Joel out in the park; I discussed it with Diana.

Diana refused to accept it. She didn't want the house to be in our children's names.

"But, Diana, why are you against the kids' owning the house? Certainly, they won't kick you out. And some day they'll end up with a piece of property worth a lot of money."

Diana suddenly showed an irrational side that I'd never seen before. "That's not the way things happened between my mother and father."

"But, Diana, we're not married. We're divorced. Suppose you marry some guy who is suddenly in terrible financial straits, and he gets you to sell the house. The kids would be deprived of a house that I want them to have."

Diana was adamant. She felt that it should be in her name, and I couldn't explain it to her. Another beautiful dream punctured. The brownstone that I wanted to buy for $90,000 then would be worth millions today.

I went back to the Sherry Netherland Hotel to pack my bags. Waiting for the limousine to come to take me to the airport, I felt blue. Here I was, headed for something that should have been a great adventure. Going off to Europe to see Pier and the Old World should have filled me with joy. Instead, I was uneasy. I tried to think of someone I could call to say good-bye to. Marlene Dietrich! I called her.

She said, "Where are you?"

"Here in New York. I'm on my way to Europe, my first trip."

"When?"

"Any minute now, I'm waiting for the limousine."

As if she had divined what I wanted, she asked, "Who's taking you to the airport?"

"No one, just the limousine driver."

"I'll be right over!"

"Marlene, my bags are packed."

"Darling, no one should make a trip to Europe for the first time without someone seeing them off." She hung up.

Marlene and the limousine arrived simultaneously five minutes later. She rode with me to the airport, arranged to get on the plane with me, to keep me company until takeoff. I was glad she did; the flight was delayed an hour. We sat and talked. She gave me a gold St. Christopher medal with her initials on the back. That act of extreme kindness meant a lot to me. I still have the medal.

They started to rev up the engines. Marlene kissed me good-bye and got off the plane. I was alone, frightened and elated at the same time. Then I was up in the air, literally, laughing at myself: a thirty-five-year-old divorced Jewish movie star clutching a St. Christopher medal like a lost five-year-old. No turning back now. Like it or not, I was on my way to Europe.

Eleven

IN PURSUIT OF PIER

I was exhilarated. I had crossed the Atlantic. I was in Europe, approaching the Fiumicino Airport in Rome. I pushed away any lingering problems from the States, looked forward to Pier, a year and a half abroad. Three movies in three countries: Israel, France, Italy.

We were coming in low. I looked down. My God! The Colosseum. I couldn't believe it—the ruins of the Colosseum, precisely as I had seen them so many times in pictures and in the movies. In the noonday sun, the shadow of the airplane went right straight through the Colosseum. My heart was racing.

At the airport, people from the De Laurentiis—Ponti group met me, thrilled to have an American movie star in their first movie, *Ulysses*, based on Homer's epic *The Odyssey*. We drove like a cavalcade through the heart of Rome to the Excelsior Hotel. I was glued to the window, gawking at the Old World, so new to me: streets crowded with people strolling, or sitting at outdoor cafés. And always, talking, gesturing, singing, laughing. I liked Rome immediately. Everybody was a performer.

I had a tremendous desire to express myself in a foreign language, tried to think of the Italian words and phrases that Pier had taught me. As we got into the hotel elevator, I said, "*Buona sera,*" to the operator.

He responded in Italian.

I said, "*Stanco?*" which means "tired."

Again he responded with something I didn't understand.

Then I said the only lengthy phrase that I had learned from Pier: "*E una cosa triste, bisogna lavorare per vivere, eh?*" ["It's sad to have to work for a living."]

And he answered again.

By that time we had arrived at my floor. As I exited the elevator, I said, "*Ciao.*"

The De Laurentiis—Ponti people all looked at me. "Do you speak Italian?" one of them asked in English.

I said, "Perfectly." Of course, I hadn't understood a word he'd said. But there was plenty of time for me to learn, and later, I did.

I had a huge suite filled with flowers, fruit, bottles of wine, liquor. As they graciously left the room, I was filled with a feeling of well-being. I quickly looked into my inside pocket to get Pier's number. How lucky that she was here in Rome! We would go to the little restaurants and bistros that she had told me about, walk up and down the Spanish Steps, the Via Veneto, sip coffee at the sidewalk cafés. All these thoughts went through my head as I waited for someone to answer the phone—Pier, I hoped.

A man said, "*Pronto.*" I had difficulty explaining to him that I wanted to speak to Anna Maria Pierangeli. Finally, he told me in broken English that she was not there. She was with her mother and the rest of her family in Venezia—Venice. I was stunned. She had known I was coming. What was she doing in Venice? And how far was that from Rome? The nice feeling was beginning to seep away. I learned the number of her hotel in Venice and finally got through.

"Pier! What are you doing in Venice? You knew I was coming to Rome."

"I'm so sorry. But my mother and sister wanted to come, and you know that I have to go with them."

"No problem. I'll come to Venice."

She said, "Oh no. It's very difficult."

I hadn't seen her in a long time. I insisted.

She said, "Maybe it would be better to wait until you come back from Israel."

Anyone else would immediately have realized that something was up. But when you're in love, you don't think clearly. You don't see clearly. I blamed it all on her domineering mother, even after I called the airport and found that there were flights to Venice almost every hour on the hour. I took the earliest flight to Venice the next morning.

Pier, filled with youthful gaiety and charm, greeted me in the hotel lobby, and seemed happy to see me. We went up to the suite to say hello to the rest of her family. All over the mirror in her room were pictures of me from *A Story of Three Loves,* and shots of the two of us in our trapeze costumes. That pleased me.

As usual, it was very difficult for us to be alone. She still always had to be chaperoned, could never be alone with me at night. "Things will be different when you come back," she whispered. I treasured the few embraces, the few kisses stolen in furtive moments. I left her with her charming giggle and her high laugh, and returned to Rome to prepare myself for Israel.

Twelve

ISRAEL

Israel in the fall of 1952, right after the War of Independence, was a new and struggling nation. A two-hour flight from Rome, and quite a different country. Unlike the lackadaisical, relaxed Italians, these were people with tremendous vitality and energy, rushing in every direction.

In Jerusalem, I stayed at the famous King David Hotel, which had been attacked by both Jews and Arabs at various times, depending on who was occupying it. Jerusalem was split in half by the Mandelbaum Gate. During the war, the British had turned over most of their posts to the Arabs, cutting off Jerusalem, and making it very difficult for Israel to gain control. The road between Tel Aviv and Jerusalem was called "the Bloody Way." During the war, it had been navigated by trucks crudely fitted with steel plates attempting to bring food and support to the Jews trapped in Jerusalem. Many trucks hadn't made it. The Arabs would picnic in the steep hills on either side of the valley, and pick off the trucks like ducks in a shooting gallery. Now, the road was littered with rusted trucks, like animal skeletons. Little wreaths of withered flowers decorated them.

That Israel won the War of Independence was a miracle. People like to think of Jews as meek and humble, walking docilely to the gas chambers. It's hard to realize that the atrocities committed in civilized Europe were so enormous that they were beyond comprehension. It's hard to believe that human beings were capable of leading other human beings into a room, and under the guise of giving them showers, gas them to death, then take the gold from their teeth, shave off their hair, turn their bodies into soap and their skin into lampshades. I've seen the concentration camps, now so neatly kept, with their manicured lawns and trees and a little trough to catch the blood as the Jews were shot. And of course, the ovens where they were so efficiently cremated.

Those who like to think of Jews as passive manage to overlook the tremendous brutal struggles that went on in the ghettoes of Poland, where—alone—they withstood the onslaught of the Nazis for so long, where they fought to the death. If you were paying attention, the ability of the Jew to fight was displayed long before the War of Independence in Israel.

The Israelis are strong, outspoken people. Sometimes quite exasperating. Once we were driving down a road taking some publicity shots. We stopped to take a picture with a little Arab girl. As we were taking the picture, suddenly four Arabs in flowing robes and headdresses descended upon us, robes flapping, like birds of prey.

I said, "Let's get the hell out of here. Something's going to happen."

Our Israeli driver said, with an Israeli accent, "Fuck them. We won the war."

When the Arabs arrived, he and they engaged in an acerbic conversation in Arabic, which the Israeli spoke perfectly. The result: the four Arabs went their way and we took the picture and went our way.

History was all around me. From my hotel room, I could see across the border to the other side of Jerusalem. Always, not far off on one of the rooftops, would be an Arab in a dirty uniform patrolling back and forth with a rifle. On the Israeli side, there were no guards. They were busy cleaning up the country and trying to live.

Ben-Gurion, the new Prime Minister of Israel, was working out of a very bare, spartan room, wearing an open-necked shirt, sleeves rolled up. He talked to me for a short time, delighted that we were making the first American movie in Israel. But after a few minutes, he dismissed me. He had a new country to run.

Israel was teeming with immigrants from all over the world—immigrants who spoke different languages, ate different foods, wore different clothing, had different customs, different skin colors. The government had revived the dead language of Hebrew and made it the living language that would unite all of these immigrant settlers in the new land of Israel.

But with all the struggle and hardships, the Israelis were saved by a sense of humor. There was a joke making the rounds about the fanaticism to learn Hebrew: Two Yeckis, German immigrants, were standing on the bank of a river. A third Yecki was rowing across. In the middle of the river, his boat capsized. He couldn't swim. As he was drowning, he kept yelling in Hebrew, *"Hutseelu! Hutseelu!"* ["Help."] On the bank, one Yecki turns to the other and says, "Hebrew he's learning. Swimming he should learn."

On a crowded bus, a mother was speaking to her son in Yiddish. An Israeli woman reprimanded her. "You should be speaking Hebrew. Why are you talking to him in Yiddish?"

The mother answered, "I don't want he should forget he's a Jew."

As a Jew, it was exciting to be in the land of my ancestors, my heritage. It was exciting to realize that thousands of years ago, my people, slaves to the Pharaoh of Egypt, had been led by Moses through the Sinai and arrived here. The land of Canaan. The land of milk and honey. Except this time, it certainly was no land of milk and honey. It was arid, barren. There was extreme poverty; food was rationed. But you didn't hear any complaints. Because in spite of all this, it was wonderful, finally, to be in the majority.

Our spoiled American film crew, however, bitched constantly about the food. We got mostly cheeses, eggs, slices of cold meat. Not very good, and not much variety. The Israelis didn't have enough to eat, but they gave the best of it to us. I found out from my driver that for them, eggs were limited to one per person per month. I fed him after that. At breakfast one morning, the crew was mumbling and grumbling about "this lousy food." I stood up. "You guys are in the minority. If you don't like it, get out." Everybody looked at me, amazed.

But it was one of the great shocks of my life to discover that there were no delicatessens in Israel. In New York, after the theater, I used to go to one of the great Jewish delis and get a thick hot pastrami or corned beef sandwich, and cream soda. I assumed that this was real Jewish food, and that it would be even better in Israel. They had never heard of a hot pastrami sandwich.

I had prepared myself months in advance, as I always did before a movie, this time to play the part of a juggler. I would stand in my bedroom in Beverly Hills, with three oranges over a bed, and keep trying to juggle them over and over again. It was hard. I didn't think I'd ever get to feel comfortable with it. Finally, the rhythm of juggling came to me; I even had a talent for it and was able to convincingly portray a professional juggler. My character, Hans, was a clown/magician/juggler in Munich before the war. Then, after surviving a concentration camp—which his family did not—he emigrates to Israel to try to start a new life. But he is so devastated that he asks every woman he sees if she is his wife, and mistakes every person in uniform for a Nazi, even the people who are trying to help him.

When Stanley Kramer first talked to me about doing *The Juggler*, he said that he was very anxious for me to meet the director, Eddie Dmytryk.

"I know Eddie."

He was quite surprised. "You know him?"

"Yes, very well."

"That's strange. I've mentioned your name many times. He's never shown any sign of recognition."

I found it strange, too. Eddie was one of the Unfriendly Ten, had served a year in jail for being a Communist, and had tremendous problems readjusting when he came out. Charlie Feldman asked me if I would help Eddie get a job. I didn't just help him get a job, I gave him one. I paid Eddie a weekly salary and had him work on scripts. I took him to restaurants, football games. I brought him to my house, despite many, many people telling me I was foolish to associate with him and could ruin myself. But I felt deeply that this was such a terrible wrong. Time passed. Eddie started to function, directed a couple of pictures, one in France. I never heard from him, never saw him.

When we started *The Juggler*, this man I had befriended when he needed help looked at me as if I were a total stranger. He made no mention of our past friendship, so I certainly wasn't going to bring it up. Maybe he was embarrassed about how he had gotten work again: by becoming a fink. He was the only one of the Unfriendly Ten to recant, say that he had been a Communist, and name names— twenty-six names.

Maybe I shouldn't pass judgment. I've often wondered what I would have done in that position. Years later, before I could start *Lust for Life*, MGM made me sign a paper saying that I had never been a Communist. Well, I never *had* been a Communist, but I resented their making me sign that paper. I argued heatedly. Nevertheless, I *did* sign.

But Eddie didn't ignore the female lead, a very young, pretty Italian girl named Milly Vitale. They were very close.

I found Israeli girls attractive, tough. Nothing meek and shy about them. Very direct. If a young girl wanted you, she made it very clear. She felt a right to choose her mate, just as men felt that they had a right to choose whom they wanted to be with. Most of the young girls were in uniform, because men and women all had to be soldiers.

I met one, Leah, eighteen, in her soldier's uniform. She

always carried a gun with her, which intimidated me. All soldiers had their guns with them, even off duty. I was trying to romance her, get her to go on a little trip with me when I had a few days off. I wanted to see Eilat, the southernmost tip of Israel, close to the Egyptian border, famous for its clear waters and scuba diving. When I finally got around to making my proposition, I didn't realize how easy it was. She just told her parents that she was going down to Eilat with me, and away we went.

We had a wonderful time, swimming and lying on the beaches during the day, making love at night. Then I went back to work and she went back to the army. It was all done with such ease—so honest and direct—that it startled me.

It didn't occur to me that my beloved one, my fiancée, Pier, might be engaging in any such activities. No, my virginal loved one was just sitting, waiting for me while I was off pursuing a man's destiny, my biological right.

But where *was* Pier? She had an uncanny habit of suddenly sending me a card from someplace when I thought she was someplace else. I was frustrated, wanting to write her a letter, not knowing where to send it.

Most of the time, we were shooting the picture up north, near the Lebanese border in a place called Shivizion, a minor resort area. The woman who cleaned my room was an old German immigrant. I'm sure she'd seen better days, but now in Israel, she was a chambermaid. She spoke to me in German, which I had studied in college, and told me with great nostalgia how much she missed those wonderful days in Germany. This drove me mad. Here was a woman who was lucky to have escaped what millions of others hadn't. And yet, as she was going around making beds in her new land of Israel, all her thoughts were of those romantic, wonderful days in Germany. I found it baffling.

Not far from Shivizion was Nahariya, a settlement of German Jews, a very beautiful little town, immaculate, with that Germanic quality of impeccable care. German performances or songs were forbidden in Israel. But one evening, they had a bootleg concert given by a member of our company, Oskar Karlweiss, a famous German entertainer and singer. All the German Jews of the town came and sang along with the old German songs, tears streaming down their faces.

I tried to understand it. They were yearning for the country where they had grown up, where they had spent their childhood. But then there was always another side of me that said "How could they? How could even all those strong sentimental attachments outweigh the tragic things that had happened to so many of their relatives, so many of their friends?" In Jerusalem, I had visited the Yad Vashem museum where records of the atrocities were kept. I had mixed feelings as I watched the rapture on the faces of those Germans in Israel as they listened to *Deutsche lieder*, forgetting for the moment what their homeland had become.

Moshe Dayan, the famous general of the War of Independence, with a patch over his eye—an eye that he had lost fighting for the British—would come to visit and watch the shooting of my film. He brought his attractive wife, who ran a store called Mesquite, in Tel Aviv, where artifacts were sold. They were accompanied by their three children: two sons, and their precocious twelve-year-old daughter, Ya'el, who would write her first book when she was seventeen.

I visited the Dayans at their modest home in Israel. The general showed me around his garden, a treasure trove of beautiful antiques, some dating back thousands of years, that he had collected in various parts of the country, while Israel was going through this tremendous surge of reconstruction. Most of General Dayan's soldiers were working building roads, or excavating, and whenever their digging unearthed some artifacts, they let him know immediately. Very often, Dayan would be there before anybody in the government. His collection of antiques was priceless. Really, I suppose, it belonged to the government, but on his death, his wife sold it to the Israeli museum for about a million dollars. A cheap price, I would imagine, for all the treasures that it contained. But it was interesting to see the love and dedication that he had for these pieces of antiquity, to see boxes of tiny shards of vases and different things that he would patiently put together, like a complicated jigsaw puzzle.

Ya'el was a very bright girl, sexy even at that young age. Jokingly, I said, "Listen, Ya'el, here's a dime. When you get to be seventeen or eighteen, if you're around Hollywood, call me." Sure enough, about five or six years later, I got a call in Los Angeles. It was Ya'el Dayan. "Well, here I am." Israelis are amazing people.

The picture was winding down. Eddie had his wife come over. He dropped Milly Vitale flat, without any preparation. When the picture was over, we all left on the same plane—Eddie holding hands and cuddling with his wife; Milly sitting next to me and crying on my shoulder. Milly was a casualty of location shooting. It's one of the sad things about movie making: you live so intimately, so intensely with the people making the film. Then, as soon as it's over, you separate. It's like a summer romance. I tried to explain to her what had happened. I don't think she understood it clearly, but I tried.

But as I comforted one young Italian girl, my thoughts were of another: the girl I was going to marry, Pier Angeli.

Thirteen

IN PURSUIT OF PIER, PART 2

I was in Rome again. Now, more than ever, I looked forward to seeing Pier. Now, we would go to little restaurants and bistros, walk up and down the Spanish Steps, sit at sidewalk cafés. I called her number.

"Pier no here." In broken English, I heard that she was with her family in Sardinia. Déjà vu. What was she doing in Sardinia? And how far was that from Rome? I finally got through to her.

"Pier! What are you doing in Sardinia? You knew I was coming to Rome."

"I'm so sorry. But my mother and sister wanted to come, and you know that I have to go with them."

This sweet child with the giggle in her voice could easily persuade me that black was white. And of course she was always the poor little helpless girl who had to obey the whims of her mother. So I suffered in silence, thinking, Well, when you're in love with a young girl that you want to mold into the woman you're looking for, these are things that happen.

So I became engrossed in the preparations for *Ulysses*, which I would come back to Rome to do after I finished *Act of Love* in Paris. One night, we went to a dinner in an old castle, very reminiscent of *La Dolce Vita*—tall, slim Romans, their fat wives left at home, holding hands and gazing into the eyes of beautiful women in low-cut dresses while white-gloved butlers served them. It was a very elegant party.

We sat down to dinner. I was next to a beautiful, dark-haired girl with an extremely low-cut dress, which revealed a generous bosom. Between the two mounds was a big, black cross, which was connected to a gold chain around her neck. We became engrossed in an animated conversation during the dinner. I don't know what cued in the conversation, but the subject of Jews came up. And this beautiful, sexy woman on my left, whose thigh rested comfortably against mine, was telling me, "There's something about Jews that I always recognize. I seem to know them the minute they walk into the room. Maybe it's a smell. But there's something about them. I can't stand them." She went on quite a bit, and I kept listening.

I interrupted. "Well, of course, being Jewish myself, I feel quite differently."

I felt her intake of breath, her leg tighten against mine. She looked at me as if she wasn't sure she had heard correctly. I said nothing, just looked at her. She said, with great incredulity, "You're Jewish?"

I said, "Yes, I am." And tossed it away. "But nevertheless, I would find it very difficult to understand how you could easily be able to identify a Jew. You certainly can't identify them by their noses. Many Romans have hooked noses. Many Italians have swarthy skins."

She just looked at me, her beautiful lips parted. She couldn't believe it. Every once in a while, she would mumble, "You're Jewish" Then she said the inevitable line: "You don't look Jewish."

This really made me laugh. I laughed so loudly, everybody at the table turned to look at me. "What does it mean, to look Jewish? What does it mean to look Italian? Over the years, there has been such a mixture of bloods. In Sicily, there are redheads, fair skins. In Morocco, the Jews are very dark. In Scandinavia, they're very light. Where I came from, Israel, I saw Jews of every shape and color—Jews with turned-up noses, Jews with hooked noses, Jews who seemed to take on the coloration of their environment."

She kept looking at me. Then she said, in a timid voice, "You're really Jewish?"

I took a good look at her: dark, nose slightly hooked, which could be considered a Roman nose, the cross—a little bit too big—that she wore between her voluptuous breasts. I don't know what telepathic wave went through my body, but suddenly I said to her, "Yes, I'm Jewish. And I'll tell you something else. You are a Jew."

She flushed. The redness started in her neck and flowed up to her forehead. She looked at me. She wanted to say something. Suddenly she got up from the table, stumbled, and walked away.

Sure enough, some time later, I discovered that this beautiful woman really was Jewish. I felt sorry for her. I remember times in my youth when I didn't want to carry the burden of being a Jew.

I liked Rome, walking along the streets. I loved the Etruscan colors of the buildings, especially at twilight. I loved the fountains. And I loved Pier. But she wasn't there. Finally, just before I had to leave for Paris, Pier came back to Rome. We had very little time to be alone. I couldn't keep her out late at night. And always there were things she had to do with her mother.

Pier and I had to leave at the same time. We could go on the same plane. I would get off in Paris, she would continue on to the United States. At least I could hear her girlish laughter and hold her hand on the plane—all under the watchful eye of Mama.

We started for Paris in terrible weather and had to land in Ireland. I wanted to go into Limerick with Pier, but her mother wouldn't let us. It was frustrating. Here we were together, so near and yet so far. We were at the airport all night. Irish coffee, that wonderful drink made with whipped cream, almost heavy schlag, coffee, and good Irish whiskey, was the only consolation I got before Pier boarded her plane to the United States and I boarded mine to Paris.

Fourteen

MONSIEUR DOUGLAS

I was in Paris for the first time. The City of Lights. One of the most beautiful cities in the world. I was excited to be staying at a real old-fashioned small hotel, with plush red velvet furniture, the Hotel Raphael, on Avenue Wagram, within walking distance of the Champs Elysées, Place de l'Etoile, the Arc de Triomphe. I walked out into the December twilight, *l'heure bleue*. Soft snow was falling on the cobblestones at the Place de la Concorde. The lights around the Place twinkled above the soft blanket of snow. I stopped, awestruck to be standing inside an Impressionist painting. Snowflakes wet my cheeks. I reached a hand up to brush them away—tears. Issur was in Paris. No more garbage cans, no more mill smoke and train shrieks. Happy Birthday, Issur.

The book *The Girl on the Via Flaminia*, by Alfred Hayes, was about a tragic love affair between an American GI and a poor girl in Italy during World War II. But the director, Anatole Litvak, changed the title to *Act of Love*, and the locale to Paris, because he liked working there. I think this was done to the detriment of the movie, which would have worked better set in the roughness of the peasants of Italy, than in the more refined atmosphere of Paris.

They were going to shoot *Act of Love* in two versions, French and English. They only wanted me for the English version; another actor would do the French version. I said, "Why would you want to do that? I play an American soldier. He's supposed to speak French with an American accent. Why not let me do the French version?"

"Because you don't speak French!"

"So, I'll learn."

They laughed. "Go ahead, try."

I found a French teacher, Mme. LaFeuille, which in French means "the leaf," like the leaf of a tree. We worked every day, two hours a day, six days a week from a book called *Assimil*. Each day we would take a chapter, sometimes two. Being a pupil again with an older woman as teacher made me think of Louise Livingston and of how important women had been in my life, how encouraging at crucial times. It was not a sexual relationship, but I think Madame fell in love with my determined efforts. She was ecstatic about the progress I was making. She told me (in French) that she could actually see me chewing away, biting off big hunks of the language. At the end of the day, my head would be aching, ready to split open. I was just dying to say something in English.

Learning French was also difficult because the French weren't very helpful. In the early 1950s, they were all trying to learn English. If you spoke to them in French, they answered in English. You were always running into people in hotels, or cab drivers, or telephone operators who were anxious to learn English. Most Americans immediately became intimidated and lapsed into English.

But as anxious as the French were to learn English, I was even more anxious to learn French. I realized very quickly that I would never learn the language if people kept talking to me in English, so if I spoke to someone in French and he answered in English, I just went ahead and kept speaking French. Very often, I would be amazed to find that my

French was better than his English. I learned tricks—if someone said something to me in English, I would respond *"Qu'est-ce qu'il a dit?"* ["What did he say?"] and force him to speak French.

One night I was supposed to make a personal appearance at the Paramount Theater in Paris, and I wanted to get there by myself. I went out of the Hotel Raphael. The doorman got me a taxi, and I said to the driver, *"Je voudrais aller au cinéma Paramount."*

He looked at me, uttered the French equivalent of "Say what?"

I repeated it several times.

He shrugged, cigarette hanging out of his mouth.

I couldn't believe that my French was so imperfect that he didn't understand my simple request. Finally, the doorman came over, and I told him. He said the exact same words I had said to the taxi driver, except he said "Paramount" with a French accent.

"Ah!" said the taxi driver, "Pahr-ah-mont!" and took off.

French on the telephone is very different—no aid from lip reading, no gestures for context. I made the operators my teachers. I would tell them in French that I was trying to learn, and ask them to correct my mistakes. Otherwise, they would have been babbling away in English.

After two months of this, I spoke French fluently, could read the newspaper. My graduation exercise—Mme. La-Feuille and I went to Fouquet's for lunch. I ordered in French, and the whole luncheon was carried on in French, with Mme. LaFeuille looking at me, eyes gleaming at her prodigy who had mastered the French language in two months, and spoke with an accent that was not American, but possibly slightly Dutch.

We started shooting *Act of Love*. Anatole Litvak—"Tola" —was a sweet man. But it surprised me how close-knit the French were. After a party at the beginning, and one dinner, no one made any effort to introduce me to people in France. It was my first time in the country. I knew no one. I was lonely.

The Hotel Raphael was lovely, but I wanted an apartment of my own. Everybody told me it would be impossible to find one, given the conditions in postwar Paris. But I found three in one day. I was tempted to take the one on Ile St. Louis, where you had to go down a rope ladder to get into one of the bedrooms. But the best was at 31 Boulevard d'Auteuil, near the Bois de Boulogne, very elegant, the ground floor of a very beautiful home with French windows giving out onto a garden.

Then I tried to get someone to handle public relations for me, and be a general assistant. Everybody said, "It's too bad that Anne Buydens isn't here. She'd be wonderful for it." But this Buydens person was in the United States. Tola had wanted her to work on *Act of Love*, but she had the opportunity to go to the United States for the opening of *Moulin Rouge*. She had been director John Huston's assistant when they shot the movie in Paris. She loved the United States, so she chose that instead.

When she came back, Shim, the still photographer, and Bob Capa's partner, arranged an interview. Anne told me later that Shim said, "Let me take you into the lion's den." I walked into my dressing room, and there she was—blue suit, white collar, very delicate wrists and ankles, which the French call *les attaches très fines,* signs of beauty in a woman. She sat there very poised, an elegant manner about her. I found her striking. We talked for a while. She spoke English with a slight accent. She also spoke German and Italian. I told her what I needed. She very politely said she did not think that the position was right for her, but she could suggest other people. This miffed me. I was an American movie star doing a picture in Paris. I expected her to be anxious to get the job. But she seemed not to be at all. I walked her to her car and said *"Au revoir."*

Alone in my apartment that evening, I kept thinking about this gal who had turned me down. I'd been invited to dinner by Claude Terrail, who owned the Tour d'Argent, an exclusive restaurant that looked out on Notre Dame cathedral. I called Anne, lowered my voice. "What are you doing this evening?"

"Oh, nothing."

"I thought you might like to join us, have a little something to eat. There will be about five of us for supper at the Tour d'Argent."

Very politely, she said, "No, thank you, I'll just stay in and make myself some eggs."

I hung up, and thought, Fuck her. She turns down my offer to work for me, she turns down my offer to have dinner with me. The hell with her.

The picture occupied most of my time. I had to work very hard trying to keep up with everybody in French. But I couldn't get Anne out of my mind. I swallowed my pride and asked her again to help me. Finally, she agreed to work for me temporarily.

It was a victory. She was extremely capable and efficient, got along very well with everyone, was well liked, and very helpful. I continued with what I thought were my very subtle plans to seduce her. But whatever I tried failed. Finally, I thought to myself, Look, you can't win 'em all. Forget it. She's a great gal. You either break off the relationship completely, or let her do her job. I wanted her there.

Once I gave up pursuing Anne, I behaved differently. I became genuinely interested in her, asked her about herself. Wary at first, she gradually began to open up to me. Like Scheherazade, she unraveled skein after skein of stories. And like the sultan, I was spellbound.

Fifteen

ANNE

It was afternoon, at my apartment.

"Would you like some tea?" Anne asked.

"Good idea," I said.

"I've told you enough about me," I said. "So, you're Belgian?"

"No."

"Oh. I thought you came from Brussels."

She took a deep breath. "I was born in Hannover, Germany, but so much that happened there was horrible. I consider myself Belgian."

"I'm sorry," I said.

"Oh, I had a happy childhood for a while. Then everything began to crumble. My parents got divorced. My mother moved to Berlin, where she lived with one handsome young man after another. I went to visit her once. There was no room for me. I had to sleep on the couch."

A happy childhood I didn't understand. Sleeping on a couch I understood.

"But I was happy living with my father," she said. He

taught me that honesty is the most important quality in life. We were very close. There were no secrets between us." She paused. "And then one day he told me that he had married my best friend. She was much older than I, but the idea that they had been going around together and keeping it from me . . . I felt betrayed, left out of everything. It was like I had no father, and no mother. When the opportunity came up to go to Belgium, I jumped at the chance. I hated Hitler, and having to do that stupid salute to him, and everybody talking about war all the time. In Belgium, I could start a new life. I would be safe." She smiled ironically.

"I was awakened by a blast one morning, hurled out of bed, flung across the room, slammed against the furniture. I was terrified. What was happening? I heard explosions, and I knew: the Nazis were bombing Brussels. It was May 1940. I was fifteen years old, and I was alone.

"Out in the street was a mad exodus: people abandoning homes, belongings, fleeing the invasion of the Nazis. The entire country was on the road. A man I knew was engaged to a girl whose family had a house in La Baule, on the Atlantic coast in northern France. He, his brother, and a lawyer friend were going to try to drive there. I joined them.

"The Germans were bombing and strafing the Belgian army on the main roads. So we took back roads. We rounded a bend—roadblock, one Belgian soldier on each side checking passports.

"We were in trouble. The three men in the car were placing themselves in terrible jeopardy by having me along, with my German passport. I was sitting in the front, in the middle between two of the men; the third was in back with the luggage. At the roadblock, I took the passport from the man on the right and gave it to the soldier on the left, took the first passport back, gave it to the other soldier, took the passport from the man on my left . . . You see?" Anne asked. I did see. This young girl had bluffed the Belgian army with passport razzle-dazzle. The Harlem Globetrotters couldn't have done better with a basketball. It took incredible guts for all of them.

"Did you get through?"

"Three times we did this, through three roadblocks. Finally, we reached the coast of France. Simone's family took us all in. We only stayed in La Baule for about ten days. The Germans had advanced right behind us. We fled south to their house in Hossegor, near the Spanish border. But by the time we got to Hossegor, there was no place to hide. The Germans had totally invaded the country. The government collapsed; Pétain took over and set up his government in Vichy. We found out that there was as much truth in the French propaganda, 'The Maginot Line will protect you,' as there had been in the German propaganda, 'We will never bomb Belgium.'

"German soldiers were everywhere. Two days later, our eighteen-year-old maid was walking into town. She went through the woods because the roads were dangerous—clogged with German military vehicles, and people driving to Spain to avoid them. She saw a German soldier, naively spoke to him, eager for news of her hometown. 'Have you been in Alsace, at such-and-such a place? My parents live there.' He raped her. She came running home, crying, told what happened. Simone's grandmother was outraged; she had promised the girl's family to take care of her as if she were her own daughter. 'They cannot do this! They cannot do this!' The grandmother pointed at me. 'You! You speak German. You go, and tell them.'

"One of the brothers drove me into town. I got in to see the commandant, an officer and a gentleman. I was lucky. I wouldn't have stood a chance three or four months later, because by then the Nazis controlled everything. There was a huge difference between the regular German army and the Nazi party. After I told the commandant what had happened, he said there would be a trial.

"The court-martial was a very big affair; generals came in from headquarters. I interpreted for the maid. The soldier, a young boy, was sentenced to life in prison. The commandant ripped off all his medals, slapped him. At the end of the trial, the soldier said, 'I only want to find out why, when I asked her for a date for the next day, she said "yes." ' "

I looked at Anne and burst out laughing.

"It wasn't funny. He had a gun to her head."

No, it wasn't funny, but it explained a lot about Anne. As a teenager, she had stood up to the invading German army. She certainly wasn't going to have any trouble turning down a dinner invitation from me. She had incredible nerve and spirit. "So you spent the war in Hossegor?"

"No, we decided to try to get to Paris. But again, my passport was a problem—I might be accused of spying, or be sent back to Germany. One of the brothers had the solution —he offered to marry me. I was sixteen when I married Albert in Hossegor. I became a Belgian."

"Did you love him?"

"Love? I was trying to survive. Albert and I agreed to stay married for six months or a year, and then get our freedom."

"Where did the newlyweds go for their honeymoon?"

She ignored my bad joke. "We had three cars and no gasoline. I went back to the commandant. 'We would like to go to Paris, but we don't have enough gasoline.' He said, 'That's not a problem at all. Come by tomorrow morning and fill up the cars.' I was suspicious. But the next day, we drove all three cars into the depot, filled our gas tanks, and they gave us six full jerry cans for the road. Off we went.

"I spent the rest of the war in Paris, putting German subtitles on French movies. Under the Nazis, French film production was encouraged. The Germans were very eager to see spicy French movies. I did three to four movies a month —a lot of work. I'd never done it before. I sat in a projection room, saw the movies three or four times in a row, stop and go, stop and go, made notes on dialogue and timing—a sentence, the numbers behind it. Often, I took the work home. That's how I got arrested for being a spy."

"What?! What are you talking about?!" She'd said it so matter-of-factly.

"Yes. A knock at my door in the middle of the night, men

in uniforms. In France, they don't need search warrants. It's the opposite of the United States—you're guilty until you prove that you're innocent. They came across the papers I was working on—sentences followed by numbers. 'What is this? It looks like a code.' They arrested me, took me to the Sûreté—jail. I was there a couple of days. Miserable. Worse, they confiscated all the hard work that I had done. I didn't get my papers back until they had them 'decoded' and found there was nothing behind it except a movie."

I looked at this delicate, beautiful girl. All this had happened to her when she was younger than Pier.

"What about Albert?"

"Poor Albert. He couldn't make a living. I supported him. He even came to me for change to go to a movie. He was very charming, good-looking. You'd think he could have done something. I lost respect for him. I said, 'I think we should get a divorce.' He said, 'I'm very happy. Why don't we stay married?' He'd been in danger for me, had helped me when I needed it. I felt obligated to him. Then I met Ramon Babbas, the industrialist and the head of the parfumerie Patou. Ramon was so kind, so helpful."

"Are you still married?"

"We got separated after I met Ramon."

"Is Babbas married?"

"Yes."

"Why don't you get a divorce?"

"Albert said, 'You want a divorce, get a lawyer. You pay for all of it.' I don't have the money."

"Babbas does." Anne said nothing. "I see. He doesn't want you to get divorced. He's married. It's perfect for him if *you* stay married. He sees you, has your company when he wants."

I could see that Anne was chafing under the unfairness of both relationships. Babbas was treating the relationship like a business deal—giving only the minimum required to keep it going. She was a working girl, he was a very wealthy guy, but the most extravagant gift he had ever given her was grapes out of season. The minute he found out I was interested, he upped the ante—gave her a new car, a beautiful wristwatch. He saw the threat in business terms—somebody coming in for a takeover. He never put it in human terms: "I love you, I want you, no matter what."

We had started talking after lunch. It was now about six o'clock. I had to do a charity event that evening at the Cirque d'Hiver, the Winter Circus. Anne came with me.

The Cirque d'Hiver is a one-ring circus, seats ascending to the ceiling around it. All the men in the audience were in black tie, the ladies in elegant evening gowns to watch the movie stars of France performing on the trapeze, or with animals. Then I came out on stage with a camera. Pictures were forbidden; immediately officials came as if to take me away, yelling at me and asking what I was doing—all in French. Then one of them said, "Wait a minute! Stop! This is our American colleague, Kirk Douglas, La Brute Chérie!" —"The Darling Brute," the French press's nickname for me. The audience was delighted. Then they said, "Would you like to participate in our circus?"

"Yes, I would. But what can I possibly do in a show like this?"

"Oh, a man of your great talents . . . We'll certainly find something suitable. Why don't you come backstage with us?"

We left the ring, and the next act came on—elephants. When the elephants exited, I entered, still in black tie, with a broom and shovel, like a giant pooper-scooper, and went around cleaning up after them, looking at the audience and shrugging my shoulders. They loved it. Little did they know that I had been trained almost from the cradle to perform that particular function.

I took Anne back to her apartment at 11½ Rue Lord Byron, just off the Champs Elysées. I gave her my perfunctory good night kiss, but it turned into something more. I thought, "My God! I've got her! I believe I've got her!" That was the beginning of our romance.

Lying in bed together the first night, I asked her, "Why were you so difficult? What did I do wrong?"

She said, "I was determined to have absolutely nothing to do with an American movie star. I've seen too many stars come here, have a little 'flirt,' and then go back home. I wanted no part of that. I got my fill on *Moulin Rouge*, having to deal with John Huston's affair with the leading lady, and her jealous husband and everybody getting black eyes and chasing around and shooting guns."

"What changed your mind?"

"You became a human being. You were really interested in me and my problems. I found that very charming and attractive."

I had been piling on all this charm, and all this malarky, which didn't amount to anything. I learned something: men never realize that they are more attractive after they give up their tricks and become themselves.

I liked Anne very much. But I *was* engaged to Pier Angeli.

Sixteen

AFFAIRS

The peripatetic Pier was now in South America. Anne said nothing about her, so I assumed she accepted it. Our friendship grew; she spent a lot of time at my house near the Bois de Boulogne. But she kept her own apartment. Anne was always independent. She was also strictly a one-man woman. She broke off her relationship with Babbas immediately when our affair started, and told him why. But they remained friends. That intrigued me.

My two boys were coming to visit me at Easter time. Diana was going to send a nurse with them. I said, "Why send a nurse? Why don't *you* come with them, take a trip to Paris? Forget a hotel. You can all stay at my place." So they came. Diana immediately got the chicken pox. Both boys had it just before they arrived, and now the big blotches were all over their mother. She stayed in bed upstairs in the house; Anne brought her chicken soup.

When Diana recovered, we went to Maxim's for dinner— Anne and I, Diana, Willy Schorr, a couple of others. In the middle of the multicourse meal, the waiter handed me a

note. It said: "Please get away and meet me in the vestiaire."
It was signed by an elegant society lady. It was dramatic. I
was impressed. And eager. I put the note in my pocket,
waited an appreciable length of time, excused myself. I went
out, and she was there in the vestiaire, waiting for me. But
she hadn't written the note. She had a note from me that I
hadn't written. Somebody in the restaurant had set us up—
written both notes, and was watching the two of us. How
could we go back knowing someone was there snickering,
"Here they come now." We were both so embarrassed, it
ruined our relationship before it started. I never found out
who did it.

When I got back to the table, Anne was gone. Diana said
that Anne had excused herself, pleading work early in the
morning. I went to Anne's, rang the doorbell. She wouldn't
let me in. Through the door, she said, "I don't want to talk to
you. You are cheap."

I agreed.

She went on. "Leaving a restaurant like that! Somebody
sends you a note, and you fall for the trick right in front of
my eyes. I don't go out with people like you. Forget it."

I pleaded and apologized. It took me several days to open
that door.

Another evening, Diana and I, Anne and Ramon Babbas
took a box at the opera. As a child, Anne had been a musical
prodigy. She preferred the piano, but her father pushed her
to play the violin. During a recital one day she suddenly
went blank. This ten-year-old girl found herself standing on
the stage in front of a hall full of people, improvising Mozart.
Finally, somebody came onstage and very graciously led her
off, while she continued to saw away.

The opera was *Les Indes Galantes*, with great special effects. In one scene, a man was singing an aria, while behind
him on one side a volcano was erupting, spewing out smoke
and sparks, lava flowing down over a mountain; while on the
other side, a ship was staggering across the stage as it sank
into the sea. It was a very serious scene, but I started to

laugh. As a performer, I was thinking of this poor tenor rehearsing his song day after day on a bare stage, working so hard to say the words precisely, to sing the notes accurately, with great emotion. The night of the performance, he sings his heart out, but nobody notices—he's being upstaged by the scenery. Diana, who has a contagious sense of humor, started to laugh, too. The same thought hit her. The more we tried not to laugh, the more we laughed. Anne kept glancing at me; the distinguished French industrialist looked at me with disdain. It was a nervous, hysterical evening, because of the strange combination of people: I'm there with my ex-wife; the woman I am having an affair with is accompanied by her ex-lover. It was a little bit too French.

Just before Diana and the boys left, we all took a walk in the Bois de Boulogne one afternoon. I was holding Michael's hand. Michael took my other hand and put it in Diana's and said, "Now the family is together."

My heart broke along with Michael's.

Act of Love finished shooting. The last scenes were on one of the most beautiful bridges in Paris, the Pont Alexandre Trois. Then I found out that Alexandre Trois was Czar Alexander III, who ruled Russia from 1881 to 1894—the height of the pogroms, and the reason my parents had to leave Russia. He was a world-class anti-Semite, right up there with Hitler. I spit on his bridge.

Anne had to go to the South of France, where she was in charge of protocol at the Cannes Film Festival. I tagged along, took the script for my next film, *Ulysses*, to study. I loved to watch Anne work, talking in Italian to the Italian contingent, switching to German with the German producers, back to French, then English with the British and Americans, switching languages as easily as shifting gears in a car. I admired her greatly.

While Anne was working, I lay around on the beach, studied my script, and encouraged my beard to grow for *Ulysses*. Once, a yacht pulled into dock, and I helped them tie up.

The owner came off, saw this unshaven bum in a bathing suit—me—and tipped me a couple hundred francs. I was between pictures; I kept it.

One day, Anne said she had to go to the airport to meet some producers. She came back with an ex-boyfriend, Joe Drown, who owned the Bel Air Hotel in Los Angeles, and told me that she was going to have dinner with him that night. I realize now that she was attempting to protect herself from her feelings for me. It embarrasses me to remember that all during this great romance, whenever I felt we were getting too close, I would remind her that I was engaged to Pier Angeli. I continued to communicate with Pier as best I could. Sometimes I had Ray Stark call her up and tell her our secret code: "1-2-3," or "Because yes." He'd write back that trying to get through Pier's mother was like trying to get through the Iron Curtain, that Pier said "1-2-3" back, and what was he doing in the numbers racket anyway? But Pier wasn't there, and Joe Drown was. I was furious. The only reason I was in Cannes was to pursue Anne, and she was going off with somebody else.

I had met a beautiful blond French girl, called her on the spur of the moment, invited her to go to St. Tropez with me for the evening. We took a room in a very quaint, charming hotel. I was still studying French. As we lay in bed together, I read to her from St. Exupéry's *Le Petit Prince*. A strange look came into her eyes—"What kind of a kook is this, who takes me all the way to St. Tropez and then reads *The Little Prince* to me in French?" But I had a reputation to protect. I didn't read *The Little Prince* to her *all* night.

The next day, back in Cannes, I called Anne to gloat about my marvelous evening. Then I said, "Did you have a lovely evening last night, too?"

She started to cry.

I said, "What's the matter?"

"Oh, he got drunk and gambled recklessly, and it was an impossible evening."

"Good. Serves you right, for what you did to me."

Suddenly, through her sobs, she blurted, "Today is my birthday!"

Two hours later, we were in the most beautiful little restaurant, candlelight, flowers. All had been forgotten. The romance continued.

Seventeen

SIGNOR DOUGLAS

After Cannes, we went to Italy to do *Ulysses*. The producers had hired Anne to do public relations for the picture a year earlier. Pier was still in South America making a film.

I was tired from shooting one film in two languages. While they finished preparations for *Ulysses*, they arranged for me to have a holiday at Carlo Ponti's home in the hills of Amalfi. Anne and I took off in a big chauffeur-driven Lancia, another Lancia behind us with the luggage. We tittered about the opulence of it. Our stay at Amalfi was lovely, even though we were aware of the tension between Ponti and his wife because of his affair with Mai Britt. Anne and I would go out in a little rowboat. I'd lie back and sing Italian songs and have Anne row me around—very much the Italian macho with his woman doing his bidding. We spent a week in Amalfi, drove around Positano, and then took a trip to Capri. An idyllic, perfect vacation.

We started shooting on May 18, 1953, in Porto Ercole, a little fishing village on the Adriatic, with men drying nets on the wide, sandy beach. I always joke that I discovered it, because when I first saw it, I said, "This is charming. I think I'll buy some land here." I wish I had. Now it's like Palm Beach.

We lived in a charming, clean house right on the ocean. Every morning was beautiful and sunny. A launch would come to the dock in front of the house and take us to the replica of a Greek ship where we were shooting, ten miles out to sea. Anne would lean against the cabin, reading a book. I'd swim for a mile or two, and then lie down beside her for the rest of the trip. Or sometimes I'd water-ski. All day we shot on the replica. At sunset, the day's work done, I would climb up to the topmost mast of the ship and dive into the sea. Anne would pretend not to be impressed. Then I'd swim alongside the launch for a mile or so before climbing aboard for the rest of the trip back to Porto Ercole.

One day when we got back I went into our bedroom. Propped up on the nightstand next to the bed was a big picture of Pier, signed: *Kirk, I'm watching you.* I thought she was in South America. I'd had such difficulty trying to get together with her. And yet, when she found out that I wasn't alone, she got someone to drive her all the way up to Porto Ercole, two hours from Rome, and brought that picture with her! It was a dramatic gesture, but there was madness in it. At the time, I didn't realize the extent of the madness. Back in Rome, I tried to locate Pier. Gone.

I had been in Rome twice before and been disappointed at not seeing Pier. This time, I went to the little restaurants and bistros she had told me about, walked up and down the Spanish Steps, the Via Veneto, had coffee at the sidewalk cafés. I did all those things. But I did them with Anne.

We found a beautiful villa, Villa Gioia—"Joy House." It was huge—terraces, gardens, swimming pool, a staff of three. Anne stayed with me most of the time, but always retained her independence—she had a room at the Hotel de la Ville, where a lot of French people stayed. I was thrilled with the villa; it was on the Via Appia Antica, the road that Caesar's legions used to march in and out of Rome. It was country, surrounded by fields, lovely places to take long walks. Everybody had the same idea; you stumbled over lovers everywhere. The young lovers of Rome would ride up on their little Vespa motorscooters, the girls sitting behind the boys, arms wrapped around them. They'd lean the scooters against a tree, go off into the bushes and make love. One day, while we were taking a walk, Anne and I saw a young fellow masturbating as he watched two other young people make love. It certainly was stimulating.

The world was filled with romance. I put Pier out of my mind. Everyone was singing romantic songs like "Come bella far l'amore quando è sera" ("How beautiful it is to make love in the evening"). We ate wonderful pasta, walked everywhere. Very few cars in Rome in those days; everyone zipped around on Vespas. But Anne and I preferred to walk up and down the old cobblestone streets—to the Colosseum, the catacombs.

We entertained at the villa. All my friends liked Anne very much. Charlie Feldman came, tried to talk me into a three-picture deal with his buddy Twentieth Century–Fox president Darryl Zanuck. I pissed him off when I told him I wasn't interested in doing *The Robe*. Michael Wilding played the part. I asked how Sam Norton was, mentioned what a great guy he was to come up with the idea that I should go to Europe for the tax break, and here I was living like a king. Not bad, Charlie agreed, after a look around. But how was I handling my business affairs in the States from so far away? I told him I wasn't worried; Sam had my power of attorney. Charlie was aghast. "I wouldn't give my power of attorney to my mother." But Charlie had always been a shark. He just didn't understand friends. Sam was the only one who wrote regularly to keep me posted, the only one I could count on to handle everything competently.

Ray Stark visited and brought a guitar. He also brought better advice: do the live-action picture Walt Disney wanted me for, the four-million-dollar Cinemascope version of Jules Verne's *20,000 Leagues Under the Sea*.

The work in Rome was bedlam. During the filming, everybody spoke his own language—English, French, Italian,

Russian, Spanish. No need to be quiet when you did a scene
—it was all going to be dubbed later. I got used to playing
intimate scenes with noise all around. And they were tough
about paying people. The less you made, the tougher they
were. They always held back. Every week, the set was
clogged with extras clamoring for their money.

Two of the biggest female stars in Italy were in the movie.
Rosanna Podestà played the Princess Nausicaa, who finds
Ulysses washed up on the beach and decides to marry him
after she sees him cleaned up. Silvana Mangano, Dino de
Laurentiis's wife, who just had a huge hit with *Bitter Rice*,
played the dual roles of Circe, the witch who turns Ulysses'
men into swine, and Penelope, the good wife who fends off
ardent suitors, most notably Tony Quinn, while waiting ten
years for Ulysses to return home.

One day, one of the other biggest female stars in Italy
popped onto the set unannounced—Pier Angeli. Being in
her presence changed everything. We had a few days together, went out to restaurants and nightclubs, before she
had to leave for London to finish a picture. By the time she
left, I was more in love with her than ever. I flew to London
to celebrate her twenty-first birthday with her, and to give
her a diamond ring that I bought at Bulgari, the Tiffany's of
Rome. It was an enchanting few days; we attended a Command Performance before the Queen. Then I flew back to
Rome to resume shooting. Anne understood—from her room
at the Hotel de la Ville.

There was a lot of action in *Ulysses*. We hunted dangerous
wild boar that were actually painted pigs. We stomped
grapes into wine. Very expensive hothouse grapes, imported
from Holland, because Italian grapes were not yet in season.
But the wrong color grapes, too purple, so we reshot the
scene, adding tomatoes. I was supposed to steal a meek little
sheep—it struggled, hit me in the nose and arms with its
sharp little hooves. I got even in the next scene—I ate the
sheep. Cheese was not so much fun. We did seven takes of a
scene where I had to taste giant white cheeses. They used
the real thing, strong Italian goat cheese. I was so nauseated,

for the eighth take, I had them slip in little pieces of banana. Then we had to reshoot the wine-stomping, this time with real Italian grapes, the right color, because the tomatoes were—surprise!—too red.

We took a break from shooting to attend the Venice Film Festival, and a ball at Contessa Volpe's palace on the Grand Canal. Silvana Mangano and I arrived in grand style: flower-festooned gondolas powered by singing gondoliers. At a screening of *The Bad and the Beautiful*, a photographer took a picture of Silvana and me, dubbed us "The Beard and the Beautiful." It was Anne's job to handle the public relations for all this, too. She showed great dignity and professionalism in hiding her personal feelings as she did her work.

There were lots of fans in Venice, mostly young girls clad in that scandalous new bathing suit that no American girl would wear—the bikini. They all wanted my autograph, but of course had no paper. In the interest of public relations, I was forced to sign my name around their navels, their thighs, their . . .

Suddenly, I heard "Keerk! Keerk!" and saw the most gorgeous creature—long, silky blond hair, beautiful breasts, never-ending legs—running toward me in a bikini, a sight I will remember long after my eyes fail me. I didn't recognize her until she said her name. She had done a bit part in *Act of Love*, bundled up in a heavy coat. But even then there was a beautiful quality about her—long, graceful neck, angelic face. I said to Anne, "I think I'll take this girl back to California with me. She could be a star." Anne didn't agree with me. Standing there on the beach, I looked at the girl and thought, My God, that body was underneath the big heavy coat! I wonder if Anne's appraisal was completely professional when she dismissed this seventeen-year-old French girl—Brigitte Bardot.

Back in Rome we filmed the wrestling match. The scenes looked authentic—I was undefeated college champion; my opponent, Umberto Silvestri, was undefeated Olympic champion.

In *Ulysses*, we had monsters, ships, pigs, grapes, goats, and handled them all, but the most difficult scene was with a little dog. Ulysses comes home in disguise after years of war and wandering, and goes unrecognized by everyone except his faithful dog, now old. I tried to make friends with this dog weeks in advance. I gave him food, petted him, had him live with me at the villa. I *like* dogs. I've always *had* dogs. But this was an Italian dog, *un cane Italiano*, totally indifferent. We shot the scene where the long-lost Ulysses enters the courtyard and the dog runs up to him. I entered, the dog exited. Fifteen times we shot the scene. Fifteen times the dog walked away from me. I have never been so snubbed by a four-footed creature. Finally, we had to go on to something else. The next time we shot the scene, they drugged the dog, so at least it wouldn't run off. Now, it merely turned its head aside whenever the camera was on it. We did get enough footage so the editors could cut something together.

Mike Todd visited the set with his Todd-AO Magnascope company, then hosted a dinner party for Evelyn Keyes. I enjoyed meeting some of the other guests—Ingrid Bergman, Ernest Hemingway's ex-wife Martha Gellhorn, and Irene Selznick, among others.

Pictures of Soraya, the beautiful wife of the Shah of Iran, were on the covers of magazines all over the world that summer. The Shah was divorcing her because they had not had any children. And now she was living in Italy. I wanted to meet her, but didn't know how. Finally, somebody pointed out the obvious: "You're a movie star. Call her up."

I invited her to a cocktail party at my villa. She brought her mother, a German woman who drank quite a bit; and a couple of male attendants—bodyguards? Soraya was certainly very attractive. We spent a pleasant enough time together, but in person she didn't possess the special quality that I had perceived in all those pictures. Another instance where I would have been better off leaving my dreams alone.

I threw a big party at the end of the picture, when Sam Norton and his wife were visiting. It was a theme party at the restaurant Apuleius on the Ostia Antica: waiters in pre-

236 The Ragman's Son

Christian costumes; place-card replicas of Ulysses' ship, each an original work of art; a special feast with the menu in ancient Greek. I made a short speech in Italian; there was much singing and dancing. The director and I had been on the outs. He refused to come to the party, but the producers persuaded him to show up. I wanted to make up with him. I liked him. After the spectacular dessert—a huge ice cream sculpture of Ulysses' ship, complete with Ulysses and his men—I sang the old Italian favorite, "Mama." But I called it "Papa" and sang it to him on my knees, my hand over my heart. But when it came to the line *Quanto ti voglio bene* (How much I love you) I looked at Anne. The song did the trick all around. Everybody left happy—and tired. I needed a vacation.

Eighteen

IN PURSUIT OF PIER, PART 3

Anne and I took a trip to Belgium. We had a magnificent, multicourse luncheon in a beautiful restaurant overlooking the main square in Brussels. We had plans to spend that evening with Anne's ex-husband (she had finally divorced him) and his girlfriend. But in our hotel room as we were getting ready to go out, I suddenly felt sick. "Anne, I feel terrible. I can't go out tonight. Why don't you go ahead, and I'll wait for you?"

Anne went out with her ex-husband while I stayed in the hotel. Suddenly, I became violently ill, and called for a doctor. He rushed up, examined me, gave me medication. The diagnosis: "You have had a heart attack, but you're out of danger. You are not to exert yourself in any way."

"But I'm flying to Baden-Baden tomorrow!" We were supposed to meet Tola Litvak.

He said, "Absolutely not. You cannot fly. That would be very dangerous for you."

Reluctantly, I agreed not to fly. But I flatly refused when he wanted to put me in the hospital. After he left, I lay in bed feeling sorry for myself. "Look at me. I'm lying here dying of a heart attack. My girlfriend's out with her ex-husband. I don't know what the hell she's doing. I'll probably be an invalid for the rest of my life, and I'm still in my thirties."

Around midnight, Anne returned, very gay. "How are you feeling?"

"Oh, I'll be all right. I hope *you* had a wonderful time, darling. *I* had a heart attack."

"What are you talking about?"

I told her what the doctor said.

Anne said, "That's ridiculous!" Her diagnosis: indigestion from eating so much.

I was furious. Indigestion!

Nevertheless, the next day we canceled our flight, and took the train directly to a famous heart clinic in Schwarzwald, the Black Forest, near Baden-Baden. One of the top doctors there, a movie fan, examined me. "I've never seen a man in better shape than you."

"But what about my heart?"

"Your heart? Your heart's like an eighteen-year-old boy's. You're a very strong man."

I tried not to see the smile creeping around the corners of Anne's lips.

I said, "That's not what the doctor told me in Brussels last night."

"What did you eat yesterday?"

Anne butted in with the menu. As she recited it, I almost got sick again, listening to how much pâté and oysters and everything else I had eaten.

He said, "Indigestion. He should have given you bicarbonate of soda, and you would have been fine."

Anne was ready to burst out laughing.

"Don't you dare say a word," I warned her.

So that was the end of my infirmity. We had a lovely time for a few days with the Litvaks in Baden-Baden.

Until I saw a copy of *Paris-Match*. Pier Angeli was on the cover. I fell in love with her all over again. And in spite of all the peculiarities of our relationship, we *were* engaged to be married. Everywhere we went, she was staring at me from the magazine. I stared back longingly. Anne stared at me staring at Pier, and said, "She is very beautiful."

I said, "I'm sorry, Anne. I guess I'm still in love with her."

Anne said, "What am I doing here? This is ridiculous! You go to her, and I'll go home and let's finish this!" Anne returned to Paris. I went to Munich, did several broadcasts for the American Forces Network, then back to Paris. I left messages everywhere for Pier. No answer.

I got word that my father was in the hospital. I wrapped things up to go back to the States. I had one more day of post-production on *Act of Love*. I was kept late at the studio; a series of minor foul-ups by one of the crew. I was annoyed, because I was supposed to meet Tola Litvak at his house, which had been my house while we were shooting *Act of Love*. I felt like a displaced person—Pier off somewhere, Anne estranged. I hadn't seen my boys in months. And it was my birthday, and nobody had even said "Happy Birthday" to me. Maybe it was better that way. My birthday always makes me sad. I was almost glad to be alone.

I got to Tola's, opened the door. Fifty people yelled "Surprise!" The party *was* surprising, beautiful girls everywhere. Then I looked closer, and Oh my God. There was a girl I had had a "flirt" with, as the French say, some time ago. Then I turned to the other side. Another girl I had been with. And another. And another. Tola, with a grin.

I said, "You set this up!"

He shook his head. Behind me, I heard "Happy Birthday." I turned. Anne. She had rounded up almost every girl I had gone out with, even the one from the night before. I was flabbergasted. I had not gone to any trouble to conceal my trysts with most of these women, but there were some that I thought I had been very discreet about. I couldn't figure out how anyone had found out. I didn't know whether to be furious, or chagrined, or what. It gave me an eerie feeling about this woman, Anne Buydens, and her strange way of saying good-bye.

Men think they're so clever. They think they're so smooth. They think they're getting away with everything, with no one noticing. And the woman knows everything. Once, Anne and I were in a crowded restaurant, sitting at a table of ten people. I was anxious to tell her an interesting story. As everyone around us was talking, I leaned over and told Anne the story. That night, at home, she said to me, "Do you know that at the next table, this girl said . . . " and she recounted an entire conversation that she had overheard.

I said, "I didn't hear that. When did you hear that?"

"When you were telling me the story."

"You mean that while I was telling you what I thought was a very important story, you were listening to some stranger at another table?"

"I heard everything you said." She repeated my story to me.

But she also heard everything that the lady next to us had said. I've talked to other women about that. They understand it, can do it. But I have never met a man who would be capable of it. Women baffle me.

Pier called, happy to hear from me. We made a date to spend New Year's Eve in Paris. But still, on the plane back to New York, I wondered, Will she be there?

I went directly to Albany to see my father in the hospital.

Issur entered the room. Pa was sleeping. Issur sat in a chair opposite him. He looked at his father, so small and shriveled in the big hospital bed, his pale face blending in with his white hair. Now his father was the child in need. Maybe it would be different this time. Maybe his father would say to Issur the things people said in movies or plays: "You know, son, how much I've always loved you, how proud I've always been of you. I'm sorry I never told you before. But everything can be different now." Then Issur would embrace his father and say, "Yes, Pa, I understand."

Issur closed his eyes, tired from the long trip. He remembered years ago walking across a field in Albany with Pa, on their way to Betty's house. It was at the beginning of Pa's illness. He wanted to live at the nursing home where Ma was. Issur was trying to arrange it, but Ma didn't want him there. Issur felt that no matter what had gone on before, at the end of their lives, they should be together. But Ma was stubborn.

Issur had been sending his father a monthly allowance. Pa said he needed more money. Could Issur give him some?

Shy, timid, reserved Issur suddenly erupted like an enraged animal. "You son of a bitch! You always want me to give you something! I gave you all my Bar Mitzvah money. I helped you stuff those goddamn ragbags. I helped you pile horseshit around the house. I gave you my love. What did you give me? NOTHING! NOTHING! All I ever wanted from you was one lousy pat on the back, just a pat on the back! But you never gave it to me!"

Issur opened his eyes in the hospital room.

Pa was staring at him.

Issur looked into his father's eyes, so, so black, like the hard pieces of coal Issur used to pick up by the railroad tracks. He knew that his father, big, strong Harry, the bulvan, toughest Jew in Amsterdam, was dying. Issur was afraid. How could someone who had always been so strong become so weak? Issur wanted to run away.

Pa said, "Stay with me."

If only Pa had said, "Stay with me" on Eagle Street. How different Issur's life would have been. Issur said, "I have children of my own now, Pa. They're waiting for me. They need me." There was cruelty under the piety; Issur didn't know why he'd said it. Did he still hurt so much that he wanted to remind his father, even now, of what he hadn't done? Was he still so mean, after so many years?

Pa looked at him, his eyes blacker than they had ever been. "I'll never see you again." His eyes burned into Issur.

Issur left.

I spent Christmas with my boys, then flew back to Paris. *Finally* my fiancée, soon to be my child bride, Pier, was coming to Paris to spend New Year's Eve with me. Alone.

Senza mamma. We had never had sex. Now it would happen. Would she be there? She called me, as charming and bubbly as ever, from her apartment at the Hotel George V. We went to a New Year's Eve party at the Tour d'Argent, the first restaurant I had invited Anne to. It was pleasant, excellent food and drinks. At midnight, Pier and I kissed. No passion. I couldn't figure it out. I finally had what I'd always wanted: to get this sweet young thing away from her mother, alone with me. Here we were alone in Paris. We could be together for the whole night, for several nights. And I felt—I didn't know what I felt. Finally I put a name on it: unhappy. We left the party, took a walk along the Seine. It was apparent to Pier that something was bothering me. I said that I just felt strange—so many peculiar things had happened in our relationship. When I came to Rome to see her the first time, she was in Venice. When I came back to Rome, she was in Capri. Or London. I was always running after her, and she was just a little child her mother led around by the hand. The whole relationship was a silly fantasy built on nothing but an adorable little giggly girl who was just playing a game with me.

Pier said, "If that's the way you feel, maybe we shouldn't be engaged."

I said, "Maybe so."

And there, under the moonlight, in one of the most romantic spots in the world, she took the little engagement ring off her finger, held it out to me. I took it. Tears were in her eyes —not mine. I took her back to her hotel.

She said, "Will I see you tomorrow?"

I said, *"Domani è troppo tardi."* ["Tomorrow is too late."] It was over.

I went back to my place, picked up the phone—and remembered that I didn't know where to reach Anne. I called her apartment. She was gone, with strict instructions to the maid under no circumstances to let me know where she was. I wheedled, pleaded. The maid hung up on me. I went to Anne's apartment to beg in person. I got the number.

I called Anne at her friends' place in St. Paul de Vence in

the South of France. "I broke off my engagement with Pier. I miss you. I want to see you. When can you come back to Paris?"

"I'm just about getting over you, so why don't you leave me alone? I don't want to get hurt anymore. And I have been hurt—badly."

"I'll wait for you in Paris. Please come back.'"

She hung up.

Anne came back to Paris on the afternoon train. She told me what she'd known all along about Pier, and what I would have known, too, if I'd bothered to read the foreign papers after I'd gone to the trouble of learning the languages: Pier was always with a man; Pier was photographed in Venice with a little poodle in her arms, given to her by her new boyfriend; Pier was in London with Dean Martin, when she had told me she was with Mamma. Anne was torn. Should she leave the clippings lying around for me to find "by accident?" Tell me outright? Say nothing? I had told Anne so many times that I was in love with Pier, was going to marry Pier. She didn't want to break my heart. But she knew that she had to get out of the relationship to save *her* heart.

Years later, I was shocked when Marisa, Pier's twin sister, told me in a fit of disgust that just fifteen minutes before I had visited Pier in Venice, Pier's mirror was plastered with pictures of a young Italian boy. You might expect this of some women, but Pier Angeli seemed so pure that even now when I think of it, it's hard for me to believe. It was incomprehensible—innocent, childlike, virginal Pier. As I think back on it, I was a fool not to have seen this other aspect of Pier. I didn't see it because I didn't want to.

Anne had arranged, as part of her cure of Kirk Douglas, to go skiing in Klosters. I was just waiting to start *20,000 Leagues Under the Sea*, so I asked to go with her. Still wary of me, she thought it best for us to be apart. I followed her anyway. Some friends of mine, and friends of Anne's—Bob Capa, Irwin Shaw—were also going to Klosters. I had never been skiing in my life. I borrowed pants, boots, sweaters;

rented skis and poles. When I got to Klosters, a girl came up to me and said, "Are you the ski instructor?" What a compliment!

Anne tried to be annoyed when I showed up, but I could see that she was pleased. The next few weeks were heaven. She had planned to stay two weeks—we stayed four. I loved it! I had a Swiss ski instructor, but learning was frustrating. I blamed everything on him. If I couldn't do something, it was his fault. "Make me do it! You make me do it!" And he did. I made all the runs, even the toughest. I entered a slalom race, just for the hell of it, and came in second.

Then I left the snows of Switzerland to do *20,000 Leagues Under the Sea* in the Bahamas.

Nineteen

STATESIDE

20,000 Leagues Under the Sea was the first movie Walt
Disney did with live characters. When they were negotiating
my contract and mentioned a price, Walt asked, quite sincerely, if that was my fee for six pictures. "Uncle Walt" was
very easy to work with. If you had a suggestion, and it was
good, he took it. I played Ned Land, a lusty sailor, quite a
ladies' man, but the picture was all aboard ship. I said,
"There are no women in this picture. Why don't we start off
with my character and two gals in a barroom scene, leaving
on their way to the ship?" He agreed immediately. The
scene is in the picture.

Walt was a fascinating guy, very happy, engrossed in the
planning of Disneyland, which was going to open the following year, 1955. He showed me sketches and took me for a
ride on the carts they would use. I asked about the submarine from *20,000 Leagues Under the Sea*. Movie props are
usually disposable; they're built to last only until the end of
the picture. But the submarine was built so solidly, so expen-
sively. "Isn't that a waste of money?" I thought I was being

smart. But Walt was way ahead of me—planning to use the submarine in Disneyland. He built it well, and charged it to the picture.

We shot the underwater sequences in the clear waters of the Bahamas during the day. One night, I was in a casino in Nassau, throwing dice at the crowded craps table. At the other end of the table was an extremely attractive girl watching me intently. I looked up, our eyes locked.

I love watching women. Sometimes I do strange things when I see an attractive girl. And I'm intrigued by the different ways boy meets girl. I see Bogart leaning on a lamppost; it's night, a little mist, he's smoking. A beautiful girl passes by, hesitates. Bogart gives her that "thin eyes look." I like that "thin eyes look." "Got a light?" the girl asks. And before many puffs, they walk off into the fog together.

There in the casino, I got that Bogart feeling. I kept looking at her while throwing the dice, disdainful of whether I won or lost. As the dice passed to the next player, I walked toward her, slowly, whispered in her ear, "My car is in space 402. Five minutes." Without looking at her, I slowly walked away. I should have been smoking a cigarette, except that I don't smoke. But I certainly felt like Bogart. I didn't look back. I didn't dare.

I waited ten minutes—to keep her waiting—then left the casino and walked out to my car. I saw a bundle of fur enclosing a face, blond hair glistening in the night lights.

I got into the car, didn't say a word. If I had been smoking, I would have taken one last drag. I drove her to my hotel. Without uttering a single word, I took her up to my room. I was Bogart all night long.

The movie company went on to Round Hill, Jamaica, to film the beach sequences where the cannibals chase me. There were beautiful, young (I hate to think how young) copper-colored girls dancing and singing Calypso songs— "Please, mister, don't you touch my tomatoes." Afterward, I would take them up to my bungalow. I'm glad I never asked them how old they were. I think I should have been in jail.

Peter Lorre was there, too, a sad, hapless fellow, all

bloated and puffy. I found out later he was a morphine addict. In those days, drug use was much less common. And I have always been dumb about such things. But I loved Peter, and we had a great time together.

After shooting, I went to the Yucatán peninsula, and Chichén Itzá, and saw all the Aztec ruins. I met a beautiful young woman in a temple where they had sacrificed virgins. Then she and I climbed the steps of a pyramid that was devoted, as far as I could tell from the decor, to the worship of male genitalia. On the top of the pyramid, she became a worshipper.

The next day, I went on to Acapulco. All the hotels and beaches were crowded and noisy. I hated it. I was going to leave. But I ran into Mike Todd. He invited me to stay at his house in Las Brisas. At that time, it was isolated, but now it's a developed area. Todd was going with Evelyn Keyes. Chomping on a big cigar, he said, "I know you used to be the boyfriend of my girl. But that's the kind of guy I am— classy. I invite you to come on over, be my guest." He was very charming, and I stayed at his house for a couple of days before I went back to California.

Sam Norton and Fran Stark had fixed up a little tract house for me at 1609 San Ysidro Drive, not far from Danny Kaye's house. Really, Fran did all the work, because she's an interior decorator. Fran had my initials embroidered on all the towels and bed covers. I was touched. It was my beautiful little bachelor pad.

I kept thinking of Anne. I called her at the Cannes Film Festival, invited her to visit me before my children came to spend Easter vacation. She agreed to visit for two weeks after the film festival was over.

Then I got word that my father died.

I cried bitter tears, selfish tears. I would never get that pat on the back. But I didn't go to the funeral. They found in his bedroom drawer a bankbook. He had secretly saved fifteen hundred dollars in the Amsterdam City Bank. I took it—all of it. My sisters were surprised. They didn't realize how much I needed something from Pa.

Anne called, tired from the Cannes festival. She would travel by ship from Europe to New York, then fly to Los Angeles.

Mike Todd and Evelyn Keyes came to visit me and stayed as my house guests. After they arrived, Mike was suddenly called overnight to Las Vegas on business, leaving Evelyn and me alone in the house. After dinner, we went to our separate bedrooms. I don't know what went on in her head that night, but it was a rough night for me. I locked my door. Not to lock her out, but to lock me in. Mike Todd trusted me, and I was not going to sleep with his girl. That much of a shit I am not.

One night around eleven o'clock, my doorbell rang. Pier. Pier, who could never go anywhere without her mother's permission, had driven up to my house all by herself. She wanted to see me. The game she was playing was clear to me. I said no, it was too late, we could talk some other time. She was devastated. She couldn't accept the fact that it was over, couldn't believe that she could be rejected. That was part of her sickness. I closed the door on Pier. In 1971, at the age of thirty-nine, Pier closed the door on herself, permanently, with pills, another casualty of Hollywood.

Anne arrived, beautifully dressed as usual, but with a veil over her face. She looked mysterious, intriguing. I lifted it up to kiss her, saw four dark spots of raw skin beginning to crust over. "My God! What happened?"

"I'd rather not talk about it."

I was curious, but I didn't push it. I was just glad that she was safe with me, although she had reserved a room at the Bel Air Hotel.

The next day, we drove into Beverly Hills for lunch. Anne was looking out the window, absorbing the view.

"Do you like it here?" I asked.

"Yes. But who's this man, Walking, that everyone is against?"

"What do you mean?" I asked, perplexed.

"Look!" She pointed to an intersection. " 'No Jay Walking.' "

Gee, I realized, she's really a foreigner.

I gave a cocktail party to introduce Anne to my friends. The house looked wonderful, but the walls were bare. Anne had run an art gallery in Paris after the war and knew a great deal about art. She and Fran Stark went to a gallery and talked the owner into loaning them some paintings to hang in the house. The day of the party, the house was hung with beautiful paintings—a man on a horse with a rooster by Chagall; some Vlaminck flowers. I liked the Chagall so much I bought it. That was the beginning of my art collection, the first piece I had bought since Aristide Bruant graced the house on Vado Place.

Among the guests at the party was Joe Drown, Anne's friend who had visited her in Cannes. He was about six feet tall, good-looking, and drunk when he arrived. I was reclining on the floor, a usual position for me, my left arm in front of me. He walked by and STOMPED on my hand with all his weight. I grabbed it and jumped up, afraid it was broken. I wanted to smash him with my right. But I didn't. I said to Anne later, "About your goddamn boyfriends . . . " I guess he was still madly in love with her.

Anne was set to do a picture starring Marlene Dietrich, and was booked on a flight back to Paris. My next picture, *The Racers*, was going to be shot in the United States. Working on different continents, we probably wouldn't see each other for a while. Although nothing was said, I knew that if she went back, I would lose her. I didn't want to lose her.

It was a Thursday. She was in the bedroom. I walked in, all eloquence. "Uh, I have to talk to you."

She sat in a little boudoir chair. "O.K."

I sat in a chair in the other corner, continued my flowery speech. "Uh, uh, I have to talk to you." I already said that. I better say something else. "Uh, I think we should get married." I was on my knees. Anne joined me.

She was stunned. She had thought I was going to say, "My kids are arriving, I think you'd better leave." She was prepared to be mortified.

I suggested we get married on Sunday, my day off. Anne said, "What's wrong with Saturday?" So Anne, Sam and Bea Norton, and Warren and Ronnie Cowan, picked me up on Saturday afternoon, May 29, when I got through work at Disney, and we flew to Las Vegas. We went straight to the License Bureau, open twenty-three hours a day. It closed just as we got up to the window. We went to the Golden Nugget and shot craps. An hour later, Anne, very nervous, said, "Come on, let's go." We got the license, and then went to our suite at the Sahara Hotel. The Justice of the Peace was waiting for us—Honest John Lytell, a good ol' boy from Texas, with a drawl as wide as the state. "Ah'm runnin' fo' sheriff. Sure hope Ah git y'alls votes."

Anne, who spoke perfect English in France, seemed to have developed an accent in the United States. She repeated the vows after Honest John: "Ah, Anne, take thee, Kirk, fo' mah lawfulwedhusbin." She said, "I, Anne, take thee, Kirk, for my *awful* wedded husband." She thought he meant "aweful," as in "full of awe." Everybody laughed, Anne blushed and looked more beautiful than ever, and we were married.

We flew back to Los Angeles after breakfast the next morning. I had to be at work the next day. We'd had our honeymoon in Klosters.

That evening, Mr. and Mrs. Douglas cuddled up together in their little house on San Ysidro Drive. I kissed the faint scars on Anne's face. She told me what had happened.

"I was in Paris, taking care of a lot of last-minute things so that I could come to see you. Ramon Babbas said, 'I think you should take a ship. Sail to New York, then fly to Los Angeles. That would give you a few extra days just to relax.' He offered to treat me to the difference between the boat ticket and the airfare. I thought that was a considerate, generous thing to do, and was glad that we had stayed friends. I took the boat, was going to stay overnight at the Sherry Netherland Hotel in New York before flying out the next day. I was very surprised to find Babbas waiting for me at the hotel. He had flown to New York. He suddenly realized how serious I was about you. He always figured the whole thing would peter out, and then I'd come back to him and everything would be fine. Except that here I was, going to California. And if I went, I might not come back.

"We had dinner, then went up to his suite to talk. He was very agitated, chain-smoking, and drinking. He begged me not to see you. I said, very calmly, 'I appreciate everything you've done for me. But I want to get married again, and I'd like to marry Kirk. But if it doesn't work, I'll come back to you.' He turned insanely jealous. He forbade me to see you. I told him, 'This is my last try. I have to find out if Kirk wants me.'

"He said, 'I'll make sure he doesn't want you!' He stuck his burning cigarette into my face, fast, right through the skin, four times, until I bled. He ran to the window, screaming, 'I'LL KILL MYSELF IF YOU LEAVE ME!' He started to climb out on the ledge. We were on the eighteenth floor. I grabbed him. Bleeding from my face, in shock, I wrestled with him, got him back inside the room. He collapsed."

"You should have let him jump." She didn't seem to hear me.

"I closed the window and locked it. Then I called the manager of his New York office. 'You have to come. You have to come right now.' He came with a doctor. They gave Ramon a shot, helped me. I left the next day, wearing a veil."

What a terrifying experience for Anne. I was glad it was all over and that the marks on her face were almost gone.

Anne and I were married. But it didn't sink in. I had to tell myself, "I'm divorced from Diana. I have two children from that marriage. Now I'm married for the second time, and I don't know what's going to happen." I didn't allow myself to think about that. I got wrapped up in my work. I didn't permit myself the luxury of reflecting, looking directly at Anne, my new wife, and saying, "She is my wife and I am her husband." The ring felt strange on my finger for a few months. Then, like Anne, it was a part of my life.

When things get too complicated, I tinge the realities of life with make-believe, dull the line between what is real, what is fantasy. It's a protective measure, letting a little bit of the unreality of my profession creep into the reality of my life. It softens the focus. The characters I play in a movie are much clearer to me and I know them much better than I know myself, or people who are close to me. It's as if I don't want to look at anything too clearly. Part of the reason I'm writing this book is to force myself to look more clearly, to sharpen the focus.

But isn't it true that actors become actors partly to escape reality, to be grown-ups who still play childish games? Acting allows you to spend time lying in bed at night thinking about make-believe people, always so much easier to deal with than real ones. It allows you to escape from the realities of life. Sometimes life becomes too harsh. Sometimes personal relationships become too overpowering. Then you can get lost. When you play tennis, you miss the ball because you're seeing things in your peripheral vision, and not concentrating. Writing this book is a way for me to get on the ball. Anne has always helped me to get on the ball, stay focused.

After *20,000 Leagues Under the Sea,* I had commitments for two more pictures with studios, then I was going to start my own production company.

Twenty

THE BRYNA COMPANY

Before I could start my own company, I had to get some things out of the way. One was the Russians. They did a radio broadcast: "Kirk Douglas, the American actor, is making a film called *Ulysses*, based on *The Odyssey* by Homer. Mr. Douglas was so impressed with the script that he asked if Mr. Homer had written any other scripts." In Russia, every child knew who Homer was, while this idiot actor, Kirk Douglas, a product of American education, did not.

They picked on the wrong guy. I rebutted over the radio, in Russian, phonetically. I hired coaches, studied Russian for weeks, then made my broadcast. I told the Russian people about my parents, illiterate Russians; about my education in a country that gave you a chance to work your way through college—America. I told them the *truth*.

The other piece of business was also exploitation of me, but closer to home. "Uncle Walt" Disney invited Michael and Joel and me to his house. He was a bug on trains. He had a toy train that went all around his property on real tracks and bridges, operated by a regular engineer. We spent one

Saturday afternoon riding around. My kids enjoyed it, I enjoyed it. We had a pleasant few hours there, thanked Uncle Walt, and left.

A few weeks later, I was surprised to see film of my two kids and me on Walt Disney's TV show. He hosted a regular program, which was basically an hour of commercials for his projects. He spent an entire program on the making of *20,000 Leagues Under the Sea*. Then he had film of "Kirk Douglas and his sons Michael and Joel riding toy trains all around my home." I was shocked at Disney's audacity in exploiting my children. He had never mentioned it to me; never asked my permission. I wrote him a letter saying that I would prefer that he never use film of my kids and me on a commercial program. I received a letter of apology.

Two months later, he broadcast the shots again. I was furious. I talked to my lawyer, Sam Norton. He advised me to sue. We instituted a suit against Walt Disney. If I won, I would give the money to charity; this suit was on principle. My deposition was taken. Uncle Walt came down, calmly; his deposition was taken. We were all set to go to trial. Then I thought, What am I doing? There are some people in our profession—Bob Hope, Walt Disney—who can do no wrong. Most people think that Walt did things for children out of the goodness of his heart, that he wasn't making millions of dollars on them. Over Sam's objections, I decided to drop the suit. Anne agreed with me. I doubt if I could have gotten anywhere with it. You can't sue God.

I also had two pictures to get out of the way. Darryl Zanuck wanted to make a deal with me to do three pictures at Twentieth Century–Fox, which I declined. But he did talk me into doing one picture for him, *The Racers*.

Bad decision. The main purpose of *The Racers* was to make a star out of Darryl Zanuck's mistress, a Polish-French girl named Bayla Wegier. Zanuck had changed her name to Bella Darvi—"Dar" for Darryl, "Vi" for Virginia, Zanuck's wife. This, and the fact that he was so open about his relationship with Bella, led to much speculation in Hollywood.

All I know is that Bella was a nice gal, but certainly not an actress. She eventually went back to France, got fat, gambled compulsively, and committed suicide. A sad example of the Andy Warhol syndrome—everybody in the world can be famous for fifteen minutes. Bella Darvi was famous for a little longer than fifteen minutes, but in the great scheme of things, not much longer. Very sad.

And it is sad that the Twentieth Century–Fox backlot where we filmed *The Racers* is gone now. Once so far west of Hollywood that people thought of it as out in the country, it turned into some of the most prime real estate in the world —Century City between Beverly Hills and Westwood, with skyscrapers over forty stories high, shopping malls, movie and legitimate theaters, and the Century Plaza Hotel, where fund-raising dinners for President Reagan are held. It's ironic—when the President comes to Los Angeles on business, he's back home on the Fox lot.

After *The Racers*, I went to Universal to do *Man Without a Star*, a simple, fun, commercial western, written by Borden Chase and D. D. Beauchamp, good writers. I was looking around for a good director. Ray Stark pleaded with me to give his client King Vidor a chance. Vidor, a famous director in the old days, in Hollywood since 1915, hadn't done anything for quite some time. I was reluctant to let him direct it, because he had done so many big important pictures in the past—*The Big Parade, The Champ, Duel in the Sun.* We were making a little film on a tight schedule and a tight budget. Ray Stark assured me that Vidor could do it. I took the chance.

I got the feeling that for Vidor, directing *Man Without a Star* was slumming. He always arrived a little late. I'd be there waiting. I was the producer, as well as the star of the picture. It was my gamble to make the picture. I had to keep pushing him. "Look, King, this is a little picture. We've got to get going." He'd be telling me about the good old days, and I'd be saying, "Can we get on with it?"

I had some difficult physical scenes: a beating from a gang

of bad guys led by Richard Boone; a fight against barbed wire; lots of riding. In my favorite scene, I twirled a gun: flipped it in the air, from side to side, behind my back, and fired it. This was basically juggling, with some additions. We filmed it in one take, no cuts, so you could see that there was no magic, no special effects, to it. You get to do gun-twirling the same way you get to Carnegie Hall—practice. We pushed through, and it turned out to be a very exciting little picture which did very well, and which helped Vidor. The next picture he directed was more his style—*War and Peace*.

Man Without a Star was a new concept in film financing: the fifty-fifty picture. The star got no salary, but, when the studio recouped all its expenses, shared the profits, fifty-fifty. Sounded great. Was great—for the studio. I made a little money. Universal made a *lot*. They controlled the bookkeeping and the distribution.

Recently, I picked up the *Los Angeles Times* and saw that *Ruthless People*, starring Bette Midler and Danny DeVito, has grossed $90 million worldwide. The picture cost $17 million. But the way Disney figures it, with distribution fees, prints, advertising, etc. the picture is actually $11 million in the red. Not much has changed: as the song says, the studio gets the gold mine, you get the shaft.

In *Ishtar*, the participants were smarter—Warren Beatty took $5.5 million up front; Dustin Hoffman did the same. Poor Elaine May—she only took a million and a half up front. Almost $13 million in fees before the picture started. The picture was a flop. So what? Their money was in the bank. That's the way to do it!

Anne and I were still living in the house up on San Ysidro. In the first stages of our marriage, Anne was uncertain. It's quite an adjustment to be married to a movie star, a man who goes off to work to make love to beautiful women. And his wife is home, pregnant, vulnerable. Anne was pleasantly shocked at being pregnant for the first time in her life. I was all for it; I felt this would give her security, a feeling of permanence in our marriage. We were both looking forward to having this child.

My father, a horse trader in Russia, became a ragman, buying old rags, pieces of metal, and junk for pennies, nickels, and dimes. And I, Issur Danielovitch, was the ragman's son.

1

My mother, Bryna Sanglel, from a family of Ukrainian farmers, wanted all her children to be born in this wonderful new land, where she thought the streets were paved with gold—literally.

2

I acted in the high school plays, and in my junior year, I won the Sanford Prize Speaking Contest with a very dramatic recitation about a dying soldier. It was called "Across the Border." They gave me a gold medal.

3

4

Ma was proud as they called off my name for Best Acting Prize and Best Speech at Commencement. I also won a prize for my essay, "The Play's the Thing," in which I wrote: "Art can only be obtained through hunger—hunger for beauty or harmony or truth or justice." Idealistic, but I still believe it.

5

Wally Thompson, six feet four, Indian-looking, was a friend of mine at college. When I left for New York City, he gave me his overcoat, which was much too long for me.

I felt a desperate need to express myself physically. So even though I had a rough schedule and worked to support myself, I went out for one of the major sports—wrestling.

For the first time in its history, a student not connected with any fraternity was elected president of the student body at St. Lawrence University. And he was Jewish. I was the BMOC.

Charles Jehlinger, the great director, the great teacher of acting at the American Academy of Dramatic Arts, who had taught Spencer Tracy, Katharine Hepburn, and Sam Levene. Everyone was intimidated by him.

8

I was graduated from the American Academy of Dramatic Arts in June of 1941. But no agents seemed to see any quality in me.

9

The Three Sisters
*opened at the Ethel
Barrymore Theatre on
December 21, 1942. One
of the pictures in* Time
*magazine was of me in
the center with a
samovar, in my white
tunic, looking very
important surrounded by
Katharine Cornell and
Judith Anderson and
Ruth Gordon and all the
others.*

*The Army turned out
new officers in three
months—"Ninety Day
Wonders." The Navy
took 120 days, and
nobody called us
wonders.*

*I happened to see the cover of
Life magazine. "Hey, I know
that girl!" I said. There,
wearing a checked blouse and
carrying a parasol, was Diana
Dill. We were married
November 2, 1943, by the Navy
chaplain.*

12

13

DOUGLAS, KIRK
S. S. No. 118-03-7480

LExington 2-1100
TELEPHONE EXCHANGE

224 West 11th Street, New York City

KIRK DOUGLAS

DIALECTS: Western, Southern, Tough, German, Russian.

RADIO: Molle Mystery Theatre, My Best Girls, Bright
Horizon, We, The People, Silver Theatre.

Leads, Character, Straight,
Comedy, Heavy.

STAGE: Broadway: Spring Again, Katherine Cornell's
Three Sisters.

Age	27
Height	5'11"
Weight	163
Hair	Blonde
Eyes	Green
Voice Range	20-45

CURRENT SHOWS: Broadway: Lenny Archer in "Kiss
And Tell." Radio: Kenzie Bates in Bright Horizon.

B/44

*My picture and résumé for
Broadway auditions. I finally
landed a part with Mercedes
McCambridge in* Man Bites Dog.

14

15

I went out occasionally with Betty Bacall, who later became Lauren Bacall. I was a senior and had been in summer stock, so Betty looked up to me, and I think had kind of a schoolgirl crush. Now she was in Hollywood to be in To Have and Have Not.

16

Without my knowledge, Lauren Bacall had been doing kind deeds for me. She had told Hal Wallis about me, and he had called me about doing a role in The Strange Love of Martha Ivers, a movie he was producing, starring Barbara Stanwyck.

17

Everyone had told me how nice Barbara Stanwyck was, but she was indifferent to me. I was young, scared, trying to look older than I was.

18

Out of the Past was a picture I did on loan-out for RKO with Robert Mitchum. I don't remember much about him, except that his stories about being a hobo kept changing every time he told them.

19

I went back to work for
Hal Wallis in I Walk
Alone, *co-starring
Wendell Corey and
another young actor,
Burt Lancaster. Burt and
I got along just as we do
now: we argued, we
fought, we talked, we
made up.*

20

*After Joel, our second
son, was born—Michael
was our first—things
started to get more
difficult between Diana
and me.*

21

Joe Mankiewicz, the director of
A Letter to Three Wives, *had a
great sense of humor. The three
wives were Jeanne Crain, Linda
Darnell, and Ann Sothern. Linda
looked like a Mata Hari, but was
really just a charming girl from
Dallas bewildered by
Hollywood. She rose fast and
faded faster. Ann Sothern
played my wife. We rehearsed
the relationship offstage.*

22

23

Midge Kelly in Champion *was probably one of the first antiheroes.* 24
My co-star was Marilyn Maxwell, who later sang with Bob Hope
for many years. Champion *was a success, a surprise hit.*

I was shocked to find I was taller than Pa. He had always seemed such a huge man.

In 1910, 1912, and 1914, my sisters Pesha, Kaleh, and Tamara were born. Then me, Issur, in 1916. Then three more girls: the twins Hashka and Siffra in 1918, and finally Rachel in 1924, when my mother was forty.

Irene Wrightsman had the look of a little girl playing grown-up. When she spoke, I saw that she had a slight overbite and I was gone.

I had misgivings about doing Detective Story *at first. I did it anyway.* 27

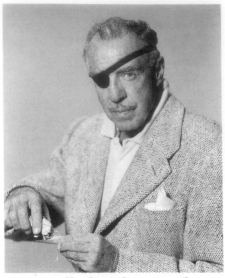

I enjoyed working with Billy Wilder on Ace in the Hole. *He's a brilliant director and a great raconteur.*

Critics talk about how Raoul Walsh movies have such great pace. They have great pace because he was always in a hurry to finish them. Along the Great Divide *was my first western. It was awful. I hated the whole picture, but I learned.*

29

30

31

Sometimes Marlene Dietrich would come over, cook soup, cuddle me. Affectionate sex. Marlene is an unusual person. She seemed to love you much more if you were not well. When you became strong and healthy she loved you less.

I was offered a part that Clark Gable had turned down.

32

33

Vincente Minnelli was directing, John Houseman was producing The Bad and the Beautiful *for MGM. I was the "bad" movie mogul.*

34

When they announced that Lana Turner was the "beautiful," the papers were filled with "When these two get together." But she was going with Fernando Lamas, who was terribly jealous. Nothing happened.

I played the part of a trapeze artist in one segment of The Story of
Three Loves. *My co-star was Pier Angeli, a nineteen-year-old
Italian girl who looked much younger. Our romance started thirty
feet above the earth.*

36

I liked Anne Buydens very much.
But I was engaged to Pier Angeli.
I married Anne on May 29, 1954.

37

I had wanted to go on a junket
to New York with Mike Todd;
Anne didn't want me to go. She
didn't object to my taking the
trip, but to my flying in Mike's
private plane. I don't know what
made Anne fight so hard, but she
saved my life.

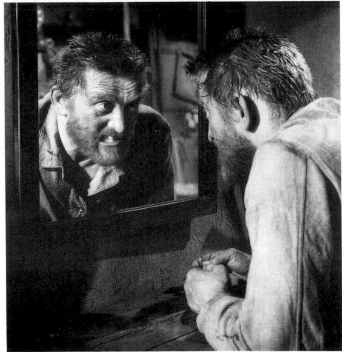

The next picture I wanted the Bryna Company to produce and me to star in was Lust for Life, *Irving Stone's 1934 bestseller about Vincent Van Gogh. Making* Lust for Life *was a wonderful but very painful experience for me. Not only did I look like Van Gogh, I was the same age he was when he committed suicide.*

40

41

During Lust for Life
*our baby was born.
We called him Peter.
Peter's middle name:
Vincent. Yes, as in
Van Gogh.*

*Academy Awards
time rolled around.
I was nominated for*
Lust for Life, *my
third nomination. I
won the New York
Film Critics Award
instead. Ingrid
Bergman won both
for* Anastasia.

42

I was intrigued by a small picture called The Killing *and wanted to meet the director, Stanley Kubrick. He said he had a script called* Paths of Glory. *It was a truly great film with a truly great theme: the insanity and brutality of war.*

We planned to shoot The Vikings *mostly on location in Norway.*

Burt Lancaster wanted to do a commercial picture with me. I said, "Why not do something classy?" The Devil's Disciple *could have been much better. But it was a noble attempt. And Larry Olivier was so brilliant he stole the picture completely.*

45

44

46

I now had four children. That was enough. I had fulfilled my biological destiny.

While Burt and I were in London we were asked to participate in the Motion Picture Relief Fund charity gala, The Night of a Thousand Stars, *at the Palladium. We did a song-and-dance routine.*

THE ELECTRIFYING
SPECTACLE THAT
THRILLED THE
WORLD!

KIRK DOUGLAS · LAURENCE OLIVIER
JEAN SIMMONS · CHARLES LAUGHTON
PETER USTINOV · JOHN GAVIN
AND TONY CURTIS
AS ANTONINUS

SPARTACUS

TECHNICOLOR®
PANAVISION®

DIRECTED BY
STANLEY KUBRICK

MUSIC COMPOSED
AND CONDUCTED BY
ALEX NORTH

SCREENPLAY BY
DALTON TRUMBO

PRODUCED BY
EDWARD LEWIS

EXECUTIVE PRODUCER
KIRK DOUGLAS

A BRYNA PRODUCTION · A UNIVERSAL RELEASE

Original soundtrack album
available only on DECCA records!

After The Vikings, *I swore I would never do another epic period picture. But big pictures and big money-makers were what Hollywood was turning out in the 1950s.*

On the set of Spartacus *with director Kubrick and Tony Curtis. In the end I kill Tony. We figured this was simple justice, since he had killed me in* The Vikings.

47

48

Dalton Trumbo, one of the Unfriendly Ten. Dalton had to hide while he was writing, using an alias. When he was working on Spartacus, for the first time in ten years he walked onto a studio lot. He said, "Thanks, Kirk, for giving me back my name." The blacklist was broken.

49

50

Lonely Are the Brave *is my favorite movie. The cast was perfect. Gena Rowlands plays the woman I'm in love with, and she was superb.*

51

52

*I was on my way
home—Broadway. We
got a great cast—
Gene Wilder as the
innocent Billy Bibbit.
I loved the role of
Randle P. McMurphy.
The audience was
spellbound. The
reviews were
murderous.*

53

54

I first met John Kennedy at a party in the mid-1950s. John and Jacqueline were so beautiful, the two of them. The prince and princess.

President Kennedy encouraged me to visit foreign countries to talk about the United States. In twenty-five years I've made trips to dozens of countries for Democratic and Republican administrations, paying my own way.

55

It pleased me that when my son Michael did his first TV series, "The Streets of San Francisco," he worked with Karl. And Michael admits he learned an awful lot working with Karl Malden. 56

The head of the Motion Picture Actors Association asked Anne and me to throw a cocktail party for Baragavoi, the famous Russian cosmonaut, when he made a visit to the United States with the civilian scientist Feotisoff. 57

58

*I loved working with Kazan
on* The Arrangement. *He
loved actors, would do
anything to seduce them
into giving the best possible
performance.*

*Coming to grips with what
it means to be a Jew has
been a theme of my life.*

We shot The War Wagon *in
Durango, Mexico, where
Wayne owned a lot of land.
We were always trying to
one-up each other.*

59

60

The Villain *was a sort of cartoon, like the Road Runner. My character was like the Coyote. I thought that if it was well done it could be very funny.*

I thought I ought to try my hand at directing. I directed two films. Both unsuccessful. The first was Scalawag. We went to Italy to set up the deal. Anne and Eric and Peter were there. Peter, sixteen, was going to be the still photographer. He insisted that he bring his dog, Shaft, a six-month-old black Labrador retriever. I played the leading role, with one leg. It was the most effective thing about the movie.

63

On January 16, 1981, President Carter put the Medal of Freedom around my neck in a ceremony at the White House.

64

I went out to meet with some refugees up near the Khyber Pass. I sat on the ground with elders of an Afghan tribe. We were all eating with our fingers out of a common bowl. It was Thanksgiving Day.

65

To my friend Kirk,

Best Wish

In 1980 I flew in the first private jet from Jerusalem to Cairo, met with Egypt's President Anwar Sadat. We talked for three hours on the banks of the Suez at Ismailia.

When Ronald Reagan ran for President, I couldn't believe it. You just don't think that somebody you've known as an actor is going to become President of the United States. I resent the criticisms that are made of Nancy. My wife helps me in all situations. Here we are when I received the Legion of Honor in France.

Amos is a character in 68
his eighties who ends
up in a nursing home. 69
Grant Tinker said that
"Amos" changed the
networks' thinking
about movies.

At my expense my staff and I flew to
Washington, D.C., and I testified before
Congressman Claude Pepper's Select
Committee on nursing homes.

Burt and I teamed up again as presenters at the 1985 Academy 70
Awards. In the audience were two young writers, James Orr and
James Cruikshank. They were struck by the same thought: "I'd like
to see these two in a movie again." So they wrote one—Tough
Guys.

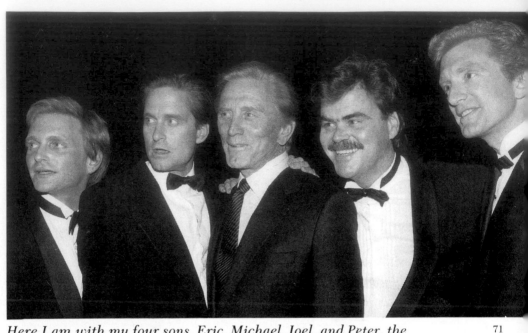

Here I am with my four sons, Eric, Michael, Joel, and Peter, the 71
night I was honored by the American Academy of Dramatic Arts.

In the garden I have a collection of statues made out of scrap
metal. Fitting for the son of a junkman. There's a bronze horse
with legs folded up. I named him Bill, after my father's horse.
Anne took this picture. 72

And I was about to produce my first movie on my own.

I named my production company the Bryna Company after my mother. I had visions of ads with her picture in the middle, oval, like an old-fashioned cameo, a serene picture of my mother, the way she used to look when she sat on the porch on the Sabbath. It tickled me to name a moving picture company after my immigrant mother, who had never had the advantages of an education, even when she came here. With seven kids, she had no time for night school. Her son gets an education, forms his own company—Bryna. When I told Ma, she sent me the longest note she ever wrote. How she must have labored over it: "God bless you, my son. Mother." I still have it.

I had no ambitions to become a tycoon in the motion picture industry. I wasn't even aware that I was one of the first actors to form his own production company. My purpose was to participate more in the creative process of making films. I would have preferred to be handed a beautifully written script, with a role I wanted to play, and a director I liked to work with. But I couldn't just wait around for it to happen. I had to *make* it happen.

Producers, and sometimes directors, get angry at me because I insist on being heard. I don't object if they don't accept my suggestions. All I ask is that they listen to me, then accept or reject what I've said. Of course, they have the last word. Forming my own company gave *me* the last word.

It was a gamble. I have never been a big gambler. When I go to Las Vegas, I enjoy gambling, but in very limited amounts. I'm much more reckless in my own profession. I gamble with my own money—buy a book, develop the property, pay the writer, and take my chances. Of course, I never made a move without Sam Norton, my best friend, lawyer, and adviser. I paid all his expenses, and he got 10 percent of everything I made in any field—investments, movies, anything. I counted on him. Like most actors, I was anxious to shove whatever money I was making into someone else's hands—"Please, take care of it. I don't want to think about it. Let me think about making a movie!"

The first movie my company made was *The Indian Fighter*, written by Frank Davis and Ben Hecht, based on a story by Ben Kadish, with André de Toth directing. There was a good part in it for Diana, my ex-wife. I asked Anne if she would mind. I don't know exactly how it happened, but somehow pregnant Anne ended up in Los Angeles baby-sitting Michael and Joel while Diana and I were up in Bend, Oregon, making a movie. I thought this was amazingly broad-minded on the part of my wife. Later, Michael and Joel came up to Oregon. They played a couple of parts in the movie, small bits that ended up on the cutting-room floor.

Walter Matthau, a successful actor on Broadway, played a villain in *Indian Fighter*. He had just made his screen debut in *The Kentuckian*, doing an excellent job under Burt Lancaster's skillful direction. Walter is a wonderful actor, but he was not yet used to working in a movie, where you do things in bits and pieces. He would stammer before he made a speech. I told him he had to stop doing it, because we would never be able to cut the picture together.

He got mad at me. "Don't you want me to think? You want me to just say the lines?"

I said, "Yeah. Just say the lines."

"All right. I'll just say the lines."

Usually, telling an actor to just say the lines gives him nothing to work with. But I knew that Walter was such a good actor, he would be fine. He did eliminate those introductory sounds, and he was excellent, as he is in everything.

I did most of my own riding in *Indian Fighter*, but occasionally, for long rides, or snatching something up from the ground, I used a stuntman. Bill Williams was an excellent rider, and in silhouette looked a lot like me. But he was not a very good stuntman. Anybody can do a stunt and get hurt; a stuntman is supposed to do it and not get hurt. Bill got hurt several times. I said, "Bill, you shouldn't be a stuntman. You should stick just to riding horses." He didn't listen to me; he was trying to make a living. Stunts are paid commensurate with the danger involved. The more stunts a stuntman does, the more money he makes. So, he kept doing stunts, and kept getting hurt. A few years after that, he was working on a western with Burt Lancaster, *The Hallelujah Trail*, and did a comparatively easy stunt. Two men ride a horse-drawn wagon toward a cliff. Horses separate, men jump off, wagon goes over the cliff. It's done often, not considered very difficult. Bill's wife was visiting the set, taking motion pictures of him at work. She was filming, looking through the camera, when Bill did the stunt. But Bill didn't jump clear. He went right over the cliff with the wagon and was killed.

It's always terrible when things like that happen. And they do. What's amazing is that there aren't more tragedies. Because directors, as well as actors, get carried away.

People think of me as a guy with a nose for danger. I smell that something might happen. But that nose doesn't always work—I broke it doing a stunt on *Indian Fighter*, a horse fall. To make a horse fall, you yank his head around by the reins. You're supposed to lean back in the saddle. I leaned forward. The horse's heavy head swung around and bashed me in the face. The horse fell, and was fine. I broke my nose. I've also broken a rib and a finger. But after seventy-five pictures, that is minor.

I was very pleased with the cast we assembled for *Indian Fighter*, except for the lead of the Indian girl. We thought it would be easy to get somebody who fit the part. It was impossible. Every girl we auditioned seemed to be just some little starlet with a feather stuck on her head.

Then one day, Anne was looking through *Vogue* magazine. There was a shot of an Italian girl—long dark hair, dark eyes —coming up out of the water soaking wet, a man's shirt clinging to her voluptuous body. Anne said, "This girl would make a fantastic Indian." She did look terrific. We tracked her down—a model named Elsa Martinelli. She was in New York, just arrived from Rome. And she was going with Oleg Cassini. I had to laugh at the way Oleg kept popping in and out of my life. When I met Gene Tierney, she was just being divorced from Oleg. When I met Irene Wrightsman in Palm

Springs, she was with Oleg. Now, I try to get Elsa Martinelli, and here's Oleg.

So I talked to Oleg. He said, "She hardly speaks any English, and that with a terrible Italian accent." I looked at her picture. She looked like a beautiful Indian girl to me. Besides, how does an Indian girl talk? Precisely what is an Indian accent, and how many people have ever heard a real one? And how bad could Elsa's accent be? I called her in New York, and told her who I was.

"No, no beeleeva you, no beeleeva you." She had just come back from seeing *20,000 Leagues Under the Sea,* and thought somebody was playing a joke on her.

I said, "Really, I *am* Kirk Douglas, and I want you to come out and test for a part in a movie I'm making."

"No, no. You no Keerka Doogalas."

I didn't know what the hell to do.

Then she had an idea. "You Keerka Doogalas, you singa da song inna da movie."

Over the telephone, I had to audition for Elsa Martinelli, three thousand miles away. I started to sing. " 'Gotta whale of a tale to tell you, lads.' "

Elsa started to shriek. *"Dio mio!* Keerka Doogalas! Keerka Doogalas!"

I arranged for her to come out to California to test. She was gorgeous and had a wonderful gamine quality that was perfect for the part. She had the potential to become a big star. I put her under contract to Bryna for several pictures. We gave her only about a page and a half of dialogue, never more than a couple of words at a time. She was a big hit in the picture, got a lot of publicity, including the cover of *Life* magazine.

People were after her. She was getting movie offers, became very impatient at the chance to make more money than I was paying her. I kept saying, "Elsa, if you are patient, I will make you a big star." I wanted her to play the female lead in a book I had just bought—*Spartacus.* But it was a big project, and would take time to set up. Elsa kept hounding me, saying I was holding her down because I had her under contract. Finally I thought, the hell with it. I said, "I don't make my money by putting people under contract. You're too much trouble. Here! You're free!" I tore up the contract.

After that, she did some bad pictures that went nowhere and did her no good. She was very unhappy, and realized that maybe I could help her with her career. She wanted to come back and be under contract to me.

I said, "O.K., Elsa, how much money are you going to pay me?"

"Whadda you mean?"

"How much money will you pay me if I put you under contract?"

She said, "No, no, no. You supposed to pay me."

"Oh no, Elsa. You're too much trouble. If you want me to put you under contract, *you* have to pay *me*."

And that was the end of my contract with Elsa Martinelli.

Before I did *The Indian Fighter* in Bend, Oregon, David Susskind sent me a play that he wanted to do on Broadway, *A Very Special Baby* by Robert Allen Aurthur.

I liked the play very much. It was about a father-son relationship. The father subconsciously hates the son, because his wife had died in childbirth. Now the son is grown up. And he has always had this strange feeling from the father. In a very dramatic scene, the son says to the father, "Let me hear you once say, 'I love you.' Even if you don't mean it, just let me hear you say it." That scene was so touching, so poignant, so much a part of me, that based on that scene alone, I guaranteed the financing of the entire play. The father was going to be portrayed by Ezio Pinza, very hot after doing *South Pacific* on Broadway. Then Pinza became ill and had to be replaced. This was not very long before he died. They got Luther Adler. I still didn't back out.

While I was making the movie, the play opened. It ran for about a week and folded. It won a prize as best American play of the year. I lost all the money I'd put into it, and I had guaranteed all the subscribers who financed it. An unusual deal. From time to time I run into one of the investors who says, "I'd love another deal like that." I joked that I didn't mind paying for the entire play. I just wish I'd had a chance to see it.

Sam Norton advised me that for tax reasons, the Bryna Company had to make movies in which I did not appear. This wasn't anything I wanted to do, and it was time-consuming. I reluctantly set up several low-budget pictures, like *Spring Reunion*, with Betty Hutton; and *Lizzie*, based on "The Bird's Nest," a story by Shirley Jackson that starred Eleanor Parker.

In one scene in *Lizzie*, I wanted a young black man to play the piano and sing. I found him in a little dive in Greenwich Village. Wonderful voice—smooth, mellow, romantic—presence and face to match. Totally new, totally unknown. I told him what we needed, asked if he had any songs that he thought would work. There were three that he was trying to get recorded. One song knocked me out. I said, "That's it. Sing it in the picture." I was such a neophyte, I didn't know anything about getting rights to music. I just paid him for singing the song in the movie; he kept all the rights to the song. The movie didn't do a nickel's worth of business, but Johnny Mathis singing "It's Not for Me to Say" is still making money.

My work on *Indian Fighter* didn't end when shooting stopped. In those days, stars were expected to appear at openings all over the country. My public relations man, Stan Margulies, and I barnstormed:

December 14	New York
December 19	Boston
December 20	Cleveland
December 21	Columbus
December 22	St. Louis
December 23	Denver
December 24, 25	Los Angeles
December 26	New Orleans
December 27	Dallas

December 28   Houston
December 29   Los Angeles

It paid off. *The Indian Fighter* did well. I was pleased. The Bryna Company was on its way.

Twenty-one

LUST FOR LIFE

The next picture I wanted the Bryna Company to produce, and me to star in, was *Lust for Life*, Irving Stone's 1934 bestseller about Vincent van Gogh. The first time I thought of doing it was when Jean Negulesco, a Rumanian director (*How to Marry a Millionaire*, *Three Coins in the Fountain*) who was also an artist, took a picture of me and drew a beard and a straw hat over it. The resemblance to Van Gogh was amazing. Negulesco was very anxious to do the picture, and so was I. I announced that my company would do a movie of *Lust for Life*.

I got a call from MGM. "Guess again. We own *Lust for Life*."

And so they did. MGM had owned it for years, had almost filmed it with Spencer Tracy in 1946. After a new script by Norman Corwin, MGM and I finally came to an agreement. The picture was produced by John Houseman, directed by Vincente Minnelli. The three of us had worked together before on *The Bad and the Beautiful*.

Making *Lust for Life* was a wonderful but painful experience for me. The wonderful part was working with Vincente Minnelli. Minnelli was high-strung and impatient with actors. But I felt like the teacher's pet. I always seemed to do the right thing; Vincente looked with pleasure on everything I did. Was it because we had worked together successfully in *The Bad and the Beautiful*? I don't know. But it was a wonderful feeling from my point of view, to have supportive looks coming from a demanding director.

The painful experience was probing into the soul of a tormented artist. Van Gogh was a prolific painter—1,600 paintings and drawings, one sold in his lifetime. But after his death . . . In 1986, *Sunflowers* sold at the Christie's auction for over $40 million, then the highest price ever paid for a painting. It was bought by the Japanese to replace the *Sunflowers* that was destroyed in the bombing of Yokohama during World War II. In 1987, Van Gogh's *Irises* topped his *Sunflowers*, selling for over $50 million.

Van Gogh was also a prolific writer, pouring his heart out to his brother Theo in letter after letter. You could read between the lines to Van Gogh's feelings, even the jealousy and betrayal that he revealed when Theo got married. I went to the cemetery and looked at the two simple gravestones— Theo and Vincent, the two brothers, side by side. Theo hadn't outlived Vincent by much. There is no doubt that Van Gogh was an extremely complex, difficult person with self-destructive impulses. But he had a great desire to give of himself. He started out wanting to be a preacher, becase he wanted to give himself to God and to humanity. What a tragic life!

We shot the movie in many of the places Van Gogh had lived and worked. It was eerie to be at the bridge that he had painted, to be at the yellow house in Arles, to be at the spots in Les Beaux. In Auvers-sur-Oise, I lay in bed in that little room above the bar (now Café Van Gogh) where he actually lived, and looked out the window and saw what he had seen: the town hall that he had painted, with all the flags just as he had painted them. We put the local peasants into period costumes. They looked like they'd walked out of Van Gogh's paintings. When I walked down the street, some of the old peasants who had known Van Gogh crossed themselves and said in shock, *"Il est retourné"* ("He's come back"). It was painful to be in the mental institution in San Rémy where Van Gogh had had himself committed, to be in the garden where he painted those swirling cypress trees that reach toward the sky like flames. I saw myself in those swirling masses of color leaping up from a fire deep within his guts. And it was horrible to be standing in the field where he painted his last painting—the crows in the wheatfield— leaning on the same tree with a gun in my hand, to hear the noise of the shot. It was the most painful film I ever made. I was almost gasping for the film to finish.

Playing Vincent van Gogh shook up my theory of what acting is all about. To me, acting is creating an illusion, showing tremendous discipline, not losing yourself in the character that you're portraying. The actor never gets lost in the character he's playing; the audience does. When you're playing the role, you try to think of the thoughts of that character. When it's over, you become yourself. You must control it.

But I was close to getting lost in the character of Van Gogh. While we were shooting, I wore heavy shoes like the ones Van Gogh wore. I always kept one untied, so that I would feel unkempt, off balance, in danger of tripping. It was loose; it gave him—and me—a shuffling gait. My wife always said that it took me a long time to get out of that character. She would hear me still walking like Van Gogh every night when I came home from shooting, and even after the picture ended.

I felt myself going over the line, into the skin of Van Gogh. Not only did I look like him, I was the same age he had been when he committed suicide. Sometimes I had to stop myself from reaching my hand up and touching my ear to find out if it was actually there. It was a frightening experience. That way lies madness. I've never said that before; these are things that I don't want to admit to myself or to think about. The memory makes me wince. I could never play him again.

For a long time after I finished the movie, I didn't see the picture. I had to get him out of my system. Maybe that was why I agreed to have my beard shaved off on the Perry Como Show; I needed a public ritual to help rid me of the character.

Marc Chagall was touched by *Lust for Life*. He sent me his autobiography, *Ma Vie*. He wanted me to play him. I am a great admirer of Chagall's works. I have four of his paintings. In my room, I am surrounded by more than twenty lithographs, Chagall's *Bible* series. I love his childlike approach—floating flowers, and animals and sensuous figures. I met Chagall in the South of France, at the Hôtel du Cap. From a distance, I watched him painting under an umbrella on the rocks close to the sea. My wife tore a picture of a Chagall painting out of the book she was reading, asked Chagall if he would autograph it to me. He took it to his room. The next day, he gave the page to me. But he had extended the little painting with flowers and floating figures. It hangs by my bed.

He invited us to his home in the mountains. He took us on a tour of the paintings on his walls. One fascinated me. It was a kitchen scene with a large, buxom woman dominating the scene. Next to her was a tiny man with a mustache. I pointed to the woman. "Who's that?"

"Ah, that," he said with pride, "is my mother."

"And this?" pointing to the little figure.

He dismissed it with, "That's my father."

I understood Chagall. But after Van Gogh, I never wanted to portray another painter.

During *Lust for Life,* our baby was born. Anne woke me up at three-thirty in the morning on November 23, 1955; she was in labor. When we reached Cedars of Lebanon Hospital and they had Anne settled in a room, the nurse handed me a pad and pencil, told me to write down the times of the pains. The contractions were about forty minutes apart when I started, then all too rapidly got closer together. I scribbled numbers down furiously. Where was that nurse? Where was the doctor? The nurse finally came in, looked at what I had written. "What is this?" she asked. I looked. The numbers didn't make any sense. "I don't know." She threw me out. In the hall, I did what I'd done twice before: pace. Just like my father in the kitchen, up and down, up and down. They wheeled Anne down the hall. The baby was breech, the cord wrapped around its neck; they were going to do a cesarean. I continued to pace. What was taking so long? We had wanted a girl, but at this point I just wanted Anne and a healthy baby. A little after 1:00 P.M., the doctor, "Red" Krohn, poked his head out the door, motioned me in. A boy, almost eight pounds. A boy with red hair like the doctor's. Hmmm. But with a very distinctive dimple in his chin. We called him Peter, the nickname Anne's father, who had always wanted a boy, had called her. Peter's middle name: Vincent. Yes, as in Van Gogh.

Van Gogh made an impression on others. There was a private screening of *Lust for Life;* quite a few members of the industry attended. We had a dinner party later at Merle Oberon's house. John Wayne was there. He kept looking at me. We had not worked together yet. He seemed upset. He had a drink in one hand, motioned to me with the other. Out on the terrace, he berated me. "Christ, Kirk! How can you play a part like that? There's so goddamn few of us left. We got to play strong, tough characters. Not those weak queers."

I tried to explain. "Hey, John, I'm an actor. I like to play interesting roles. It's all make-believe, John. It isn't real. You're not really John Wayne, you know."

He just looked at me oddly. I had betrayed him. I took it as a compliment; the picture had moved him, or at least disturbed him. I understand that—Van Gogh disturbed me, too. I own a lot of art work, but nothing by Van Gogh. Aside from the fact that I can't afford to buy his paintings now, it would be too weird—I'd feel as though I'd painted it myself.

Twenty-two

GUNFIGHT AT THE O.K. CORRAL

It was a relief to get into my next picture, *Gunfight at the O.K. Corral,* and play Doc Holliday, who was merely a consumptive, a former dentist whose practice had vanished when his illness manifested itself. Hal Wallis had bought a story outline from ex-newspaperman Stuart Lake, a friend of Wyatt Earp's, and his biographer. I read the script. I didn't think it was brilliant, but it could be an interesting relationship between two men. And Wallis, who had dropped me years ago because I would not sign a term contract, was now offering me ten times the salary he would have been paying me if he still had me under contract. I said I would play Doc Holliday (Wallis had been trying to get Bogart) if Burt Lancaster would play Wyatt Earp. Burt was still under contract to Wallis, with one more picture to go. I think that Burt had no particular desire to play Wyatt Earp, but with me playing Doc Holliday and the picture finishing off his contract with Wallis, that was all the inducement he needed. So he agreed to play Wyatt Earp, the lawman, and I played Doc Holliday, the gunslinger with thirty notches on his belt.

They had considered staging the shoot-out in the real O.K. Corral, right where it had occurred, but it was small and we would have been cramped for angles. The real gunfight, on October 29, 1881, was smaller than ours, and duller: thirty seconds, thirty-four shots, three men dead. In our version, the shoot-out took four days to film and lasted five minutes.

I had to cough a lot in *Gunfight at the O.K. Corral*, and I had to choreograph every cough. Since movies are not shot in sequence, I had to plan where I was going to cough, how lightly or deeply, and where I was really going to have an attack. In some scenes, I didn't cough at all. Nothing would be more annoying than to be coughing in every scene. A movie is not real. You create the illusion you want to create. My worst coughing, the coughing that nearly kills Doc Holliday, was just before the shoot-out. I have a full-blown attack just as I'm about to beat up my hooker girlfriend, played by Jo Van Fleet, who had just won a Best Supporting Actress Academy Award for *East of Eden*.

Jo wanted to be pumped up before she went on to do a scene. She asked me to slap her.

I said, "What?"

"Slap me."

"You sure?"

"Yeah, yeah. Go on. Hit me."

"O.K." I whacked her.

She went on and played the scene. They did the scene over and over, never quite right. Every time, she came to me and asked me to hit her. And hit her harder.

I told Burt what was happening. He couldn't believe it. I said, "Burt, come over and watch what happens." So, again, she got ready to play the scene, and asked me to hit her really hard. I said, "You really want me to?" And I hauled off and whacked her. Her head spun. Burt stood there with his jaw dropping, watching this sadomasochistic ritual. She shook her head, went and played the scene. Actors are willing to do anything that will help them get a good performance. They're almost willing to sell their souls. If Jo felt that getting slapped charged up her energies . . . Well, she got the performance. It was a take.

My friendship with Burt really started on *Gunfight at the O.K. Corral,* although we had made *I Walk Alone* ten years earlier. After the day's shooting in Tucson, and dinner at the hotel, we would just sit around and talk. Almost every night, we talked for hours. Sometimes it would be one-thirty or two in the morning before we said, "Hey, we'd better get to bed. We've got to get up and shoot tomorrow." After about a week of this, Hal Wallis came up to me. Hal was a rather taciturn, lonely fellow. Very perplexed, he asked, "What is it that you and Burt talk about night after night?" How sad that Hal Wallis, a great selector of talent, a man who knew people so well that he could pick stars, including Burt and me, had no friends with whom he could hold lengthy conversations after dinner. He didn't know that between friends, the well of conversation never runs dry. You get too tired to talk, maybe, or you don't have the time. But to Hal, the camaraderie between Burt and me was one of the mysteries of the universe.

I admired the wonderful relationship Burt had with little Nick Cravat, his acrobatic partner in the circus, and then in *The Flame and the Arrow* and *The Crimson Pirate*. Nick was a strange, very proud fellow. Burt said to me once, "Kirk, why don't you put Nick in your next movie?" I said, "Sure." He said, "Handle him gently."

I had Nick come over to the office, had a nice talk with him, then said, "Nick, I'd love you to be in my next picture. There's a good part for you." He burst out, "Go fuck yourself! Don't give me any crumbs! I don't want your fuckin' picture!" Before I could say anything, he left. I told Burt. He laughed. "Well," he said, "that's Nick."

The success of *Gunfight at the O.K. Corral* really depended on the love between the two men, which has been the most important theme in many movies—starring Spencer Tracy and Clark Gable, Dean Martin and Jerry Lewis, Robert Redford and Paul Newman. They're just starting to make female buddy movies now—*Crimes of the Heart, Outra-*

geous Fortune, Black Widow. But it does seem that very often, going back to Humphrey Bogart characters, you find movies with a great affection between two men. I remember a favorable review of *Gunfight at the O.K. Corral* in the *New York Times* which concluded with the observation that at the end, Burt Lancaster was very sad to see his buddy Kirk go off to San Francisco, while he was stuck with Rhonda Fleming.

There was a very tense dramatic moment in the film: Burt, alone and without a gun, is facing a saloon full of tough cowboys. I come in, pull my gun, snatch a gun from one of the cowboys, toss it to Burt, and the two of us subdue the entire room. We go out on the porch and Burt says to me, "Thanks, Doc." I was supposed to say, "Forget it." When I came to "Forget it," the ridiculousness of the scene—our great bravery, our machismo—made us howl. We did the scene over and over. It just made us laugh harder. Finally, we were laughing so hard, they had to stop shooting for the day and send us home like bad boys.

I enjoy working with Burt. We always have plenty to talk about. By no means do we agree on everything. On the contrary, we very often disagree. At the American Academy of Dramatic Arts tribute to me in New York City on April 6, 1987, Burt said: "Kirk would be the first person to tell you he's a very difficult man." He paused. "And I would be the second."

Twenty-three

HERR DOUGLAS

I saw a small picture called *The Killing*. It was made for very little money, and it made very little money. It was an unusual picture, and the studio had no faith in it and handled it poorly. I was intrigued by the film, and wanted to meet the director, Stanley Kubrick. He had started out as a photographer for *Look* magazine when he was seventeen; he was twenty-eight now, but looked much younger. I asked him if he had any other projects. He said he had a script called *Paths of Glory*, by Calder Willingham and Jim Thompson, based on Humphrey Cobb's 1935 novel about the greed for fame in the high command in World War I France that led to the needless deaths of so many men. Stanley told me he'd had no success setting the picture up, but he'd be glad to let me see it. I read the script and fell in love with it. "Stanley, I don't think this picture will ever make a nickel, but we *have* to make it."

I tried to get the financing. It wasn't easy. The project had been turned down everywhere. But I had a good relationship with United Artists. I trapped them into doing it, by saying I had a deal with MGM, and if they didn't want to make the movie, to let me know immediately. They finally decided to make it on a limited budget, about $3 million.

We thought the best place to shoot, in terms of the look we needed, and the budget we were working with, would be Germany. They had castles that looked French, and were bound to have a field that we could use for the battle scenes. The whole picture was shot in and around Munich.

Stanley Kubrick and his partner, James Harris, the man who put up the money to develop the script, went ahead to Germany to prepare *Paths of Glory*. When I arrived at the Hotel Vierjahrzeiten in Munich, I was greeted by Stanley and a completely rewritten script. He had revised it on his own, with Jim Thompson. It was a catastrophe, a cheapened version of what I thought had been a beautiful script. The dialogue was atrocious. My character said things like: "You've got a big head. You're so sure the sun rises and sets up there in your noggin you don't even bother to carry matches." And "And you've got the only brain in the world. They made yours and threw the pattern away? The rest of us have a skullful of Cornflakes." Speeches like this went on for pages, right up to the happy ending, when the general's car arrives screeching to a halt the firing squad and he changes the men's death sentence to thirty days in the guardhouse. Then my character, Colonel Dax, goes off with the bad guy he has been fighting all through the movie, General Rousseau, to have a drink, as the general puts his arm around my shoulder.

I called Stanley and Harris to my room. "Stanley, did you write this?"

"Yes." Kubrick always had a calm way about him. I never heard him raise his voice, never saw him get excited or reveal anything. He just looked at you through those big, wide eyes.

I said, "Stanley, why would you do that?"

He very calmly said, "To make it commercial. I want to make money."

I hit the ceiling. I called him every four-letter word I could think of. "You came to me with a script written by other people. It was based on a book. I love *that* script. I told you I didn't think this would be commercial, but I want to make it. You left it in my hands to put the picture together. I got the money, based on *that* script. Not this shit!" I threw the script across the room. "We're going back to the original script, or we're not making the picture."

Stanley never blinked an eye. We shot the original script. I think the movie is a classic, one of the most important pictures—possibly the *most* important picture—Stanley Kubrick has ever made.

Stanley could be exasperating, but what a talent. And a tremendous ego. Nothing wrong with that. Ego, not carried to excess, is healthy. I'm interested only in talent. But wherever we went, Stanley made sure they stuck signs saying HARRIS-KUBRICK all around like FOR RENT signs. I was tempted to say, "Get rid of all those signs and put up a sign that says BRYNA." It was the Bryna Company that put the picture together and signed Kubrick to a three-picture contract. But I dismissed that petty thought. It amused me that he was so anxious about the HARRIS-KUBRICK signs. I'm surprised that he didn't want the signs to say just KUBRICK. It amused me less years later when Stanley told people that I was only an employee on *Paths of Glory*.

Academy Award time rolled around. I was nominated for *Lust for Life*, my third nomination. I had been nominated twice before—for *Champion*, and for *The Bad and the Beautiful*, which I had also done with Minnelli and Houseman. Everyone wants to win an Oscar. It's a meaningful award, because it's given by your peers. It's your colleagues saying, "You deserve this honor." You can't predict when you're going to get nominated, or when you're going to win. But when I was nominated for *Lust for Life*, everyone was telling me that I was a shoo-in—third time's the charm. Besides, everybody was telling me that I had no competition. You believe what you like to believe. Mike Todd guaranteed that

I would win, as if he had advance information from Price Waterhouse, the accounting firm that added up the ballots. It didn't take much to convince me.

The press must have been speaking to Mike Todd, too, because they were convinced that I was going to win. The night of the Oscars, at least fifty photographers were assembled in the lobby of Munich's Hotel Vierjahrzeiten as I went up to my room. There they were, patiently waiting to catch the winning smile as word flashed across from the United States that I had won the Oscar.

It was difficult for me to sleep that night. I rehearsed the look of surprise on my face as I woke up from a sound sleep to find that I had won the Oscar. Visions of Oscars danced in my head, like a little kid on Christmas Eve. When I woke up, the look of surprise on my face was real—I hadn't won. Yul Brynner had, for a musical—*The King and I*. The photographers and journalists, tired from staying awake all night, straggled home in the early morning, emptying out the lobby.

I was all alone—no Oscar, family far away. There was a knock on the door. A stranger handed me a package and left. A present after all. An Oscar. Inscribed: *"To Daddy, who rates an Oscar with us always. Stolz and Peter."* "Stolz" was my pet name for Anne. It means "proud." I kept the Oscar by my bed at the hotel and everywhere, all the time. Some day, if I ever get a real Oscar, I'll give it to Anne.

I went out for dinner alone one night in Munich, came back around eleven, was lying in bed, reading. A little before midnight, the phone rang. "Yes?"

"I hope I'm not disturbing you." A soft, feminine, well-modulated voice.

"Not all," says I, lowering my voice. And thinking, "Here I go again!"

"We saw you having dinner here and I wanted to get up the nerve to ask you to join us for a drink."

"That was very thoughtful of you." I tried, really tried, not to lower my voice.

"Is it too late?" she cooed.

"Yes, it is." I was the boss, in complete control.

"Oh, I'm sorry," she whispered.

"But how about coming over here for a drink?" I tried to stop myself from saying it, but it came out.

"If it's not too late?"

"Room 502." I hung up the phone, tried not to look at the Oscar that Anne had sent me. Would I never learn? I was in a foreign country. Anything could happen.

Like the time in Boston, on the road with *Woman Bites Dog.* We had just finished the performance and were all back in the hotel. It was a bitter cold winter night. Some of the cast went off to a bar. I wasn't invited. The minute you start making movies, most stage actors don't like you. You're an interloper. Is it contempt? Jealousy? I don't know, but whatever it is, you're apart. I was feeling lonely as I got into bed.

The phone rang. Some of the actors asking me to join them for a drink? No, a low, sexy woman's voice. "Mr. Douglas?"

"Yes."

"I hope I'm not disturbing you." Chopin in the background.

"Not at all." My voice got lower.

"I loved your performance tonight."

"Well, thank you." My voice got lower yet.

"Didn't you look right at me at the curtain call?"

"Well, I . . ."

"Second row, very light skin, auburn hair."

Light skin, auburn hair, Chopin, snow falling. "I, ah, think so." My voice couldn't have gotten any lower.

"I've been sitting here, listening to the music—and thinking of you."

"Could I listen to the music with you?"

"Oh, would you?"

Within minutes, I was in front of the hotel, giving a taxi driver the address she had given me. Her place was much farther from the hotel than she had led me to believe. Or was it my impatience? The taxi let me out. "Don't wait." I dashed up to the third floor, knocked at the door of apartment 3F.

She had auburn hair all right, right out of a bottle. And

white skin, too. A lot of it. She was fat. Through thick, heavily rouged lips, she asked me to come in. "Take off your coat." Her voice had lost the tinkling quality it had on the phone.

I hadn't moved far into the room. As I took off my coat, I kicked myself for not having the taxi wait. I thought I heard something at the door. My titian-haired beauty threw a look in that direction, smiled at me and asked, "What would you like to drink?"

Suddenly, a panic came over me. I grabbed my coat, burst out the door, startling two men leaning against it. "Hey! Where you goin'?" one yelled, grabbing my coat. I left the coat in his hands, ran without looking back.

"WHAT ARE YOU DOIN' WITH MY WIFE?" was the last I heard as I tore down three flights of stairs and into the street.

I felt ridiculous running down the icy cold street, no taxi, no coat, nothing in sight. The old shakedown. At the next intersection, my lungs bursting, I found a taxi. I slid in, not bothering to check if anyone was following. At the hotel, I saw the actors still happily drinking at a table in the bar.

I went straight to my room, double locked the door, tore off my clothes, and jumped into bed, happy to be alone. I slept well.

And here I was, about to do a rerun of that scene. I reached for the telephone to call the concierge to intercept her—a knock at the door.

"Who is it?" It couldn't be the girl. The restaurant was twenty minutes away.

It was the girl. She had called from the lobby.

What the hell. I opened the door. She was beautiful. Ravishing. Slightly Eurasian-looking. "Come in," I said. "Take your coat off." We talked for a while. She told me she was a princess from Afghanistan. I wasn't sure where Afghanistan was, but if she had told me she was the Pope, I wouldn't have cared. She had led a very interesting life. After three days and nights, I knew a lot about her. Then she walked out of my life, just as she had walked in. Or so I thought.

Years later, Anne and I were invited to a small dinner party Greg Peck was having for a well-known art dealer and his fiancée. Peck introduced us. "Mr. Wildenstein, this is Mr. and Mrs. Douglas, and this is Princess Safia Tarzi from Afghanistan." I looked into those beautiful eyes. "How do you do?" She looked right back at me. "Pleased to meet you." And we spent a pleasant, formal evening together.

I never saw her again. She was an adventurous girl; she died shortly after that in a hot air balloon. It saddened me. I was grateful for that brief period that I spent with her.

What a strange coincidence! As I write this, I hear Willie Nelson singing "All the Girls I've Loved Before"—

To all the girls I've loved before,
That travelled in and out my door,
I dedicate this song.
I'm glad they came along,
All the girls I've loved before.

Did I use them? Did they use me? Or did we use each other?

Infidelity. I remember an elegant Parisian lady saying, "The most embarrassing thing I can think of is to be caught in bed with your own husband." That's a little far out, but attitudes toward infidelity vary around the world. Sex is a powerful drive, and it rears its ugly—or beautiful—head at unusual times. For a man, anyway, it's got something to do with proving himself. An erection is a mysterious thing. There's always that fear, each time one goes, that you won't be seeing it again. Man is not a monogamous animal. You get lonely, far from home, from family. I've been guilty, during my marriage, as much as anyone else. Maybe more. And probably much less than lots of people might think, because I've always had a tremendous sex life with my wife Anne.

Anne and Peter joined me in Munich. In 1957, it was not the beautiful city it is now. Destruction from aerial bombardments during the war was still evident everywhere. A vigorous rebuilding program was in progress. Nevertheless, the shop windows were filled with all kinds of goodies. This seemed odd—there was a much greater shortage of supplies in England, a country that had won the war, than in Germany, which had been defeated. Germany seemed to be recovering more rapidly, with the help of America's Marshall Plan.

The war was too close, and I still had deep feelings that I tried to hide. I kept telling myself that not all Germans had participated in the Holocaust, the massacre of Jews, all Germans were not like that. Anne and I met a very nice couple, Mr. and Mrs. George Niedermeyer. The wife was very young, the husband about twenty years older. They seemed intelligent and charming; "good Germans." I wanted to try to establish a relationship.

Then I went to Dachau, the concentration camp in the Munich suburbs. There was the iron gate with the obscene words over it: *Arbeit Macht Frei* ("Work Will Make You Free"). One of the most hideous things about the place was that, considering the thousands who had suffered misery and torture and death there, it was so small. So very small. Dachau was open to the public; the Germans had scrubbed it clean. All the lice- and disease-infested barracks had been torn or burned down and a model one built new, so you could see what it had been like—sort of. The rest of the area was planted with grass, like a football field. But behind a slightly raised mound of ground, you could see wooden troughs where the blood was caught and drained off when the Jews were shot. The troughs had all been cleaned out, too. We saw what looked like shower rooms—gas chambers, the ceilings low, so not too much gas was wasted in the extermination. So efficient. Nearby was the stone building with two parallel furnaces, as clean as barbecues, where the bodies of the Jews—men, women, and children—were burned. The high chimneys must have given off quite a stench, close to the city of Munich. When we discussed this with our German friends, they both looked at us wide-eyed. What were we talking about? Were they telling me they were not aware of what had happened in Germany, even at this late stage? Yes. They refused to acknowledge that the Holocaust had ever taken place. Were they pretending? Or had they actually blocked out everything?

Incidents like that sicken me. It wasn't the only one.

The Bryna Company had taken over the Geiselgasteig Studios, dilapidated studios on the outskirts of Munich. Geiselgasteig had once been very active, but had seen no activity during World War II, and very little since. Shooting the interiors of *Paths of Glory* was the only game in town. I was also arranging to shoot the interiors of *The Vikings* there. So the studio was delighted to have me.

Every morning, I got into a highly visible white Cadillac, and a German chauffeur drove me to the studio. And every day, a tall guard stood holding a chain across the gate, forcing us to stop. The guard would pause, look in the car at the driver, look at me, then drop the chain and allow us to go into the studio. After several days of this, I became quite annoyed. It all came to a head the morning after my Dachau conversation with the Niedermeyers. As the white Cadillac approached the studio, I saw our old German friend standing there, holding the chain across the entranceway. I wondered to myself, what part did he play in the war? What did he see? What did he do? He stood there like a German general.

I said to my driver, "If you stop this car, you're fired."

He looked at me.

I said, "You go right straight through that chain."

He looked at me again.

"OR YOU'RE FIRED."

"*Jawohl.*" He floored it.

I saw the look of surprise on the German guard's face as he dropped the chain. As soon as we were inside the gate, I told my driver, "Stop the car!" I got out and, in my inadequate German, yelled at the guard. "You Nazi dog! How dare you?" I grabbed him, held him close to my face. "Do you know who I am?"

"*Jawohl.*"

"You recognize me?"

"*Jawohl. Jawohl.*"

"Have I been here every morning in that white Cadillac? You know who I am?"

He nodded vigorously.

I said to him, "The next time I come to this gate and that chain is up, YOU—RAUS."

"*Jawohl.*"

Then suddenly, this arrogant guard lost all of his arrogance, and I felt like an idiot, because my rage was so out of proportion. I had just snapped at his taking advantage of his menial position to stop me every day. That was his satisfaction. Well, needless to say, whenever he saw that white Cadillac zooming toward the gate, that chain went down.

I don't know whether he was a Nazi or not. But nobody was. It was impossible to find a Nazi in Germany after the war. As far as I could tell, no one in Germany had ever voted for Hitler. No one had ever believed in the philosophy of the Nazi Party. And yet, there must have been millions of them during the war. Occasionally, you did meet a German who felt shame for what had happened to his country, who gave you a little bit of hope that perhaps there was some remorse, and from it, maybe some humanity.

Paths of Glory opened on September 18, 1957, the first world premiere ever in Munich. It was a truly great film with a truly great theme: the insanity and brutality of war. Hollis Alpert of the *Saturday Review* said it was "unquestionably the finest American film of the year. It is so searing in its intensity that it will probably take its place, in years to come, as one of the screen's most extraordinary achievements."

As I had predicted, it made no money. A picture can't make money unless people pay to see it, and people can't see it if it's been banned in their country. Oh, they never banned it outright in France. Just the usual "high level talks" between the French government and United Artists. It was also banned from the Berlin Film Festival in 1958 when France threatened to pull out. Even the Swiss were not neutral on *Paths of Glory.* They called it "subversive propaganda directed at France," refused to screen it for journalists, and declared that they would confiscate any prints that were not immediately exported from the country. *Paths of Glory* was not shown in France and Switzerland until the 1970s, almost twenty years later. I never thought of *Paths of Glory* as anti-French. I love France, have done many things for France, for which they gave me the Légion d'Honneur. More important—they gave me my wife.

The other project that I was anxious to do was *The Vikings* —what the *New York Times* called a "Norse opera." It really was a western set in the days of the Vikings.

I felt that the English characters should be played by English actors, to give it a certain elegance, and the Vikings should be played by Americans, who would give it a rougher quality. Ernie Borgnine, two years younger than I, played my father. Tony Curtis played one of the parts with his wife, Janet Leigh, the only one in the cast with any Scandinavian blood. James Donald, who had played my brother Theo in *Lust for Life*, was also in the cast.

We planned to shoot *The Vikings* mostly on location in Norway, and at the Geiselgasteig Studios in Munich. I thought Richard Fleischer, who had done such a good job on *20,000 Leagues Under the Sea*, would be good to direct *The Vikings*.

I wanted to make a good film. I employed experts from Norway, Sweden, and Denmark to give me an exact historical feeling about the period of the Vikings, the exact dimensions of the boats that they used, how the houses and the mead hall were built, etc. The experts disagreed, and finally I had to make the decisions myself.

I felt very romantic about the film, and about how everybody should work, like a team. I decided, on impulse, that we would all make a grand tour. I wanted the cast to get a feel of what these countries were like. We all assembled in London—Janet Leigh, Ernie Borgnine, Tony Curtis. I told them, "There's a fjord in your future." We flew to Scandinavia. Tony was terrified of flying; I think this is one of the first times that he actually flew in a plane. Instead of going directly to Norway, we stopped in Denmark, Stockholm, Oslo, and then on to Bergen, the closest city to where we would be shooting.

Soon we were sending letters back home: "Greetings from Norway, where the sun shines at midnight and seldom any other time." One beautiful, sunny day, we had gorgeous shots of the Viking ships taking off in a breeze, white sails flapping, from the deep blue Hardanger Fjord. Then the weather went bad. We weren't sure we'd be able to match those breathtaking shots. We had to make a decision. We gave up the shots, reshot the whole thing in the rain, with the sails tightly rolled up and the oarsmen powering the boat. That proved to be the right decision, because so much of the weather was bad. I was standing one day with a group of the actors, watching a bright sunny sky turn to rain. This is very exasperating for a producer. I said to one of the Norwegian boys who was playing a part in the picture, "Does it always rain here in Norway?" He said, "I don't know. I'm only eighteen."

Dick Fleischer told me to take a day off—he was going to shoot a stunt, a scene where my character performs an old Viking tradition, "Running the Oars." They would get drunk on the ship, lock the oars into the oarlocks, then climb off the boat and run on the oars. They all told me I couldn't do it. That was all I needed to hear. "I'm going to do it." I watched them do it, saw that you needed to get a rhythm going, keep the momentum from oar to oar. If you slowed down, you had time to lose your balance—and fall into the freezing waters of the fjord. I did the stunt myself, and only slipped once—deliberately. After all, my character was supposed to be drunk.

A lot of the filming and living conditions were hard. But it was fun, and we all had terrific rapport. We had a lot of help from the Norwegians. We built a Viking town; we paid Norwegian rowing clubs to be the oarsmen on the Viking ships. It's not an easy thing to row one of those boats. They worked for months to prepare. They were so wonderful to us that I thought we should show our appreciation. One Sunday, I threw a party with terrific food and lots of booze. All the members of the cast pitched in and put on a show. I juggled, Tony assisting me. The audience applauded like crazy. Of course, supposedly unbeknown to us, Janet Leigh was behind us doing a striptease. The audience applauded, I bowed. "Do you want more?" They all yelled, "Yeah! More! More!" So I'd start to juggle again, and Janet would take off more clothes. They loved the show. We did different routines. The party was expensive, but was worth it. The three weeks of shooting we had left in Norway would fly by. We would be sorry to leave to shoot interiors at Geiselgasteig Studios in Munich. It was a warm, wonderful evening. I was very happy.

The next morning, the entire Norwegian crew went on strike. They wanted more money. I was shocked. After this wonderful party of camaraderie? This infuriated me. I called a meeting of my staff. We went through every single shot remaining in Norway. Could we do this on the stage? Yes. Could we do that on the stage? Yes. Was it possible to alter this scene? I decided that there wasn't anything left we couldn't do in Munich.

I said, "It's a wrap! Get everything together. We're leaving." The Norwegians were dumbfounded. They immediately rushed up, willing to work for their original salaries. But I refused to even discuss it with them. I was angry and hurt. I had thought they really liked us, that we were friends. I had been betrayed. They had been working for me for months, making more money than they ever had. I had seen this quality in other places, but never in any Scandinavian country. I was really hurt, and I wouldn't listen to any of them.

We headed for Munich. Because my wife spoke perfect German, she was a big help to me during the shooting of *The Vikings*. I moved from the Vierjahrzeiten to a large apartment at the Bayerischer Hof Hotel, partially destroyed in the war, and being rebuilt. Now it's a gigantic modern hotel. But at the time, we had an old wing of the hotel. What I remember most is my son Peter, about a year and a half old, running down the hall. He'd always fall on his mouth, and have a big thick lip. I was afraid he would grow up with this thick lip; it was getting to be a permanent feature. I tried to give him lessons in falling, teach him to put his arms out in front of him to break his fall. But no. He would just fall over like a log and land right on his lip. And all I could do was watch. Parenthood is hell.

Twenty-four

MY FRIEND SAM

Anne and I had been having arguments, increasingly worse, for a couple of years. All about Sam Norton, my best friend, business manager, lawyer, and agent. It started when Anne asked me, "Who handles your business? Who takes care of your affairs?" Sam took care of everything. All my income went directly to him, and he paid the bills. If I needed money, I just picked up the phone. "Sam, send me a couple hundred dollars pocket money," and that was it. He was a godsend. I loved to stop by his office on the ground floor of my building and just talk with him. He was never too busy to see me. He gave me the feeling that I would have liked to have had with my father.

One day, I laughingly said to Sam, "My wife wants to know how much money I have."

"You're a millionaire."

I reported this good news to Anne. She said, "Where is it?"

"What do you mean, where is it?"

"If you have a million dollars, it should be in the bank, or invested, or . . . Where is it? There should be statements, stock certificates, *something*."

I was annoyed. I called Sam. "Anne wants to know where the money is."

"Oh, for heaven's sakes, I'll take care of it. Come on over and I'll show you."

He showed me papers with figures, columns, subtotals, accounts receivable, debits—stuff I didn't want to see and didn't understand. Anne wasn't satisfied, and Sam knew it. He gave me a piece of paper, told me to sign it, that it would settle everything. It stated that I was giving outright to my wife all the paintings and art objects that we owned, that they did not belong to any community property, but were her sole property. I signed it, then took it home and handed it to Anne. Anne looked at it. "What is this?"

"I don't know. Sam gave it to me. He said you would be very pleased to have it. He knows it's because of you that we have some art. You bought most of it."

"But it doesn't matter. It's ours. Why should it be just mine? This seems like a bribe."

"Bribe! For what?"

"To keep me from asking any more questions."

"That's ridiculous. What are you saying?"

"Kirk, when we got married in Las Vegas, Sam shoved a paper at me a split second before the ceremony and said, 'Sign here.' Of course I signed. I wasn't going to read anything at the moment I was getting married. I never signed anything in my life without reading it. But I signed that, and now I want to know what it was."

"What did Sam say?"

"Not to worry about it. He said it was just a prenuptial agreement, that everybody in America has one. All it means is that what was yours before we got married is yours, and what's mine is mine."

"If Sam told you not to worry about it, don't worry about it."

"Kirk, it's a legal document. I signed it. Now I don't know

what it says or where it is. And he won't let me see it. There is something wrong with Sam Norton. I feel it in my bones."

"You're talking about my best friend."

"I don't think he's a friend. I think he's a crook."

"Look, I've known him almost fifteen years. Now DROP IT."

But Anne didn't drop it. Several days later, Greg Bautzer, a lawyer, called Sam, said he represented Anne, and he wanted the prenuptial agreement.

I was furious. She was implying awful things about my friend Sam. And she had gone behind my back. "How dare you?"

"Kirk, I'm trying to protect you. You're not a business-man."

I slammed out of the room. Anne got the prenuptial agreement. She objected to the part that said that she and her children had no right to any of my income for the first five years of our marriage. "My God! I have a child! God forbid something happens to you tomorrow!"

"Don't be silly. You know we're going to stay married. And after five years, the document means nothing."

"Yes, but we're not immortal. And besides, if I get nothing, where does everything go? To Sam Norton?"

I couldn't understand all the fuss. Sam had been trying to protect me. He was there when my first marriage ended in divorce, and wanted to make sure I didn't lose everything if this one did, too.

Things got worse. Sam had done his job well: the agreement was irrevocable and couldn't be rescinded without going to court—a lot of time, money, and publicity that nobody wanted. Anne's lawyer insisted that I take out a huge life insurance policy naming her and Peter as beneficiaries. It cost me a tremendous amount of money and was totally unnecessary, as far as I was concerned. I began to doubt. Not Sam. My marriage.

I didn't want to deal with this any more. Burt Lancaster wanted to do a commercial picture with me. I knew that his company, Hecht-Hill-Lancaster, owned George Bernard Shaw's play *The Devil's Disciple,* and that Burt had put about $800,000 into it. I said, "Why not do something classy? Let's do Shaw." I was willing to do it for a nominal sum. Larry Olivier was interested in the role of General Burgoyne. It would be shot in London, thousands of miles from Los Angeles and my problems. I would go over alone; Anne would join me in a few weeks. We needed the break. With great relief, I left for London.

For many years, after one of my pictures opened, a very intelligent letter would arrive from a woman living in Stratford-on-Avon, Shakespeare's birthplace. The letters were well written, in a beautiful feminine hand in lavender ink, each a favorable critique of the movie. Intrigued, I answered. A correspondence sprang up which became warmer and friendlier over the years. I wondered what she looked like. I pictured someone like Louise Livingston, tall and dark, walking along the banks of the Avon, composing verses. One day, a book of verse did arrive, *Poems for K,* each poem inspired by a scene from one of my movies. The tempo of our correspondence increased. We both fell in love —with me. Now, more than ever, I was anxious to meet her, face to face, "breath to breath, where hushed awakenings are dear."

I rented a lovely flat in Belgravia, with a little garden. When I got settled in, I called her on the phone, lowered my voice. "Hello, Kirk here."

"Yes, of course, that same voice."

And she sounded just the way I thought she would. I invited her to my flat for tea. That seemed the proper invitation. I would send my car and driver.

"Five o'clock," she said.

"That would be fine." My voice got lower.

It was a typical London day, drizzling. The butler lit a fire in the fireplace. I wore a velvet lounging jacket with an ascot. I wanted our first meeting to be perfect. The doorbell rang. "I'll get it," I told the butler.

I slowly walked to the door and opened it. I wasn't quite

prepared. She was extremely short, ugly, and leaned on a cane, looking up at me through very thick glasses. I tried to conceal my shock. "Please, come in."

She hobbled past me into the room. That's when I noticed the hump on her back. I tried to cover my hysteria by being overly polite and solicitous, pouring tea and offering sandwiches. She had the same musical voice I had heard on the telephone, but she didn't say much, because I did most of the talking, hastily, perspiration on my hands and forehead in spite of the cold London afternoon.

She didn't stay long, and politely bade me good-bye. I never heard from her again. Maybe she was disappointed in finding something ugly in me that could not see something beautiful in her. I've often wondered.

The Devil's Disciple could have been much better. There were constant problems. But it was a noble attempt. And Larry Olivier was so brilliant, he stole the picture completely. Burt and I played Americans during the Revolutionary War, caught in a comedy of mistaken identities. I'm the good-for-nothing who is mistaken for Burt, the good preacher, when the British soldiers, led by Olivier as General Burgoyne, come to arrest him. I go along with them, save Burt's life, redeem myself, and get to kiss Rev. Burt's pretty wife good-bye in the bargain.

They cut two of my most important scenes because they said the picture was too long. I rethought my entire approach to the role. A week later, they put them back in; they said the picture was too short.

Larry and his wife, Vivien Leigh, lived nearby and were very kind and hospitable. Vivien's beautiful face was the same, in spite of the weight she had gained. She was not well emotionally. Everyone pretended there was nothing wrong, in spite of her strange behavior. In a restaurant one day with a group, including director Terence Young, she turned to Olivier and said, "Larry, why don't you fuck me anymore?" Then she started coming on to me, very seductive, with Olivier sitting right there. At first, I didn't believe it. It made me uncomfortable. She was behaving like

Blanche du Bois in *A Streetcar Named Desire*—sexual, bizarre. Shortly after that, they were divorced, and several years after that, at the age of fifty-four, she committed suicide.

While Burt and I were in London, we were asked to participate in the Motion Picture Relief Fund gala charity, *The Night of a Thousand Stars*, at the Palladium. We wanted to be part of it, but what to do? We had had a very successful evening at the Academy Awards, doing a song-and-dance routine called *"It's Great Not to Be Nominated."* We decided to do something similar. We rehearsed and rehearsed. But backstage, the night of the show, we were frightened. What the hell were we doing there with this all-star cast? It wasn't bad enough that Laurence Olivier and all the big English actors were there; the act preceding ours was Sid Caesar and Imogene Coca, the hottest comedy team in the United States. Standing backstage listening to their act, hearing not one laugh from the audience, Burt and I looked at each other, certain of the doom that awaited us. Too late to back out now. That's show biz. They announced us.

As the orchestra played the whistling theme from *The Bridge on the River Kwai*—DA-da, da-da-da, DA-DA-DA— Burt and I walked out from opposite sides in bowler hats, cutaway coats, and canes. We walked right past each other, as if we hadn't seen each other. Then, we stopped, turned around, faced each other, acknowledged each other by doffing our bowler hats. Together we walked down to the footlights. There was such an ovation from the audience that we had to stop. I turned to Burt while they were applauding, whispered, "Let's get off now. It can't get any better." The applause subsided; we went into our routine. Leaning on our canes and swaying to the music, we sang "Maybe It's Because I'm a Londoner That I Love London So." For the second chorus, we went into a delicate soft-shoe routine, ending with me climbing up on Burt's shoulders. We went off that way, with me standing on Burt's shoulders, waving my hat, the two of us really belting the last chorus. A tremendous ovation. What a thrill! That is a nice memory.

And I was getting letters from Sam about my oil invest-ments: "Oil continues to flow like liquor at a fireman's ball." But when I returned to Los Angeles, Anne informed me that in my absence, she had had my books audited by Price Waterhouse.

"Oh? The company that added up the Academy Award ballots wrong the three times I lost?" But it was no joke when Price Waterhouse presented us with the findings of their in-depth audit:

1. I had no money in the bank.

2. I owed the IRS $750,000. The eighteen months I had spent in Europe in 1952–1954 did not qualify for the tax-free income break that Sam had told me they did.

3. The solid investments I thought I had, including the oil wells, were dummy corporations that received a percentage of every investment. All the corporations were owned by Sam Norton. The list went on and on.

This was in addition to the 10 percent that Rosenthal & Norton took off the top for being my lawyers, and the 10 percent that Sam got personally for being my agent. There had been a lot of money; I had worked steadily, and we had lived modestly. The studios paid airfare and living expenses when we traveled. Diana was remarried, so I didn't pay ali-mony, just child support.

The bottom line: Sam Norton had bled me dry, stolen all my income, every cent. Years ago, to get out of a contract with Warner Brothers, I had done one picture for nothing. Sam Norton had fixed it so that I had done twenty-seven other pictures for nothing, too.

I was penniless and in debt.

Heartsick, Anne and I sat down with a new lawyer we had hired without Sam's knowing about it. He gave us more bad news: Sam had been giving me very bad advice about every-thing. It was not true that The Bryna Company needed to produce films in which I did not appear. And Sam had cross-collateralized *The Indian Fighter*, a profitable picture, with *Spring Reunion*, a picture with no profits, which meant that *Indian Fighter* made no money. The worst part: my contract gave Rosenthal & Norton the same percentage of my income on *The Vikings* and all future pictures.

Greed motivated Sam. The only way to get him to loosen his grip on what he already had was to dangle a bigger piece of the action in front of him. He didn't know that we had done an audit in such depth. Sam was not suspicious of me. He had always been able to manipulate me.

I went to see Sam.

Issur stood in front of the door to his best friend Sam's office, a place he had always enjoyed coming before, a place he had felt warm and protected. He wanted it all not to have happened, wanted Sam to say it wasn't so.

Issur was destroyed; he wanted to weep. Sam had been the new father who would love Issur and take care of him. Sam even looked like Issur's father—was stocky, had dark hair and a mustache. Issur had given his father his life savings, and his father had never paid him back—not in money, not in affection. When he found Sam, Issur had been happy to say again, "Here, Pa. Here's the money." It was supposed to be different this time.

But it was the nightmare all over again. Issur was reduced to a skinny, dirty, snotty-nosed little kid, in the agony of knowing that all those times he had sat in Sam's house and talked and laughed, all those dinners and lunches, and conversations, all those years that Issur had loved Sam, Sam had never loved Issur, had never even seen Issur. He had seen only dollar signs.

Kirk Douglas, actor, grabbed the knob on Sam Norton's office door, took a deep breath, and made his entrance.

Sam was sitting behind his desk. He looked up and smiled.

I waved the auditor's report under his nose. "YOU SON OF A BITCH! YOU'RE MY BEST FRIEND! HOW COULD YOU DO THIS TO ME? I'LL PUT YOU IN JAIL!"

Sam went white. "If you do that, I'll kill myself."

I leaned forward, looked him in the eye. "Sam, tell me the

truth." Big pause. "It was Rosenthal, wasn't it? He made you do it."

Sam breathed. "Yes, yes. He's my partner. You know how it is. I didn't want . . . I tried . . ."

"Sam, you and I don't need Jerry Rosenthal. I want to branch out into more independent production. I want you to come with me, be my right-hand man, work for me exclusively. You'll be my lawyer, my agent, produce all my pictures. Not Rosenthal. Just *you*."

Sam was taking the bait.

"I don't want Rosenthal to have any part of *The Vikings*, which I think is going to be very successful. If you take care of me on this, I'll take care of you."

Sam nodded. He was hooked. And he was petrified.

It made me sick, but I persisted. "If you sign a paper saying that Rosenthal & Norton are not entitled to anything from *The Vikings*—commissions or percentages or fees—then you and I will start fresh. Whole new deal. You'll become the president of my company. We'll work out a salary. You're the lawyer, you draw up the contract. O.K.?"

Sam drew up a document selling out his partner, Jerry Rosenthal.

Jerry Rosenthal, furious at the loss of future contracts with me, forced "My Friend Sam" not to practice law for many years.

For what Sam had done to us, Anne and I could have had him put in jail. But I was afraid that he really would commit suicide. And we were advised not to, because then he couldn't earn any money to pay us back if he was in jail. He did have to pay us back—about $200,000, with interest. It was a fraction of what he had taken, but it was all we could claim. He had arranged things very well for himself. The $200,000 was only the most obviously stolen—money he had used to buy things for his wife and children and himself. He paid us $2,500 a month.

After a few years, he started writing me little notes, saying that, for old times' sake, we should let bygones be bygones. I considered it, uncertain. We were lucky to get away with our future. Maybe we could forget about the past. Anne made up my mind. "Never. Never. Never. Never."

Sam stopped paying anyway, just stopped sending the checks. We went back to our lawyers to try to get him to pay the rest of what he owed us. But Sam had put everything in his wife's name, or his kids'; it was inaccessible. Our lawyers couldn't do a thing.

Anne got the rest of the money, ten years later. She was in Palm Springs, trying to figure out how to get to Indio, about twenty-five miles away, to pick up her station wagon, which was being repaired there. She mentioned this to a woman friend who said, "No problem. I have to go to court in Indio tomorrow for my divorce. I'll take you."

At ten the next morning, the friend called. "My lawyer says you wouldn't ride in the same car with him."

"Who's your lawyer?"

"Sam Norton."

"You're damn right I wouldn't ride in the same car! I'd rather walk!" Anne immediately called our lawyer in Los Angeles, Karl Samuelian, and said, "Sam Norton is practicing law again. He's handling a very important, very expensive divorce case with enormous legal fees."

He said, "I'm dispatching somebody right this minute to Riverside to file with the county courthouse."

Within hours, we attached Norton's salary from the divorce. Our legal fees were more than what we got from Sam. But to Anne, it was a matter of principle. "Justice has to be done. Until the last penny is paid, I will not sit still."

Anne is this way about me, a protective lioness. And I try to be like that about her. Each of us will do things for the other that we would not do for ourselves. She was relentless about making Sam pay for what he had done. When that last check arrived, small as it was, the look of satisfaction on Anne's face was worth it.

If Anne hadn't caught Sam, there's a real possibility that we would be destitute now. Doris Day stayed with Jerry Rosenthal and lost a lot of money. In her autobiography, she says that I advised her to get rid of him. On July 14, 1987, after nineteen years, she finally succeeded in having him disbarred, and won a judgment of $22 million. He's still protesting his innocence; she's still waiting to collect. Unfortunately, everybody in Hollywood has stories like these. You learn the hard way that the old joke is no joke:

"How do people in Hollywood say 'Fuck you'?"

" 'Trust me.' "

Twenty-five

BRYNA

The Vikings opened on May 9, 1958, and, thank God, was a tremendous hit. United Artists was happy, I was happy. I was able to pay the IRS the $750,000 I owed them.

Anne and I were going into production immediately—another child. I wanted to be in the delivery room for this one —no more pacing out in the hall. On June 21, 1958, I scrubbed, got gowned and masked, and went into the operating room for the cesarean. Another boy. No dimple. But huge blue eyes, Anne's eyes, and blond almost to whiteness. We gave him a good Viking name: Eric.

In those days, visiting hours were short. Husbands were not allowed much access to wives and newborns, and were never supposed to be around during feeding, because of germs or something. I thought this was ridiculous. I wanted to be with my wife and my baby. When visiting hours ended and everyone was supposed to leave the floor, I went into the closet. I did this when Peter was born, and again with Eric. The nurses, of course, caught on, and would say to Anne, "Mrs. Douglas, is your husband in the closet?" And

Anne would say, "Oh no, he's gone home." The nurses went, and I came out, germs and all, to be with my family. Now, of course, everyone realizes how important it is for husbands to help with childbirth. But then they made you feel like a criminal.

I now had four children. Anne had had two cesareans. That was enough. I had fulfilled my biological destiny. I thought about a vasectomy. The prospect was a little frightening. I worried, like any man, that it might affect my potency. I was reassured that many doctors had had the operation themselves, and I went ahead. Now I can say with authority that my fears were unfounded.

I did a lot of work to help sell *The Vikings*. I was even hauled up in a boatswain's chair to the top of a Broadway billboard several stories high and almost a block long. The prow of a Viking ship stuck out of the sign; I christened it with a bottle of champagne. People thought I was crazy, going ten stories up. But in those days, that seemed like nothing to me.

I wanted my mother to see that sign. Whenever I'd gone back to visit her in Schenectady, when she was living with my sisters, or in Albany, in the nursing home, she'd have her immigrant friends around. She was so proud of me. "Look at my son, his name in lights. America is such a wonderful land." I was embarrassed by the adulation. "Ma, America's such a wonderful land, I'll put *your* name in lights." Now, I had done it. I brought her to New York, rented a big limousine. We drove to Times Square and I had the driver stop the car. There was the gigantic billboard. I pointed through the window. "See, Ma, the name I taught you how to write, in lights. B-R-Y-N-A. BRYNA PRESENTS THE VIKINGS."

My mother looked at it in awe. "Oh, America is such a wonderful land."

I was glad I had done that, because just a few months later she called me on the telephone. Very quietly, she asked when I was coming back East, because she wanted to see me. She'd never been like that before. I knew.

I headed for the airport, fortified myself with a few drinks in the Ambassador Room before boarding with the first-class passengers. A "first-class passenger." On an airplane, yet. I thought of Ma, and Pa, and the years on Eagle Street, when I had watched the trains whizzing by and had wondered if I would ever go anywhere.

It was late. Time to lie down in the sleeper berth, take one of those "first class" sleeping pills, try to get some sleep before we arrived in New York. But I couldn't sleep—I couldn't find a pleasant thought to gnaw on. I kept thinking, "Where should I be buried? What should I do about my children, my wife, my estate?" I decided that I wanted to be cremated. I didn't want a grave that people would have to visit.

At the airport in New York, there was a limousine to meet me. There were always limousines now. It took me to Grand Central Station, where I boarded the deluxe train to Albany, the one that didn't stop in Amsterdam. A taxi from the train in Albany, and I was at the hospital. As I walked in, I realized that it was December 9, my birthday.

Issur walked slowly toward his mother's hospital room, down the long linoleum-carpeted corridor. He pushed open the door to the hushed, dark room. Ma was in bed under an oxygen tent—a transparent plastic dome, the kind of thing his son Peter would like to play under. She lay there breathing heavily, suffering from pneumonia on top of a heart condition and diabetes.

"Hello, Ma. It's me," he whispered.

She gave a feeble smile. "My big-shot son."

Issur was glad that Ma was alert. "Oh, I'm not so very big, Ma."

"Yes, you are." Her head turned a little toward the nurse. "This is my son. The whole world trembles when they say his name."

Rustling, whispers, giggles from the hallway. Issur looked up. People peeking through the door, pointing. "Look! There he is! That's him!" They didn't see Issur with his dying mother; all they saw was somebody from the movies. Issur's problems were not theirs.

Issur remembered as a child thinking that if his mother died, he would die too. He had seen his mother lose control only once. They were seven starving children, squalling for food. Ma had started screaming, too. "There is nothing! I have nothing! What do you want from me?" twisting her flesh as if she would pull off chunks to feed them, as she ran from the house. Issur and his sisters stared at each other, suddenly silent. If Ma was gone, they would die.

Issur and his sisters stayed with Ma for days as she got weaker and weaker, drifted in and out of consciousness. At dusk one day, she roused herself. "What day is it?"

"Friday."

"Don't forget to light the candles for Sabbath."

They didn't want to leave Ma, but she insisted. So they all went to Betty's house and lit candles. Issur said the evening prayer. They all returned to Ma and told her they had done as she asked. She beamed at them, her daughters and son at her bedside. "Gut Shabbas," she said.

Issur's sisters returned to their families that night. Issur stayed. He sat with Ma, held her hand tightly. He was over-whelmed by his mother's composure and dignity, remembered the look in his father's dying eyes: fear. That same look must have been in Issur's eyes. Ma looked up at him, a clear, serene smile on her face, the smile that was there every Sabbath as she sat on the porch in her rocking chair, Bible open on her lap.

"Don't be scared, Issur. It happens to all of us."

Issur choked. Holding his own breath, he watched his mother breathe so slowly, in, then out, each breath causing her pain. Until a long, deflating exhale followed by . . . nothing. Issur reached a finger out, touched Ma's forehead. It felt strange. When you're dead, you're really dead, he thought. Issur's mother was like the chair, the table, the bedpan: an inanimate object. Issur cried.

The private nurse came in and handed him a bill. She

wanted to be paid immediately. Numb, Issur reached into his pocket, pulled out some money. He handed it to the woman without looking at her.

Both Issur's mother and father were dead. He had only his sisters now, and his mixed feelings about them. They buried Ma apart from Pa. Ma wanted it that way. Issur resented it. Why, even in death, could the two of them not be united? After the funeral, Issur never went to visit his mother's grave; he didn't like that cemetery. But he found great solace at the grave of his father in the Jewish cemetery in Amsterdam, New York. It was a peaceful little place.

A parent's death makes you grow up, and growing up is hard. You think that when you do grow up, something wonderful will happen. No more problems, like magic. Then, you grow up. You become a "big man." Your voice is lower. But inside, you're still a child. But you look like an adult, and other people think you're one, so you pretend to be one; you return the favor by pretending that they're one. You all buy into the same fiction.

The truth was that Issur was a forty-two-year-old orphan pretending to be Kirk Douglas, a grown-up, flying back to the heart of the world of make-believe so he could pretend to be a man who lived two thousand years ago—a slave called Spartacus.

Twenty-six

THE WARS OF
SPARTACUS

After *The Vikings,* I swore that I would never do another epic period picture again. But big pictures and big money-makers—*The Robe, Samson and Delilah, Quo Vadis, The Ten Commandments*—were what Hollywood was turning out in the 1950s. Then I read a script. The leading role was perfect for me—Ben Hur!

MGM was remaking their 1927 movie, William Wyler directing. I had enjoyed working with Wyler on *Detective Story* and went to see him. Yes, he would like me to be in *Ben Hur.* Great! But not the lead. Oh? He wanted me for Messala, Ben Hur's friend turned to-the-death enemy in the chariot race. I wasn't interested in the role of a one-note bad guy. But Wyler was firm. He wanted Charlton Heston for Ben Hur, and he got him. I was disappointed.

Then, at the end of 1957, Eddie Lewis, a very talented filmmaker who worked for me for eight years, brought me a book called *Spartacus.* The author, Howard Fast, had spent some months in jail because of his association with the Communist Party. Now Fast was not exactly on the blacklist; it was more like the gray list. He had changed that by writing blatantly patriotic books on George Washington and Tom Paine.

Spartacus was a real man, but if you look him up in the history books, you find only a short paragraph about him. Rome was ashamed; this man had almost destroyed them. They wanted to bury him. I was intrigued with the story of Spartacus the slave, dreaming of the death of slavery, driving into the armor of Rome the wedge that would eventually destroy her.

I'm always astounded by the impact, the extent of the Roman Empire. Caesarea, Israel—full of Roman ruins. In Tunisia, a coliseum. Roman ruins in England. How did the Romans get to so many places? Aqueducts everywhere. Travel is difficult now, by jet. But on horseback, or on foot? It always amazed me *how* they did that, and how *much* they did.

Looking at these ruins, and at the Sphinx and the pyramids in Egypt, at the palaces in India, I wince. I see thousands and thousands of slaves carrying rocks, beaten, starved, crushed, dying. I identify with them. As it says in the Torah: "Slaves were we unto Egypt." I come from a race of slaves. That would have been *my* family, *me*.

Spartacus would make a terrific picture. I took an option on the book with my own money. I was sure I'd have no difficulty getting United Artists to finance *Spartacus*. They were very happy with *The Vikings*, now in the final editing stages and shaping up to be a big picture. And I had taken a tremendous financial risk for them in personally guaranteeing completion of *The Vikings*.

I went to Arthur Krim, the head of United Artists. I told him my idea to make a movie about *Spartacus*. I got an abrupt "NO." I was taken aback—hurt, angry.

On January 13, 1958, I received a telegram from Arthur:

DEAR KIRK: "SPARTACUS" COVERS THE SAME STORY AS "THE GLADIATORS" BY KOESTLER. WE ARE ALREADY COMMITTED TO "THE GLADIATORS" WITH YUL BRYNNER TO BE DIRECTED BY

Now I understood. Then we got a call from Marty Ritt.
How dare we try to make a movie about Spartacus when he
was developing a screenplay based on *The Gladiators*? He
wanted us to give up our movie.

Eddie and I talked it over. Ritt and Brynner seemed to be
way ahead of us with their project, already developing a
screenplay. And they had funding from a major studio.
Maybe we could join forces. There were two wonderful
parts, adversaries—I could play one, Yul the other. Certainly, United Artists would be happy with a Yul Brynner-
Kirk Douglas picture.

We called Marty, made our proposal. He would talk it over
with Yul.

He got back to us. No way. Yul Brynner hated my guts. I
thought that was odd—*he* had beaten *me* for the Academy
Award.

A few days later, Eddie tossed a copy of *Variety* onto my
desk. There was a picture of Yul Brynner dressed as Spartacus, and the words:

"THE GLADIATORS"
Next From United Artists

Production would begin as soon as Yul Brynner and Marty
Ritt finished Faulkner's *The Sound and the Fury* at Fox. *The
Gladiators* was budgeted at $5,500,000.

I was depressed—all the work I'd done, all the money I'd
spent. But what did they *really* have? Yul Brynner went
down to Western Costume, rented a gladiator suit, took a
picture, and put it in the paper. On February 11, 1958, I sent
a telegram to Arthur Krim:

WE ARE SPENDING FIVE MILLION FIVE HUNDRED AND TWO DOL-
LARS ON SPARTACUS. YOUR MOVE. KIRK.

But what did we have—an option, about to expire, on a very difficult novel; no director, and no deal. And no title: United Artists had registered *Spartacus* at the same time they'd registered *The Gladiators*.

I went to other studios. How naive of me. Nobody wanted to touch it. Buck United Artists? We were dead in the water.

Howard Fast agreed to extend the option on *Spartacus* for another sixty days "for one dollar and other considerations." The "other considerations" included letting Howard write the screenplay, something Eddie and I agreed to very reluctantly. But until we got a deal set up . . .

March 22, 1958. Anne and I were driving back from Palm Springs in deafening silence. We had been arguing for several days. I had wanted to go on a junket to New York with Mike Todd and some of the boys; Anne didn't want me to go. She didn't object to my taking the trip, but to my flying in Mike's private plane. Anne insisted I fly a regular commercial airline and meet them in New York.

"But that's just the point!" I said. "The flight is the fun! We'd be going *together*."

Anne was adamant. She did not want me flying in Mike's plane. I had been on the verge of ignoring her and just telling her that I was going anyway. But I didn't go. I fumed instead. Liz Taylor, married to Mike Todd, had a bad cold and didn't go either.

I turned on the car radio to drown out the silence. It was like a bad plot device in a B-movie: my hand left the knob just as the announcer broke in with a newsflash—Mike Todd was dead. His private plane had crashed. Everyone on board was killed.

I pulled over to the side of the road. Neither of us could speak for quite a while. I don't know what had made Anne fight so strongly, but she had saved my life. We got so wrapped up in thinking that the decisions we make in our lives are all-important that we forget that bigger decisions are being made for us.

But I didn't linger on it. My thoughts were on *Spartacus*. My agent was the brilliant Lew Wasserman, head of MCA,

Music Corporation of America. Lew said the only way we could get the picture made was to involve a top director or an important cast. Kirk Douglas alone was not enough.

We went to directors. David Lean, finishing up *The Bridge on the River Kwai,* graciously declined: "I can't somehow fit myself into it style-wise. I couldn't bring it off."

Sixty pages of Howard Fast's screenplay arrived—a disaster, unusable. He hadn't used the dramatic elements he'd put in his own book. It was just characters spouting ideas; speeches on two legs. Very often, the one who writes the book is not the one who should write the screenplay. He's given it his best shot when he's written the book. The same thing had happened with *Lust for Life.* The book by Irving Stone was wonderful. The script by Irving Stone was not.

We were losing precious time in our race with United Artists. To attract stars or a top director, we needed not just a good screenplay, but a great one. And we needed it fast.

Over the years, I'd read a lot of scripts, rarely anything I liked. But when I did say, "I like this script. This is really good," it often turned out to be by Dalton Trumbo, using one of his many *noms de plume.* We knew he was a brilliant writer; we'd heard he was phenomenally fast. He could turn out 40 rough pages a day, a 150-page script, polished, in a week. On a manual typewriter.

Dalton *had* to write fast: he was on the blacklist, making only $2,500 per script. His pre-blacklist salary as a contract writer at MGM in the 1940s, when he wrote *Kitty Foyle* and *A Guy Named Joe,* had been $3,000 a week.

At the time, the studios were terrified; they had knuckled under early, passed the Waldorf Amendment in 1947, pledging not to hire anyone with Communist affiliations.

Some of the people accused of being Communists were Communists, but that is not against the law in the United States. The House Un-American Activities Committee, HUAC, cross-examined people from Hollywood. Twenty-three went willingly and testified to the political affiliations of others. Among them were Gary Cooper, Ronald Reagan, George Murphy, Robert Montgomery, Adolphe Menjou. Because of their testimony and others', ten men went to jail. I think we spend too much time fighting communism instead of fighting to make democracy better. Let's be more confident that we have the best system of government in the world. We become too concerned about the possibility of a pocket of communism in Central America or Vietnam and ignore our contiguous neighbors—Mexico, Canada, even Cuba. We lose track of what democracy is all about.

Dalton Trumbo was one of the Unfriendly Ten. He stood on his rights under the First Amendment, the right of every American to free speech. He went to jail for a year. That was in 1950. Now, almost ten years later, he still couldn't set foot on any studio lot. Senator McCarthy's public discrediting at the hands of journalist Edward R. Murrow on national television, and his death shortly afterward in 1957 did nothing to put out the wildfire. The blacklist was still in place.

Dalton had to hide while he was writing and use an alias on every script. For ten years, he wrote under assumed names, including stories for women's magazines using his wife's name. At the Academy Awards in 1956, the year I didn't win for *Lust for Life*, Dalton Trumbo *did* win Best Screenplay for *The Brave One*, under the alias "Robert Rich." The ceremony was a joke. "Accepting the Oscar for 'Robert Rich,' who unfortunately can't be with us tonight . . ." Everybody in town knew what was going on. Such hypocrisy.

Trumbo hated Howard Fast. Would he want to adapt Fast's novel? Eddie and I approached Trumbo tentatively. Yes, Trumbo said, he thought Fast was just as narrow-minded in his Marxist views as the people who were against communism. The only time they had met, Fast had berated Trumbo for not holding Marxism classes in jail. But Dalton also said he would write the treatment, because "You cannot fight a blacklist for as many years as I have and retain any desire to install a new one." Dalton started writing the outline. Nobody knew, not even Howard Fast.

Very delicately, I presented Dalton's treatment to Howard Fast as Eddie's work, explaining that this was the direction we saw the screenplay going. Fast blew up, called his agent, wanted out of the whole deal. His agent set him straight and Howard returned to work, unwillingly following "Eddie's" outline, but with no better results. It was still terrible.

We knew now that Dalton had to write the full screenplay, and quickly. We set everything up very carefully. Eddie would "front" for Dalton, put his own name on whatever Dalton wrote. Bryna would pay Eddie. Eddie would pass the money on to "Sam Jackson," the alias Dalton had decided to use on *Spartacus*. This was dangerous for me and for Eddie. "Sam Jackson" explained what happened to the money after that:

> For several years I have kept a checking account at the United States National Bank on Colorado Avenue in Pasadena, under the name of James and Dorothy Bonham. I used it as a clearing house for all checks made out to me under pseudonyms. A check would reach me payable to [some pseudonym]; I would then forge my pseudonym's signature, endorse the check as James Bonham, and deposit it. When it had cleared, James Bonham would then draw a check payable to Dalton Trumbo's Bank of America account.
>
> I went through this ridiculous routine because I have *never* endorsed with my own name any check, lest the looseness of Hollywood banking clerks would cause it to be known that DT was working for this or that producer.

Communists might not have been everywhere, but spies were. Banks rewarded clerks for giving information about anyone suspected of being subversive.

Dalton had a different alias for every project, so he could keep them all straight. We had secret meetings at my house, his house; memos went back and forth under the name "Sam Jackson." My files are filled with memos from "Sam Jackson."

It wasn't long before we came to see why Dalton hated Howard Fast. Howard was an incredible egomaniac, the only person who was always right. Everybody else was wrong. Howard asked us to call a meeting of all the department heads—set designers, wardrobe, props, etc. He asked for a chalkboard, different colored chalks, and a pointer. He then proceeded to lecture these people—all at the top of their profession—about how everything they had ever done was wrong. But now he would show them the way. This time, with his guidance, they would get it right.

Without Fast's knowing, Dalton was writing at breakneck speed. He was wonderful to work with, never had any hesitancy about rewriting a scene. If you didn't like a scene, he'd just rip it out of the typewriter, crumple it up, throw it in the wastepaper basket, and start again. He never fought or balked at making changes or taking a different approach. I liked him.

He worked at night, often in the bathtub, the typewriter in front of him on a tray, a cigarette in his mouth (he smoked six packs a day). On his shoulder perched a parrot I had given him, pecking at Dalton's ear while Dalton pecked at the keys.

Eddie and I sat around the office dreaming: wouldn't it be miraculous if we could get Laurence Olivier—*Sir* Laurence Olivier—and Charles Laughton and Peter Ustinov to be in our movie?

While I was in London working on *The Devil's Disciple* with Olivier, I gave him the book of *Spartacus*. He read it and reacted very favorably. He thought Spartacus would be a terrific role—for him. Uh oh. He liked Howard Fast's vision of Spartacus as a character with an aura of divinity about him, looked up to and called "Father" by the men in the mines. But his concept was completely different from mine. In the script Dalton was working on, Spartacus is an animal at the start, illiterate, evolving into a man reacting against circumstances, then acting on his own ideas and becoming a leader. Larry also thought he could direct the film, which we felt would be a tremendous burden for him. But he was interested!

Both companies were racing to get scripts finished. Ira

Wolfert was writing for United Artists. It didn't occur to us that he was just United Artist's front for *their* fast-writing blacklisted writer, Abe Polonsky. The whole system was ridiculous.

The first batch of pages arrived from Dalton—just dialogue, endless dialogue. We panicked. Then we got a note from him: "I know you are gravely alarmed, but there's no need to be. The only way I can write a script is from beginning to end, dialogue only. Then I make first corrections. Then I do the script—that is, fill in shots and description and action." He went on to assure us that our August deadline would be met. He was true to his word.

Dalton worked at top speed, came up with a first draft. Now we needed Lew Wasserman's help in getting our script to Olivier, Laughton, and Ustinov. I thought I'd better tell Lew that Dalton Trumbo was writing the script. He said, "I know." It was becoming the worst-kept secret in Hollywood. Copies went to Olivier and Laughton in London. Lew got a copy of Dalton's rough draft to Peter Ustinov in Switzerland. Lew promised that all three would read it.

Much to our surprise, United Artists' script of *The Gladiators* was finished at the same time—and went to the same three actors. Eddie and I got on a plane to London.

Charles Laughton was doing a play. We went backstage to see him before the performance. We waited as Charles received various guests with joviality and ease. I had always admired Charles, a brilliant actor who played Quasimodo in *The Hunchback of Notre Dame,* and won an Academy Award in 1932 for *The Private Life of Henry VIII.* But I liked him best for his sadistic Captain Bligh in *Mutiny on the Bounty.*

His guests gone, Charles turned to us. "I glanced at the script. Really, a piece of shit." We left very depressed.

Olivier was enthusiastic about the first draft, but had many reservations. Eddie was extremely embarrassed at having to claim it as his work, especially when Olivier praised it. He felt like a terrible fraud.

Back in Los Angeles, Lew Wasserman gave us hope.

"Don't worry. That's just Laughton's attitude. It's a good role, and he'll do it. He needs the money." I couldn't believe it. That was one.

Before the end of August, we got word that Peter Ustinov had many comments and suggestions about his part, but was amenable to playing the role. That was two.

Then on September 4, 1958, a letter from Olivier:

> I have now contracted myself to go to Stratford-on-Avon for the fourth play of the season next year, which is "Coriolanus," and to start rehearsing in June. I imagine this decision will fairly knock me out for any further consideration as director of the film.
>
> If, however, you can still see your way to improving the part of Crassus in relation to the other three roles, then I should be more than happy to look at it again as it is such a gallant enterprise and one I should be extremely proud to be part of. Could you be so kind as to let me see something just as soon as you possibly can?

Three!

We were three-for-three against UA's zero-for-three. But our script was stacked. It highlighted the Romans, the characters we wanted Olivier, Laughton, and Ustinov to play. It was told in flashback, from the point of view of Olivier's character. We had had no time to develop the character of Spartacus. He wasn't even crucified. We had to entice them, allay their fears that Kirk Douglas, this actor who also owned the company, would be able to twist it in his direction. When you're an actor and the producer, wearing two hats, you must have two heads. That makes you kind of a monster. They felt that I was playing a subordinate role. They were all interested. On the basis of these commitments, we made a deal at Universal.

Another phone call from Marty Ritt. They had been rethinking the suggestion we had made months earlier. Oh? Perhaps we were right—maybe we ought to pool our resources. My tone said what my words didn't: "Fuck you, boys."

We had the better script, but they *did* have a script. They also had a director, Yul Brynner, and now Tony Quinn. And they had scouted locations in Europe. They weren't totally out of the picture.

That year's meeting of studio heads and theater owners from all over the country was in Miami. The studios, in alphabetical order, plugged their forthcoming pictures. Down at the end, United Artists talked about their big picture, *The Gladiators*, with Yul Brynner, based on the story of Spartacus. Then Universal talked about *their* big picture, *Spartacus*, with Kirk Douglas. Everybody laughed at the suicidal idea—two studios making huge pictures on the same subject.

They couldn't start shooting in Europe until the weather eased up in the summer. But you can shoot all year round in California. The script needed a lot more work. But it was now or nothing. We decided to shoot—and knock them out.

I got a telegram from United Artists on October 27, 1958:

DEAR KIRK—AT ARTHURS [KRIM] REQUEST YUL BRYNNER HAS AGREED IN THE INTERESTS OF GOOD WILL TO YOUR USE OF TITLE "SPARTACUS."

Yul consoled himself by making *The Magnificent Seven*. That was good news. At that time I was getting extremely bad news from the accountants who were examining my arrangement with Cantor-Fitzgerald and Norton & Rosenthal. My financial situation was a complete disaster. And then I went back East, and my mother died. I returned, and plunged myself into *Spartacus*.

Tony Curtis came to me. He really wanted to be in *Spartacus*. It would be a big picture, and get rid of a commitment he owed Universal. I didn't think there was anything for him, or that he was right for this kind of picture. Since *The Vikings*, he had done *The Defiant Ones*, playing a runaway from a chain gang, shackled to Sidney Poitier. Then two comedies: *Operation Petticoat*, and *Some Like It Hot*, in drag. But Tony was insistent. We made a role for him, a poetic young man named Antoninus who becomes like a son to Spartacus. In the end, the Romans force the two of us to fight to the death. The survivor will be crucified. Neither of us wants the other to have to undergo that agony, so we try to kill each other. I kill Tony. We figured this was simple justice, since he had killed me in *The Vikings*.

If we hadn't had to rush, we would have been much better prepared and had a more finished script. My role of Spartacus was a myth. It didn't exist. I came up with the idea of combining his character and the character of David the Jew. But we had no time to do that now. Contracts were being drawn up.

I sent the script to Howard Fast for suggestions. We talked on the telephone.

He said, "This is the worst script I ever read. It's so bad it's insulting. It's tragic. Actors cannot read the dialogue. None of the scenes can be played."

"You're calling Olivier, Laughton, Ustinov, and me idiots?"

"The only similarity is character names. I don't know why you bought the book. Who wrote this script?"

I gulped. "Eddie Lewis."

"Then Eddie Lewis is the world's worst writer—no talent, no imagination, ignorant. He has a compulsion to prove he can write."

"I was hoping for a more detailed, reflective evaluation from you. This is only a draft, not the final version."

"The only barrier to getting a good script is Eddie Lewis. He is a literary and dramatic half-wit. A film based on this script will be a disaster."

Dalton laughed when he heard this. The parrot cackled.

I had a language scheme worked out for the picture, as I had in *The Vikings*: the Romans would be played by British actors, the slaves by Americans. For Varinia, the slave girl Spartacus marries, who is supposed to be foreign to all of them, I wanted a real foreigner. I had wanted Elsa Martinelli, but she was long gone. Ingrid Bergman turned it down: "too bloody." Jean Simmons wanted the role, but I didn't want her because she was British and didn't fit in with my linguistic scheme.

Jeanne Moreau could play the part. She was not yet a big star, but I had seen her in a movie called *The Lovers*. She exuded sexuality without trying. I went to Paris. Dancing together at Maxim's, I literally kept her at arm's length. I was afraid to hold her body close. She had such sensuality. Raoul Levy, a producer in Paris, committed suicide over her. Jeanne was in a play that had one more month to run. I offered to buy it out. But Jeanne, like United Artists, said "NO." Or rather, *"Non."* I couldn't understand it. Then I found out she was in the middle of a love affair. That's a quality I've found in many French actresses: they fall in love, and that takes precedence over everything. I admire that. Anne has that quality.

We looked at thousands of feet of film of foreign actresses, finally settled on a stunning German girl named Sabina Bethmann. We flew her to Hollywood to test. She looked great on film, but was not much of an actress. We got dialogue coaches to help her lose her accent, Jeff Corey to coach her acting. Jeff was another victim of the blacklist, an actor who had turned to teaching acting to support himself.

I wanted everything about *Spartacus* to be special and authentic. I went to see Jay Sebring, a genius with hair. Jay was a charismatic, tiny little fellow. Good-looking. Well built. Quite a ladies' man. Jay came up with the distinctive look for the slaves—hair cut butch on top, long in back with a tiny ponytail. I don't know if that haircut set any trends in the early sixties, but everybody is walking around with a Spartacut in the eighties.

Jay Sebring and a pregnant Sharon Tate were killed by Charles Manson and his "family" in the Bel Air slaughter in 1969. Jay went with Sharon Tate before Roman Polanski did. There was talk that their romance still continued, even that the baby might have been Jay's. I knew Sharon Tate. Beautiful, naive young girl. I heard it over the radio. The shocking story was the sort of thing you read about in fiction, see in movies. It doesn't happen to people you know. It was incomprehensible, even if a lot of it was drugs. Jay was a tremendous guy. My barber now, Little Joe, was Jay's eighteen-year-old protégé then.

Everything was coming together. Then Universal insisted that I use Anthony Mann as the director. I was against this. Mann had made several successful pictures—*Winchester 73, The Glenn Miller Story, Strategic Air Command*—westerns or soap operas. He was wrong for *Spartacus*. I like people who come up with ideas to make things better; Tony Mann had very little to say. He seemed scared of the scope of the picture. I fought with the studio to replace him. But they had done well financially with him, and ignored all my pleas.

We started shooting on January 27, 1959, with that auspicious cast, with the Dalton Trumbo (I mean "Sam Jackson") script, and with Anthony Mann as director. The first week, shooting the mine sequence in Death Valley, went fine. I was pleasantly surprised. But when we got to the gladiator school, it all started to fall apart. It was clear that Tony Mann was not in control. He let Peter Ustinov direct his own scenes by taking every suggestion Peter made. The suggestions were good—for Peter, but not necessarily for the picture. Peter was a witty man, and got many laughs at Hollywood dinner parties remarking that on a Kirk Douglas picture, "You have to be careful not to act too well." Ironically, Peter was the only one to win an Oscar for acting in *Spartacus*.

The studio came to me. "Kirk, you're right. You have to get rid of Anthony Mann." I balked, unprepared for this sudden shift. I hated making a change when we were already shooting. A commitment is like a marriage: you try to make it work. You don't get a divorce immediately. I tried to keep him. Besides, who could I get to replace him? But they were adamant: they wanted him fired. And they wanted me to do it. At the end of shooting on Friday, February 13, 1959, I sat down with Anthony Mann. It was not easy. "Tony, I'm sorry, but the studio doesn't feel you're right for this movie." I was so touched by the way Tony accepted it, his graciousness.

Maybe he was relieved. I said, "Tony, I owe you a movie." I also owed him $75,000. We paid him in full.

There I was with a distinguished international cast, two weeks of film in the can, a twelve-million-dollar budget— and no director. I wanted Stanley Kubrick, who had directed *Paths of Glory* for Bryna. Stanley had been in pre-production on *One-Eyed Jacks* for Marlon Brando for more than six months, and then Brando decided to direct the film himself. Not exactly a recommendation. Universal said "NO." I fought. The clock was running. In desperation, they capitulated. Stanley read the script, we had meetings all weekend, and at the beginning of the next week, Monday, February 16, we resumed. We lost no days of shooting. You can't switch horses in midstream faster than that.

Monday morning, the principals, in costume, were sitting in the balcony of the gladiator arena. Rumors were flying. I took Stanley into the middle of the arena. "This is your new director." They looked down at this thirty-year-old youth, thought it was a joke. Then consternation—I had worked with Stanley, they hadn't. That made him "my boy." They didn't know that Stanley is nobody's boy. He stands up to anybody.

It was clear that Sabina Bethmann wasn't going to work out as Varinia. She lacked emotion. Kubrick suggested he do an improvisation with her. The scene: he would tell her that she had just lost the part in the movie. Stanley figured this would smoke her out—if she had any talent at all, she would cry or scream or get mad or something.

Eddie and I looked at each other. This was cruel, and Stanley wanted us to participate. Eddie excused himself from the room. I excused myself from the improvisation, but, fascinated, stayed to watch Stanley in action. He explained the scenario to Sabina. Nothing happened. The poor girl froze. That was the end of Sabina. She had worked two days, but we paid her what we owed her—$35,000. She was upset. "What am I going to tell everybody back home?" I told her to tell the truth—"I tried out for a movie, but it didn't work out." Even Olivier said he was up for a role opposite Greta Garbo once, and she didn't want him. She wanted John Gilbert. There was no disgrace in that. Every actor had been through it.

Jean Simmons had always been eagerly waiting in the wings. Only my stubbornness about the linguistic scheme had prevented us from hiring her in the first place. I called her at her ranch in Nogales, Arizona. As she tells it, "Kirk told me to get my ass on out to Los Angeles. I did. Pronto."

Shortly after she started the picture, she had emergency surgery and couldn't work. We shot around her. We would do my scenes with Tony Curtis. Then Tony, relaxing one Sunday afternoon at my house with his new sport, tennis, hurt his leg. He limped off the court, laughing. "I'm not like you," he said to me. "Some goddamn Cossack who can ride a horse for ninety hours straight." The next day he was in the hospital, in a cast from hip to toe. He had nearly severed his Achilles tendon. He couldn't work.

In the middle of all this, Charles Laughton waddled into my dressing room, preceded by his belly. I thought of Bertolt Brecht's poem "Laughton's Belly:"

> *Here it was: not unexpected, but not usual either*
> *And built of foods which he*
> *At his leisure had selected, for his entertainment.*
> *And to a good plan, excellently carried out.*

"Yes, Charles. What is it?"
"I am very unhappy."
"What's the matter, Charles?"
His famous lower lip pouting, Charles said, "I'm going to sue you."
I was stunned. "Why, Charles?"
"I will cause you much trouble."
It was so outrageous, I started to laugh. My mother had

recently died; my business manager, who I thought was a father to me, had ruined me financially; Jean Simmons had been out sick for over a month; Tony Curtis was in a wheel-chair; I was in the middle of an epic movie written by a blacklisted ex-convict, directed by a twenty-nine-year-old; I was months over schedule, 250 percent over budget. And now Charles Laughton was going to sue me? I couldn't stop laughing. Charles looked at me strangely. I was now laughing hysterically. As he waddled out, sputtering, I called, "Go ahead! Sue me! What the fuck do I care!" I never did find out why he wanted to sue me.

We couldn't shoot around people any more, so we shut production down at the studio, and sent Olivier up to William Randolph Hearst's castle in San Simeon to film some exteriors.

Tony came back to work. Jean came back to work. I got a virus. For the first time in my career, I was too sick to work. They shot around me.

I made overtures of friendship to Stanley. One Saturday afternoon, I brought him with me to see my psychiatrist. I had been in analysis for over four years. I wanted Stanley to know everything about me. During that session we talked about silent films, how they used music to set the scene for the actors. We tried it in several scenes of *Spartacus* that would have only music under them. It really helped.

But sometimes Stanley got hooked on things. One day he decided that he wanted to raise the ceiling of the stage two feet. I said, "What, are you crazy?" It was impractical, expensive, time-consuming, and not essential. But overall, his selectivity and his concepts were wonderful.

Dalton had written a brilliant seduction scene between Olivier's character, the wealthy Roman aristocrat Crassus, and Tony Curtis's character, the sensitive, poetic slave boy named Antoninus. It was very subtle; nothing explicit. The censors weren't quite sure it was about homosexuality, but just in case, they wanted it out. We argued, hoping to keep it in. It was just another way Romans abused the slaves.

INTERIOR CRASSUS' PALACE—MARBLE BATHROOM—CRASSUS AND SLAVES—NIGHT

A sunken tub in its center dominates this magnificent apartment. Crassus lolls at his ease in the tub. Two slaves stand at his head, alert to his every want. A third slave, on hands and knees, shampoos his master's hair. Some distance away stands Antoninus, silent and watchful and withdrawn, holding a folded robe over one arm. Crassus, as we come in on the scene, is in the course of a gentle, ironic inquisition of his new, young slave.

CRASSUS
Do you steal, Antoninus?

ANTONINUS
No.

CRASSUS
No, *Master.*

ANTONINUS
No, Master.

CRASSUS
Do you lie?

ANTONINUS
No, Master.

CRASSUS
Have you ever dishonored the gods?

ANTONINUS
No, Master.

CRASSUS
Do you refrain from these vices out of
respect for the moral virtues?

ANTONINUS
Yes, Master.

CRASSUS
Do you eat oysters?

ANTONINUS
When I have them.

CRASSUS
Do you eat snails?

ANTONINUS
No, Master.

Crassus laughs softly.

CRASSUS
Do you consider the eating of oysters to
be moral, and the eating of snails to be
immoral?

ANTONINUS
I—I don't think so.

CRASSUS
Of *course* not. It's a matter of appetite, isn't it?

ANTONINUS
Yes, Master

CRASSUS
An appetite has nothing to do with morals, has it?

ANTONINUS
No, Master.

CRASSUS
(to servant)
I'm finished.

*One servant assists him from the tub, while another swathes
him completely in a deep-pile towel. Crassus, paying them no
heed, continues to keep his eyes on Antoninus, and addresses
him throughout the above action.*

CRASSUS
Therefore no appetite is immoral, is it?
It's merely different.

ANTONINUS
Yes, Master.

*While the two servants are patting Crassus dry through the
swathing towel, a third powders his feet.*

CRASSUS
My robe, Antoninus.

*Antoninus slowly approaches his master, unfolds the robe, and
holds it forth for him. As the towel is removed, the robe re-
places it.*

CRASSUS
My appetite includes both snails and
oysters.

The rest of the scene with Olivier and Curtis continues with Olivier talking about "The might, the majesty, the terror of Rome," and we know he is speaking of himself. "There is the power that bestrides the known world, like a colossus. No nation can withstand Rome. No *man* can withstand her. And how much less—a boy. There's only one way to deal with Rome, Antoninus. You must serve her. You must abase yourself before her. You must grovel at her feet. You must *love* her."

We argued and argued, and finally the censors hemmed and hawed and said that the scene *might* work if we changed "snails and oysters" to "artichokes and truffles." They were also uncomfortable with the word "appetite." We shot it, hoping to convince them. They looked at it, stood firm. We had to cut it out of the picture.

Film writers have never been treated with much respect. When I first came to Hollywood, writers had to stay in their cubicles, like prisoners in pens, writing all day. At the end of the day they were asked: "How many pages did you write today?" One writer, Jerry Wald, worried that the big dog he left behind in his apartment wasn't getting enough exercise. Then he hit upon the solution. When the phone rang, the dog ran around the apartment like crazy, so twice a day, Jerry would pick up the phone in his cubbyhole at the studio, call his own apartment, and let the phone ring for quite a while, knowing that the dog would run around. Then he'd hang up.

Slaving away in the cell next to Jerry were the Epstein brothers, Julius and Phil, identical twins and practical jokers. That was how they had gotten their reputation as terrific lovers. According to Hollywood legend, one would be in bed with a girl, get up, go into the bathroom—and the other twin would come and get into bed, ready to go. They wowed a lot of women that way.

The Epstein brothers were aware of Jerry Wald and his dog problem. One of them somehow got the key to Jerry's apartment, went in, and waited. When Jerry made his morning call to the apartment, Epstein let it ring a couple of times, then picked up the phone and said, *"Woof! Woof!"*

Stanley, Eddie Lewis, and I had a meeting. A sticky subject came up. What writer's name should we put on the screen for *Spartacus*? The script now said, "By Eddie Lewis and Sam Jackson." The options: (1) leave the credit the way it was. Eddie vetoed this. (2) Use only Eddie's name. Eddie vetoed this violently. (3) Use only Sam Jackson. This was much more difficult. Eddie Lewis was a real person. Sam Jackson didn't exist. We would have to fabricate a string of lies around him, the way the producers did when Dalton wrote *The Brave One*. And besides, it fooled no one. What to do?

Kubrick jumped in with his solution. "Use my name."

Eddie and I looked at each other, horrified. I said, "Stanley, wouldn't you feel embarrassed to put your name on a script that someone else wrote?"

He looked at me as if he didn't know what I was talking about. "No." He would have been delighted to take the credit.

The whole business of the blacklist angered Eddie and me, but Stanley's eagerness to use Dalton revolted us. That ended the meeting. That night it all suddenly became very clear. I knew what name to put on the screen. Eddie did, too. The next morning, I called the gate at Universal. "I'd like to leave a pass for Dalton Trumbo." The masquerade was over. All my friends told me I was being stupid, throwing my career away. It was a tremendous risk. At first, nobody believed me. Dalton did. For the first time in ten years, he walked onto a studio lot. He said, "Thanks, Kirk, for giving me back my name." The blacklist was broken.

Otto Preminger called me from New York. He was annoyed that Trumbo was working on *Spartacus* instead of *Exodus*, his project. He was amazed that I was using Dalton Trumbo's name openly.

Soon after, he held a press conference announcing that Dalton Trumbo would be the writer of *Exodus*.

I wasn't thinking of being a hero and breaking the blacklist; it wasn't until later that I realized the significance of that impulsive gesture. I was just thinking, how unfair for someone to say, "Put my name on it. Let me get the credit for someone else's work."

And yet, of all the directors I've worked with, Stanley places second to none. He is a brilliant director. A brilliant director is the one who makes the right choices. William Wyler is a perfect example. He never told me what to do on *Detective Story*. He'd just squint and say, "Do it again." Then we did it. And he knew when it was right; he knew which take to choose.

My association with Stanley is a strange one. I don't know of any other director that I did more for, to get him started in filmmaking. Harris-Kubrick shared offices in my building. The Bryna Company signed Stanley Kubrick for three pictures in addition to *Paths of Glory* and *Spartacus*.

The first project Stanley submitted was his original screenplay, *I Stole 16 Million Dollars*, based on Willie Sutton, the famous bank robber who, when asked, "Why do you rob banks?" answered, "Because that's where the money is." I thought the script was poorly written. I told Stanley I didn't want to do it. He shrugged. "I'll get Cary Grant." No one has ever heard of that script since.

While *Spartacus* was being edited in the fall of 1959, I made another picture, *Strangers When We Meet*. It was directed by Richard Quine, a very talented director who was having a relationship with Kim Novak, the leading lady. One morning, we were shooting a scene down at the beach. Obviously, Kim and Dick had been discussing the scene, and she was excited about a wonderful idea she had come up with. Apparently, Dick had agreed with her wholeheartedly. I listened to her argument, told her exactly why it was impossible to do the scene that way. She looked at Dick. He looked at me and said, "You know, Kim, he's right."

Kim went berserk. She ripped up the pages, started to

make incoherent sounds, screamed, went nuts. It was impossible to shoot with her for the rest of the day. The next day we shot the scene the way it was written.

We got through the picture, and I enjoyed working with her, although I do think that she convinced Richard to give the picture the wrong ending. The original ending in the book, very powerful, was that after our love affair had ended, Walter Matthau, who was playing a heavy, comes to pick her up in a car, and she decides what the hell, and goes off with him. Life goes on. Instead, she preferred to spurn him, pull her trenchcoat up around her neck, and walk off like Charlie Chaplin. I didn't think that was the right ending, but those are the hazards of working with someone who's romantically involved with the director.

We looked at Kubrick's first rough assembly of *Spartacus*. Everyone was unhappy. Dalton wrote a word-by-word critique.

It was a detailed evaluation of the director, the changes in dialogue, the scenes and performances. It was over eighty pages, all typed by him, divided into two sections—"The Two Conflicting Points of View on Spartacus" and "Scene-by-Scene Run-Through." It is the most brilliant analysis of movie-making that I have ever read. It should be studied by every filmmaker. After reading it, Kubrick must blush with shame at his hubris in suggesting his name be used as the writer. Now we had to restructure, to reshoot.

We needed more money from Universal. We had just gotten more money to shoot battle scenes. The battle was only suggested in the first screenplay: you saw them about to begin, then a time dissolve and the bloody aftermath. But it was apparent now that we needed to see the battle. We would do the reshoots when Stanley came back from filming the battle scenes in Spain, where we had received the cooperation of the government to use their army as the Roman army.

And we needed sound—male voices saying "Hail, Crassus!" and "I am Spartacus" in English. We needed thousands of voices. We came up with the idea of getting the lines at a college football game during half-time. We settled on Michigan State in East Lansing, because, as I said, "It's only natural for Spartacus to go to the Spartans for help." So, on Saturday, October 17, 1959, 76,000 screaming fans at the Michigan State–Notre Dame football game made history when they yelled and made noises that were recorded on three-channel sound equipment and laid into the *Spartacus* soundtrack back in Hollywood.

Stanley came back with incredible footage of the battle, so wide that he'd had to shoot from almost half a mile away. At the end of the year, we started reshooting the other scenes.

Jokes were flying; extras were paying off their mortgages; some were building swimming pools. *Spartacus* would be shooting forever. At the beginning of *Spartacus*, Lew Wasserman at MCA was my agent; he worked for me. In the middle of shooting, MCA bought Universal; I worked for him. For an entire movie studio, MCA paid $11,250,000, three-quarters of a million dollars *less* than the budget of *Spartacus*.

I was getting tired, real tired. One Friday, Eddie looked at me. "What are you doing this weekend?"

"I'm going to drive to Palm Springs and just rest."

He said, "What do you mean, *drive*? You're a *star*. You *own* Bryna. Let me get you a limousine and a driver."

He's right, I thought. Yeah. "Go ahead."

A long, shiny black limousine pulled up and I climbed in, still dressed in my dirty burlap slave tunic. I just plopped down on a silver blanket in the back, and we breezed on down the freeway. I thought, by God, Eddie's right. I *am* a star. I wish the kids in Amsterdam could see me now. Here I am, my company producing *Spartacus*. I'd come a long way from hitchhiking to college on that truckload of fertilizer. I was dozing off when the driver pulled of the freeway into a gas station.

He said, "I'll just be a minute. Men's room."

After he left, I got out and stretched. There was a little café. I went in to get a beer. Then I realized I didn't have any money in my tunic. As I headed back to the car, I saw the driver get in, start the car, and drive away. I stood there. This can't be. He'll come back in a minute. I waited. Nothing happened. I felt like an idiot. I went back into the café, bummed some change for the telephone. I called the sheriff in the next town, Redlands. "My name is Kirk Douglas, and my driver is going to be driving through Redlands in a minute, in a big black limousine, and he thinks I'm asleep in the back, but I'm not. When you see this limousine, will you please stop him?"

"Don't be a wise guy. We'll run you in." Click.

Now I was angry. I knew it was too good to last. I went out to the freeway, stuck out my thumb. Here I was, back to hitchhiking. Two girls recognized me and picked me up, all excited. It was a frightening ride. They were driving and talking, and mostly looking at me. "Oh, wow! The girls in the office will never believe this!"

"Keep your eyes on the road. Eyes on the road."

They got so excited they missed the turn-off to Palm Springs and were headed out to Indio. I made them hang a "U" in the middle of the freeway and go back.

In the meantime, the limousine driver went merrily on to Palm Springs. My wife and I were supposed to go out to dinner at Dean Martin's that night, and she was waiting. The limo pulled up to the house. Anne came out, all dressed for dinner. The driver opened the back door of the limo, got a strange expression on his face, closed the door, jumped back in the car and started the engine.

Anne said, "What happened? Did you lose my husband?"

"Yes."

She thought it was funny.

The chauffeur said, "I'll go back and get him."

"Don't bother. I know my husband. He won't be there." She went to dinner, figuring that I would get there somehow.

The girls finally dropped me off at my house. I was late, looked for the keys so I could drive over to Dean Martin's. I couldn't find car keys. I found something else. Spartacus bicycled to Dean Martin's house. Issur laughed at him all the way. I was *so* glad Eddie had talked me into that relaxing limousine ride.

Spartacus went back to the editors after the reshoots, and I went to Mexico to film another Bryna production, *The Last Sunset*, based on Howard Rigsby's novel *Sundown at Crazy Horse*. The story about incest fascinated me. Television deals with this subject in the 1980s, but in 1960, you had to treat it very delicately. I played O'Malley, a drifting cowhand in the Old West pursued by lawman Stribling. O'Malley stops in to visit a woman he hasn't seen in years, falls in love with her beautiful sixteen-year-old daughter, has an affair with the girl, and then finds out that he is the girl's father. Guilt-ridden, O'Malley commits suicide by walking into a shoot-out with Stribling with no bullets in his gun.

Rock Hudson, the biggest box-office draw in the world, played Stribling. So of course he had top billing. Universal, financing and releasing the picture, worried about the parts being even. We had to beef up Rock's part, put in scenes that really didn't suit the story, just to satisfy Universal.

I had a problem working with Rock Hudson that I did not understand at the time. He avoided any kind of direct contact with me. I was aware of how difficult it must have been for him—his co-star also the producer, the boss. I tried everything I could to make him feel comfortable. But Rock always had a strange attitude toward me, never dealt with me directly. He would make demands to the studio. Then the studio would come to me and say, "You have to do this and this." When I saw him socially, it was all pleasant. But there was never any feeling of friendship—or of animosity. Just this strange distance and neutrality.

In Rock, I saw what the rest of the world saw: a tall, dark, husky actor. It never occurred to me that he was homosexual. I don't think that way. I don't draw a sharp line between masculine and feminine. We all have both sides. And we need them, especially artists. An artist needs what people refer to as feminine traits—sensitivity, intuition. And I'm attracted to women who have what are sometimes called masculine traits—efficiency, capability. Like Anne. I find those traits attractive, so I never pass judgment.

I'm glad I didn't know, until I read Rock's autobiography, published posthumously, that he was most attracted to blond, blue-eyed, rugged men.

Rock Hudson's death of AIDS in 1985 made headlines on front pages everywhere. Pictures of a sickly Rock Hudson kissing the beautiful Linda Evans of "Dynasty" were published in every country. The world of the arts has probably suffered the greatest loss from this plague. Gays are a vital force in the arts, have made tremendous contributions in theater, dance, movies, music. Almost every day now, the obituary columns in *Variety* and the *Hollywood Reporter* list deaths from AIDS. How sad that young people, who should be carefree, have to live with this. When I was growing up, fear of pregnancy was the main problem. Condoms were the answer. Then came the pill. But fear of death from sex is something that people of my generation, sexually active after the discovery of the antibiotics that conquered syphilis and gonorrhea, have never had to live with.

I sent the script of *The Last Sunset* to Lauren Bacall. I had enjoyed working with her in *Young Man with a Horn*, and I never forgot her kindness in giving me her uncle's coat when we were in drama school. My psychiatrist once said to me, "Don't you ever stop repaying?" Betty's reaction was strange. She was indignant. She berated me for even submitting the script to her. I said, "Betty, it's the leading female role. You have Rock Hudson in love with you, Kirk Douglas in love with you. I think it's a very good part." She was not convinced. I gave the part to Dorothy Malone, who did a very good job. Carol Lynley played the part of my incestuous daughter.

We decided to shoot the movie in Mexico. Eddie Lewis suggested a director he thought was very talented, Robert Aldrich. Then, (on Friday, November 27, 1959) I got this letter from Aldrich:

Naturally, I am more than emotionally anxious . . . I am completely dedicated to the hope that somehow, some way, you will decide that it is in our collective best interests that I direct "THE LAST SUNSET." I have no possible way or wish to influence your final decision, but . . . if there were ever a happy marriage between the right time, the real need and the true talent to exploit another's efforts in your own behalf . . . Now is such a time. I *have* to do your picture, and I have to do it better than any picture you have ever made before.

He made notes that he wanted me to have even if I decided he shouldn't direct the picture. No strings attached.

This approach was unprecedented for me, and I was moved by his enthusiasm. With Eddie Lewis urging me, I said, "O.K."

Robert Aldrich arrived in Mexico with five writers—all working on other projects. I couldn't believe that a director who was so desperate to direct a picture with two major stars would arrive on location and work on other projects. I was furious. I told him to concentrate on the movie he was being paid to do. I made him get rid of the writers. Aldrich never forgave me for that. It was a cool relationship, but he proved himself a competent director.

Shooting in Mexico, everyone's always careful of the water and the food. Joseph Cotten was very finicky, brought canned food from America, drank only bottled water. He never touched any food from Mexico. And, of course, he was the first one to become sick. He became violently ill, completely dehydrated. You can take all the precautions in the world, and still get the bug.

The Last Sunset is another example of how a studio operates. Universal insisted on controlling the production. The publicity department sent over pages and pages of suggestions for titles, most of them atrocious:

The Magnificent Two
The Majestic Brutes
The Tragic Brutes

Seething Guns
The Fuel and the Fire
Thunderblast
Two to Make Hate
Lion in My Path
Back Against the Wall
Trigger Talk
Death Is My Middle Name
Appointment with a Dead Sun
A Commotion at Sunset
Shoe the Wild Sea-Mare
Long Day, Short Sunset
All Girls Wear Yellow Dresses
A Primrose from O'Malley
My Gun, My Life!

Unfortunately, this was not the worst of my problems with the studio. I stuck strictly to their budget, finished the picture exactly on their schedule—and suddenly was informed that the picture was a million dollars over budget. To this day I don't know why. I protested that I'd done everything according to their rules, fulfilled all my obligations to them. Nevertheless, there was an overcharge of a million dollars.

When I got back, the editing of *Spartacus* was in the final stages, and the scoring. We got Alex North to write the music. Alex had worked on a long string of excellent pictures, and been nominated for Academy Awards for six of them.

Strangers When We Meet, my picture with Kim Novak, opened well in July 1960. *Spartacus* was going to open in the fall. We considered opening in Rome in early September, at the end of the Olympics, with a reception at the Roman Baths. But the weather is unpredictable, we'd be rushed, etc. We decided to open in New York on October 19.

The American Legion, the world's largest veterans' organization, attacked me. They sent a letter to 17,000 local posts: "DON'T SEE *SPARTACUS*." They named me as bad guy for employing Dalton Trumbo.

Hedda Hopper got into the act. She blasted *Spartacus*:

> It has acres of dead people, more blood and gore than you ever saw in your whole life.
> In the final scene, Spartacus' mistress, carrying her illegitimate baby, passes along the Appian Way with 6,000 crucified men on crosses.
> That story was sold to Universal from a book written by a Commie and the screen script was written by a Commie, so don't go to see it.

She was applauded.

And Stanley Kubrick was giving interviews to the press saying that he "improvised a lot on the set"—an insult to Dalton, who was furious.

I later talked to Malcolm McDowell, the star of *A Clockwork Orange*. "How did you like working with Kubrick?"

"That son of a bitch!"

"Why?"

"I scratched the cornea of my left eye. It hurt, I couldn't see. Kubrick said, 'Let's go on with the scene. I'll favor your other eye.'"

He had many more stories to tell me.

Over the years, Stanley has gone out of his way to disown *Spartacus*, and knock me. Recently, in London, I spoke to a group of journalists on the opening of *Tough Guys*. One of them said, "What does Stanley Kubrick have against you and *Spartacus*?" This is almost twenty years after *Spartacus* was made.

I answered, "I guess Stanley was annoyed that I handed him a film already in production with Olivier, Laughton, Ustinov, Douglas, and a great script by Dalton Trumbo that he was anxious to claim as his own."

Stanley is not a writer. He has always functioned better if he got a good writer and worked with him as an editor. He was great at developing a concept. For example, in the scene where we see Jean Simmons for the first time, as she's ladling out food to the slaves, originally, there was dialogue.

Stanley came up with the idea of losing the dialogue, just using music. It worked much better. But that's not the same as writing a script. I have a copy of the terrible script of *Paths of Glory* that he wrote to make it more commercial. If we had shot that script, Stanley might still be living in an apartment in Brooklyn instead of in a castle in England.

All this only proves that you don't have to be a nice person to be extremely talented. You can be a shit and be talented and, conversely, you can be the nicest guy in the world and not have any talent. Stanley Kubrick is a talented shit.

In the fall of 1961, Louis Blau, a very pleasant lawyer, came to see me with his client Stanley Kubrick at my home on Canon Drive. Stanley said nothing. Blau did all the talking. He said that Stanley wanted to get out of his contract with me. I thought about it. People advised me to hold him to the contract. But I knew how much I chafed when I was under a contract that I wanted to break. You can't keep someone committed to a contract against his will. We made some minimal arrangement, and on December 15, 1961, I released him. In the nearly thirty years since *Spartacus,* Stanley has made only seven movies. If I had held him to his contract, half of his remaining movies would have been made for my company.

The Hollywood premiere of *Spartacus* was held on Wednesday, October 19, 1960. The 8:00 P.M. black-tie premiere at the Pantages Theatre, and the midnight supper that followed at the Beverly Hilton were a benefit for Cedars of Lebanon Hospital. Movie premieres always look glamorous on newsreels and TV. That's because the best ones are planned just as carefully as any movie, and cost a lot.

Anne revolutionized charity premieres. In the past, studios had offered the movie to be used for charity and would insist on receiving a block of free tickets. Anne pointed out to them that the publicity they were getting was worth a lot, and she convinced them to pay for their tickets *and* make a contribution to charity.

Spartacus was a big hit, even in Russia. They saw it as

their revolution, the uprising of the slaves against the masters. I felt as though my life had come full circle: Russian immigrants come to America, where they have the freedom to make the story of the Russian immigrants. Ma and Pa would have liked it.

President Kennedy sneaked out of the White House in the middle of a snowstorm one night, to go see *Spartacus* at the Warner Theater. I would have been glad to provide him with a print, but he was impulsive and wanted to see it right then.

He never mentioned it. But Bobby Kennedy later kidded me about it. He said, "You know, my brother helped you with *Spartacus*."

I said, "Yes, he did." He became a number-one fan of the picture.

At that time, I was averaging three movies a year. A strange life, 90 percent concerned with making movies. If you're starring in three movies a year, and producing most of them, there's an enormous amount of work in the preparation and selling of each one before you even get to the actual filming. Then there is the work of post-production. It was a terrible life for my wife, living with me under those circumstances. And for my children. Now, averaging one picture a year, I have much more time to look around and see what's happening. When I comment to my wife that I wasn't aware of these people, or that event, she says, "It was always that way. You were just too busy making movies." It was an unnatural life, just being wrapped up in make-believe characters.

Spartacus took three years out of my life—more time than the real-life Spartacus spent waging war against the Roman Empire.

Twenty-seven

LONELY ARE THE BRAVE

My love affair with Dalton Trumbo continued. After *Spartacus,* he was supposed to start writing a script for me based on Edward Abbey's novel *The Brave Cowboy.* Instead, he was working on *Exodus* for Otto Preminger. I called him on it. He said, "Remember when we were working on *Spartacus,* we fucked Preminger? Well, now it's your turn to get fucked." I could deal with that kind of openness. So I went off to make another movie.

Town Without Pity, set up by the Mirisch Company in conjunction with Bryna, was directed by Gottfried Reinhardt. I think it's the best thing he's ever done. I had enjoyed working with him on *Equilibrium,* where I met Pier Angeli. Now, I was working with him and another beautiful young girl, Christine Kaufmann.

Town Without Pity was a contemporary story about the problems of American troops in Germany. A girl charges four GIs with rape. I'm the army lawyer in a dilemma: in order to keep the GIs from receiving the death penalty, I have to put the girl on the witness stand and cut her to ribbons. If they let the GIs off with life in prison, I won't have to cross-examine her. I beg her father to settle for the lesser penalty, so that she won't have to testify, but he insists, and I have no choice. As a clever lawyer, I do what I have to do—rip her to shreds. She breaks down and later commits suicide. One life for four. My character is devastated when he learns this.

We shot the movie in Munich and in Vienna—home of Sacher torte, Wiener schnitzel, and Hitler. Vienna reminded me of an aging courtesan, with its decaying baroque buildings, enormous doors inviting theatrical entrances. The city was charming and schmaltzy, but underneath corrupt and insidious. A perfect setting for Kurt Waldheim. I heard Brecht's *Threepenny Opera* there for the first time, and was particularly taken with one song, "Mack the Knife." I thought it could be a big hit in the United States. So did Bobby Darin.

At one point, a whole group of Americans came to visit us in Munich. There were Lew Wasserman, his wife Edie, Ray Stark, Charlie Feldman. About twenty people. Anne and I took them to a restaurant, the Schwarzwalder, the Black Forest restaurant, famous for its wine. It didn't serve beer, a unique thing in Germany. I was feeling very Continental, and wanted to impress my American friends with my linguistic abilities. In my best German, I ordered the wine that I thought my wife, who knows much more than I do about wine, had ordered a few days before. When they brought it to me, I went through the ritual of sniffing it, commenting on the bouquet, the aroma; tasting it and declaring it to be excellent. Then the waiter went around the table filling glasses.

During all this, Anne was on the opposite side of the table talking with Lew Wasserman, paying no attention to my pompous act of being the Continental. When the wine came to my wife, she sipped it and immediately called the wine steward over. He took it, smelled it, and immediately started to pick up all the glasses that he had poured. All eyes turned to me as he went around collecting glasses, coming closer to me. As he came to pick up my wine, I put my hand over the glass. "I like it." That ended my career as a wine connoisseur.

Recently, a young fan came up to me and said, *"Lonely Are the Brave* is my favorite movie. I thought you were terrific in it."

"Thank you," said I modestly. "I thought so, too."

Lonely Are the Brave is my favorite movie. I love the theme that if you try to be an individual, society will crush you.

Pictures come in strange ways. At a cocktail party, Joe Berry, an acquaintance not in the film industry, suggested that I read a book called *The Brave Cowboy*, by Edward Abbey. I picked up a paperback copy. One look at the cover and I almost never opened it: a cowboy with a gun in his hand, his bandaged head oozing blood. It had nothing to do with the story. But once I read about this modern-day cowboy still living by the code of the Old West, who breaks into jail to help his friend, then flees on horseback and is pursued by helicopters, I had to make it into a movie.

Whenever I loved a book, the studios hated it. But I had a contract that permitted me, if I did not go over a budget of three million dollars, to make what they called a "disapproved picture." This was a disapproved picture.

Again, I got into arguments with Universal about the title. I thought *The Brave Cowboy* was ironic. I wanted to call it *The Last Cowboy*. But again, the publicity department at Universal bombarded me with pages and pages of titles.

In Fury Bred
Rugged Justice
Wild Gun, Wild Heart
Forked Trail
The Granite Cage
High Is the Trail
The Jailbreak!
Trail of Murder!
When I Say Go!

Pursuit!
Relentless!
Ride the Man Down!
Give Me a Gun!

And a leftover from *The Last Sunset* title fest, *My Gun, My Life*, but this time minus the exclamation point. They finally decided, over my objections, that it should be called *Lonely Are the Brave*. To this day, I'm not quite sure what it means. Very often, people say, "Gee, I love . . . what's that picture? You know, with you and the horse going over the mountain." The picture sticks in their minds, but not the title.

My dear friend Dalton Trumbo finally wrote the screenplay. Of the seventy-five movies I've acted in, and all the others I've produced, and all the movies I've ever heard of, it's the only time that I know of a writer producing a perfect screenplay: one draft, no revisions. Like a hole-in-one. We shot it. It was a plus that Edward Abbey liked the screenplay, too. He was magnanimous enough to say that he thought it was an improvement over the book, particularly the dialogue. But he liked his title better.

And the cast was perfect. We wanted a semidocumentary feel to the movie, realism. Black and white photography. Gena Rowlands plays the woman I'm in love with, the wife of my best friend, who's in jail for helping illegal aliens get into the country. She was superb.

Walter Matthau was wonderful as the sheriff who hunts me down while having to put up with Bill Schallert's not-too-bright deputy. A marvelous relationship emerged between my character and Matthau's. He develops tremendous admiration and respect for this character whom he tracks but sees only at the very end of the picture. The driver of the truck filled with toilets that runs me down on the highway was Carroll O'Connor in his screen debut.

I get into a bar fight with a unique heavy, a brilliant idea of Edward Abbey's—a vicious one-armed man. He was played by Bill Raisch, Burt Lancaster's stand-in, who had done almost no acting at all. Bill had been an adagio dancer in the Ziegfeld Follies, and had lost his arm in a shipboard explosion. He was dynamic and articulate, not mean at all, and dedicated to the idea that amputees can lead full lives.

Even now, I'm constantly running into people who tell me they named their horse "Whisky," after my beautiful palomino mare. I used the name again for my horse in *The Villain*, in 1978. We got a joke out of it. I walk into a saloon, pound on the bar, demand "Whisky!"—and my horse ambles in through the swinging doors.

Lonely Are the Brave is one of the most physically difficult pictures I have done. We shot the movie in and around Albuquerque, the same terrain we'd covered in *Ace in the Hole*, aka *The Big Carnival*, but up in the mountains this time. We ran into snow, fog, and freezing rain—in May. I hadn't seen such bad weather in the summertime since *The Vikings*. Crew members passed out or got sick from the lack of oxygen 11,000 feet up. Or we couldn't shoot because of strong, dusty winds. We took to carrying a wind machine around with us, so that we could have wind when we needed it, and match shots to the wind that Mother Nature provided unasked. It was also one of the first times that a helicopter was used as a camera mount; working it out was very tricky.

I took David Miller as a director, and regretted it. I felt that he did a far from brilliant job. He was unhappy on location. I played pimp and introduced him to a girl. Anything to try to keep him happy and get through the picture. I thought he was the only one who didn't come up to the high standards of all the other elements in the picture.

In the middle of the filming, David got word that his father had died. He left for a couple of days, but we couldn't afford to stop. Eddie Lewis took over as director, did a good job. I asked him, "Were you nervous?" He replied, "When you have a great script, excellent actors, a good cameraman, and no special effects, the director can go home."

I had many arguments with David while we were shooting. Once, he had me with the horse right on the edge of a very narrow ledge with a steep drop. He wanted me to walk around the horse on the outside. I said, "David, are you crazy? If the horse just bumps me, off I go. If he just shifts a foot, he could knock me right off."

He muttered.

I said, "Please, David, if you don't mind, let me go around the horse on the inside. Against the wall." The horse wasn't going to fall, because the horse protects himself. In movies, I've gone through a narrow pass and had my legs cut, because the horse could get through. If there's an overhanging branch, and the horse can get through, *you* have to duck. A horse never looks out for anything but himself.

This annoyed David. And I was annoyed that he was annoyed, that he didn't see, that he was so insensitive to human safety. I would have expected a director to say, "You know, you're right. Go around this way."

It's this kind of thinking—or lack of it—that leads to accidents like the disaster that occurred in *Twilight Zone.* People just don't stop to think that something might be dangerous. Filmmakers get so caught up in what they're doing, it impairs their judgment. I followed the *Twilight Zone* trial. What a tragedy! The leading actor was decapitated and two children, working illegally, were killed. All unnecessarily.

Like Jack Burns, the cowboy I played, the best relationship I had on the picture was with my horse. Of course, the horse couldn't talk back. And probably the horse didn't know I was the producer.

We had sneak previews of *Lonely Are the Brave* at a theater in Glendale, California, that was playing *Breakfast at Tiffany's,* starring Audrey Hepburn. The sneak was more successful than any other sneak for a Bryna picture, including *Spartacus.* And with two completely different audiences —teenagers, and sophisticated adults. It was talked about as an Academy Award contender, along with *To Kill a Mockingbird,* starring Gregory Peck as a humanitarian southern lawyer; Montgomery Clift in *Freud;* and Eugene O'Neill's autobiographical *Long Day's Journey into Night,* with Katharine Hepburn playing his drug-addicted mother.

Even the people at the Production Code Administration (the censors) were praising it:

"Lonely Are the Brave" is proof that outstanding films can still be made without the immorality and decadence which pervade so many of today's movies. This is an exciting story which reveals the very heart of the American spirit. Kirk's performance is not only different, it's superb.

I pleaded with Universal not to release *Lonely Are the Brave* like a cheap little Western, which is how they saw it. Please release it modestly, like an art film: spend no money on advertising, put it in one or two theaters and give it a chance to grow, to find its audience by word of mouth. This was not a ridiculous request. I had asked Walter Reade, Jr., president of Walter Reade theaters, to look at the movie and let me know what he thought. He wrote, very frankly:

I must say I was terribly impressed with the film. . . . First of all, as to the title. I am sure you and your associates have spent a great deal of time on the title, but I think it is a real rotten title and can't do anything for box-office at all. . . . I think it is a word of mouth picture; it has to have a lot of exposure and a very slow release before a decision is made as to just which route it can go. . . .

Instead, Universal threw the movie out fast into mass release—no press screenings, no big campaign, no first-run movie theaters. Within two weeks, at the same time it was breaking box-office records in London, and getting rave reviews from *Time, Newsweek,* and other publications, they pulled it out of theaters in the United States because it was doing so badly. The egos of the studio heads wouldn't let them admit they had made a mistake, and capitalize on the publicity. They just dropped the picture flat. Bewildered press people were writing things like, "Lonely is a picture called 'Lonely Are the Brave,'" and "Everybody thinks

'Lonely Are the Brave' is terrific except the people at Universal."

Eddie Lewis and I were so furious that we wrote a nine-page letter to Universal, detailing how badly we felt they had handled the picture, and suggesting remedies. Nothing came of it.

Lonely Are the Brave has become a cult classic. It is still my favorite. Years later, Artie Shaw, a brilliant musician, came to me and said, "I'd like to take *Lonely Are the Brave* all around the country and sell it, distribute it right." He loved the movie that much.

In 1967, Warren Beatty had the same problem with *Bonnie and Clyde* at Warner Brothers—the picture was just tossed out into mass release and it died. But Warren had the guts to buck the studio and get the picture rereleased in smaller theaters until it could find its audience. It became a huge hit.

Incidents like these have caused independent production to increase. The power of the studios has slowly eroded, from the beginning, when they controlled everything, until now they have, for the most part, become distributing organizations that get independent filmmakers to make a movie.

In the fall of 1961, Anne and I went to Rome. *Two Weeks in Another Town* was the third movie that I made with Vincente Minnelli as director, and John Houseman as producer. The two previous movies, *The Bad and the Beautiful* and *Lust for Life,* both had won me Academy Award nominations.

Two Weeks in Another Town, by Charles Schnee, based on the novel by Irwin Shaw, could have been a powerful movie about modern life. It was really a form of *La Dolce Vita,* very daring in its concept of one man who finds redemption and leaves behind the shallow, hard people he knows. Cyd Charisse played my bitchy ex-wife.

Edward G. Robinson played a movie director who gives my character, broken-down actor Jack Andrus, another chance. Eddie was in his sixties now, still bruised from being caught in the meat grinder of the blacklist in the early

1950s. Nobody had formally accused Eddie of anything; innuendoes ruined him. Among Eddie's "crimes" was his membership in a group called "American Youth for Democracy" and a loan of $2,500 he had made to Dalton Trumbo. Eddie testified before HUAC three times that he had never been a member of the Communist Party. Then he realized that wasn't what they wanted to hear. They wanted him to grovel. He finally did what they wanted, but hated himself for it.

Most of *Two Weeks in Another Town* was shot in Rome at night. Minnelli could easily sleep during the day, sometimes until six o'clock in the evening. I couldn't, so there were three unpleasant weeks of night shooting and not much sleep.

Liz Taylor was also in Rome, doing a little picture called *Cleopatra*. She and Eddie Fisher threw a cocktail party and black-tie dinner for two hundred people at the Grand Hotel to celebrate the first anniversary of *Spartacus*. The cake weighed over twenty pounds.

In addition to the casts of both our pictures, the guests included Jack Lemmon, Joan Collins, Anthony Quinn, Jack Palance, Charlton Heston, Robert Wagner, Elsa Martinelli, Lex Barker, Rory Calhoun, Dorothy Malone, Hume Cronyn, Barbara Rush, Kenneth Haigh, Gina Lollobrigida, and Anthony Franciosa. And Liz's *Cleopatra* co-star, Richard Burton. At the party, it was easy to see Fisher was out, Burton was in.

Two Weeks in Another Town had some scandalous scenes. In one, set in a depraved nightclub in Rome where society people sit around drinking, watching a sexual act being performed (off screen, of course), they wanted to have a black singer. They brought to the studio a beautiful young girl chaperoned by her parents. She had a beautiful voice, as well—Leslie Uggams. I saw her again in January 1987, in Sacramento, California, at the second inauguration of Governor Deukmejian.

Vincente Minnelli was a wonderful man who worked within the framework of the old-fashioned studio system. He never did a lot of work on the post-production of a film. He was basically through with the picture when the shooting ended, leaving it to the producer and the editor to finish. And now, suddenly, a new head of the studio took over, Joseph Vogel. He decided that MGM should make only family pictures. Now, one thing *Two Weeks in Another Town* was not, was a family picture. It was very sexy, had some wild scenes. But he decided that the film would be edited differently—he was determined to make a family picture out of what we had shot. In the middle of these discussions, I wondered where John Houseman, the producer, was.

When I saw them emasculate the film, I wrote to Vogel, even though I was just an actor in it. I implored him, argued with him, told him that if he had wanted to make a family picture, he never should have made *Two Weeks in Another Town*. Margaret Booth, now Ray Stark's chief editor, was working on *Two Weeks in Another Town*. I went to Margaret, pleaded with her. She agreed with me that what they were doing was wrong, but she worked for MGM and was frightened of losing her job. She burst into tears. I never could keep my mouth shut.

They cut out the most exciting scenes. I felt this was such an injustice to Vincente Minnelli, who'd done a wonderful job with the film. And an injustice to the paying public, who could have had the experience of watching a very dramatic, meaningful film. They released it that way, emasculated.

The Hook was a small film. I helped Robert Walker get a part in it. I saw his screen test, and I pushed to get him in the picture. The other kid, Nick Adams, was a good friend of mine. He was a funny guy, who started out as Andy Griffith's sidekick in *No Time for Sergeants*, and had a hit playing Johnny Yuma in his Civil War TV series, "The Rebel." Nick used to do wonderful imitations of me. Charming guy. Killed himself with an overdose of paraldehyde when he was thirty-six. Who can determine what goes on in the mind of a seemingly happy-go-lucky fellow?

We shot a lot of the movie on Catalina. One day, I thought

I would do what the big movie stars do: I rented a yacht, about 120 feet long, and took a group of people sailing to Catalina, including Gene Kelly, and Janet Leigh, who was going with Arthur Loew at the time.

Arthur Loew was from the very rich Loew family that owned MGM and so many other things. He was a very bright, talented fellow, who really could have been a stand-up comic. Suddenly, he started to ad-lib. "You're always hearing about the problems of poor people. What about the problems of rich people?" And he went into a whole routine about "How do you think it feels to be driven to school in a Rolls-Royce, and have people make fun of you when you get out of your car?" and other problems that a rich kid faces. It was hilarious. But, at the same time, poignant. That was the funniest thing about the voyage to Catalina. The rest of the trip was disastrous. The water became very rough and people got seasick.

I thought that *The List of Adrian Messenger* could have been a really big commercial success. The idea—using stars, heavily disguised, in bit parts—was funny. I was able to get Robert Mitchum and Tony Curtis. Burt Lancaster played a woman. A large woman. He was hilarious. Frank Sinatra played a small part. I also played my role in disguise, a minor part.

Elizabeth Taylor agreed to play a sailor called "Chesty." I thought it would be fantastic to have this grizzled sailor peel off his mask, and see the beautiful face of Liz Taylor underneath. I made all the arrangements to send the makeup man from Universal to Switzerland, where she was at the time, to make a mask of her face. And then something happened and she dropped out.

It was one of the first movies that George C. Scott worked in. I had seen him in *The Andersonville Trial* on the New York stage. The play was not a success on Broadway, although Scott was magnificent in the lead role, slim as a razor blade. Oddly enough, the play was produced by Bill Darrid, the man who eventually married my first wife, Diana. Bill was a very talented writer, producer and actor, who to this day is a dear friend of mine.

The director of *The List of Adrian Messenger* was John Huston, certainly one of the most talented men in the industry. But John could also be a charlatan. If he wanted to slough something off, he could slough it off. I don't think he really felt the spirit of it. I had never worked with John before. My only knowledge of him was indirect: what Anne had told me about the escapades during the making of *Moulin Rouge;* and what I had heard from Evelyn Keyes when they were getting divorced.

John convinced us that one of the scenes should be shot in Ireland, where he had a house. So there was an inconsistency about the movie; it didn't have the continuous energy it needed of bouncing from one person to another, not being sure who was who, with the audience playing the game of "Is that Mitchum? Curtis? Who is this big woman?" Some people did enjoy the movie. But it never became the commercial success that I had hoped for. It could have been exciting. A lot of it I blame on myself, because I didn't have the time to focus on it.

My interests were elsewhere. I had bought two books I loved: *Seven Days in May* to make into a movie; *One Flew Over the Cuckoo's Nest* to do as a play. But first, Anne and I were flying down to Rio for the Mardi Gras!

Twenty-eight

SEVEN DAYS
IN MAY

Rio. February 1963. One of the most beautiful cities in the world. I was overwhelmed—not by the beauty, but by the people. It was the night of the big Mardi Gras ball, everyone in elaborate, fanciful costumes. I was dressed as Spartacus. Trying to get up the steps into the hotel ballroom, Anne and I were squashed like sardines, could hardly move. I watched helplessly as Anne got pulled away from me into the crush, makeup pouring down her face from the heat. I was jammed into the middle of six Brazilian guards, my protectors against the screaming mob trying to touch a movie star. Suddenly I felt somebody groping my groin under my tunic. I grabbed the hand, lifted it up—and looked right into the face of one of my guards. Holy shit! Who's going to protect me from the goddamn guards?

Brazilians certainly are warm and friendly. When there was a party, which was frequently, the whole family would turn out—grandfathers, children. Everybody mixed in. That part of it was fun.

We stopped in Belo Horizonte on our way to Brasília, the

new capital city inland. Coming in for a landing at the airport, we saw a huge mob, twenty-five thousand people. We didn't know if it was a natural disaster, or a religious festival, or Lindbergh landing in Paris. I asked what the hell had happened.

"They are waiting to see Kirk Douglas, the American movie star."

I had no idea. I had never experienced such a reaction. There, a movie star was like a god descending from Valhalla. I was petrified. Do you know what it feels like when a mob that size surges at you?

In Brazil, I received a wire from Bobby Kennedy asking if I would go to Cartagena, Colombia, to represent the United States at a film festival. I went gladly. My appearance apparently was very successful and led to many trips around the world that I would later take for our government.

Movie stars have a tremendous impact. We forget that a roll of celluloid film travels all over the world, seen by many millions of people. People make heroes out of the stars they see on the screen, and heroes have power. Politicians are eager to line up movie stars, like hunks of meat. And there's a great danger of movie stars abusing this power themselves. Every day, stars turn down requests for interviews, photo layouts. If a star wants to keep punching ideas, he has an unfair advantage, because he has access to the media, much more than politicians.

I think Jane Fonda is guilty of abusing this power. During the Vietnam War, she called me and asked for my support for her trip to Hanoi. I was never in favor of the Vietnam War. I didn't want my sons Michael and Joel dying for a corrupt regime. But I said to Jane, "What are you trying to do? Negotiate a separate peace with North Vietnam?" She was adamant. I suggested she fight our government's point of view through her congressman, senator, or a personal appeal through the press. "A little learning is a dangerous thing. Drink deep or taste not the Pierian spring." A few weeks later, I saw a picture of Jane Fonda in Hanoi, sitting on an antiaircraft gun that had probably shot down some of our planes.

I read the book *Seven Days in May* by Fletcher Knebel and Charles Bailey, and thought it would make a wonderful movie. Many people strongly advised me to stay away from it. The subject—an attempted military takeover of the United States government—was risky. How would the government react? Of course, this was years before Ollie North and his entourage set up shop.

I went to Washington to talk with the writers. Before I did, I attended a fancy buffet dinner. I was standing with a plate full of hot food, ill at ease. A voice next to me said, "Do you intend to make a movie out of *Seven Days in May?* "

I turned. President Kennedy! "Yes, Mr. President."

"Good." He spent the next twenty minutes, while our dinner got cold, telling me that he thought it would make an excellent movie. If I had had any doubts, this one strong "yea" drowned out all the other "nays."

I bought the book. The writers were rather stiff at our lunch meeting, not friendly. Then it came out: "You're not going to make a typical Hollywood movie out of our book, are you?"

This nettled me, to say the least. I looked from one to the other. "I will make a much better movie than your goddamned book." I paid the check and left.

I resented their pocketing the money I was paying for their book, then questioning what I was going to do with it. I think by that time I had sufficient credentials. They could have looked at *Spartacus, The Vikings, Lonely Are the Brave, Paths of Glory.* I resented their pompous attitude. I never talked to the writers again. They wrote an interesting book. I made a better movie.

Later, Fletcher Knebel wrote a book called *A Night at Camp David*, about a president who seems unbalanced, and the loyal aide afraid he is going to push the button starting World War III. A major Hollywood star was interested in making the book into a movie, and the deal was almost closed when word got out in the industry that President Lyndon Johnson didn't want the topic—and the portrayal of the president—put on film. It was never made.

We proceeded to develop the script. Rod Serling wrote it. There were two parts that I could have played: General James Mattoon Scott, the bad guy behind the takeover plot; and Colonel Jiggs Casey, the good guy who blows the whistle by going to the president. I sent the script to Burt Lancaster. "I'll play either part. You choose."

Burt elected to play the general, which was fine with me, because it was the part that I usually played, the heavy. I enjoyed playing the role of nice guy.

We had a great cast. Fredric March played Lyman Jordan, the President of the United States. Fredric March was an excellent, professional actor. I consider him in a class with Laurence Olivier.

Edmund O'Brien, always one of my favorites, played a southern senator with a taste for booze. Although underrated, Edmund O'Brien was one of the best Shakespearean actors. I remember the movie *Julius Caesar*, where he played Cassius to Marlon Brando's Marc Antony. In simple-sounding American speech, Edmund made the words of Shakespeare sound as if they had just occurred to him, really came out of him. A tremendously talented actor.

Everybody was good. Martin Balsam played the President's aide, John Houseman was the treacherous Admiral Barnswell, George Macready, Hugh Marlowe, and Andrew Duggan were the supporting cast.

I wanted John Frankenheimer to direct, and he agreed . . . until he found out that Burt was in it. He had just finished working with Burt on *Birdman of Alcatraz,* and swore he'd never work with him again.

I was surprised. "Why? What happened?"

John and Burt had gotten into a heated argument about how to shoot one scene. Finally, John gave instructions to the camera crew.

Burt said, "What are you doing?"

John said, "The camera goes here."

Burt picked Frankenheimer up, carried him across the room, plunked him down. *"That's* where the camera goes."

I was shocked. "John, how could you take such a humiliating experience?"

"That's why I don't want to work with him again."

"John, I promise you will not have any problems with Burt during the shooting of *Seven Days in May*." I was the boss, and I understood Burt. I had worked with him before. And I felt that I could prevent an unpleasant situation from occurring.

With a certain amount of trepidation, John agreed to direct the picture. His agent insisted that it had to be called "A John Frankenheimer Film." It amused me. I've always been intrigued with this *auteur* theory that came across the ocean from Europe and contaminated our system. The *auteur* theory holds that the director is the creator of the film. A film is a collaborative effort. It is rare that a movie is ever one person's film. Perhaps people like Charlie Chaplin, Orson Welles, Woody Allen, Barbra Streisand, who write, direct, and star in their pictures, are entitled to that billing. Yet even they need help—producers, casting directors, editors, technicians, location managers, other actors. But when a picture like *Seven Days in May* is presented to a director with the script already written, with all the financing and distribution arranged—and what a cast!—all set, it seems unfair to bill it as his film. Nevertheless, I capitulated and the credits read: "A John Frankenheimer Film."

And yes, John had no problems with Burt. He *did* have problems with Ava Gardner. One night after shooting, John and I were in my dressing room, discussing the progress of the film. The assistant director poked his head in. "Mr. Frankenheimer, Miss Gardner wants to see you in her dressing room."

John looked up to the sky.

I said, "What is the matter?"

He said, "It happens every night."

"What happens every night?"

"She gets a few drinks in her, and then I have to go in

there and she chews my ass out. She complains about what's going on. Nobody is doing anything right. She's even accused you and me of having a homosexual relationship."

I said, "Listen, I've known Ava for years. She must be just a little high."

"Well," he said, getting up, "I have to go over and see her."

"No you don't, John."

He stopped in his tracks, looked at me.

I said, "This is a Bryna film. I'll take the responsibility. You don't have to go and see her."

"Well, she might not come—"

I said, "She'll come to work tomorrow because she's paid to come to work. John, I don't want you to be subjected to that. I think it's humiliating."

Nevertheless, he went to see her.

We shot the picture mostly in Hollywood. The President's Maine hideaway was Lake Arrowhead; the aircraft carrier in the Mediterranean was in San Diego; the secret army base in Texas was outside of Yuma. The Washington, D.C., scenes were real: we filmed in Dulles Airport and outside the White House.

We needed just one crucial shot of the Pentagon to make it authentic. No filming allowed there. We had to get it. No way. So we stole the shot. We concealed the camera in a van, parked on the street opposite the Pentagon. I strode up to the entrance, dressed in my marine colonel's uniform. The guard on duty saluted me. I saluted back. I walked into the Pentagon, waited a bit, then walked out. The guard looked at me a little strangely, but he was well trained, and not about to question a superior officer. The shot is in the film. Very authentic.

We also shot an ending that I liked very much, but which we didn't use. General Scott, the treacherous Burt Lancaster character, goes off in his sports car, and dies in a wreck. Was it accident or suicide? Coming up out of the wreckage over the car radio is President Lyman Jordan's speech about the sanctity of the Constitution. Instead, the last time we see

Burt is in his confrontation with me. He regards me as a traitor to him; I know he has been a traitor to the country. He says to me, "Do you know who Judas was?"

I answer, "Yes. He's a man I used to work for and respect, until he disgraced the three stars on his uniform."

After *Seven Days in May*, Burt went to France to do a World War II movie called *The Train*, about a special train loaded with all the great artworks of France being shipped to Germany. Burt got in a bind with the director and wanted Frankenheimer to direct the picture. And Frankenheimer, who hadn't even finished editing *Seven Days in May*, was delighted to drop everything and go to France and work with Burt again.

It's ironic. I arrange this rapprochement between Frankenheimer and Burt, and then the two of them go off, great buddies.

In interviews later, Frankenheimer played the role of the great *auteur*—and I was just some actor working under his tutelage, grateful for his guidance. He twisted the whole thing around. This was not the frightened man I had talked to in private—"How am I going to get along with Burt Lancaster?" "Oh my God, how am I going to deal with Ava Gardner?"

Why is it that often the people you do the most for resent you the most? Maybe you remind them of their weaknesses. The hell with them.

I was going to Africa on a great adventure.

Twenty-nine

KILLER DOUGLAS

True, the men's adventure magazine, had invited me to go big-game hunting. I thought, Wow! Africa, big-game hunting, yeah, sounds great. I'll go. So I went to East Africa (now Kenya and Tanganyika) for three weeks.

First, they had to teach me how to shoot. Usually the guns I fired were loaded with blanks; the guns I'd juggled had been totally empty. They showed me what to do, and I discovered that I had a natural aptitude. My first shot with a high-powered rifle, I got a bull's-eye. And a black eye. I wasn't prepared for the recoil. The gun slammed back into my face. My eye got black, my nose bloody. But before long, I was using .264, .375, and .468 caliber rifles. It wasn't that difficult. The sites had crosshairs; if you lined the crosshair up on the animal, and you weren't nervous, you just squeezed the trigger, and you got it.

I shot everything—guinea fowl; gazelles; impalas; oryx; zebra; leopard; a 1,200-pound eland, the largest of the antelopes. I tracked them, killed them, skinned them. Once I got started, it mushroomed. I experienced a feeling of power. I looked at something and BANG! I had total control over it. I enjoyed it. Ostensibly, because I was a fearless warrior, our guides, the Masai, the tall people who stand on one leg like flamingos, inducted me into their tribe. They gave me a shield and a spear, and made me their blood brother. They called me "Killer Douglas."

For some people, killing is an aphrodisiac. The white hunters told me stories of rich women who wanted to have sex with them on top of animals that were dead or dying. The women loved it; it was a turn-on for them. I thought of Nina Foch and Joanna Barnes playing the two bloodthirsty Roman ladies in *Spartacus*, picking out big muscular gladiators, and licking their chops as they watched the men kill each other. You can't imagine anything in your wildest dreams that somebody hasn't already done or thought of.

They also told me about one macho guy out hunting lions. When they got close to the lion, he gave the professional hunter his camera. "When the lion charges, you get a picture of the two of us as I shoot him." The dumb professional hunter put his gun down, took the camera. The lion charged, the guy shot and missed, the lion killed him. And the professional hunter didn't get the picture.

We camped one night near the village of a very beautiful native Boran tribe. The men seemed to enjoy a life of leisure, while the women, with glistening, supple muscles, did all the work, including building huts. I took a turn at pounding maize with a heavy pestle. It was hard work. All the Boran men laughed their heads off at this crazy white man doing women's work.

There was one girl who would have turned heads anywhere in the world. She was walking topless, with great dignity, her beautiful breasts pointing to the sky. I fantasized about bringing her to London or Paris, bathing her in a tubful of bubbles, dressing her in the finest gowns, and taking her out in society. But these Pygmalion thoughts were brief.

One day, I watched, fascinated, as one of our native guides looked through the field until he found two smooth, flat stones, and used them to hold his penis while he relieved himself. Then I discovered that the Boran, although illiterate, were devout Mohammedans, and it was Ramadan, their holy month. They fast from sunrise to sunset, and are forbidden to engage in sex. Our guide never touched himself.

Our safari was as luxurious as you could get under the circumstances. There was always plenty of food, either steak, or something we'd shot, plus an assortment of beverages: vodka, bourbon, scotch, beer. White man's food. I wanted to know what the natives ate. I watched after we killed a wildebeest in an open field. They broke open the bones, sucked out the marrow. I told our white guides I wanted to try it. They scoffed at me. Why should I eat *that*, when we had all this perfectly good food? Because I was curious. I knelt down in the field with the natives and sucked out a hunk of marrow. It was warm, a little salty, but probably more nourishing that what we were eating. Besides, in the finest restaurants in the world, people pay top dollar for osso buco, veal bones, which they eat with sterling silver marrow spoons. Here I was enjoying it without the high overhead—osso buco tartare, on the hoof.

It was fun. It was exciting. I particularly loved tracking elephants. We wanted to get one with tusks of about 125 pounds. Very large. I got pretty good at tracking. Where elephants have rubbed their bodies against tree trunks tells you how tall they are. The size of the dung tells you how big they are. You put your finger in the dung, the temperature tells you how recently the elephant passed by.

One time we came upon a whole herd of elephants. The professional hunter said, "Let me see you take aim." He told me where to hit the elephant, about a foot below the top of his head. "That's where you get the brain. A black liquid oozes out."

I lined up on the herd, picked one out, all ready to shoot. He yanked my gun down.

I said, "What the hell—?"

"Are you crazy? You can't shoot that elephant!"

"Then what the hell did you tell me to take aim for?"

"I just wanted to check you out. Most people, when I tell them that, they shake, they throw up. You shoot that elephant, we could get killed in here, stampeded."

I'm glad I didn't shoot.

I shot everything else, though. And I found out something about myself: I'm a hyper guy, but when there's a real emergency, I get very calm, very steady.

I thought it would be macho to shoot something and make a coat for my wife. A leopard was the most exciting, because it was the most dangerous. Leopards are smart, so you have to set an elaborate trap. You shoot a wildebeest for bait, hang it from the branch of a tree so the hyenas can't get at it. The leopard has to jump up, climb the tree, crawl across the branch, and reach down to get the meat. You sit in a blind at dusk, waiting for the leopard to come, hungry after his afternoon nap in the African heat. So I was sitting there in the blind, reading Louis Nizer's book, *My Day in Court*, which they wanted me to do on Broadway. It grew dimmer and dimmer. I couldn't see very well. Suddenly I looked up. There was a leopard, staring right at me from that branch. I never heard him or saw him climb the tree. He just *appeared*. It's very tricky. You have to wait until the leopard gets in exact position sideways, so that you shoot him just below the chest, in the heart. You only get one shot; you don't want a wounded leopard charging you.

I shot him, one shot. I felt really macho. My wife would parade around in this coat that I shot for her. Then I found out that one leopard skin makes a coat for one leopard. To get a coat for a human, you have to have *five* leopard skins. No problem. I'd just shoot more leopards. Five *matching* leopard skins. "What do you mean, matching? Aren't all leopards the same?" No—there are all different kinds of leopards, with all different kinds of spots. You've got to get skins that match. It's not easy to do, and it's very expensive. Exasperated, I bought five matching skins, sent them to Maximilian, the furrier, in New York, had Anne make trips back and forth for fittings. She had the most beautiful leopard coat you ever saw. And the most expensive.

In Nairobi, I attended the premiere of *Spartacus*. We donated the money to Albert Schweitzer.

When I came back from the big game hunt, I put the skin of the leopard I shot on the floor of my den, his head still on, eyes glassy, teeth bared. But over the years, my dogs chewed the hell out of it. I put the trophies of all the other animals around my projection room. Then one day, about a year later, I was looking at all these dead animal heads on the walls, when I heard a voice. A voice I hadn't heard in a long time.

"What are you doing surrounded by all these dead animals?" Issur asked. "They were so beautiful when they were alive."

"It's macho. That's what a man's supposed to do—hunt, bring home the bacon."

"It wasn't even dangerous."

"What about the leopard?"

"You can bullshit youself, but you can't bullshit me. How could you have killed them?"

I pulled down the trophies, gave them all—including Anne's coat—to the Museum of Natural History in New York City.

I'm not a vegetarian. I'd shoot any animal if I was going to eat it. Or if it was going to eat me. But on the safari, at night when you're in your tent all zipped up, you hear the animals walking around, leading their animal lives, minding their own business. They're not stupid. They're not out to attack you. When an animal smells a human being, it goes away, unless it's rabid or enraged. Those animals are not out there looking for people. We're looking for *them*.

Every year, Anne and I go fishing in Alaska. About a half hour by seaplane from Ketchikan are miles and miles of deserted islands in an inland sea fed by melting snow from the mountain tops. How beautiful, how peaceful. We live in Yes Bay lodge, a rustic dwelling by the side of the bay.

Every day, we go out fishing in a little boat. It amazes me that Anne, my Parisian wife, loves it so. It annoys me that she catches more fish than I do. With the rain pouring down, we sit in rain gear, mesmerized by the bobbing tip of our fishing poles. The fish we catch are cleaned and frozen, given to our friends at home, and all year round we eat salmon—silvers, kings, chums.

At least once during our week's stay, we visit San Ann where the river rushes over the rocks and falls and empties into the sea. Here a miracle takes place.

The salmon, from as far off as Japan, make their pilgrimage to the exact river where they were born. They take this long voyage, overcoming larger fish, professional fishermen with nets, amateurs like us with poles, bears scooping them up as they converge toward the falls leading to the river where they were born.

Anne and I walk for a mile into the woods, led by a guide with a gun. There is a possibility of running into some curious bears. We come to a ledge overlooking rocky falls. The water from the river roars down over the rocks. The salmon must fight against the force of this water. We see them— hundreds of them—leaping into the air, throwing their bodies against the rocks to scramble over the falls to reach the river. They fall back and hurl themselves again.

A little farther down, in a quiet, shallow pool, we see a black mass—hundreds of salmon resting before they begin their attack.

As we peer down from the ledge, watching the salmon repeatedly making their assault, we see eight black bears on the water's edge, scooping up salmon with their paws or snouts.

The salmon that make the successful journey swim up the river. In a quiet spot, the female deposits her eggs in the sand. The male fertilizes the eggs. When they are hatched, the grown-up salmon die, the carcasses fed upon by swooping eagles, gulls, and fish. And with the newborn salmon, the cycle begins again.

In this age of highly specialized computers, what can compare with the instinct in the brains of salmon that leads them 10,000 miles through the ocean to find the riverbed where

they were born? What mechanism compels them to overcome overwhelming obstacles to fulfill their mission: fertil-
ize the eggs and die.

No one could stand on the ledge overlooking those rushing
falls, watch those salmon hurl themselves against the rocks
to fulfill their destiny, and walk away an atheist.

I went hunting again only once, years later. In an office.
Jack Clayton was directing *Something Wicked This Way
Comes;* my son Peter was producing. Clayton's a little bit
macho. He had a long office, with a target on the wall way
the hell over at the other end. While he was talking to people
he would nonchalantly shoot an arrow at this little target. He
loved to intimidate and impress people that way, loved to
see the looks on their faces.

I said, "What's that?"

He said, "Try it"

I threaded the arrow, pulled the bow, and—zing! BULL'S-
EYE! I was more amazed than he. But being an actor, I
covered it up. I calmly put the bow down and continued
talking as if nothing had happened. He just stared at me.

But I didn't tell him that I was blood brother to the Masai.
He was upset enough as it was.

Thirty

ONE FLEW OVER THE CUCKOO'S NEST

I finished reading *A Case of Libel* and decided I didn't want to play the part. There was no character development. He was a brilliant Jewish lawyer in Act I, a brilliant Jewish lawyer in Act II, a brilliant Jewish lawyer in Act III. Then I was offered a million and a half dollars to do *The Fall of the Roman Empire*. A lot of money! That's like seven million dollars today. Nobody had ever been offered that much. But the Bronson Group in Spain was desperate for a star.

I tried to make a deal. I said, "For a million dollars, I'll do *Montezuma.*" This was a Dalton Trumbo script I owned, about Cortez conquering the Aztec empire, and as he is dying, questioning the morality of what he had done. John Huston wanted to direct it. But *they* didn't want to do *Montezuma.* They wanted to do their script of *The Fall of the Roman Empire.* I couldn't understand it; I had a much better script. But that's not the way it works. Sophia Loren finally agreed to be in it, because they offered her a million dollars.

Harold Mirisch said to me, "For that kind of money, I would have hit you over the head. How dare you turn it down?'' He was right. Turning down that much money is nothing to be proud of. That money would have permitted me to do all kinds of things. Instead, I prepared myself to go back to Broadway.

My agents nearly killed me. Why was I giving up millions of dollars in movies to do a play for nothing? Why? Because I was still a failure. I wanted to be a star on the stage. Flesh and blood, not a shadow on the screen. The eye of the movie camera is an evil eye. When you act in front of it, that cyclops keeps taking from you, until you feel empty. On the stage, you give something to the audience, more comes back. When the curtain comes down in a theater, you have a feeling of exhilaration—something's been completed, fulfilled. It's so different from an exhausting day of shooting at the studio. You come home tired, drained. Making a movie is like making a mosaic—laboriously putting little pieces together, jumping from one part of the picture to another, never seeing the whole, whereas in a play, the momentum of the continuity works with you, takes you along. Doing a play is like dancing to music. Making a movie is like dancing in wet cement. And besides, I had never had a real success on the stage in a role that I had originated.

I left *Seven Days in May* in the hands of Eddie Lewis and the editors, and headed for New York to do a dramatization of a book that I was crazy about—*One Flew Over the Cuckoo's Nest*. I bought the book from the writer Ken Kesey, the son of an Oregon dairy farmer, a crazy, talented guy. His first novel. If Kesey had written the book back East, it would have been treated with the respect that it deserved when it came out. Instead, it went almost unnoticed until years later.

I found out that Dale Wasserman, who had written the first draft of *The Vikings*, and the initial script of *Cleopatra*, had also been anxious to buy the book of *One Flew Over the Cuckoo's Nest*. I figured he felt the same way about it that I did. I asked him to write the play, even though he had never had anything produced on Broadway. In exchange I gave him all the rights to the play; I kept the movie rights.

Wasserman came up with a good play, and we went into

rehearsals. I was excited. We got a great cast—Gene Wilder as the innocent Bill Bibbit, and William Daniels, as the browbeaten husband doubting his sexuality. I played Randle P. McMurphy and I took no salary. We tried out in New Haven, Boston—rave reviews. A hit! I couldn't wait to get to Broadway.

Then I almost got sidetracked. I received a letter from a professor at Harvard, Timothy Leary, inviting me to participate in a mind-expansion program using something I'd never heard of—LSD. I was intrigued. If I hadn't been in the middle of a hit play, I would have joined his experiment. I wanted to expand my mind.

I had tried marijuana many times in the past. Years ago, it was not considered an addictive drug. I thought of pot as less dangerous than alcohol. If you drink down a bottle of scotch, it can kill you.

I even found marijuana bushes growing in the backyard, planted by my boys. I stopped it, but I didn't consider it a serious offense. I felt they would have to learn to deal with illegal pot the same way they would have to learn to deal with legal alcohol.

At a party at Malibu beach one night, a famous star was snorting cocaine. I had never tried it. I was curious.

"Try it," he said. And I did.

He taught me how to use a straw or roll up a dollar bill and sniff up a line of the white powder. I experienced a mild, euphoric effect that didn't last long. Then I had to sniff again. I tried it several times, and felt it was too much work for the rewards. There are others who obviously feel differently. But dope had never played an important part in my life.

Of course, I can talk this openly about it, since I have no intention of running for the presidency or the Supreme Court.

Meanwhile, we were all high from the success of the play. Euphoria took over the whole cast. We had done so well on the road that we canceled our dates in Buffalo and went straight to New York. I was on my way home—Broadway.

November 14, 1963. Opening night in New York. Excitement, hope. Ken Kesey flew in from Oregon, as my guest. It was our first meeting; his eyes looked sort of glazed. It wasn't just the thrill of seeing his baby born on the stage, or even the discomfort of the tuxedo he had bought for the evening. It was the beginning of his involvement with drugs that would lead Tom Wolfe to write *The Electric Kool-Aid Acid Test* about him.

The house was packed. The audience was spellbound.

The reviews were murderous. Walter Kerr in the *Herald Tribune* said, "*One Flew Over the Cuckoo's Nest* is so preposterous a proposition for the theater that it could be dismissed very briefly if it weren't for the extraordinary tastelessness with which it has been conceived. Tastelessness of this caliber should be talked about." He also said that the role of McMurphy, my role, was "written from the gut downward," and "The play is adapted from a novel by Ken Kesey, unlucky man." Howard Taubman of the *New York Times* wrote: "Do you find the quips, pranks and wiles of the inmates of a mental hospital amusing? If you do, you should have a merry old time at *One Flew Over the Cuckoo's Nest*." He went on to say, "As an objective reporter, I should tell you that people were chuckling and roaring at a lot of these gags last night. I should also add that I found them either embarrassing or in appalling taste." His summation: "How can a thread of compassion stand out in a crazy-quilt of wisecracks, cavortings, violence and histrionic villainy?"

I wished I were in Boston expanding my mind on LSD. Those two reviews were death to the play. If *one* of them had been good, we would have had a chance. They canceled out the so-so reviews and even an ecstatic review on TV. The critics didn't understand the play. They were giving rave reviews to light comedies like Jean Kerr's *Mary, Mary,* and *Never Too Late,* about a middle-aged woman who gets pregnant. But even worse than their cruelty to the play, they were indifferent to me. Love me or hate me, but don't be indifferent.

Van Heflin, who was a hit in the Louis Nizer play I turned

down, had warned me. "Kirk, the first time you go back to New York they'll kick your ass. They may forgive you the second time. But not the first." One of the few actors to withstand such treatment is Jack Lemmon. He had the hell kicked out of him a few times, but he kept coming back.

Critics. Not that they should bend over backward when a movie star comes to New York, but they should at least encourage movie stars to come there and do plays. I took comfort from the words of Teddy Roosevelt:

It's not the critic who counts. The credit belongs to the one who is actually in the arena; who know the great enthusiasm, the great devotion; who at best knows in the end the triumph of high achievement; and who, at the worst, fails while doing greatly, so that his place shall never be with those cold and timid souls who know neither victory nor defeat.

The same thing happened to my son Michael when he produced and starred in *The China Syndrome*. *Newsweek*'s George Will wrote a scathing essay on the impossibility of a breakdown in a nuclear facility. A few days later, Three-Mile Island happened. Will never acknowledged it, or printed a retraction or an apology. Michael could have capitalized on Three-Mile Island for publicity, but he didn't. He felt that would be ghoulish.

Lee Strasberg, the great guru of the Actors Studio, came one night. Gene Wilder and William Daniels, members of the Studio, were excited and awed. Strasberg coming to see them was like Jelly coming to see me. Strasberg was very kind. He told me that I had an unusual quality—when I came onstage, there was a space around me. He asked me to do a play for the Actors Studio. The last thing in the world I wanted was to do another play. In spite of Strasberg's good opinion, the reviews had taken their toll; we were not doing well. But, instead of asking the cast to take a cut—standard procedure in a weak show—stubbornly, I kept everybody at full salary.

Maureen O'Sullivan, in *Never Too Late*, at the Playhouse

Theatre, opposite the Cort (where we were), was doing better. Her daughter, seventeen-year-old Mia Farrow, spent many nights watching *One Flew Over the Cuckoo's Nest* while she waited for her mother. Several times, after the theater, I took them both out to dinner. I didn't know which way to turn, they both were so beautiful.

Mia is really bright. It wouldn't surprise me if Mia has the highest IQ of any actress I know. When she was married to Frank Sinatra, we were at a dinner party at the home of Edie and Bill Goetz, the head of Universal. And there were about twenty people around the table. I was sitting next to Mia. I said, "Mia, tell me, what do you think of these people?" She went right down the table, person by person, and gave the most amazingly accurate character appraisal of each one. I was flabbergasted. She always looked so naive, wide-eyed, angelic. But she was a rapier. Concise and to the point. I'm a big fan of Mia's. She's just had a baby boy, Satchel, with Woody Allen.

Friday afternoon, November 22, 1963. I hailed a cab. The driver swerved to the curb. As I bent my head to get in, he said, "Isn't it terrible about President Kennedy?"

"What are you talking about?"

"He's been shot."

I was devastated. The world was devastated. There was a numbness in the people on the stage and in the audience. For quite a while there was a numbness over the world.

Years later, I talked with Yevgeny Yevtushenko, the Russian poet. I asked him, "How did Russia react when President Kennedy was shot?"

"People cried in the street. They cried perhaps more for his youth than for anything else. But they sensed that, in him, there might be a chance for our two countries to get together."

I had met John Fitzgerald Kennedy for the first time at a party at Charlie Feldman's house in the mid-1950s. Charlie said to me, "See that guy?" He pointed out a slim, handsome fellow in his early thirties. The girls seemed to be taken with him. Charlie said, "He's going to be President of the United States." I didn't know what he was talking about.

Then in January 1963, Gene Kelly and I had been co-masters of ceremonies at the celebration of the anniversary of President Kennedy's second year in office. It was a wonderful evening. Everybody was in great spirits. The President and the First Lady were handsome. Then the weather turned bad; we couldn't get a plane out. Anne and I were stuck in Washington for the weekend. So were the President and First Lady. They were supposed to be at Camp David, but the weather was so bad they stayed at the White House.

Attorney General Bobby Kennedy invited us to his house in McLean, Virginia, for dinner. After dinner, Bobby said, "Let's go over and see my brother." He said it very casually, as if we were dropping in on a next door neighbor. I was excited. And nervous. "But do we need to . . . are we supposed to . . . "

"Oh," he said, "you're fine."

So we all hopped into station wagons, and off we went to the White House.

The President had just finished dinner with Ambassador Olgivie from England and his wife, who were great friends of the Kennedys. Later, he became Lord Harlech. We all trooped in, sat around in the living room on the floor. Everybody had to perform. Teddy Kennedy was very adept at singing songs accompanied by his wife, Joan, at the piano. And even the President and Bobby got up together and sang, almost in a monotone, a camp song that they used to sing when they were kids. Most of the evening, the President sat in his famous rocking chair, head back, thoroughly enjoying the performances. George Burns did some patter. Carol Channing sang "Diamonds Are a Girl's Best Friend."

Some people declined to perform, including Anne. I tried to compensate by giving a corny rendition of "I'm Red Hot Henry Brown, the Hottest Man in Town." I gave it all I had. It's difficult for an actor. If you're a pianist and someone says, "Play the piano," you play the piano. But it's different if someone says, "Oh, you're an actor? So act." We had been at the White House before, to formal state dinners. But that evening was a magnificent experience.

During the evening, someone wanted to see the famous Lincoln bedroom. Jackie Kennedy obligingly took a group, including Anne, to see it. After they went off, the President said to me, "Jackie doesn't know that my mother is sleeping in that room." So Jackie walks into the Lincoln bedroom with a group of people, and there's Rose Kennedy propped up in bed reading a book. But they all took it in style. And when they came back out, Jackie and the President had a good laugh. It was an evening of gaiety, of youth, a bunch of camp kids sitting around on the floor, drinking beer, everybody getting up to entertain. Bobby dropped us off at our hotel that night. Anne and I were awed by the whole evening.

All these thoughts went through my head when I heard that the President had been assassinated. It was tragic. You don't feel that way if your recollection is of an infirm person. But here was someone vital, full of health, handsome. They were so beautiful, the two of them. The prince and princess.

Seventeen years later, in 1980, I was making *The Man from Snowy River*, the only American in the Australian company. Ten thousand miles away from home, sitting on a horse in the hills above Melbourne. An excited Australian came running up to me. "President Reagan's just been shot!" I galloped off, pulled up under a tree. I was angry. I started to cry. I was a Democrat, but someone had shot my President. Not until the end of the day did I learn that he had not been killed. That day, I also learned the meaning of the office of the President. He's the President of all of us—the people who voted for him, the people who voted against him, the people who didn't vote at all.

Cuckoo's Nest limped along for five months. My sons Michael and Joel made their stage debuts as orderlies one night during school vacation. When five-year-old Eric, watching from the wings, saw them wheeling me out on a gurney, he thought I'd really died, and burst into tears. I couldn't keep the play afloat financially any longer, not singlehandedly. I did what I had been putting off for so long: suggested that the cast take a cut in salary. They held a meeting, refused to take the cut—"Let the rich movie star pay." I was hurt, immediately posted a closing notice on the backstage bulletin board. When they saw the notice, they came to talk. I remembered the *Vikings* strike. I refused to listen.

January 25, 1964, the night *Cuckoo's Nest* closed, I gave the first sneak preview of *Seven Days in May*, in the same Broadway theater, for all the actors on Broadway. At midnight. This theater, which I could not fill as a stage actor, I filled easily as a movie star.

I crawled back home to Los Angeles like a wounded animal, defeated in my last battle to become a star on Broadway. I licked my wounds and moaned to Anne, "I gave New York a classic and they don't even realize it." Anne consoled me.

I loved the role of Randle P. McMurphy, and I was determined to see *One Flew Over the Cuckoo's Nest* on the screen. I knew the book hadn't been a best seller. And I knew how bad the odds were for turning a play that hadn't done well on Broadway into a movie.

But I didn't know it would take more than ten years.

Thirty-one

AMBASSADOR DOUGLAS

President Kennedy encouraged me to visit foreign countries to talk about the United States. In twenty-five years, I've made trips to dozens of countries, for Democratic and Republican administrations, paying my own way. Talking about America. Agreeing sometimes with their criticisms. But trying to show them, through my life, what our country is all about.

After my initial experience in Colombia, I was ready for something bigger: a trip around the world for the United States (at our own expense, of course). Anne and I spent a lot of 1964 on the road for the U.S. government.

February 20, 1964. Germany. The dead of winter. But it didn't feel like winter in bustling, prosperous West Berlin, with the energy of rebuilding everywhere. We visited Axel Springer, the big German publishing firm; they took us up on the roof and pointed—the Berlin Wall. A thick, ugly concrete scar severing the city. You could look right over the top into East Berlin. I was anxious to go to the other side.

We crossed at Checkpoint Charlie. An entirely different

atmosphere. Shocking. Rude guards stopped the car. In addition to ordering us around, inspecting the inside and the trunk, they stuck a mirror underneath the car to see if we were smuggling anything.

In East Berlin, it felt like winter. Gray, gray, gray, gray, gray. The winter of the soul—oppression, deprivation. In stores, you saw washing machines with hand wringers. Everything antiquated. A total lack of joy.

We couldn't wait to get back to West Berlin, didn't even stop to change our money at Checkpoint Charlie. We were glad to hand them whatever we had at the border and get the hell out of there.

We went on to India. India. The huge palaces, where the colonial rulers had stayed, where Mountbatten and that whole English group had love affairs. And not just the English—Nehru was a big ladies' man, too.

We had tea with Mrs. Gandhi. We were obviously an obligation for her; she kept sneaking looks at her wristwatch. We got the feeling that she was wondering how long she had to put up with these Americans.

I'm always surprised when people in high positions don't realize how they reveal themselves. Maybe because I'm an actor, I'm used to observing people, picking up clues. Years later, we were at a state dinner for Margaret Thatcher at the White House, going through the receiving line. I'll never forget her grip: as she shook hands with me, she grabbed my hand and pulled me down the line at the same time. The iron fist in the velvet glove. I was tempted to take her arm and push it the other way. But I didn't want to take the chance that she was stronger than I was.

I returned to India in January 1987 to film the ABC miniseries "Queenie," based on Michael Korda's best seller. Not much had changed—still palaces and poverty. We went to Jaipur, in the desert southwest of New Delhi. The pink city, they call it, constructed of beautiful pink bricks. But the poverty, the poverty. I dined with the Maharajah of Jaipur, who's called Bubbles, because so much champagne flowed at his birth. You say, "Pleased to meet you, Your Highness." He says, "Oh, call me Bubbles." Everybody calls him Bubbles. He's in his fifties.

I heard all the stories about the affairs of Bubbles and his stepmother, the Maharanee, affairs of the heart and of revenge. They play out their own little "Dynasty"–"Dallas" scenarios. They still possess great wealth, though not as much as in the past. They're down to one or two ancient palaces. On mountaintops, beautifully built, inlaid with glass and stones. All slave labor. And then, as if the view weren't sufficient, they've built a big artificial lake.

In Thailand, we were met by a man from the U.S. Information Agency. Our schedule seemed sparse, considering that we were to be goodwill ambassadors, and that we had done much more in other countries. There had to be something we could do. I said, "Aren't there any events that we can participate in?"

"Oh no."

That evening, at a party with Thai friends, we were invited by a Lady-in-Waiting to the Queen for the dedication of a new hospital. We told our USIA guy about it. He didn't even know where it was. Driving there, we had to ask for directions. So many of the USIA employees were just little people in little jobs. No imagination. They kept in their own little group, had their own PX, their own white clubs, didn't mix with the people in the country they were in, didn't speak the language, didn't care.

When we arrived, the King and Queen were there. Their protocol people brought us up to an honored position on the dais, sitting just a little bit behind the King and Queen. There were speeches and ceremonies, names of those who had contributed to this worthwhile cause. So I made a personal donation for a room at the hospital in honor of our country and our President. I donated that much whatever the currency was. They were all very pleased. Then I looked at my wife. How much did I donate? I had no idea. Oh my God. It turned out to be something like eleven thousand dollars. I was afraid I had given them a hundred thousand.

The Philippines intrigued me. Universities were open twenty-four hours a day; students were on eight-hour shifts. American jeeps, remnants of World War II, were zipping all over the place. So much traffic—bicycles, cars, taxi-jeeps. Constant activity night and day.

I was talking to a group of students in Manila. I gave my speech, then came questions and answers, the mike handed around the audience. One fellow got up, obviously a well-trained young Communist, and said, "What the hell are you doing in our country anyway? You don't even know anything about our country. Who needs you here?" I listened. Then I said, "Look, we in America know a lot about your country. We're aware of the three-hundred-and-fifty-year domination of the Spanish. We know that, for fifty years, you've been under the influence of America. And we're proud that now you're out of that and you're all independent." I threw in all the facts that I knew. And then topped it off with, "But one thing I do know. Even though I've been here only one day, I've been here long enough to know that you are not a typical Filipino, because the Filipinos are a very polite and hospitable people. And have treated me with great . . ." By this time they were glowering at him.

You have to prepare yourself. Each country is different. Before I visited a country, I always briefed myself. I read up on it. That was part of the excitement of taking the trip. You never knew what you were going to run into. Besides, it's just rude to go somewhere and not know anything about the people you're talking to.

A lot of the young people I spoke to at universities are probably leaders of their countries by now. Might I have had a little effect on them? Expressing my viewpoint about America? I hope so.

We visited Hong Kong to open a canteen on behalf of President Kennedy to feed the poor. My first trip to Hong Kong. That was exciting. I was intrigued by one of those mammoth restaurants. The food came around on trolleys. All different kinds of food, in different-shaped wicker baskets.

You picked what you wanted. At the end, when it came to your bill, they would just look at all the baskets, and each size had a different price. That's how they added up the bill.

Shortly after Anne and I returned from the trip, on April 30, 1964, I was cited in the Congressional Record for "service on behalf of [my] country as a good-will ambassador on behalf of the State Department and the United States Information Agency."

That fall found us on a plane again, this time bound for the eastern Mediterranean. These trips were hard on Anne. Just the decision was difficult—should she go with me, or stay home with the children? How to divide her time, herself, her love, between a globe-trotting husband and two sons? And what's left for her?

November 4, 1964. Yugoslavia. They took me to the home of a USIA official. Over coffee and cake, I talked with eight or ten students who were studying cinema. After the students left at the end of the evening, I turned angrily to the USIA official. "I didn't come here to talk to a handful of special students about movies. I usually encourage people not to go into movies. I'd like to talk to a large, general group."

"Oh no," said my host. "In a Communist country, you cannot have a large gathering."

That was hard for me to believe. The next morning, I called the university in Belgrade. That evening, I gave a talk before several thousand students. It was wonderful. They love American movies. They loved having an American actor talk to them.

The next day, at a luncheon at the American Embassy, I asked if my wife and I might be able to meet President Tito. The British ambassador interrupted. "My dear boy, I've been waiting for six weeks just to have ten minutes to present my credentials to President Tito. President Tito is not that easy to see."

Oh. Pardon me. I called President Tito's office.

The next day, President Tito sent his private plane to fly my wife and me to his villa at Liubiana. We spent three hours with him, drinking wine and talking. Tito was a movie fan, especially westerns. He'd seen every western I'd done, loved *Gunfight at the O.K. Corral*. Pictures of us together were all over the newspapers.

When I got back to the American Embassy in Belgrade, the British ambassador was there again. "My dear boy, I don't understand. You spend three hours with President Tito, while I have been waiting to spend ten minutes with him. Tell me, how does that happen?"

"Mr. Ambassador, how many movies have you made?"

The Queen of Greece was a movie fan, too. She didn't seem like a queen, this pretty little starstruck bobby-soxer. I don't think she was more than eighteen when the king married her. The King of Greece was a very charming man. He liked sailing. Anne and I were attending an intimate luncheon at the palace, only five or six people. I did a bit of diplomacy. The king wanted to talk to Jacob Javits, the United States senator from New York. I happened to know that Javits was nearby at the time, in Turkey. I called him and arranged a meeting. I don't know what they discussed.

I saw the King and Queen of Greece again quite a few times at dinner parties in the United States and in London after they were deposed. Although they don't seem to be going hungry, there are not many jobs available for ex-kings.

They gave me an interpreter when I went to Turkey, a young woman. Although she spoke English quite well, something made me wonder about the accuracy of her translations. Then at a school, my fears were confirmed. After she translated something for me, a kid in the audience jumped up. "Wait a minute! That's not what you said!" he spoke in perfect English.

I looked at her. "What . . . ?"

She zigged and zagged. I became very suspicious. Very uncomfortable. I felt that she was distorting whatever I was saying, interpreting according to her own beliefs, which were not pro-American.

At the next meeting, with thousands of students in an auditorium, a student stood up and started reading a prepared statement, in English, about the sins of Hollywood. I hadn't come all the way to Turkey to hear this kid tell me what he found out reading fan magazines.

I said sarcastically, "How long were you in Hollywood?"

"I've never been."

"Now that's strange. You've never been to Hollywood? Well, you know, I have been there. Would you like to hear my feelings, whether you agree with them or not, and then we'll discuss it?"

My interpreter translated. Suddenly a bunch of students were coming at me, climbing over a railing. Three huge Turkish secret service police grabbed me, hustled me out. Squeezed me into a car and brought me back to the hotel. Thank God Anne was not with me at that time.

I called the American Embassy, furious that they'd stuck me with some third-rate interpreter. "Who the hell is this woman?"

The official interpreter for the United States Ambassador. And she was a Communist. I don't know if anything was ever done about it, but I made a point of it in my report when I got back to Washington.

Deep down within me, Issur spoke up. "I'm proud of you and Anne for taking those trips around the world for your country."

"Oh, I don't know," I mumbled. "Do you think they do any good?"

"Sure, if you keep doing them, others will do them. It all adds up."

"Well, I hope you're right."

"I know I'm right," said Issur with an unusual note of conviction. "Remember Ma saying 'America, such a wonderful land.'"

"Yeah, and look at the hardships we all went through here."

"Nothing compared to what Ma and Pa went through in Russia."

"Yeah. I guess you're right."

One of the rare times that Issur and I agreed.

Thirty-two

GENERAL DOUGLAS

I was a much more effective military man on the screen than in real life. I've saved most of the countries in the free world in *Seven Days in May, In Harm's Way, The Heroes of Telemark, Cast a Giant Shadow, Is Paris Burning?* and *The Final Countdown.*

In *In Harm's Way* I played a naval officer, a bitter flier under John Wayne's command. After raping Jill Haworth, the girlfriend of Wayne's son, played by Brandon de Wilde, I sacrifice myself on an air mission.

The most exciting thing about the production was that we got to shoot on the USS *St. Paul,* a cruiser, as it sailed from Seattle to Hawaii. And there was Otto Preminger, the director, treating the personnel like his own personal crew, the boat like a prop, yelling to the captain, in his German accent, "Push the boat the other vey, so ve get the sunlight!"

I shared a bunk with one of the officers, Josh Nelson, who I was surprised to learn was Jewish. I never think of naval officers as being Jewish, maybe because I didn't know any others when I was one. I asked Josh if many of the crew were Jewish.

He said, "A few."

I said, "Do you ever hold religious services?"

"I tried to, but it's hard to get them interested enough."

"Suppose I conduct the religious service?"

"Would you? *Could* you?"

"Yes." I said, "Why don't you tell your friends that tomorrow, Friday night, I'll conduct the service."

That Friday evening, we were all dining at the captain's table—John Wayne, Burgess Meredith, and of course Otto Preminger—when over the loudspeakers:

NOW HEAR THIS, MEN. AT 20:00
THERE WILL BE FRIDAY EVENING
JEWISH RELIGIOUS SERVICE
CONDUCTED BY KIRK DOUGLAS.

Well, this caused a little ripple. Heads everywhere bobbed. And I, very dignified and nonchalant, stood up and said, "Would you excuse me, Captain? I have to officiate at this service." John Wayne and Burgess Meredith, curious, came over later. Otto Preminger, a Jew, didn't. In a borrowed yarmulke and prayer shawl, I conducted the Friday evening service, remembering the old Hebrew prayers that I had learned when I was a poor boy living in Amsterdam, when the people in my synagogue wanted little Issur to become a rabbi, and I didn't know how to tell them that I wanted to be an actor. That one night on the USS *St. Paul* was the fulfillment of my debt to them.

In Harm's Way was the first movie I did with John Wayne. He was a strange fellow. I'll never forget the talk we had about my playing in *Lust for Life*. Although emotionally we were not close, and politically we were antipodal, he asked me to work with him several times. We would usually have dinner together only once or twice during the entire shooting of a movie. And yet we got along quite well. We were two completely different kinds of people, but there was a mutual respect. Wayne liked to hunker down with the crew —the stuntmen and special-effects guys. I was much more of a loner. When my work was over, I went home. I didn't hunker down with anyone, except a few friends, if any were around, or my wife and my family.

Anne, Peter, and Eric were with me in Hawaii. We had a house on Diamond Head Road, right on the ocean. The boys spent every day in the surf; Peter got a terrible sunburn. Whenever I made movies during summer vacations, my four sons were with me. They traveled to many countries while they were still children.

Michael was supposed to join us in Hawaii, but I was mad at him. He was almost flunking out of the University of California at Santa Barbara, so I wouldn't let him come. Michael got his act together, even got a job at a gas station, and became "Attendant of the Month."

In Harm's Way was the first time I'd worked with Otto Preminger. Otto was a brilliant producer, with a great sense of showmanship. It had been very clever of him, after I decided to use Dalton Trumbo's real name on *Spartacus*, to call a press conference to say *he* was going to use Trumbo's name on *Exodus*, when it was a *fait accompli*.

I'd known Otto only socially, and he was extraordinarily charming. Professionally, he was an absolute bully. He looked and acted like the sadistic Nazi commandant he played in *Stalag 17*. Bald as a bullet, he bragged, "I'm the man with no hair that shoves around the people with hair." Otto was unmerciful to Tom Tryon, who played one of the military officers. Once, Otto was so insulting and cruel to Tom that I walked off the set. "How can you take it, Tom?"

"I can't. I really can't."

Otto would SCREAM. He would come right up to Tom, saliva spitting out of his mouth, and he would just yell. I've never seen anyone treated that way. Tom was shattered. I felt sorry for him. I thought, Otto is going to kill him. Literally. Tom is going to have a heart attack. I said, "Tom, will you let me help you?"

"Oh God, yes. Please. Anything."

"Listen to me. The next time Otto screams at you, just yell right back 'OTTO, GO FUCK YOURSELF!' and walk off the set."

He looked at me. "I couldn't do that."

"Tom, I'm telling you, if you do that, it will be over. He's a bully. But he's got to finish the picture. What the hell? If he wants to replace you, tell him to replace you."

I could never get Tom to do that. He went through the picture continually insulted. He had a three-picture deal with Preminger, but he never worked with him again. Tom became a best-selling author—*The Other, Harvest Home, Lady,* and *Crowned Heads.*

I never liked Otto after that. Once, he raised his voice in a nasty way toward me. I walked over to him, nose to nose. In a very low voice, I said, "Are you talking to me?" That was the end of it. He never insulted me again.

In addition to his infamous handling of actors, I didn't think Otto was a very good director, in spite of his Academy Award nominations for *Laura* and *The Cardinal.* But he was a very interesting man, born in Vienna, the son of a wealthy Jewish lawyer. He had an illegitimate son with Gypsy Rose Lee. He did a lot of provocative movies—*The Moon Is Blue, The Man with the Golden Arm.* But I never thought that directing was his forte. The special effects in *In Harm's Way* were terrible and phony. I said, "Otto, you can tell they're goddamn little toy boats. There's nobody on deck. Couldn't you have at least put a couple of toy soldiers on the ship?"

Otto ended very sadly. He sold a lot of wonderful paintings and pieces of art that he owned to get the financing for his last movie, *The Human Factor,* which was a complete flop. He lost all his money, had a stroke soon after that, and died.

Out of the blue, I got a call from Anthony Mann, the director I had fired on *Spartacus.* He was preparing a film.

Before he could say any more, I said, "You got me."

"But let me tell you about it first."

"Tony, I told you I owe you a movie. You've got me. I'm ready to play the part."

The part was Dr. Rolf Pederson, a Norwegian scientist reluctant to join Richard Harris and the underground against the Nazis in *The Heroes of Telemark*. It was exciting to make the movie, because it was based on the true story of a heavy-water plant in Norway that was crucial to the Nazi effort to create an atomic bomb, and the partisans' destruction of it. We shot where it had really happened, in a little town in a valley near Rjukan, north of Oslo, and used Norwegians who had been involved in the event.

The script is credited to Ivan Moffat and Ben Barzman, but Harold Pinter also worked on it. He wrote a really good battle-of-the-sexes scene where I'm trying to seduce my ex-wife. Unfortunately, since the picture runs a little over two hours—131 minutes—when it is shown on television, this scene is sometimes cut.

The climax of the movie was the blowing up of the ferry bringing the heavy water to Germany. The captain of the ferry in the movie was the captain of the ferry that had been blown up during the war. He had escaped by swimming to safety, as several others did.

I was glad I did that picture for Tony Mann; it was the last complete picture he directed. He was in the middle of *A Dandy in Aspic* with Laurence Harvey and Mia Farrow when he died. Harvey finished directing the picture.

I was in London finishing up *Telemark* when John Wayne called again. He had a project, *Cast a Giant Shadow*, about Mickey Marcus, the American West Point graduate and lawyer who went to Israel and helped them win the War of Independence. He said, "Kirk, if you play the lead, Mickey Marcus, I'll play the other American general, and we'll get an all-star cast." Which we did. We got Frank Sinatra to play a small part, and Yul Brynner. Angie Dickinson played my American wife, Senta Berger my Israeli mistress. Also in it were James Donald, Luther Adler, Gary Merrill, and Chaim Topol. As a matter of fact, there were too many stars in it. It took away from the significance of the piece.

In Israel, people went out of their way to do everything they could for me. I thought I had the largest apartment in the hotel. When Yul Brynner arrived, he said, "Come on up to my apartment, have a drink."

I said "No, no, why don't you come to mine?"

He insisted. So I went up to his apartment, and was astonished to find that it was exactly twice as large as mine. Yul had sent his assistant ahead to find a place to live, and had them knock down a wall, so he could have two apartments made into one.

Mel Shavelson, a very bright writer-director, was at the helm. Though Mel was Jewish, he was not Jewish enough. The movie needed to be done by someone with deep conviction, but Mel was cynical about being Jewish. And I think had he not been so, the picture would have been stronger. His cynicism was better expressed in the book that he wrote about the making of the movie, *How to Make a Jewish Movie*.

The underlying theme of *Cast a Giant Shadow* was a Jew who doesn't think of himself as one, and eventually finds his Jewishness. Mickey Marcus, in helping the Israelis, discovered his Jewishness, came to grips with it, and acknowledged that he was a Jew. His death, the night before independence, was tragic. Mickey Marcus was killed by an Israeli sentry because he did not understand the sentry's command—he did not speak Hebrew.

Coming to grips with what it means to be a Jew was also the theme of *The Juggler*, which I had done in 1953, and *Remembrance of Love (Holocaust Survivors)* which I did in 1982 with my son Eric.

It has also been a theme of my own life. Years back, I tried to forget that I was a Jew. I remember saying, "Oh no, I'm half Jewish," to minimize the stigma of being a Jew, one hundred percent. When my children were born, technically, they were not Jews, because the religion of the mother is the determining factor, and neither of my wives was Jewish. But they were aware, culturally, of my deep convictions. I never tried to influence them; I allowed them to make the choice, because I think that religion should be a personal decision. A while back, I asked Michael, "What are you?"

"I'm a Jew."

"Why?"

After a long pause, "Because I feel that I am."

My sons Michael and Joel were with me in Israel working on *Cast a Giant Shadow*. Joel, a big burly fellow of six feet two, often acted as my bodyguard. Once, I went into a barber shop to get a haircut and lots of people collected. Joel pushed them aside to clear a path for me. He loved playing that role.

In one scene, we needed an Israeli soldier to drive a jeep at breakneck speed up a mountainside, and stop at an exact spot for the camera. The Israeli playing the soldier said it was too dangerous, and wouldn't do it. But American boys are brought up with cars. Quickly, I said, "Michael, get a costume, get into that jeep, drive it up the mountainside, and stop on the mark." Michael jumped into the uniform, into the jeep, tore up the mountain, hit his mark perfectly.

Michael was an expert driver. He later took a course at the Bondurant racing school in Riverside, California, and broke all speed records. He was great with an automobile, which came in handy on his TV series, "The Streets of San Francisco," but which terrified Karl Malden. Once, after playing scenes where they ran a name through the computers to check a license plate, Karl wanted to see how it was really done. He ran his own name through, came up with a twelve-year-old parking ticket. Then he ran Michael's name through the computer. It printed out *pages*.

My sons have been with me year after year as I made movies. Now they create movies, too. I used to make three movies a year. Most actors now, the stars, make a movie once a year or once every two years.

Last October 1, I was lying in bed watching TV—an interview with my son Michael discussing the great success of *Fatal Attraction*. Then—the inevitable questions about his father and comparisons. On the screen came clips of me as Spartacus. I was Michael's age then.

Suddenly, the house began to shake—violently. Earth-quake. I cuddled my wife. Banshee, our Labrador retriever, jumped on the bed beside us. He wanted reassurance, too.

The earthquake subsided. Of course, the TV interview was interrupted to give a report of the quake.

"Now, we resume our scheduled program."

The face of Michael again appeared on the screen.

"How do you feel about always being compared to your father?"

Michael's face could be seen absorbing the question, and then he answered, "I don't mind looking into the mirror and seeing my father."

I was touched.

Michael came to visit me while *Fatal Attraction* was play-ing everywhere—a giant hit. He was in Los Angeles to make arrangements for publicity on *Wall Street*, the picture he had just finished shooting, and was about to get into preproduc-tion on the sequel to *Jewel of the Nile*. He was also involved in a new financial deal for his production company. After dinner, we started talking.

"You did a great job in *Fatal Attraction*, but I'd like to see you play an S.O.B. Remember, virtue is not photogenic."

Michael looked at me and smiled. "Wait until you see *Wall Street*."

We said nothing for a while.

"Michael, how was I as a father?"

"Gee, Dad, you were loony, jumping from one picture to another. You were so uptight."

I looked at Michael—the lines of fatigue around his eyes, the tension in his jaw. I started to laugh.

Michael swung around and stared at me. "What's funny?"

"I must have been a lot like you are right now."

Michael broke into a grin and kissed me. It takes one to know one.

In between movies, I was busy taking *Cuckoo's Nest* to every single studio. They all turned it down. Several times I thought of just selling it outright—if I could have found a buyer. But Michael always said, "Dad, don't ever sell that movie. That's a perfect role for you." Perfect or not, I was not easy to live with while I was trying so hard to get the movie made. It was maddening for me. And for Anne? How can any woman be married to a movie star? She has to be part saint, part sexpot. My wife Anne is all that. And more.

Ray Stark was producing *Is Paris Burning?*, a World War II epic about the Allies' liberation of France and Hitler's mad instructions to burn Paris to the ground. Ray asked me as a favor to do one day's work playing General George Patton. He asked how much I wanted. I said, "Ray, as a friend, I'll do it for nothing, if you don't use my name. But if you use my name, I want fifty thousand dollars."

My agents thought I was being unreasonable, that twenty-five thousand would be enough. I said, "Do you think it's right for me to tell him I'll do it for nothing?" They said, "No." I said, "I do. But does he really want me to play the part, or do they just want to use my name in the picture?" I said, "Ray, I leave the choice up to you." He paid me the fifty thousand dollars.

I felt, in a sense, that was a little unfair, and even wrong, of me. But if I'm going to whore, I should be paid for it. It's like the old joke—"We know what you are, we're just talking price."

Is Paris Burning? was made for Paramount. The studio had just been bought by Gulf + Western; the beginning of the conglomerates. (They also own Simon and Schuster, the publishers of this book.) Charles Bluhdorn, the head of Gulf + Western, who knew nothing about films, was personally supervising the editing of the picture. I heard they were butchering my scene. I went and complained. "What the hell is this? Who cut this?"

Charlie Bluhdorn said, "I did."

"How dare you do that? How dare you distort a picture just because you have the money to buy the studio?"

He looked at me very oddly. But I admired how he took it. He could have kicked me out.

Even though our first introduction generated some friction, we became friends. Charles Bluhdorn was fascinated with motion pictures. I think he was, in the beginning, fascinated with me as a movie star. He was just starting in the business and didn't know many stars. We were having dinner in New York once. I told him about a play that I was very anxious to do as a movie—*The Man of La Mancha*, an adaptation of *Don Quixote*, which I had always loved. It was a very good play by Dale Wasserman, who had adapted *One Flew Over the Cuckoo's Nest*. I said, "Why don't we buy this play, be partners, make it as a movie."

"They want two million for it."

"I'll put up a million dollars."

He looked at me. "Do you have a million dollars?"

"Yes. Let's go."

I knew that if we bought this property, it guaranteed the making of the movie. After all, he owned the studio. It would probably be the safest investment I'd ever made. We went together to look at the play, beautifully done, with Richard Kiley. Charlie decided not to do it. That was the end of that project.

Around 1979, my son Peter brought me *The Final Countdown*, a script outline he owned about a modern ship that gets caught in a time warp and goes back into World War I. But Peter shrewdly knew that we had to pick a moment in history that everyone would recognize, and came up with Pearl Harbor. Imagine the USS *Nimitz*, a nuclear-powered aircraft carrier, going back in time to just a few days before Pearl Harbor. The *Nimitz* is out at sea, fully loaded with jets and bombs, and it spots the Japanese armada approaching Pearl Harbor. What do they do? Change the course of history? I agreed to play the captain of the ship.

Pearl Harbor still affects me, even to this day. I visited the USS *Arizona* memorial. There it was, still a commissioned ship, flag flying, but sunken, with only part of the turret above water. Within are the bodies of more than a thousand sailors that have never been brought out, for fear that the whole thing would blow up. It gives you an eerie feeling, especially when you see so many Japanese there with cameras taking pictures. A very eerie feeling.

The Final Countdown had a good cast—Charles Durning as a presidential hopeful U.S. senator, Katharine Ross as his aide, James Farentino as one of the contemporary crewmen who mysteriously disappears, Martin Sheen as a modern observer.

The picture had special effects as the ship gets caught in the time-warp storm. But the most exciting thing was shooting on the USS *Nimitz* for about three weeks. When the *Nimitz* was in port at Newport, Rhode Island, none of the planes were on it. And then we went out to sea, and the jets came in. It was thrilling. I watched them for hours, one after the other zooming in to the deck, the tail hooked by trip wires at the last possible second.

I had to experience the feeling of being catapulted off an aircraft carrier. I badgered the captain, a wonderful guy, and he finally relented. They gave me a crash course on what to do in emergencies. I didn't remember any of it. Then they put me in a flight jumpsuit, helmet, parachute. In no time, I was sitting behind the pilot, my earphones adjusted. As the engines were revving up, the pilot, a young midwesterner, said, "My wife and I really admire you. We go to see all your pictures."

Nervous, I said, "Thank you."

He said, "Why don't you give the signal."

"What?"

"Just salute that sailor there and we're on our way."

I saluted. We exploded off the deck, then dipped sickeningly toward the ocean. My eyes were closed, but part of my urinary tract was open. We swerved up into the sky. I began to relax. Just when I was getting used to it, the pilot said, "Ready to go back?"

"Sure," I said. But go back where? The boat that had seemed gigantic when we were on it was a speck on a wave now, a small slab like a tombstone.

We came in for our landing, hit the deck, and bounced up

into the air again with a terrible roar. Nonchalantly, the pilot said, "Golly, I forgot to lower the tail hook. That means I'll have to buy all the boys a drink."

I was just thinking, "Let's get the hell out of here."

We made another pass. The tail hook grabbed the wire, I grabbed the door handle and climbed out, knowing that I would never make a fighter pilot.

But, in spite of the *Nimitz* and the jets and the special effects (not special or effective enough), the picture did not do well.

But Peter, twenty-three, had produced his first motion picture. I have great admiration for my four sons. They come from two wives. They were brought up in affluence, but all of them have a great desire to work. They are different from me, and from each other, but we all have in common talent and independence. My Jewish dream of being the patriarch, with my children working together with me, will never be fulfilled. My need to have them sitting around me at the dinner table once a week will never be satisfied. I always wanted that to happen with Pa. Of course, one time that it did, I flipped a teaspoonful of hot tea in his face. My sons have expressed to me much love and much resentment. I feel that the resentment decreases and the love increases as they get older. Or is it because I get older? One thing about my four sons—Michael, Joel, Peter, and Eric—they're never dull.

Thirty-three

COMRADE DOUGLAS

April 1966. Anne and I packed our suitcases for the U.S. State Department again. This time, the Iron Curtain countries.

Poland. I had to give a talk in Lodz, at the famous cinema school that Roman Polanski had attended. I expected it to be like the American Academy of Dramatic Arts—intellectual, academic. When I arrived, I found billboards of me all over the place, students dressed in cowboy outfits, shooting guns to greet me. That was what they thought of Kirk Douglas—King of the Cowboys. They were convinced that I was just the biggest goddamned cowboy in the world. I thought, Aren't they interested in knowing who I am? Not at all. They knew who I was: a movie star.

In the back of the school they had a western street, complete with saloon. They led out a beautiful, enormous white horse they wanted me to get on. I approached this prancing giant steed very carefully, thinking "Holy . . . what kind of a horse is this?" I like to check these things out. Yet I couldn't lose face. I got up on the horse. This seemed to be a cue in a script I didn't have—the students dressed as cowboys rushed to attack me from all sides, just as in a movie. But there was no script, no choreography—just mob hysteria. They're thinking, "The great Kirk Douglas. Invincible." I had to be very cool. One of the Polish cowboys came at me, blood in his eye. I reached out and kicked him right in the face, and knocked him down. Another guy came over, and— pretending to be very playful—I had to give him an elbow in the throat. And knock a few of these guys off. Or they would have knocked me off the horse, and probably trampled me. And my reputation. I don't know what they would have done if John Wayne had been there. Mobbed is mobbed, whether it's in Poland by fans who adore you, or in Turkey by people who hate you.

I was dumbfounded. These were students, studying make-believe. They *know* it's make-believe, *know* how it works. But they came unhinged over a movie star. They took movies of everything I did while I was there, put together a film of my visit. It won a prize. That was Poland.

Czechoslovakia. Prague impressed me. A beautiful city. More artistic than anywhere else behind the Iron Curtain. More talented people. I went to several of their theaters. They had interesting ways of doing movies. I was particularly impressed by the work of director Milos Forman, and by his unique sense of humor. I met him, told him I wanted to send him a book that I owned and thought would make a terrific movie. He agreed to look at it. When I got back to the States, I sent him *One Flew Over the Cuckoo's Nest.* Never heard from him. I thought he was a very rude man.

Rumania. U.S. Ambassador Davis and his group greeted us at the airport in Bucharest. But there was also a Rumanian group to greet us. The Rumanians swept me off, under the nose of the Americans, almost kidnapped me. I waved questioningly to Ambassador Davis, who made a "Go ahead" gesture. So we went with the Rumanians. The first thing they did was shove a wad of money into my fist.

I said, "What's this for?"

"You are the guest of Rumania. This is for expenses."

"Wait a minute." I had a difficult time explaining to them that I pay my own way. I don't even let my own government pay my expenses. I don't want anyone to say that I'm taking trips because the government is paying. They couldn't understand that. They were disappointed that I wouldn't take their money.

It reminded me of a similar situation when I was in Moscow. They wanted me to do an interview on TV, which I did. After it was over, they gave me a wad of money. Rubles. I said, "What's this?" They said I had to be paid for the interview. I declined. They insisted. They made me take it. Not that much, but enough to buy some caviar and vodka. The Russians are more persuasive than the Rumanians.

In Rumania, there were spy types all over the place. At the USIA office, they pointed out a man sitting in a car, taking photos of everybody coming into our building. They warned us that everything was wired, so we should be careful of what we said. Whenever we went into a room, we always assumed that the microphone was in the chandelier. The first day in Bucharest, we ordered a simple breakfast. The bill came. It was outrageous. I couldn't believe it. I don't think any hotel in New York or London would have been that expensive. I looked up, addressed the chandelier loudly, "Boy, this is supposed to be a Communist country. Would you take a look at this bill? It's ridiculous. This is twice as much as we would ever pay in the United States." And sure enough, the next morning we ordered breakfast—the same food—and the bill was less than half.

We visited some beautiful castles, but never got to the castle of Dracula—Vlad the Impaler to his friends. Then the American Embassy had a dinner for us. It's a wonderful way to help to bring about communication. The ambassador and his wife were excited because there was a newspaper editor they had been inviting to dinner for two years, who never came, but who was coming that night. The ambassador said to me, wide-eyed, "How did that happen?"

I answered, "His wife is a big movie fan, and she said 'Tonight ve go to the embassy.' "

He laughed. But that's about what it was.

I found this over and over again—the embassy would have dinners when I was there, and people who never would have come otherwise showed up. Years earlier, when I was making pictures in foreign countries, I wondered why the American Embassy never called on movie stars. Movie stars are an international institution. And if the embassies want to use them as bait to get the people they want to come to dinner, that's fine. American movies are another form of bait. In foreign countries, show people an American movie, even without the star, and they'll come to dinner. Once everybody is there, you have a chance to talk. Then things can happen.

Years before, I was at a formal dinner party at the American Embassy in Rome. After dinner, they showed *Seven Days in May*. They ran it on a 16mm projector, I was embarrassed. I didn't stay to see it. I bought the embassy a projection room with a professional 35mm projector. I never saw it until March of 1987 when I was in Italy for the opening of *Tough Guys*. We had a dinner at the embassy. Ambassador Rapf and his wife were extremely pleased by the turnout. But this time we saw a movie the way it was meant to be seen.

By the time we got to Budapest, the last stop on our tour, we were thoroughly depressed by the grayness of the Iron Curtain countries, in spite of the beauty of the city. It was made worse because we liked the people, and could see what living there was doing to them. When I talk about the grayness, I don't mean the weather.

Two things were certain in the Iron Curtain countries: they always took your passport away, and you always got paranoid when they did. What if they found some ridiculous charge to pin on you? What if some demented person planted something on you or made an accusation? What if . . . ?

In Budapest, they invited us to stay for the May Day Parade. I would have the seat of honor near Kadar, the General Secretary of the Hungarian Communist Party, who had come to power when the Russians crushed the freedom fighters in

1956. Anne and I looked at each other, visions of millions of people in the United States turning on their television sets and seeing Kirk Douglas and his wife in the reviewing stand at a May Day Parade in a Communist country. We made a quick departure from Budapest.

It had been less than two weeks, but when we finally got to Vienna, we felt as if we had been granted a reprieve from a sentence of life imprisonment.

Baragavoi is the famous Russian cosmonaut who made a visit to the United States with Feotistoff, the civilian scientist. The head of the MPAA asked if Anne and I would throw a cocktail party for them. Baragavoi was a typical hearty Russian, next to me in the receiving line. We were talking through an interpreter. He spoke no English. A beautiful girl would come in, and I would say, "What about the next time we take a trip in space, we take her along?" He'd say, "Da, da, da." He loved that. He had a great eye for the ladies.

We had a tremendous turnout, about three hundred people. Most of Hollywood was there. At the end I made a little speech based on *Soyuz*, the name of one of their sputniks, which means "united." And my whole idea was that the symbol of *Soyuz* should unite our two countries. They were pleased. Baragavoi had a great time.

A couple of weeks later in New York, I heard that Baragavoi was at the Waldorf-Astoria, leaving that day for Russia. I called him, and through an interpreter explained that I wanted to say good-bye to him. The interpreter said, "Come right over. He wants to see you." So I went. His car was already downstairs to take him to the airport. And he came down. And of course the cameras and people were all there. He grabbed me and lifted me off the ground, and embraced me. "Tovarish!"

In Russia in 1977, while attending a conference to discuss film exchanges, I asked to see Baragavoi. Nobody said "*nyet*," nobody said "*da*." Nobody even said maybe.

Jack Valenti and I were in the hotel snack bar, sipping a beer. Suddenly a Russian man came up, trailing a couple of pretty girls. With tears in his eyes, he threw his arms around me, sputtering in Russian. One of the girls who spoke a little English explained that he was a great fan of mine. He had seen *Spartacus*, which had been a big hit in Russia. I smiled and nodded. While we were "talking," someone from the hotel appeared, said that something had come up and I had to go upstairs right away. I couldn't imagine what it was.

The Russia Hotel covers a whole block. It's gigantic, built to hold every member of the Politburo under one roof. They took me to another part of the hotel, which I was surprised to find was much more luxurious than where we were living. They opened the door to a sumptuous room, motioned for me to go in alone. I went in.

Baragavoi. A much more restrained Baragavoi. The difference was startling, like McMurphy in *Cuckoo's Nest* after the lobotomy. He had brought his daughter, a little shy and starstruck, who wanted to meet the American movie star. He had a gift for me, a special bottle of vodka, which he remembered us drinking together. He was very warm, but slightly repressed. The meeting didn't last long. Everything was a little bit formal, not full of exuberance. That's what happens when the room is full of microphones.

That night, Jack and I attended a big dinner with a group of Russian government officials. We all drank a lot of vodka. They asked me about my reactions to their country.

Through an interpreter, I told them. "The trouble with your country is that you don't have enough communism."

They all looked at me.

I said, "We have more communism in my country."

"What . . . ?"

I said, "Lenin said communism is based on a classless society. Here in Moscow, all I see are classes. One class has dachas, the other class has . . ." Valenti was kicking me under the table. I kept talking. "We don't have that. We wouldn't permit it. Your limousines race out of the Kremlin, and everybody runs out of the way. You couldn't get away with that in our country. Street kids would throw rocks through the windows."

There was a lot of rumbling in Russian, and then somebody changed the subject.

But I think it's true. They don't really have communism there. There's a big joke in Russia: if somebody says, "When do you think such-and-such will happen?" instead of saying "never" or "the next blue moon," they say, "That will happen when communism comes to Russia." They do have a sense of humor. They need it.

There is one synagogue in Moscow. It wasn't far from the hotel. I asked if I could visit it. Sure. They'd arrange it. I asked to go on a Saturday morning, when services would be held. I went, and sure enough, there were a bunch of old Jews. Nobody young. All old Jews, praying away. Back at the hotel, I said to Jack, "That's nice. At least they have one place where the Jews come and pray."

He said, "Kirk, are you kidding? Word got out that Kirk Douglas, the actor, wanted to see a synagogue on Saturday. So they sent to the casting office: 'We want sixty old-looking Jews. Have them there Saturday, in costume, praying.'"

Was he kidding?

Thirty-four

MOVIES

I stopped dictating into the recorder and looked out the window. The shadows were getting longer. It was quiet in my house in Beverly Hills. My wife spends much more time in the office than I do. I picked up the telephone connected to the office.

"Yes?"

"Is my wife there?"

"Yes." Silence.

"Do you mind if I talk to her?" Annoyed. A click of the phone; my wife picks up.

"Yes."

"Honey, come home."

"I thought you were working on your book."

"I am. But I'm lonely."

"Oh, you just want to make sure that I'm in the next room?"

"That's right."

"O.K." And she came home.

Actors are lonely people. Sometimes actors are friends. I

envy them. But very often actors don't seem to have other actors for friends. They live in their own world. Maybe they're ashamed of being actors. It's a strange profession.

John Wayne called me. He was producing a western, *The War Wagon*, from a script by Clare Huffaker, based on his novel *Badman*, and wanted me to be in it.

Although Wayne had made many, many movies, he had also made bad business investments; he told me he was broke. It wasn't until the late sixties that he made pictures where he was able to recoup some money. We shot *The War Wagon* in Durango, Mexico, where Wayne owned a lot of land. Very rough country. In the plane flying to Durango, he had trouble breathing. We had to put an oxygen mask on him. It was the beginning of his lung problems.

Anne flew down to Durango to visit me. I had told her that we were roughing it, living in a very modest motel. My wife's favorite spot in the whole world is the Hôtel du Cap in the South of France. Once an old château, it's now a splendid hotel with spacious rooms and a long, wide walk that leads down to the swimming pool at the edge of the Mediterranean Sea. To the right of that is a lovely restaurant. On the other side are bamboo cabañas with high fences around them. For two weeks I worked on this book in one of the cabañas. There's a roped-off dressing area, shower, and a bathroom. A path leads down to the sea. It's private. You can spend the day with a few friends and just read and lie in the sun. Or you can lie nude and sunbathe. In the evening, you can go to one of the many restaurants in the area that serve excellent French food and wine. It's expensive. That's Anne's idea of heaven.

Durango was Anne's idea of hell. She walked into this room, and was mystified by the sign on the bathroom mirror: PLEASE SHAKE OUT YOUR BOOTS BEFORE PUTTING THEM ON

She said, "What on earth does that mean?"

I explained, "That's in case there are scorpions."

"Scorpions?"

"Yes. They like to go into warm places, and you don't want to step on one. It could give you an awful bite."

The next day, after carefully shaking out her boots, Anne was on a plane back to Beverly Hills.

There were a lot of scorpions around the rocks; you had to be careful. When we were out in the wild, shooting, it was good to wear high boots. But scorpions don't go around attacking you.

It was clear that Wayne was having physical problems, but he never let them deter him. I always admired the fact that he was a professional. He was always the first one on the set, usually checking out what the special-effects guys were doing. He butted into everything. I should talk; I've been accused of that myself. But he had me beat by a long shot.

He would push directors around. When Wayne formed his own company and got away from strong directors like John Ford, who kept him under control, he became a force that dominated directors. "What, you're going to put the camera here? Jesus. Put it *there!*" This was out in the countryside. Whatever direction the camera pointed was fine. It was all beautiful scenery.

Scenes often lined up with Wayne in the center, a couple of cowboys on one side, a couple on the other. He'd turn to the left and say something, turn to the right and say something. Then they'd move forward.

I found myself in that choreography at one point, on his right. As Wayne turned to the fellow on his left, I bent down to pour myself a cup of coffee from the fire. I'll never forget the look on Wayne's face when he turned around, all set to do his routine, and had to look for me, crouched down. He said, "What the . . . ?"

"Well, John, we were lined up like the Rockettes. I just thought it would break things up."

He accepted it, but reluctantly.

The director, Burt Kennedy, was having trouble with Wayne. Burt was a very talented director, but gentle. Wayne was a less talented director, and far from gentle. I tried to get Burt to stand up to him. It wasn't easy. I thought of Tom Tryon's relationship with Preminger: director bullies actor. Here was the reverse: actor bullies director. Wayne was never that offensive, but he was rough. Either way, it was unpleasant.

I wasn't quite sure how to play Lomax, my show-off cowboy character. Then I got an idea from my son Joel. I had Lomax wear a black glove with a gaudy ring over it. The first time I got into wardrobe, with this large ring over my glove, John Wayne took one look at me and said scornfully, "Are you going to play it like a queer?"

"I'll try not to let the effeminate side of me come out, John."

Everybody called him "Duke." I called him "John." I don't like nicknames unless they mean something. When I worked with Elia Kazan, everyone called him "Gadge."

I said to him, "What does 'Gadge' mean?"

He explained that "Gadge" was short for "gadget," because he was a little fellow. How denigrating. I could never call him that. So I always called him by his name. I didn't know what Duke meant, so John Wayne was always John to me. The rivalry between the two of us worked. It was the big joke in *War Wagon*. We were always trying to one-up each other. There's a wonderful scene where Wayne and I shoot two bad guys at the same time. I look at him very coolly and say, "Mine hit the ground first." Wayne looks at me, pauses, then says, "Mine was taller."

Our strange relationship of professional respect in spite of extreme personal and political differences continued. During the picture, I made political statements for Democratic candidates, Wayne made statements for Republicans.

My character, Lomax, never got on a horse the normal way. He was always doing fancy mounts. We had stuntmen there to do them for me. They planned to do it in a long shot, then cut to me in a close shot sitting on a horse. I didn't think that was going to be very effective or fool anybody. I studied how they did the different mounts—side mounts, scissors, or over the rear of the horse. I said, "I can do all those mounts myself."

The stuntman, Hal Needham, looked at me skeptically. I

had seen that look before. It was the look on the faces of the producers of *Act of Love,* when I told them I would learn to speak French. It was the look on the faces of the directors when I said I would do my own trapeze work or run the oars.

I told him to get me a small trampoline, a minitramp. You have to learn how to manipulate a trampoline. But I have pretty good coordination. The most important thing about any mount is to lift your rear end up high enough to get your leg over the horse's rump, or the saddle. In a short while I got very handy with the trampoline, and had no problem doing trick mounts.

This annoyed Wayne. A newspaper reporter interviewing him said, "I understand Kirk Douglas is very good with a horse."

Wayne snorted. "Good with a horse! He can't even get on a horse unless he uses a trampoline!"

I thought that was a very funny way of taking me down. But I guess he had a right to be jealous, and Needham had a right to be skeptical: I was fifty years old.

I left the West and John Wayne's Batjac Productions behind and headed for Sicily to produce *The Brotherhood,* a movie about the Mafia. It might have been more commercial if it had had more violence and killing. But I was intrigued with showing the dichotomy between the family life that the members of the Mafia led, and the brutal business that they were in. The well-written script was by Lewis John Carlino, who was related to Mafia members. I thought it was a very good study of the Mafia, before *The Godfather* was made. I dyed my hair black, grew a mustache to play my character Don Francesco, of the old school; my directness and violence are an embarrassment to the "new" Mafia, represented by Alex Cord, my younger brother, who deals with Mafia business as *business.* We both gradually realize that I will have to go, and that in order to survive in the new organization, he will have to be the one to kill me.

Marty Ritt was the director of *Brotherhood.* He turned it

down at first. I worked on it and rewrote it, and then he decided to do it. But we never had a very warm relationship. Maybe it went back to *Spartacus*.

I had a scene with Irene Papas, the Greek actress, who played my wife. It was not working. The timing was off; it just didn't feel right. I said, "Marty, let me work with Irene." She and I went off together and worked on the scene. It's a bedroom scene. I come back home late at night. I'm drunk, singing a song. As I peel off my clothes, she, like a good Italian wife, follows me around, picking up after me. I become very amorous, promising a wild night of sex, but fall asleep drunk before anything ever happens. From the look on her face, you can tell she's been through this a thousand times, and knows that the only thing she's going to get out of it is dirty laundry. Very nice scene. We worked it out together, rehearsed it until it felt good.

When Marty came to shoot it, he didn't change a thing, just shot it exactly as we rehearsed it. I always felt resentment on his part. And I felt rejected. The pattern of my life. And deep inside of me, Issur hid behind a garbage can so no one could see that he was hurt. Somehow, I blame myself. I was bothered that we didn't have a warmer relationship during the shooting of *The Brotherhood*. And I never saw Marty dying to do any movies for me afterward.

We shot quite a bit of *The Brotherhood* in Palermo, Sicily. Not the most colorful place in the world. The American crew was depressed.

A friend of mine, Ralph Stolkin, was sailing his luxurious yacht down to Capri. I knew it would be filled with champagne and caviar. I called him, made Palermo sound like a wonderful place, tried to convince him to make a detour. He wasn't interested; he was waiting for Bea Korshak, wife of lawyer Sidney Korshak, and Dinah Shore, who were in Dubrovnik, Yugoslavia. I told him to let me take care of everything. I got in touch with Dinah and Bea in Yugoslavia, suggested that they come to Palermo instead of Capri. They didn't want to. They had never been to Capri, had always wanted to see it.

I said, "Capri? Capri's *nothing!* You can see that any time. But *Palermo!* Come directly to Sicily." Then I got in touch with Ralph and settled the logistics. Everybody would meet in Palermo.

I had been talking to my crew about this for weeks. "You're going to have cigars, Havana cigars. Dom Pérignon champagne! Caviar!" And they kept saying, "Yeah, yeah, yeah." But finally the day arrived. This beautiful yacht came sailing into the filthy waters of Palermo, defecation floating all around it. Condoms. Bea and Dinah were "a little disappointed. Palermo wasn't exactly what we thought it was going to be." For two days, I had the members of my cast come aboard and feast on caviar and champagne and Havana cigars. I encouraged Ralph to stay for four or five days, or a week. But the next morning I looked out and the yacht was gone. They said nothing, just snuck off during the night. I had seduced them out of two days of luxury. After the movie came out, Sidney Korshak, who had had many newspaper articles written about him and his alleged connections with the Mafia, told me that the big capos were most impressed with the picture. They felt it captured the spirit of their organization. They particularly liked my portrayal of a Mafia don. They wanted to meet me.

I was very curious about these men. But Korshak never quite got me together with them. Frankly, I felt that he was extremely considerate of me, protective, and felt that it would be better for me not to. He knew that whatever he did was watched. And if he took me someplace for a meeting— many of them were living in Palm Springs at the time—it would just give the government a record of the visit.

Korshak said that he would like to do me a favor and sell me, at a very reasonable price, four points in a Las Vegas hotel, the Riviera. And several people, when they heard about it, said, "How terrific! You have a chance to make a *lot* of money!" Anne and I discussed it, decided we didn't want to participate. We didn't want to go into business without knowing who our partners were. So we turned down an opportunity to make a lot of money. We never regretted it.

After a barbecue at Sidney Korshak's house one day, I walked into the kitchen and was astonished to find George Raft doing the dishes. I backed out and mentioned this to Sidney. He said, "Oh, George likes to do that." George had been one of the original tough guys in Hollywood. But he had made an amazing number of bad career decisions. He told Jack Warner he wanted out of his contract, because Warner was giving him lousy scripts that he kept turning down. Scripts like *The Maltese Falcon, High Sierra, Casablanca.*

The Arrangement was a best-selling novel, mostly autobiographical, written by Elia Kazan, who had directed *A Tree Grows in Brooklyn, Viva Zapata, East of Eden,* and *A Streetcar Named Desire,* and who had won Academy Awards for directing *Gentleman's Agreement* and *On the Waterfront.* He was going to make *The Arrangement* into a movie. I loved the book. But I didn't know Kazan very well, and I didn't know how to tell him. Warren Beatty, who had worked with Kazan on *Splendor in the Grass,* the doomed teen romance, with Natalie Wood, gave me a sound piece of advice: "If you want to play the part so badly, why don't you just call Kazan and tell him? If he doesn't want you, he will at least be flattered." So I called Kazan in New York, told him how much I loved the book, and that I wished he would consider me for the film. He gave me the role.

At first, Kazan was thinking of having his wife play herself in the film. That is, the woman now his wife, who was his girlfriend in the book, would play herself as his girlfriend. This bothered me. It's bad enough having to play the alter ego of a director who's written a movie based on his own novel, based on his own life. But to also have him be the producer, and have to make love to his wife, who was his girlfriend, right in front of him . . . Thank God he didn't do it. Deborah Kerr played the wife, Faye Dunaway the girlfriend. They both did wonderful jobs.

In one scene, Faye and I we were supposed to be naked, sitting in bed together after our great romance. And she came wearing these little stickers over her nipples. I said, "Faye, honestly, please take those off. They look so silly." She said, "Oh well," and ripped them off. I enjoyed working with Faye; she was a natural girl, very talented. I found her very attractive, but she had a mad crush on Marcello Mastroianni.

I loved working with Kazan. He loved actors, would do anything to seduce them into giving the best possible performance. Few directors are like that. I liked to go down to Palm Springs on the weekend. But almost every weekend he kept me in town to discuss the script, and the movie. He used me as a sounding board. It was flattering.

I enjoyed doing the picture. Kazan was trying to do something different, bold, go inside the head of my character in all his confusion over his career, his women, his father, his life. Screenings of the picture drew mixed reactions. In the editing, Kazan changed the ending. I felt that he hadn't made the movie that was based on his book, the movie that he had shot. I thought that Kazan was too close to all of it. As usual, I voiced my opinion very strongly.

Exasperated, he said, "O.K., go ahead, you edit the film."

I took him at his word, and recut the film with Stefan Arnstein, the editor. He'd been working with the great Elia Kazan. Now here comes this actor—me—to take over.

I took the footage that Kazan had shot, structured it as he had in his book. In his cut, the film ended with his father, played by Richard Boone, dying. The last shot was a close-up of my face, thinking about my father. But the book had a wonderful ending, which he had shot and not used, where I ended up with my sweetheart. It was as if each of us was being interviewed by an unseen person off camera. Faye Dunaway was expressing how she felt, and I was expressing how I felt. It is apparent from what we are saying that we are not living happily ever after. I used those scenes in editing the picture.

Ted Ashley, the head of Warners, thought my editing was a vast improvement. Then Kazan had second thoughts, which I can understand. It embarrassed me greatly, because suddenly he must have felt, What am I doing letting this actor take over my film? He cut the film back to his original concept, ending with the freeze frame on me. We never discussed that incident, but I always felt it impeded any friendship we might have had. I've never seen him since then. I felt robbed of a potential friend—or father. I have great admiration and respect for Kazan. Working with him was a fascinating, enjoyable experience.

The Arrangement was previewed for the Strasberg Theatre in New York, with a dinner afterward. Very unsuccessful. There's nothing worse than the hush that descends on a crowd when they've been disappointed by something they've been expecting great things from. Nobody knows what to say.

I admired the way Kazan handled himself, in a very charming, amusing manner. I felt crushed. Not for myself, but for the project. I still feel that parts of it, especially the beginning, are brilliant. To this day I feel that, if he could come back and take the actual film he shot and rearrange it, it would become a great movie.

Recently, I came across a photo of the two of us that I liked. We both seemed happy, engrossed in conversation. I sent it to him for his signature. He signed it and sent this letter:

Dear Kirk,
    I am aware of the darker sides of your character, as you must be aware of the darker sides of mine. No artist is devoid of these aspects and they don't really matter. A man must be judged by what is best about him; about how hard he works, how devoted he is to his opinions and how much he loves his children. In these respects, I have nothing but praise for you. Your kids are damn nice kids and they reflect you.
    I don't go on at great length about the film, "The Arrangement." It was a disappointment to me as it must have been to you. I say what I have to say in my book.
    I have great affection for you and considerable admiration.
                                        Fondly,

                        Elia

Cuckoo's Nest was always on my mind. I tried to get the financing from a businessman named Max Palevski. He had made his fortune from a computer his company developed and then sold to Xerox, almost a billion dollars. One day, he told me that he wanted to make movies.

I said, "Yeah?"

He said, "Yes. But I don't want to do anything ordinary. I want to do something special, worthwhile."

"Max, let's have lunch."

We had lunch at my home. I gave him the script of *One Flew Over the Cuckoo's Nest.* "Max, I think this is something special, and very worthwhile."

He read it and got back to me. "Yeah. But I don't think it's commercial." I thought, here's a billionaire who says he wants to do something special. I offer him something special, but his business sense says it's not good enough. Of course, *Cuckoo's Nest* turned out to be not only an artistic but a commercial success.

Max Palevski went into business with Peter Hart, made several movies. All flops, like *The Savage Is Loose.* He became disenchanted with the motion picture business and got out. Sometimes you have the opportunity, the brass ring is there, and you don't reach up and take it. Max, you had your chance.

I went from the avant-garde to the Old West in my next picture, *There Was a Crooked Man.* The director was Joe Mankiewicz. I had done *A Letter to Three Wives* with him twenty-two years earlier. Since then, Joe had directed and/or written many wonderful movies: Academy Awards for writing and directing *All About Eve; Julius Caesar* with Marlon Brando; the backstage Hollywood story *The Barefoot Contessa,* with Bogart and Ava Gardner; the musical *Guys and Dolls* with Brando and Sinatra; and, of course, the spectacular *Cleopatra* starring Elizabeth Taylor and Richard Burton.

I think Joe was uncomfortable doing *There Was a Crooked Man* in the wilds of the desert. He was much more at home with a scene in a library. It was a brilliantly written script, by David Newman and Robert Benton, their first since *Bonnie and Clyde*.

I was the robber-killer-bad guy who ends up in prison breaking rocks. Henry Fonda plays the warden, a seemingly decent, humane man. But when the chips are down, he goes for the gold, proving that he's just as crooked as everybody else. The picture was very cynical and did not do well—*everybody* was crooked, nobody to root for.

Henry Fonda was a wonderful actor, but when I looked at him, I remembered him at that party years ago, snickering with his wife, talking the girl I had brought into dropping me, sneaking out the back door with Jimmy Stewart. I never mentioned it to Jimmy Stewart, and I never mentioned it to Henry Fonda. But whenever I looked at Henry, I relived that scene. How cruel of them. And how petty of me not to forget. I always wanted to say, "You know, Henry, the way you should have handled it was just say to her, tell him, 'I have a terrible headache. Would you mind taking me home?' Then let the jerk"—me, Kirk the jerk—"take you home. And then you just get in your car and meet us." I never realized how deeply that incident hurt me. It was so difficult for me to forget it.

We shot a lot of the movie on a huge prison set that Warner Brothers built for $300,000 in the desert at Joshua Tree National Monument. I stayed at my house in Palm Springs. Henry Fonda stayed at his. A helicopter took us back and forth to the location.

Coming back from location one day, we ran into a tremendous sandstorm. You could see nothing. I looked at Henry, he looked at me, and we just sat there.

Suddenly, I heard the pilot mutter, "I don't like this."

I said, "What?"

He repeated, "I don't like this."

I said, "DOWN!"

We were able to make out a stretch of green, and landed the helicopter. It was a golf course. We walked to the clubhouse, grabbed a couple of taxis, and went home.

When you're up in a helicopter, you're completely dependent on your pilot. Henry and I both hated looking out and seeing all this sand whipping around. But I assumed that the pilot was in control. But if *he* doesn't like it, I hate it.

Nineteen seventy-one. The Jicarilla Apache Indian tribe came to me with a proposition. They had some money from oil on their lands, and wanted to make a movie. Just a commercial movie, nothing with Indians. I had seen a script called *A Gunfight*, with an interesting premise. Two old-time gunfighters run into each other by accident after many years. The whole town is in an uproar at these two former champion gunslingers coming together, making bets about who was better in the old days, who would have won if they had ever faced off.

My character says, "Look, all our lives we've taken our chances, risked our lives for a drink or pat on the back. Why not risk our lives once for winner takes all?"

We're going to have that gunfight. It turns into a major event, and we hold our gunfight in a bullfighting arena just over the Mexican border.

Johnny Cash was very hot at the time. I called him up and pitched the part of the other gunfighter to him, and he agreed to do it. Jane Alexander played my wife. My son Eric made his debut playing my son in the picture, and he was quite good. I was pleased to be working with my youngest son. One day, a horse stepped on my hand. Eric came running up. "Quick, Daddy! Bite a bullet!" But I had conflicting emotions. I didn't want Eric—or any of my sons—to become actors.

The Apaches eventually got all their money back, but I never saw any profits from the picture.

While Anne and I were taking a rest in Cap d'Antibes, producer Alexander Salkind called from Paris to try to get me to do *The Light at the Edge of the World,* by Jules Verne. I wasn't receptive. But he was persistent. One afternoon, we came back to the villa, and there, sitting by the pool, was an elderly gentleman—Mr. Salkind. A man who didn't fly, he'd taken the train down from Paris with the script.

He wanted me to read it. I had good memories of *20,000 Leagues Under the Sea*, also a Jules Verne story. And I admired Salkind's tenacity; I read it.

The Light at the Edge of the World is what sailors call the lighthouse set up in 1865 at Cape Horn, the southernmost tip of South America. The waters are treacherous, the rocks rugged. In this story, a pirate captain wants to take over the lighthouse to give out false signals and lure ships aground to kill the crews and take the cargo. I play an American soldier-of-fortune living in the lighthouse along with Fernando Rey and Massimo Ranieri. The script by Tom Rowe was good. I said I would do it.

We made plans to shoot the picture in Cadaques, Spain, a quaint little resort town near the French border. A very colorful place, with sharp black pointed rocks, like stalagmites, jutting up next to the water.

It was during the summer. I decided to take fourteen-year-old Peter, who was not very keen on going, with me. Peter and I stayed in a small house on a tiny street.

It was the turning point in his life from a boy to a man. In the movie we used an old sailing vessel, which was owned and manned by an English crew. Peter got to know these fellows, and was with them constantly. He helped them work the ship during the day; at night he'd go out with them for dinner. He would always ask me to go along. "Dad, wouldn't you like to go out and have dinner with us?" I think he was relieved when I said, "No, I think I'll just go back to the house and study my lines and go to bed." It was the first time that he got drunk. I got up early one morning and found a couple of young fellows who obviously had had too much to drink, sleeping on the couch. They took him for his first visit to a brothel. Vicariously, I was enjoying the transformation that was taking place within him.

Peter could only stay for a few weeks. When the time came for him to go back, I took him to the airport. I'll never forget —there were tears in his eyes. He was sorry to leave. It was a great contrast to the misgivings he had when we first arrived. What a difference in him. He had become a man. This English crew had accepted him. They were all older than he. The youngest were probably eighteen and twenty-one, but they had accepted him, and he had had a wonderful time. And that pleased me.

Yul Brynner played the brutal pirate captain. I got him the job, in spite of *Spartacus*. Yul always had to have the biggest everything, just as when we were shooting *Cast a Giant Shadow* in Israel. Yul found the largest house in town, on top of a hill, and rented it. He had the largest trailer—oversize. It created tremendous problems when it had to be moved around on the rough locations. It had every modern convenience, including a butler who cooked meals. Yul would invite you over, in the middle of the wilds, to have a drink, oysters, fried shrimp, all kinds of hors d'oeuvres, at his trailer. It was quite a treat. I wondered how Yul Brynner had learned to live so well.

The most interesting thing about making *The Light at the Edge of the World* was my relationship with my next-door neighbor, Salvador Dali. His house was just above mine, overlooking the sea. He was really a crazy man. Dali invited us all to a cocktail party at his unusual home on the beach. And I invited him to the set. He came several times to watch the shooting, and became quite engrossed in it. Then one night he invited me and Jean Claude, a handsome young French actor who was in the picture, to dinner. I was eager to go; I always found it exciting to look at his paintings.

It was an intimate dinner—only Jean Claude, Dali, a beautiful young lady, and me. Afterward, Dali showed us some of his works. He was in the process of painting one of his versions of *Christ on the Cross*, this one from almost a helicopterlike angle. What a brilliant talent for form. It was fascinating to wander around his house, looking at all the *objets d'art*.

He had a little film that he said he thought would amuse us. I settled down very expectantly. With Dali, you never knew what you were going to get. The lights went out, the movie came on. It was a very basic story about a woman and a banana. What that woman did with that banana after she peeled it left nothing to the imagination. Then he showed us a room full of all kinds of clay sections of the human body. Apparently he was quite a student of anatomy. With a little Cointreau in hand, he began to talk to the three of us about anatomy.

Then he picked something up. I wasn't sure. I thought, could it be . . . ? Naw. But maybe . . . Was I right? Yes. He had a plaster vagina and two penises, or penii, whatever the plural of penis is, and he went into a lecture, using these visual aids, showing how he thought it would be possible for two cocks to enter one vagina.

As Dali was talking, I looked at this young French actor, then at this smiling, lovely lady. As quickly as I could, I said, "If you don't mind, you'll have to excuse us. We have to get up *so* early for work." We left behind a rather disappointed Salvador Dali. And I think a rather disappointed young lady. Off into the night we went, laughing at the proposition we had just been offered.

Back in bed, I had second thoughts. *Was* it possible? I gnawed on that thought, smiling, until I fell asleep.

I had close to a fatal accident on the sharp black rocks of Cadaques. In one scene, I was supposed to roll off the roof of a hut. They built a platform with a mattress for me to fall on. A crew member suggested, "We could put an iron rail, like a fence, around the platform."

I said, "Not necessary. I have a stuntman on the platform to catch me."

I did the scene—rolled off the hut, grabbed onto the stuntman. I was moving with too much momentum, grabbed too hard. We both fell off the platform onto the rocks. I landed first; he fell on top of me. My head hit a rock. Fortunately, a flat one. A pointed one would have split my head open like a melon. I was bleeding. A lot. Everyone was alarmed. I kept babbling, "The shot. Did we get the goddamn shot?"

"No."

I insisted on immediately climbing back up on top of the

roof and falling off again. They tried to stop me, but I refused to listen. Their concern made me angry. I had them wipe off the blood. I went up, did the shot again.

I collapsed. They took me home. For a week I couldn't shoot, could barely move. I had a concussion. Strange thoughts kept going in and out of my head.

Issur wouldn't stay put behind his garbage can. "Why are you so hard on people?" he asked. "Why do you kick the shit out of them? You say such awful things. Why?"

"Because they're true."

"But they happened years ago. Why are you so angry now?"

"I don't know. But I'm too old to stop."

Meanwhile, I thought I was getting the financing for *Cuckoo's Nest.* But every time I came close, Dale Wasserman sued me for the movie rights. Why, I don't know. I had paid him for writing the play, given him the rights to it. He had done very well with them. The play is always being performed somewhere, all over the world. I would say, "Dale, why are you suing me? Yes, you would like to have the movie rights. But, Dale, it's my project. I bought it. I paid you. I own the movie rights." And it would have to go to arbitration. It went to arbitration twice. Both times it was decided in my favor.

The funding fell through again. I had lost another round. I was down. But I wasn't out.

Thirty-five

OLYMPICS

Mike Frankovich, an independent producer and head of Columbia, called me up one day in 1967. I was the main partner of a big apartment house on Beverly Glen, with some single rooms. Very nice. A UCLA alumni group wanted a place to live for a hot young basketball player.

I told him he was welcome to one. For nothing. I knew what it was like to work, and go to school, and be an athlete. You don't get to play pro anything unless you go to college. But no, they had to pay something. Otherwise it would be considered payment to the athlete, and they wanted to avoid being accused of breaking their amateur standing. So I let the basketball player use the apartment for a couple of years, at low rent, so the records would show that I was paid. But I never wanted him to feel that he was obligated to me. An alumnus offered me tickets to all the basketball games. I never went.

We have a hypocritical point of view about amateur athletics and professional athletics. Supposedly in amateur athletics the athletes don't get paid. In professional athletics, they get paid. Now, is the UCLA versus USC basketball or base-ball or football game amateur athletics? They put it on TV. They advertise it. They make enormous sums of money. And then they try to hide behind a facade that these athletes are amateur. They seek to find if any of these athletes are paid. Most of these athletes come from poor families. Should athletics be something just for the rich? If somebody gets a scholarship for going to college does that make him a professional scholar? Because someone is paying his tuition? Or his room and board?

When I was at college, I was undefeated wrestling champion. They talked to me about training for the Olympic tryouts. They wanted me to go to Oklahoma, where the tryouts were going to be held. I didn't have the money to do that, couldn't take the time off from work. Nobody said to me, "We'll pay for everything."

Just as scholarships are given for scholastic achievement, there's nothing wrong with athletes receiving remuneration for all the money they make for the university. Maybe they *should* get cars. Clothes. Food. And not try to sneak it under the table. The games they play in, that take them away from their studies, generate great publicity for the university, generate great amounts of money. And yet there's somebody looking, saying, "Ah hah! Somebody gave this man a free room!" I think the practice of paying athletes under the table, and then penalizing them when they're found out, is hypocrisy. It's stupid.

I never met the basketball player I subsidized, Lew Alcindor, not even when he became Kareem Abdul Jabar. I only talked to him once, on the phone. I had heard that two members of the track team were going to use the Black Power salute at the Olympics in Mexico City in 1968, and Lew was connected with them. So I called him. I said that they ought to reconsider. He said there was nothing he could do. That was it. They went ahead and did it, and they got thrown out. I still think it was wrong.

All Russian athletes are professional athletes. The state takes care of them, room and board and salary. Those boxers you see year after year—that's their job, to be a boxer on the Olympic team. A new American team comes in, they're boxing a seasoned guy who was boxing four years ago. He might have had hundreds of matches.

In 1971, I became Public Affairs Director of the United States Olympics. I helped raise money, attended banquets, did TV spots, to get our athletes to Munich in 1972. I went to Colorado, met with athletes at the training camps.

In the middle of all this, my son Michael came to me. He was doing "The Streets of San Francisco." "Dad, let me try to set up *Cuckoo's Nest.*" Ten years earlier, Michael had made his stage debut playing an orderly in *Cuckoo's Nest* for one night. I'd exhausted all the possibilities I could think of. Michael and I became partners. I hoped he could succeed where I had failed. I'd do *anything* to be able to play Mc-Murphy.

Since I was raising money for the Olympics, and I knew the athletes, I thought it would be nice to see the Olympics in Germany. I arrived in Munich, went to the offices of the U.S. Olympic Committee to arrange to get some seats, which, of course, I wanted to pay for. Couldn't talk to them. Couldn't even get in touch with them. Couldn't believe it. I was just flabbergasted. I went to the German Olympics office. Greeted me with open arms. The next thing, I'm sitting in the front row at the swimming meet, next to Mark Spitz's parents. Behind me were some of the American Olympic officials. I looked at them. They just ignored me. They had their own little group, their own private clique. And I was right back at St. Lawrence University, waiting to be brought to the fraternity house for dinner, and they just left me there.

But the Germans gave me the best seats, A-1 treatment. Sitting beside Mark Spitz's father, I watched Mark win his seventh medal. Mr. Spitz was very nice. He asked me to help him get an agent for Mark, called me several times. I helped him get in touch with the William Morris Agency.

I talked with Mark Spitz. He told me about the Olympics in Mexico City four years earlier. He thought he was just as good then. But his American competitors were rough. They called him "Jew boy." Just psyched him out. So that gentle-man's agreement is still around.

Mark Spitz's coach was a shit. The night Mark won his seventh medal, and became an American hero, we were at dinner. The coach had a few drinks and said, "You think Spitz is good? He's *nothing*. I've got a fourteen-year-old kid who's going to go right past him." What a time to be talking about that, when here's a guy who's just won seven medals, instead of just letting him savor the moment of victory.

With my German hosts, I visited Olympic Village. I visited the Israeli compound, met a handful of Israeli athletes. The next day, Anne and I were getting ready to leave, packing our suitcases, the TV on in the background. That's when I heard that eleven Israeli athletes had been massacred in the village we had just visited. Going to the airport was out of the question. We were in shock. So, I thought, was the rest of the world.

Then Avery Brundage, head of the U.S. Olympic Commit-tee, decided that we shouldn't capitulate, that the games must go on. It was a horrible thing. To this day, I don't understand. What would have happened if the eleven ath-letes killed had been American? How would we have felt, watching the rest of the world playing games as if nothing had happened, while we buried the best young men in our country?

But these weren't American boys. They were Jew boys. So the world was not alarmed, just as the world was not alarmed when terrorists tried to hijack Israeli planes. What the world forgets, but Jews remember, is that the next time—they're hijacking *your* plane. American planes have been hijacked. Russian planes. German planes. Then people become alarmed. The irony is, no Israeli plane has ever been suc-cessfully hijacked.

Anne and I went to the Winter Olympics in Sarajevo, Yu-goslavia, in 1984, with our friends Jay and Renée Weiss from Florida. The Yugoslavians were very polite, nice, hospitable. There was only one unpleasant incident.

We all went out to a restaurant for dinner. As we walked in, they couldn't have been friendlier—the owner had me take pictures with him, his children, grandmother, cousins, his *dog*. They were taking pictures all over the place. Smiling and laughing, they served us a delicious meal. Then came the bill, scrawled on a scrap of paper bag—the equivalent of six hundred American dollars for eight people. Exorbitant. I protested. "A top restaurant in New York wouldn't charge this much. And we didn't have any fancy, expensive wines. What cost so much?" They shrugged. I asked for an itemized bill. They didn't have one. They wouldn't make one. I asked to speak to the manager. Gone home. I could see that we would have to pay, or be there all night. I said to our interpreter, "I resent this. And I want you to report to the authorities that I feel we were taken advantage of." And I must say, the government came in the next day and checked. Our bill should not have been more than about a hundred and ten dollars. It seemed these friendly restaurateurs had been doing the same thing to lots of other people. The government closed the restaurant down for nine months.

Aside from that, everybody was friendly and hospitable. I hoped Angelenos would be the same when the Summer Olympics came to Los Angeles in 1984. I wrote an editorial which appeared in the *Los Angeles Times* on May 21, 1984, on *Kinderstube*, a German word that means "child upbringing," and is usually related to adults. Either they have good manners as a result of *Kinderstube*, or bad manners because of the lack of it. The editorial ended:

I think it can be said that no nuclear armory, no ocean crowded with warships, no treasury filled with precious metals can extract from the foreign visitors who come to Los Angeles a large harvest of affection and warmth for this land than the people of Los Angeles practicing, each day, *Kinderstube*. Let us begin.

Thirty-six

DIRECTOR DOUGLAS

Since I was accused so often of trying to direct the films I was in, I thought I ought to really try my hand at directing. I directed two films. Both unsuccessful.

The first was *Scalawag*. In my seventy-five movies, I have never had one with so many disasters. I thought I had chosen something very simple, with a great chance for success. It was based on the Robert Louis Stevenson book *Treasure Island*. But instead of putting it on a ship, I had it all take place on land.

I had Albert Maltz, one of the Unfriendly Ten, who of course now could use his name openly, write the script. Maltz proved to me again what had been said about the Unfriendly Ten: "Two had talent. The rest were just unfriendly." I paid him to do the script. When it was done, I felt it was much too pretentious and filled with messages. I brought in another writer, Sid Fleishman, and I wrote it with him. When the script was finished, it had both Maltz's and Fleishman's names on it. Maltz was indignant. He wrote me a letter saying that the script now had nothing to do with what he had written. He demanded that his name be taken off. I was sorry he felt that way, but I took his name off the script.

I now had the script I wanted. I thought it was a chance to make a lot of money—an inexpensive picture, very commercial. I decided to get the financing independently. I was assured that there would be no problem making *Scalawag* in Yugoslavia on a limited budget.

Meanwhile, Michael, bless him, had succeeded in some financing of his own. When no studio would put up the money for *One Flew Over the Cuckoo's Nest,* he had set up independent financing for the movie with Saul Zaentz.

I was going to play McMurphy!

And I was going to have a production credit that said, "In Association with the Bryna Company." It was finally going to happen, my dream of a production company named after my mother, working with my son, in the role of my life.

I'd met a very shrewd businessman named Dan Lufkin, of the investment firm Donaldson, Lufkin & Jenrette. This was my first experience with the big-money men. I learned a lot. Boy, they're a strange breed. Dan Lufkin seemed like a pleasant enough fellow. We talked about different investments. He said he would help me make money. I was interested. I'd made many unsuccessful investments, so I was grateful to Dan. He had a company that managed athletes and asked if I could arrange a meeting with O.J. Simpson. I did. They signed him up. I never found out whether this was a good thing I had done for O.J.

Then I came to him with an idea. I told him about my trip to Africa, about the huge parks with live animals. I said, "Everything in America is phony. Don't you think people would like to see a large park with *live* animals?" Through Elia Kazan, I had met a man who knew all about how to get animals from Africa. I introduced him to Dan Lufkin, and we arranged it.

They set up a company, Lion Country Safari. Everyone

had stock, including me. They built the park. The stock rock-eted from two to twenty.

And I found out something. Somebody can tell you when to buy a stock, or even *give* you stock. But the most important thing is to have someone tell you when you should *sell* it.

Dan sold his stock when it went up to twenty. He made a lot of money. I was shocked that he hadn't said anything to me. "Dan, why didn't you tell me that I should sell?"

He said, "That's not up to me. You've got a lawyer."

Then I found out that my stock hadn't been issued prop-erly. I wasn't able to sell it. By the time I went through all the legal processes that enabled me to sell the stock, it had dropped from twenty back to two.

Before all of this happened, I went to Dan and explained about *Scalawag*, how I thought we could do pretty well. I intended to produce, direct, and star in it. I would take no salary. We had a very commercial script, a very low budget. We would shoot it in Yugoslavia.

Dan very charmingly said, "O.K., I'm in. I'll put up the money. You run with it." It was about five hundred thousand dollars, a very low budget.

We went to Italy to set up the deal. Anne and Eric and Peter were there. Peter, sixteen, was going to be the still photographer. He was being a pain in the ass, insisted on bringing his dog, Shaft, a six-month-old black Labrador re-triever. Later, I was glad he had; the "trained" dog that was supplied for the movie turned out to be a man-eater. But Shaft disappeared after work one day. We were frantic, until a knock on the door. A couple of the local boys. "Do you own a black dog?"

"Yes."

"Is there a reward?"

Peter gratefully gave them some money, then greeted a bounding Shaft. When this happened a second, and a third time, we realized we were in the middle of a dognapping racket. The dog didn't seem to mind, so we didn't mind paying.

I went to Italy, our base. We were going to ship the film down the Yugoslav coast to Starigrad, a little town north of Dubrovnik. Then we'd take it down to Split in a car, and then across the channel to Rome for processing.

I started making my deals. And all the time my dear friend Dan Lufkin was holding back the money. This put us in embarrassing situations and hampered all of our movements. I brought the actors to location early at my own expense so that we could rehearse. When the crew became disgruntled, I said I would pay for their overtime. If I had had the money in advance, I could have presold the picture and made a deal *guaranteeing* that we wouldn't lose any money. In the meantime, I was pleading with Lufkin, "Dan, you told me, 'Go ahead, Kirk. You run with it.' " The last straw—Dan wanted to make sure the money was being spent properly, so he sent a man who had no knowledge of filmmaking to supervise me.

We hired David Lean's associate producer, who we thought would be very knowledgeable in all areas. He was a complete zero, used to expensive movies where you take your time and have anything you want at your fingertips. He didn't know how to cut corners. When I got ready to shoot, he said, "You can't shoot. You're not ready."

I said, "We're going to start shooting the movie."

He quit.

Anne had to become the producer. My respect for my wife increased—she spoke Italian and could deal with the Italians. She learned enough Serbo-Croatian to get along with the Yugoslavs. She handled innumerable problems.

The cast consisted of Americans, Yugoslavs, Italians. I played the leading role, the scalawag. I decided to play him with one leg. Being very flexible, I was able to twist one leg up and strap the foot around my bottom. Bob Schiffer, a brilliant makeup artist from the Disney studios, made a cast that covered my thigh, where I tucked the leg that was doubled up. Then he had to carefully get the correct angle for the stump. I spent a lot of time learning to walk on it, to keep my balance. It was difficult. But to ride a horse, to *mount* a horse, with my leg twisted up under me and a stick of wood attached to it, was one of the most difficult things I have ever done—and it was self-imposed. It was very effective.

It was the most effective thing about the entire movie. People were always wondering where my leg was. Usually when a character in a movie is missing an arm or leg, he wears a long coat or jacket, so that you can't see his limb tucked up behind him. Like Gregory Peck playing Captain Ahab in *Moby Dick*. I wore just a shirt and pants. I had the pants cut a little bit fuller on the side where I had no leg. But I could walk with my back to the camera, turn around. People would always say, how the hell did you do that? Where was your leg? Up my ass.

It was one of the early pictures that Danny DeVito, another graduate of the American Academy of Dramatic Arts, was in. He was very good and very funny as a character named Flyspeck. Michael tells me that to this day, Danny does great imitations of me trying to direct and produce and act in the picture on a horse, with one leg tied around my rear end.

After the picture was all over, I got a very sweet letter postmarked New Jersey.

Dear Mr. & Mrs. Douglas:

I am Danny DeVito's mother, writing to thank you both for giving my son a part in your movie, "Scallywag." My family all went to see it at the Paramount in N.Y.C. it was a great movie. Some of my friends & relatives saw it in Florida, they called me up to-day, to tell me how much they enjoyed it. & told me that Danny was great they liked his acting, so that made me feel so proud. Half of Asbury Park N.J. are waiting for it to come here. My daughter owns a Beauty Salon in Neptune N.J. & has a sign in it: "Scallywag Coming Soon." You see there is plenty of publicity out here.

Love to your son Michael, he spent a weekend at our house & we all love him, & we also watch the Streets of San Francisco on Thursday nights.

Again, I want to thank you both for giving my son a part in your movie. It's great to have a part with a big star like you.
Sincerely Yours,

Mrs. Dan DeVito

Danny became a big star: *Taxi, Romancing the Stone, Ruthless People, The Jewel of the Nile, Tin Men.* And he directed his first picture, *Throw Momma from the Train.*

While we were casting *Scalawag* in England, Anne and I discovered a young girl named Lesley-Anne Downe, about seventeen years old. She was ravishingly beautiful. This was her first picture.

Peter was going into business for himself. He talked Lesley-Anne Downe into signing a contract that allowed him to do a nude layout of her in the water, and got some beautiful shots. He probably did better than anyone on the movie. He sold the layout to *Playboy.* As Lesley-Anne became more successful, she tried to rescind the contract. But it was too late. Peter had already sold the pictures; he didn't own them anymore. She was furious. But they made up. When Peter was seventeen, he left our house to go and live with her.

Then Neville Brand, who was playing Brimstone, and who, incidentally, was the most decorated soldier of World War II after Audie Murphy, fell in love with one of the young ladies of the town. The girl's parents tried to keep her away. Neville would come running up to my room, roaring drunk, pounding on the door. "WHERE IS SHE! BY GOD, WHERE IS SHE! IF I DON'T FIND HER, I'M TELLING YOU, BLOOD WILL FLOW!"

I just looked at him.

He added hastily, "But not your blood, Kirk."

He was going through a terrible stage of being a big bully. We were on a boat one day, in the middle of a scene. He went on a rampage. I had had all I could take. I grabbed him. "If I hear one more sound out of you, I'll kill you."

He was like a pricked balloon. Just shriveled up. I felt so sad, I wanted to cry, to see a man who'd pumped himself up, a big war hero, suddenly just deflate. I never had any problems with him after that. But I felt sad at that moment when I saw him lose all of his macho quality. He wasn't a bad person. Sober, he was charming and an excellent actor.

I hate physical violence. Maybe because my father was such a practitioner of it, the toughest guy in town. And even though I became a wrestling champion, that was different; it was a controlled athletic situation. I hate bullies, people who try to make their point with their fists, or in a macho way. Sometimes it bothers me to the point of driving me mad. Like what happened with Neville Brand. Later, I was angry at myself, because he made me resort to the very thing that I hate. I was ready to punch him out. I play guys who do that. But I'm not like that.

The production had one problem after another. We asked for a single telephone line in our hotel room; we got a party line. It rang all hours of the day and night. When we picked it up—incomprehensible conversations in Yugoslavian. And we got charged for all of it. We'd ask for forty chickens, get eight. The Italian leading man and his wife got into fistfights. My son Eric became their confidant and referee. The sync sound camera would not show up the day we shot dialogue scenes.

Every day brought a hideous new surprise, as the daily production reports, kept by a Yugoslav production manager, document:

Thursday, June 22, 1972—first day of shooting.

Friday, June 23, 1972

7.15 Director Mr. Douglas wants to have set up the camera trolly but same is missing as the Director of Photography has led the camera car in a wrong direction, the truck with equipment following him, so that both vehicles still not on set.

Saturday, June 24, 1972

The weather is not good for shooting exteriors. Mr. Douglas proposes to go and shoot INTERIOR BARN but the dog is not available.

Monday, June 26, 1972
>21 horses with riders. 1 donkey. 3 lizards. 2 live parrots. 3 snakes. 3 turtles. 3 policemen & car.

Tuesday, June 27, 1972
>7.00–8.00
>>Camera set up. Some misunderstanding between Assistants whereby camera set up in wrong position.

11.30–11.35
>Parrot missing from set.

Wednesday, June 28, 1972
>39 horses with riders. 1 white horse. 2 sheep dogs with handler. 155 sheep. 2 parrots. 1 donkey. 3 packhorses.

12.00   Mr. Douglas wants to give the break, but the lunch box have still not arrived on set. Mr. Douglas wants the production to check why lunch boxes were not punctually on set at 11.30 as required from the first day.

Waiting for the camera car. Asst. Director Fabrizzio Castellani wants to make a note and to have the camera car driver permanently present on set.

12.20   Arrive the camera car

12.40   Camera car ready

1.00   The lunch boxes arrived and the production gives a break

NOTE

A shepperd dog has beaten Radomir Spasojevic's leg.

Thursday, June 29, 1972
>6.45   Mr. Douglas was kept waiting, as the driver of his car overslept and came late. Mr. Douglas was protesting and thinks the drivers should be with their cars ready before the departure time, and have their cars parked in the drive off direction.

10.35   Needing live parrot which not on set.

11.40   Live parrot arrives.

11.25–11.50
>Set up cameras. Rehearsal and waiting for parrot.

1.15–1.45

> Break (only 1/2 hour) for lunch too short for 15 packages. Italian generator-operator Mr. Dante insists to have a 1 hour lunch break and refuses to start generator before expiration of his one hour break.

Saturday, July 1, 1972

10.00 Mr. Douglas wants to know why his double is not yet arrived on set.

3.10 Mr. Douglas's double Mr. Bunjak arrives.

Monday, July 3, 1972

11.00 German Shepherd brought from Belgrade.

11.40 The German shepherd no good—Mr. Peter Douglas brings his dog instead.

Wednesday, July 5, 1972

12.20 Mr. Douglas complaining for not having the vultures on set, and therefore not being able to complete this scene. The production was informed three month ago that for this scene vultures are indispensable, says Mr. Douglas.

5.05 Shooting scene a325—1st take. After this take the vulture flies off but is catched.

5.20 Shooting scene a325—2nd take. Vulture flies off again and disappears definitely.

Thursday, July 6, 1972

8.20 The vultures being brought without handler, are trying to tie at least one to the tree.

9.10 Shoot 3 takes without vulture, having still complications to get the vulture on the tree.

9.35 Preparing another scene instead, having nobody to put the vulture on the tree.

Friday, July 7, 1972

NOTE

Mr. Neville Brand who by mistake was before departure called in his room and brought on set.

The handler for vultures still not arrived, were shooting vultures without him. 1 vulture escaped during night.

Saturday, July 8, 1972

NOTE

On a transport tour from set a donkey run into a Volvo production car and damaged the car. The donkey died.

The vulture handler who arrived last night was on set, but today no scene with vultures been shot.

Mr. Douglas ordered as his own expense beer which has been offered to Unit on set.

Monday, July 10, 1972

Mr. Douglas complains about the clappers loader [assistant cameraman], who not skilled at all for this work.

Tuesday, July 11, 1972

The vulture escaped a few days ago was catched and brought back.

The ship required for afternoon could not arrive due to bad stormy weather.

Miss Lesley-Anne Down waited 1/2 hour to get a car to take her from the hotel to the location. She was in costume and in her costume shoes, which are very difficult for walking. She had to find someone to give her a ride.

Thursday, July 13, 1972

Strong storm wind and periodical rain. Director Mr. Douglas complains about boats and motor boats appearing in background of scene and passing by—being assured by the Production that water traffic will be controlled.

Monday, July 17, 1972

Mr. Douglas protesting for having on set not the required number of sheep/130 sheep reported and having only 80. Besides this, complaining of having more skinny lambs than sheep in the herd.

Friday, July 28, 1972

Neville Brand (Brimstone) brought in hospital, and 3rd Camera Unit cannot work without Mr. Brand who indispensable for scenes around "Vultures Tree."

NOTE:

ZVONKO BUNJAK, double for Mr. Douglas, has left set without asking permission to leave.

Saturday, July 29, 1972

8 vultures w/handler. 1 vulture escapes from tree, snapping wires it was tied with.

Saturday, August 5, 1972

11.20 Director sends back to hotel Lesley-Anne Downe & Phil Brown who were per Call Sheet supposed to Stand by at hotel, but were by mistake brought on set.

Monday, August 7, 1972

Lunch Box: 102 which number was not sufficient and a part of the Unit had their lunch at the canteen on charge of the Production.

NOTE

Sound operator Mr. Cyrill Collick protesting on the bad quality of lunch box, asking whether the responsible persons in charge do know what they are getting for lunch on set—suggesting that they try to eat same food. The lunch Box becoming from day to day worse and today are not eatable at all.

Friday, August 11, 1972

Mr. Douglas wants to know when the underwater camera will arrive which was ordered by him 3 weeks ago, and which is indispensable for underwater shooting.

Friday, August 25, 1972

Director Mr. Douglas wants to have prepared the camp set with wagon, sheep, etc. Not possible any more. Director resents why sheep have been dismissed and sent home, and asks who permitted this.

Mr. Cardiff calls electricians and protests why all electricians not on set having not permitted them to stay in hotel for packing. Director resents for having no silks and satins on set, this being a very important shot planned months ago.

Mr. Sovagovic [Beanbelly] not yet on set for the next shot. While waiting for him, sending to village to bring more horses for next shot. Director protesting and objecting that today it goes worse than the first day of shooting. Director orders a break.

When the movie was finished, Albert Maltz changed his mind and demanded that his name be put back on the script. This annoyed me. My guess is that someone had told him that it was going to be a very successful picture. (It wasn't.) I refused to put his name on the movie. He insisted that it go to the Screenwriters Guild for arbitration. It came back from arbitration, and I was dumbfounded to learn that they felt his name had to be used. I couldn't believe it. I must say it has always caused me to doubt the process of arbitration. I even showed them the letter from Maltz. Didn't matter. His name had to be on the script.

We couldn't get proper distribution of the movie. I cringe when I think of the time and energy I spent making *Scalawag*, and of how much more money I could have made just taking a part in someone else's film. I saw the movie recently on television. All those great artistic shots—in my head. I should have followed the advice I spouted during *Spartacus* —American crews are the best, no need to leave home. You don't save money by using inexperienced labor.

You would think that one experience would have cured me of ever wanting to direct a picture again.

It didn't.

I said to Michael, "Who are you using as a director on *Cuckoo's Nest?*"

"I don't think you know him, Dad. This guy from Czechoslovakia named Milos Forman."

That's when I found out that Milos had never received the copy of *Cuckoo's Nest* I had sent him eight years earlier. I thought he was rude for not responding; he thought I was rude for not sending it. That's what happens in a Communist-dominated country: a book comes in; some petty official objects to it; it never reaches its destination.

I couldn't get over the amazing coincidence of Michael picking the same director. We had never discussed it. What odds would Vegas give on that?

August 9, 1974. Richard Milhous Nixon resigned the office of President of the United States. I had met President Nixon once at a White House reception. In front of me in the receiving line were Greg Peck and Sylvia Fine (Mrs. Danny Kaye). Greg said, "Hello, my name is Greg Peck." Nixon shook his hand, told Greg how much he loved him in *The Friendly Persuasion*—a Gary Cooper picture. Then Nixon greeted Sylvia: "Hello, Mrs. Kaye," and shook my hand and said, "Hi, Danny."

"My name is Kirk Douglas."

"Oh yes, yes. Of course. Of course."

So Nixon wasn't a big movie fan.

The last time I was in Las Vegas, Frank Sinatra and Dean Martin were performing. That afternoon, they insisted that I use the new Sands sauna room.

I went, took off my clothes, and walked into the steam room. Sitting next to me in the mist was a beautiful naked girl. We chatted for about ten minutes. When I came out, the "boys" were watching me and I said, "That's a real nice guy in there."

Now I had another chance to go to Las Vegas.

Frank Sinatra asked if Greg Peck and I would be character witnesses for him in Las Vegas, so he could become part owner of a casino. What character do you have to have to own a casino? Who are these people who own casinos? And what is their character?

I could see Frank was just burning. He was puffed up like a blowfish, ready to explode. It was humiliating for him. Greg gave a very serious discourse on Frank's character.

I couldn't resist. When I got up there I said, "I don't know what the qualifications are to own a casino. And I want to be very careful in delineating Mr. Sinatra's character. I must confess, I have found him guilty of professional jealousy."

Everybody's ears perked up.

"Oh yes," I said. "Years ago, I made a record of a song I sang in *20,000 Leagues Under the Sea,* called "A Whale of a Tale." And I felt that there was professional jealousy on his part."

Everybody laughed. Frank's wife, Barbara, later said, "Thank God for you. You finally got a smile out of Frank, and relaxed him a bit." And that was the extent of the so-called investigation into his character.

Cuckoo's Nest and McMurphy occupied all my thoughts. Then a blow, almost incomprehensible: they wanted somebody else for McMurphy. Why? That was *my* part. McMurphy was *my* character. I'd found him. I could create him, make him breathe. But after ten years of my telling everybody what a great role it was, they finally agreed. Oh yes, Kirk. You're right, Kirk. But now you're too old, Kirk. Well, I might have been too old then, but I'm not too old now. I could still play that part.

They went off to shoot the movie—my son, my project, my role. Without me. I was lonely. At least I would have the consolation of Joel's presence in Tucson, where I was going to produce, direct, and star in *Posse.*

I played an ambitious sheriff who was very well organized and had a traveling posse, like a small professional army. He would travel by train with the horses and the men to wherever the trouble was. He had political ambitions, wanted to be senator, and eventually President of the United States.

He pursued the bad guy, played by Bruce Dern. I had always admired Bruce as an actor. I thought that maybe this would be the movie that would make him a big star. It didn't. I realized later that he would always be a character actor, because he thought of himself that way. In the scene that opens the picture, he comes out of a barn. Walks out, looks around. The first time he did it, he came out of the barn, looked around and squinted, his face all scrunched up.

I said, "Go back in the barn. Think that you're Gary

Cooper and open the door. Walk right straight out and don't do anything. Just look around." He looked handsome!

I also cast an actor named Jim Stacy who had been on the TV series "Lancer" and had the lead in a Disney movie. *Summer Magic*. A year before *Posse*, one night in September 1973, Jim had been riding his motorcycle in Benedict Canyon, a girl seated behind him, when they were sideswiped by a drunk driver in a car. The girl was killed. Jim lived, but lost his left arm, except for a six-inch stump. His left leg was off at the hip. I had never met Jim. But Stan Kamen, my agent at William Morris, said, "Kirk, this is a terrible thing Jim's going through, and he has no money. If there's anything you can do for him . . . " I felt sympathy for the plight of the husky young actor who until the accident had enjoyed a promising career. So I created a character, the editor of the town newspaper, a man without a leg and an arm, for Jim.

Jim was a son of a bitch. He complained. He was rough with me. I was rougher. "Look, Jim, I'm not going to treat you like a cripple. You don't like me. And I don't like you, Jim. But we're stuck with each other. I'm the director, and it's my production. So we'll just have to work with each other." We had some tough times. I understood. He needed to assert himself. But he wasn't easy to deal with.

Then Joel told me he was leaving to join Michael on *Cuckoo's Nest*. I understood. It's taken me a long time to realize that most sons, especially ones as independent as mine, don't want to work for their fathers. There's that mixed feeling in me that admires their independence, and wants them to be independent, and yet wants them to be with me.

I was lonely. When you're the producer, the boss, the star, and the director, who do you talk to? It is lonely. Who loves the boss? It's tough enough being the star. It's tough enough being the director. It was so nice to have Joel there, have dinner with him sometimes. Joel never knew how much I missed him.

From September to November 1974, we shot, mostly in Old Tucson, with the railroad scenes done on the Southern

Pacific tracks outside of Florence, Arizona. Paramount had given me so little money to make *Posse* that I had to cut corners where I could. Transportation was one area. I flew tourist class to Tucson with my union Hollywood crew, bought them some drinks. Everybody seemed to be having a good time. Then I found out they were going to sue me, or fine me, because the union says the crew had to fly first class. This is one reason production is running away from Hollywood.

Posse was not a hit, but the studio didn't lose any money. Maybe I'm better at second-guessing other directors, but as McMurphy of *Cuckoo's Nest* would have said, "I tried. God damn it, I *tried!*"

The British *Monthly Film Bulletin* said, "*Posse*—that rarity of recent years—a taut, well-made Western that delivers its message about the dangers of political machines and the ambition that drives them, with a welcome lack of visual or verbal rhetoric. The connections with recent American history—from Vietnam to Watergate—are there for the asking, but it is to the film's credit that it is not begging for them to be made."

I say I'm not interested in statements. That's bullshit. I'm highly interested in statements. *Posse* made a significant statement. It presents the two sides of a coin: How those who fight for the law can become twisted and become like the criminals they are pursuing. How easy it is to become the bad guy when you think you're doing good. In our own government, people suddenly switch over and become agents, use their knowledge to work against us, like Wilson, the CIA agent who sold arms to Libya. Or the overzealous participants in Watergate. Now it's the Iran-contra hearings. Ollie North captured part of the public with his boyish looks and endearing voice. They made him a hero. Or was he a villain who lied, altered and shredded documents, corrupted his secretary? He thought he was doing the right thing. That's a better movie than *Posse*.

After *Posse* was over, Jim Stacy's lawsuit over his accident went to trial. The man who hit Jim had no insurance. Jim was suing the Melting Pot Restaurant, which owned the bar that had continued serving liquor to the man even though he was drunk. Jim's lawyer asked me if I would help them. I hesitated for a second, but then said of course I would.

I went downtown to the courthouse. Jim came into the courtroom in a wheelchair—pathos manipulation. I had seen Jim get around easily with only one arm, one leg, and one crutch.

I turned out to be the key witness. The most important task for Jim's lawyers was to prove damages. Jim's lawyers claimed that he could have become a big star, would have had a chance to make millions, and he was deprived of it all because of the accident.

The insurance lawyers had me on the stand. "Is it true that Jim Stacy was an actor in a TV series?"

I said, "Yes."

"And wasn't it also true that for two years before the accident happened, he wasn't getting much work?"

"Yes, that's true."

"Wouldn't that show that he didn't have such a big career ahead of him?"

I said, "Not at all. It takes at least two years to make the transition. For example, it took Steve McQueen about two years to make the transition from TV to movies, and he became a tremendous star. It took more than two years for my son Michael to make the transition from the TV series 'The Streets of San Francisco.' Now he's a big star. Jim Stacy could have been the same big star."

They asked me how much money I thought he could make a year.

"About two to three million dollars."

By this time I could see the insurance lawyers huddling and saying to each other, "Get that guy off the stand."

Jim Stacy's lawyer kissed me in the hallway. They won the case. He was awarded $1.9 million.

I've always had a warm feeling for Jim. Whenever I think of him, I think it's possible to adjust to very difficult things if you have the will. Now, Jim does public service announcements: "Drunk driving. It can cost you an arm and a leg." They're very effective.

Since then, Jim and I have become friends. We don't see much of each other. But he knows I have great affection for him.

One Flew Over the Cuckoo's Nest was finished. Still nobody wanted it. Michael was having just as hard a time finding a distributor as we'd had arranging the financing. Again, the picture was turned down at studio after studio. Michael went to United Artists. They hadn't wanted to gamble putting up the money to *make* the picture, but they finally agreed to distribute it. They made over $30 million.

Michael and Jack Nicholson went on a world tour and came back to receive five of the top Oscars, over $200 million at the box office—a phenomenal success. Michael did it. But I still argue with him about things in the movie that I think were done wrong. The attack on Big Nurse, for instance. In the book, McMurphy rips her top off. In the movie, Jack Nicholson chokes her. She comes back with her neck in a brace. What does that prove? That he's stronger than she is? There must be an underlying sexuality between McMurphy and Big Nurse. Onstage, I suggested what I think should have been done in the movie: rape. And have her respond. Now, when the inmates look at Big Nurse, they really see her naked, down to her soul. I say, "Michael, if you had done it my way, you might not have made two hundred million dollars. But it would have been *right*."

Jack Nicholson played my part, McMurphy—brilliantly, damn it! But he played him differently than I would have. He played a lunatic. To me, McMurphy was a charming, shrewd con artist, who finds himself committed to a mental institution. All the other inmates were there voluntarily, but McMurphy had been committed. "You guys can walk out of here. I can't." He figured he'd be there for a few months, do his time, and get out. But then he finds that he has fallen in love with these people, and sacrifices himself for them—a different version of Jesus Christ. Maybe I'm wrong. After all,

Nicholson won an Academy Award. But Ken Kesey told the press that he thought I should have played it. That made two of us.

One Flew Over the Cuckoo's Nest is one of the biggest disappointments of my life. I made more money from that film than any I acted in. And I would gladly give back every cent, if I could have played that role.

Thirty-seven

FANS

I am constantly amazed by fans—the letters they send from all over the world, enclosing photographs they have paid for to be autographed. I always sign them myself. I think of so many young—and old—people looking at a photograph in their room signed by one of their favorites.

I am amazed by fans waiting ouside theaters, restaurants, hotels—sometimes for hours—clutching a photograph they want to have autographed. They all have a need to fill some void in their life. We all have fantasies.

When they celebrated the tenth anniversary of Elvis Presley's death, it was more like a canonization. People lined up to visit Graceland. Middle-aged women—and yes, men, too —with tears in their eyes. I couldn't believe one woman saying, "Elvis's death meant more to me than a death in my own family."

Fans can look at you with love and admiration—sometimes with madness. John Lennon was shot dead by a fan. Actors are targets. Millions of people see them on screen and fantasize. Some try to change their fantasies into reality. For years, a man would try to contact me. He would walk up and down in front of my house. He wasn't loitering so the police could do nothing about it. Do you know if you keep moving, you can't be arrested? Sometimes he parked his car in front of the house for hours. If the police came, he opened up the hood and was fixing his car. He couldn't be arrested. He telephoned, wrote letters. I felt that any contact with him would make the situation worse. But I was frightened by his persistence—for my family, as well as myself.

One morning, I woke up around seven o'clock and heard splashing in the pool. I looked out the window and saw my "friend" in the pool. That is trespassing. The police arrived. They tried to get him out, but he stayed in the middle of the pool. It was funny. The police wanted to avoid jumping into the water after him.

Finally, he came out and they arrested him. He was sent to a mental institution. For a time, he wrote me strange letters and then I heard nothing more from him.

One afternoon, the doorbell rang. Concha, my house-keeper, answered the door and a woman walked in. She was well-dressed and spoke with an accent. She said she was my wife and insisted on seeing me because she knew I was ill!

I heard all this from the top of the stairs and called the police. When they arrived, they said they couldn't push her out of the house because she had not forced her way in. She had money in her purse and an Italian passport. They finally talked her into leaving.

Then the police got a call from a shop on Rodeo Drive. The woman was buying things and charging them to her husband—me. They picked her up and she was sent to the Camarillo Hospital for the mentally ill.

About a month later, I received a doctor's bill for psychiatric care for Mrs. Kirk Douglas. Who's crazy?

Crazier things have happened. While I was shooting *Young Man with a Horn,* I spent a weekend in Palm Springs with Evelyn Keyes. We were sitting around the pool reading the morning newspapers. Evelyn gasped and said, "Look at this." There was a photograph of a statuesque starlet who had mysteriously disappeared. Her purse was found in Griffith Park. Inside was a note: "Dear Kirk . . . Mother knows about it . . . I can't wait . . . Jean." I grabbed the paper. "Actor Kirk Douglas enters the investigation of the disappearance of actress Jean Spangler."

We joked about it until we heard on TV that the girl's murdered body was found near the Mexican border.

I rushed back to Beverly Hills. There was a call from Thad Brown, chief of the Homicide Bureau. He was sending over a couple of his men to question me. There were photographers at the precinct waiting for me to be brought in. He wanted to spare me that until he had more information.

Needless to say, I became alarmed. I called my stand-in.

"Larry, do I know a Jean Spangler?"

"Yes," he answered.

"I do! Where?"

"Don't you remember that afternoon you shot a scene with that beautiful extra and made a date with her?"

"Oh yes, but you talked me out of it."

"That's right. I told you she's a star-fucker and bad news."

I remembered. I called; her mother answered. Jean was not there. I left a message that something had come up and I wouldn't be able to see her that night. I never saw or spoke to her again.

I told all this to the detectives when they questioned me. They looked at their notes.

"Mrs. Spangler said you called many times."

"That's ridiculous. I called once."

The detective kept looking at his notes.

"Some of her friends said she dated you often."

I couldn't believe what I was hearing. He flipped a page.

"One of her friends said she was at a party with both of you."

I was bewildered. "Do you have the exact date of that party?"

They had the date, and I was able to prove where I had been that night and with whom.

Meanwhile, the newspapers had discovered that Jean had played a bit part in *Young Man with a Horn,* and my name began to pop up in articles about the murder.

Eventually, I learned from Thad Brown that they knew the girl was a psychopathic liar and I was not involved in the case. I was grateful to Thad Brown—the considerate way that he protected me. The case was never solved.

Sometimes I think my life is a B-movie script. I'd never make the movie.

While on a publicity tour for *The Vikings,* we were in Cleveland, Ohio. A big convention was taking place at the hotel. That evening, I entered a crowded elevator, and in the midst of the group stood a slightly inebriated member of the convention. On his lapel was a big button inscribed, TOM KENNEDY, MINNEAPOLIS. As I entered the elevator, his bleary eyes focused on me, he pointed and said, "Kirk Douglas."

I pointed back, "Tom Kennedy."

His eyes opened wide. "You know me?"

"Aren't you from Minneapolis?" I asked.

"Yeah!" he answered incredulously.

As we reached our floor, I said, "Tom, how quickly you forget."

As I left, he was saying, "He knows me! He knows me!"

This is what I call a triple: Burt Lancaster and I were sitting in a booth at Ruby's Restaurant in Palm Springs. A drunk walked in, sat down next to me. Ignoring Burt, he said, "Mr. Mitchum, I want to tell you how great you were in *Trapeze!*"—Burt's movie.

In New York, I was hurrying to a luncheon appointment. A man started yelling. I crossed the street, car wheels screeching as he ran toward me: "I'm so excited—my favorite actor!"

"Thank you," I said, as I hurried along.

He kept up with me. "Gee, I'm so nervous, your name went right out of my head."

"Douglas," I said.

"Yeah," he cried, "Melvyn Douglas, my favorite actor."

Fan letters can range from glowing love letters to requests
for money. Sometimes they offer money. This is a letter I
received recently from Germany:

As an elderly woman living alone, one thinks not only of
one's past but also beyond one's own being. In a word, I have
a considerable fortune and no heir.

For years I have been an admirer of your artistic ideas, and
now I would like to name you as my sole heir in my testa-
ment.

This is a great honor for me because in this way I want to
express my appreciation of your people. I will always remember what your country did for us during the postwar
period.

It would be a great pleasure if you would accept the inheritance after my passing. I would hope that with this help you
would be able to attend to your artistic work more inten-
sively.

> Sincerely yours,
>
> Gerda von Nussink

The return address—"Fillerschloss," her 300-year-old castle. A rendering of it was on the envelope as part of the
postmark.

I thought about the letter, read it again, and had my assistant reply:

Dear Ms. von Nussink:

I am in receipt of your letter to Kirk Douglas of April 14,
1987.

Mr. Douglas read your letter and asked that I respond to you.
He feels this is either some kind of hoax or written by someone in need of help. If it is a hoax, he feels that the people
involved should devote their energies to more productive

enterprises. If it is not, he suggests that you go to someone
for help.

There must be worthwhile charitable causes in Germany—a
country he admires—that could use the large inheritance you
refer to. He feels this is much more productive than trying to
give your accumulated wealth to an American movie actor.

Sincerely,

Karen McKinnon,
Assistant to Kirk Douglas

Months later, the news media revealed that the letter *was*
a hoax, concocted by a German man who sent the same letter
to about one hundred celebrities. He wanted to prove that
the rich and famous are also greedy. *Woman's World* in its
issue of November 3, 1987, printed replies from Meryl
Streep, Richard Nixon, Tony Curtis, Princess Anne, Sean
Connery, Donna Sommer and others. They were not all
greedy, but they were certainly gullible. My answering letter did not appear in the article.

"Frau von Nussink" now hopes to write a best-seller.

The fans around the Kempinski Hotel in Berlin are unbelievable! They stay there—morning, noon, and late into the
night waiting for an autograph. They are of all ages, with
photos they have bought or cut out from magazines and
newspapers.

If you are in a hurry, and ask the driver to pick you up at
the back entrance—they are there!

I was in Berlin to accept "Die Golden Camera"—a prestigious recognition for a lifetime achievement in films.

I made my acceptance speech in German, which pleased
the German public immensely.

On my way home from Berlin, I stopped in Paris. I was
always a big fan of Marlene Dietrich and I had heard that
she was living the life of a recluse in an apartment there. She

contacted no one, accepted no interviews. Occasionally she went out shopping for food, camouflaged by a hat, shawl, and dark glasses. The sister of Jean Gabin accompanied her. Jean had been a great love of her life.

I finally tracked down her phone number while I was in Paris. I hesitated a long time before calling. I didn't know how she would react.

"I would like to speak to Miss Dietrich, please."

"Who's calling?" That gruff, husky voice.

"Kirk Douglas."

A slight pause. "My God—no."

"Yes, and I still have the Saint Christopher medal you gave me."

"Darling, Kirk, I can't believe it's you."

"How are you, Marlene?"

"Fine," she said in a strong voice. "But I can't see. Oh, I can read the headlines, but I can't read books."

"How are you getting along?"

"They won't leave me alone. They just want to come up and stare at me. They wait with cameras. They put them up on a truck and take pictures in my window. The sons of bitches. Why don't they leave me alone?"

"Marlene, you're world-famous."

"Bullshit," she answered brusquely. "That was a long time ago. I have four grown-up grandchildren."

"Yes, I know, Marlene, they're doing well."

"I'm proud of *your* sons. That Michael, he's something."

She seemed anxious to talk. Her voice was strong, a little bitter.

"I'll call you from L.A."

"Please. You can reverse the charges."

I laughed. *"Je t'aime."*

"Moi aussi."

"Goodbye, Marlene."

"Goodbye. Oh, Kirk, don't lose the Saint Christopher medal. It will bring you luck."

I was settled comfortably in the Concorde, racing at twice the speed of sound to New York, where beautiful, sexy Marlene had given me the medal. Now she was almost blind, living in a fourth-floor apartment. All she wanted was to be left alone. But I think she liked hearing from people in her past.

Thirty-eight

MEDAL OF
FREEDOM

Ingmar Bergman had dropped out as president of the Cannes Film Festival jury; they wanted me to take over. I didn't want to. My wife, because she had been associated with the festival for years, insisted. I accepted. Françoise Sagan, president of the jury in 1979, said that people had been pressured to vote a certain way. And I had been a juror in 1970, and said at the time, "I don't know what I'm doing here. You can give prizes for cows, because one gives more milk than the other and you can measure that. But I don't believe you can give prizes for works of art." I should have listened to myself.

It started out smoothly. Everyone expressed an opinion about the films and we finally decided to give two pictures the first place, the Palme d'Or: *All That Jazz*, Bob Fosse's semi-autobiographical musical, starring Roy Scheider, Gwen Verdon, Ann Reinking, and Jessica Lange as the Angel of Death; and Akira Kurosawa's *Kagemusha*. At eleven o'clock at night, everybody left. All set.

They were going to announce the results at noon the next

day. I asked Favre Le Bret, the head of the festival, if he wanted me there for the announcement. "No, no. It's not important." The next morning at the Hôtel du Cap, I signed the official papers.

A few hours later, the head of the Cannes Festival wanted me to sign a paper saying that *Mon Oncle d'Amérique*, a French picture which we, the jury, had voted second-place, was really equal to the two first-place pictures.

I said, "We already voted and I signed the papers."

Favre Le Bret insisted that I sign this new paper making it a three-way tie.

I said, "This is dishonest. I'm not going to sign this."

He made the announcements anyway, at the press conference he had told me it wasn't necessary for me to attend. To explain the absence of Kirk Douglas, president of the jury, he told the world that I was sick, and could not be there. I was furious.

I fought to make *All That Jazz* the winning picture, because I liked it. All the people connected with *All That Jazz* decided they didn't have a chance to win and left. There was nobody there to accept the prize. If you're going to put a picture into competition, stick around for the outcome.

But Peter Sellers and his wife waited patiently. He had been assured that he was going to win Best Actor for *Being There*. He was never considered for a prize.

They announced the awards that afternoon, and he found out he hadn't won. I felt bad about it. He was alone. Everyone connected with *Being There* wasn't there. He looked forlorn. I invited him and his wife to dinner. He was pleased.

Peter's suntan looked like bad makeup over his pallor. He appeared sick. But if he was upset about not winning, he didn't show it. Socially, Peter was boring—until he started to talk about other people. Then he *became* those people, the most perfect imitation. He was a genius at that. Otherwise, he was like Chauncey the Gardener, the character he played in *Being There*.

I was glad we had that dinner. A few months afterward, Peter died.

Articles were published criticizing me. Being president of the Cannes Film Festival is a no-win situation. I was censured for not being manipulated.

In 1987, Yves Montand was president of the jury. When he announced the winner, a French film, the whole theater booed.

I should not have broken the rule I had adhered to happily since college: never be president of anything.

That trip to France, like the ones I made for the USIA, had nothing to do with politics. I don't like the word "politics," because I'm not there to espouse the particular beliefs of one party versus another, but of our country. I made trips under Democratic administrations. I did them for Republicans. I just hope that whoever is President will help the country and the world.

As an American, I have always tried to communicate with people in other countries. In 1980, I flew in the first private jet from Jerusalem to Cairo, met with Egypt's President Anwar Sadat. We talked for three hours on the banks of the Suez at Ismailia. He was a charming man. In my room I keep a beautiful silver mirror—the handle is a silver peacock—that he gave me. How different the history of the Middle East might have been if he had not been assassinated.

I was honored on January 16, 1981, for my trips around the world as a "good will" ambassador. President Carter put the Medal of Freedom, the highest civilian award, around my neck in a ceremony at the White House. I couldn't believe it. For doing something that I felt privileged to do? That I felt it was my duty to do? I had to convince myself it wasn't make-believe.

That evening, Ann and I sat with the President and First Lady up on the White House verandah, looking down as the Marine Corps Band performed wonderful maneuvers along with their music. We stayed that night in the Lincoln Bedroom. What a thrill! We remembered when President Kennedy's mother had stayed there.

The next morning as I ate scrambled eggs and bacon, just like millions of other Americans, I looked around the breakfast table—me, the son of Russian Jewish immigrants; Anne, a naturalized citizen born in Europe; a farm couple from Plains, Georgia—and the President and First Lady of the United States. Just a typical American breakfast. In the White House.

Something Wicked This Way Comes, a wonderful Ray Bradbury story, came my way from my son Peter, who loves Bradbury's imagination. Peter had a deal to produce a picture at Universal, so he wouldn't be involved. I would produce this surreal children's fantasy about good and evil, about two little boys who sneak out of the house one summer night and encounter life and nightmares in the form of the carnival and its menacing Ringmaster. I would be the Ringmaster. Steven Spielberg wanted to direct.

I kept waiting—a year—but Spielberg would never give me a start date on *Something Wicked*.

I got a definite offer to do the movie from Disney, and I took it. But by then I was leaving to do *The Man from Snowy River* in Australia, so I couldn't be the producer. I went to Peter. His picture at Universal was delayed, so he produced *Something Wicked*, and I went to Australia.

The Australians were very chauvinistic about their national poem, "The Man from Snowy River," written by Banjo Paterson, who also wrote "Waltzing Matilda." It was going to be the most expensive picture ever shot in Australia—$5 million, compared to the usual $1 million. The producers knew that they'd have to appeal to a worldwide audience to make money, so they cast me, the only foreigner. The Australians hated the fact that one American was in the movie, and playing *two* roles—a straitlaced, domineering rancher; and his brother, a crazy, one-legged (leg up my ass again) mountain man. They tried to keep me out of the country on legal grounds, questioned whether I could work under their union rules.

I saw the newspaper clippings kicking the shit out of this Yankee, and decided that I needed a good offense. At the airport in Australia, after eighteen hours of flying, I was greeted by a belligerent press. I said that Banjo Paterson wasn't just an Australian; as a great artist, he belonged to the world. Then I recited the first stanza of their famous poem:

There was movement at the station
For the word had passed around
That the colt from Old Regret
Had got away . . .

I stopped, looked at them. "What's the next line?" Nobody knew. It's like "The Star-Spangled Banner"—who knows the second verse? Many don't know the first. Then I said, "You people ought to read Banjo Paterson's beautiful poem." From then on, the tough Australian press treated me more gently.

When I returned from Australia, Director Ted Kotcheff came to me with an interesting script. It had been kicking around for almost ten years and had been through eighteen script revisions. Every male star in Hollywood had been attached to it at one time or other. Al Pacino, Robert De Niro, my son Michael, Nick Nolte, George C. Scott, Gene Hackman, and others. Marty Ritt was going to direct, then John Frankenheimer. It was at one studio, then another. Now, it looked as though it was finally going to get made. I liked the concept, but the script wasn't very good. I turned down *First Blood.*

Kotcheff kept after me to play the marine colonel who trains ex-Green Beret Sylvester Stallone into a killing machine who became Rambo. I had some suggestions about what should happen to my character and Stallone's. Kotcheff liked them, so I agreed to do the movie.

In December 1981, Anne and I went to the location—Hope, Canada, near Vancouver, to begin the picture. I was still waiting for the script with the revisions Kotcheff and I had agreed on. There were delays. When I finally got it, I was flabbergasted; it was precisely the first script that I had turned down.

I called Kotcheff. "What the hell is going on? You can't expect me to shoot a script I already turned down!"

I hadn't been talking to the right person. Kotcheff did not have artistic control over the picture; Stallone did. Stallone was happy with the first script, wanted to shoot it, and had every right to. It almost ended up in a lawsuit, but we eventually settled to everyone's satisfaction: Stallone made the movie he wanted, and I didn't have to be in it. Richard Crenna played Colonel Trautman.

What was the bone of contention between Stallone and me? Merely that I thought it would be better, dramatically, if my character realizes what a Frankenstein monster, amoral killer, and menace to society he has created, and KILLS STALLONE.

If they'd listened to me, there would have been no *Rambo*s. They would have lost a billion dollars, but it would have been *right*.

Rambo: First Blood III is about the Soviet invasion of Afghanistan in 1982. I made a movie about the real thing. After the invasion, the USIA called me. Would I go to Pakistan and make a documentary about the three million Afghanistan refugees who had fled there? Even though Anne and I had been to Tokyo, China, and Hong Kong just a few months earlier, I grabbed a suitcase—alone.

From my journal:

November 1982. Well, here I am in Islamabad, the capital of Pakistan. It took me about twenty-eight hours, non-stop, to get here from Los Angeles. It was a long, tiring trip. At Los Angeles we were in the airplane for about an hour and a half before it took off for San Francisco. I did get some sleep in the bunks. I was amazed that it was ten hours from Hawaii to Manila. And I just made the connection from Manila to Karachi.

Karachi is a very deserted, poor-looking town. I was dumbfounded to find that it's got a population of over five million.

From Karachi we flew to Islamabad in the private plane of the Pakistani Air Force's Chief of Staff. Most of the land between Karachi and Islamabad is very arid. But there's a big, beautiful river, the Indus, that snakes along. You wonder why they don't have more vegetation, when they have so much water. It's a desert with a big river going through it. What would the Israelis do if they lived here with all that water?

We landed at Rawalpindi, drove to the hotel in Islamabad. I just talked to my wife and Eric on the phone. And now I don't feel tired or sleepy at all. I'm going to read for a while, and see if I can get some rest, because tomorrow my trip begins. And I'll try to keep up this diary. Good night.

The USIA, under Charles Wick, is certainly much better organized than it used to be. For example, when I came into my room tonight, they had a television set up with a tape recorder with several cassettes on the whole Afghan situation, so that I could brief myself. I'm looking at a French documentary now. I wonder if any American ones have been made, or if mine is the first.

The Russians were Afghanistan's friendly neighbor. They helped them. They built roads that led right to their borders. And suddenly, this friendly neighbor used those wonderful roads to carry tanks and equipment into Afghanistan. The aim: to make Afghanistan a Communist country, another satellite of the Soviet Union.

The Mujahaddin (holy warriors) are fighting for their country. Their religion teaches them that if they die, they go into heaven. So they fight fearlessly. They are helped by the unusual terrain, filled with wild, sharp craters difficult for a donkey to climb over.

The Afghan people had to contend with the Russian helicopters which go about three hundred miles an hour and are equipped with all the most modern devices, and laser beams.

I look out the window this morning at Islamabad, for the first time see greenery—green hills, green trees. Much more colorful than the area between Karachi and Islamabad. Today I meet President Zia.

My journal ends here; it was too difficult to keep up. I was supposed to have a meeting with President Zia. That was changed to dinner, and could I come half an hour early? This was a big event; he had invited the American Embassy staff, which had never been invited to his house before. President Zia had maps, pictures, reports. Before the others arrived, he briefed me on the Soviet plans for the area: once they subdued Afghanistan, they would move on Pakistan, until they reached the Arabian Sea. Their goal: control of the Straits of Hormuz. Pakistan would give them the access they needed. It was crucial that the Russians be stopped.

As we started to go in to dinner, I suddenly felt very sick —chills, dizziness. I leaned against the wall. President Zia was very solicitous, helped me into his bedroom, saw that I was comfortable, took my shoes off himself. Then he sent his doctor in. I don't know what the diagnosis was; he just told me to rest, stay in my room. When I felt well enough, I could go back to my hotel. President Zia ordered me to stay in bed.

The next day, still feeling sick, I went out to meet with some refugees, up near the Khyber Pass; we could hear loud gunfire just across the border in Afghanistan. I sat on the ground with the elders of an Afghan tribe. We were all eating with our fingers out of a common bowl. Through the interpreter, I told them, "In my country, today is Thanksgiving Day, one day every year that we set aside to give thanks for all that we have in life."

The leader of the elders, a man with a long white beard, nodded his head. Through the interpreter, he said, "In my country, we give thanks every day."

That humbled me. There's a lesson there for all of us.

Back at the Hotel, President Zia descended upon me in all his fury with full entourage, something totally unheard of. How dare I not obey the doctor's orders and stay put? What did I mean, behaving like this when I was not well?

I appreciated his concern. He was right. I didn't feel any better when I got down to Karachi, on the ocean, so it wasn't the altitude. I was supposed to stop in the Philippines for a dinner with President and Imelda Marcos, but I had to cancel. I was just too sick. I flew straight back to Washington.

I delivered the documentary, which has been shown all over the world. In it, I visit children maimed by picking up bombs shaped like toys, dropped by the Russians. Some have lost hands, some have lost legs.

You see me addressing hordes of Afghan refugees. They are not clamoring for food. They want to fight. They want guns to shoot down the helicopters. (Now, they seem to be getting them.)

The documentary shows my visit to a large group of girl students. Led by one of them, they chorus in unison, "When I grow up, I will only marry a man who will kill the Russians."

Our government is far behind Madison Avenue. Charlie Wick made better use of movie people than anybody else. But I don't agree with everything Charlie Wick does. The *New York Times* called me once when they were investigating him for taping telephone conversations. "Did Mr. Wick say this and this?" And they repeated verbatim the things that I had said to him over the telephone. He thought this was an easier way to keep track of his conversations. If he had just *told* me he was taping, it would have been all right with me. I don't think he was spying on me. What's to spy on?

I left documentaries and went back to feature films. I returned to Israel for the third time in 1982 to make *Remembrance of Love*. It's about a Jew, now living in America, who goes to a convention of Holocaust survivors hoping to find the girl he was in love with and was separated from in World War II. My son Eric played me as a young man, with great restraint and much depth. We had no scenes together, but it gave me a nice feeling to be working in the same film with him.

Eric is my youngest son, very high-strung, which he says he inherits from me. He is extremely bright—too bright. Years ago, I learned never to argue with him. His mind works too fast. After graduating from Claremont College, Eric studied at both the Royal Academy of Dramatic Arts and the London Academy of Dramatic Arts. Eric has a great facility for languages. He just finished a movie in Paris—acting in French. Eric adapts quickly. He was very comfortable in Israel, made many friends, and began to learn Hebrew.

I was warned not to go to Israel to make a movie. It was dangerous. There was a war going on in Lebanon. Somehow, one felt deceptively safe in Israel—but sad. Each day in Tel Aviv, we saw helicopters bringing in wounded Israeli soldiers.

I went to visit them at the Tel Hashomer hospital. There were also wounded Lebanese and Syrian soldiers getting the same treatment, while a guard stood at the door. The Israeli woman in charge of our visit was very charming and compassionate. Her only son had been killed the first week of the war.

American marines landed in Beirut. After much prodding, I succeeded in getting the Israelis to fly me to Beirut. We drove down to the seaport. The marines were cordoned off in one section of the port. I finally got through and enjoyed talking to our marines. And they seemed glad to see an American.

The next weekend, Anne and I were driven to the Bekha valley, a long, arduous trip. We visited an Israeli tank unit camped in the camouflage of an olive grove. They took me for a ride in one of their special tanks, the Mercava, extremely effective in the battles against Syria. They even let me drive it for a few minutes. We drove to a town on the mountainside and looked down into the beautiful Bekha Valley.

They gave me binoculars and pointed out the various installations. "That's the PLO headquarters."

"PLO?" I said.

"Yes, they made a raid in this town last night." I was glad to get back to Tel Aviv, gladder still to get back to the United States.

Peter came to me with a book. "Dad, here's a role you're

too *young* to play." He always knows how to handle the old man. The book was *Amos,* by Stanley West. Amos is a character in his eighties who ends up in a nursing home after his own injury and the death of his wife in a car accident. As Amos's injuries heal and he becomes more aware of his surroundings, he realizes that the home is being run by a greedy nurse who is killing off the patients for the insurance. After the nurse beats the woman patient Amos has become involved with, he decides to do something about it. Knowing that he is now terminally ill with cancer, he arranges his death so that it will reveal the nurse's guilt.

I hired researchers to find out what was really going on in nursing homes. I got a report with footnotes. What was in it scared the hell out of me. Nursing homes had changed a lot since my mother spent the last seven years of her life in one. I had to tell somebody. I wrote an editorial, which ran in the *New York Times* on Tuesday, August 20, 1985. Then, at my expense, my staff and I flew to Washington, D.C., and I testified before Congressman Claude Pepper's Select Committee on Nursing Homes.

Amos aired on Saturday, September 28, 1985, on CBS. It was the first day of the new season; the networks gave it everything they had. NBC had the first showing of *Tootsie,* the Academy Award winning movie with Dustin Hoffman in drag and Jessica Lange in love with him. Ironically, ABC threw in with *Rambo: First Blood.* If I had been in it, I would have been competing against myself. We knew *Amos* would finish in the cellar, we just hoped it wasn't by a disgraceful margin.

It was a huge margin. But *Amos* finished *first.* Grant Tinker said that *Amos* changed the networks' thinking about movies. Why should they pay $17 million for the television rights to *Tootsie* when they could make *Amos* for $2.5 million?

The picture, the editorial, the congressional appearance had hit nerves. I received floods of mail. Some of the letters were from nursing homes, telling me that I didn't know what I was talking about, that good nursing homes outnumbered bad ones. I wish I could have shown them the other letters I got—horror stories from people with relatives in nursing homes. Some letters had to be turned over to state officials, or the police. They were really heartbreaking. I tried to answer all of them. It was like writing hundreds of condolence letters. In many cases, people thought that I, personally, had the power to fix whatever was wrong. I wish I had a magic wand, too. I may be Spartacus, but I am not Superman.

Thirty-nine

TOUGH GUYS

All my life, I had wanted to be a star on the American stage. I hadn't succeeded; I felt like a failure. Always on the lookout for a good play, I finally found one: *The Boys in Autumn,* a two-character play by Bernard Sabbath. I played Tom Sawyer, to Burt Lancaster's Huck Finn, fifty years after Mark Twain left them. There had been tragedies in our lives: Huck had mercifully killed his terminally ill wife; Tom was fixated on Becky Thatcher to the point that every time he saw a little girl who reminded him of Becky, he had to touch her. I played the banjo and sang a song called "Oh Tell Me, Pretty Maiden." I enjoyed it. We did the play for six weeks in San Francisco, but didn't think it was ready for Broadway. Two years later, George C. Scott did it on Broadway. It was a flop.

Burt and I teamed up again as presenters at the 1985 Academy Awards. My son Michael, one of the hosts, introduced us. They showed a portion of the song-and-dance routine Burt and I had done on the Academy Awards in 1958. In the audience at the 1985 Academy Awards were two young writers, James Orr and James Cruikshank. They looked at each other, struck by the same thought: "I'd like to see these two in a movie again." So they wrote one—*Tough Guys*.

The story of two robbers who get out of jail after sharing a tiny cell for thirty years and decide to "do it right this time" —not go clean, but perfect the botched robbery that landed them in jail—was perfect for Burt and me. The executives at Disney thought so, too.

But how to make it happen around the usual problems of schedules, differences of opinion? While the script was being revised, Burt went to work on a picture in Mexico. I went to Washington, D.C., to testify before Congress about abuse of the elderly. Then there was another picture Burt wanted to do in Europe.

It looked like the whole thing was going to fall apart. Disney was unhappy; they'd lost almost a million dollars in developing the project. But we hung in, managed to get everything ironed out.

The picture was fun to work on. It was good to work with Eli Wallach, Alexis Smith (looking stunning), Charles Durning, and two newcomers—ravishing Darlanne Fleugel as my girlfriend, and pixieish and tremendously talented Dana Carvey as our parole officer. Dana went straight from *Tough Guys* to "Saturday Night Live," where he created "Church Lady," among other brilliant, original characters.

We shot a scene in a disco, slam dancing. A lot of people were surprised "How'd you learn to dance that way?" I didn't know what they were talking about. I didn't rehearse anything. The music played, and I saw the other people, and away I went. You know, arms swirling, bodies wiggling, punching and kicking.

The only scene that was really difficult to shoot was the one where I run on top of the train and moon Charles Durning, the cop pursuing me in a helicopter. It wasn't difficult for me to do physically; I'd been on the tops of moving trains before. No, the problem was that the insurance company

would not insure this particular scene. And the studio refused to be responsible. Why were they so unreasonable? I
was only sixty-nine years old.

Jeff Kanew, maybe the most dedicated director I have ever
known, assumed all liability himself. He didn't tell me until
after the scene was shot. I said, "Jeff, do you know what kind
of a risk you were taking?" He nodded. If anything had gone
wrong he would have been ruined. Just as I would have
been ruined twenty-eight years earlier when I personally
guaranteed completion of *The Vikings*.

But the very best thing about the movie was the credits. A
surprise gift, a pat on the back, from Jeff Kanew, right there
on the screen. I couldn't believe my eyes:

Creative Consultant   *Issur Danielovitch*

It was the first time Issur had ever gotten public acknowl-
edgment for anything.

Forty

MUSIC BOX

Sunday, August 3, 1986. I didn't do much all day, took it easy. I was thinking about *Tough Guys*. I'd done some loop lines that week, and was looking forward to the opening at the end of September. I played a little tennis, watched TV, lolled around. A shave and a shower, and I was ready for our dinner date at Chasen's.

Anne and I pulled up to the restaurant a few minutes past seven-thirty, found the usual coterie of fans waiting. A young boy, couldn't have been more than ten, came up and asked for my autograph. Not far away, I saw two people who looked like his parents. I wondered if the kid really knew who I was, or if it was the parents who wanted the autograph. I signed a couple more autographs, and we entered the restaurant.

Ronnie, the head waiter, escorted us to the table where Mark Goodson and his ex-wife, Suzanne, were waiting for us. I shook hands with Mark as Anne said hello to Suzanne. I leaned over to kiss Suzanne on the cheek.

A sledgehammer smashed me in the head. The room was

spinning. I was dizzy, broke out into a sweat. Everything reeled nauseatingly; I didn't know where I was, up or down. My knees wouldn't hold. From somewhere, I heard Suzanne saying, "Here. Just lean over and relax, Kirk." I could vaguely see Mark, absolutely petrified and immobile. Anne immediately rushed to my side. I mumbled, "Take me home. Take me home."

They helped me into the lobby by the front door and laid me down on a couch. Curious people began to gather. The busy hour at Chasen's, now busier.

I felt miserable. A man bent down over me—"I'm a doctor." Somebody had gotten him out of a party in the room next door. He took my pulse, muttered, "My God, it's way below forty, close to thirty." Then he looked at me strangely and said, "Now, don't be afraid."

I looked up at him. "No, I'm not afraid." Something told me just to be very calm.

Suddenly I heard sirens—a fire engine with paramedics, tailed by an ambulance. They rushed in, started to work on me, taking my blood pressure, my pulse, shooting needles into my veins.

"No, no. Just take me home."

"We can't do that. You've got to go to the hospital."

People coming in for dinner were greeted by policemen, paramedics, firemen, all grouped around somebody on a couch in the lobby.

So many people were working on me, I couldn't feel what they were all doing. Finally, they lifted me onto a gurney, wheeled me out the door—right past the people I had been signing autographs for only minutes earlier. I wondered, "What do they think of Spartacus now?" and covered my face with a napkin. Maybe if I couldn't see them, they couldn't see me. The ambulance headed for the hospital, lights flashing and sirens blaring.

Inside the ambulance, they kept giving me something intravenously, reporting to the hospital on the telephone. The thought kept going through my mind: "I've seen this before.

I've done this scene. But this is not my movie. I want to get out of this."

I heard someone say, "Is he dead?"

The Cedars-Sinai Hospital emergency room was only minutes away. I was soaked with sweat. Nurses wriggled me out of my shoes, socks, pants. Young doctor—"Do you have any chest pains?" "No." "Feel any paralysis in your left arm?" "No." One of the nurses—"Can I cut your shirt?" I nodded. She ripped through my Turnbull & Asser shirt with a scissors, mopped the puddle of cold sweat on my chest. I looked up—my doctor, Rex Kennamer. How did he get here so quickly? How long had this been going on? His associate, Dr. Jeff Helfenstein. Rex—"Adrenalin." Then, "Heartbeat, thirty." Rex—"Give him another Adrenalin." Three shots altogether. Behind all this, Anne's huge blue eyes fixed on me.

Things quieted down. They pushed me down the hall on the gurney. I looked up at the ceiling—white, lights going by. "Wait a minute, I've seen this scene. But this isn't my movie. Get me out of this movie."

And then I was in one of the small rooms in Intensive Care, attached to an electrocardiograph hooked up to a monitor—a strange place for a man in perfect health. That's what I'd been told just two days earlier after a week of extensive physical examinations—electrocardiogram, blood tests, urine tests. I was so proud. I'd done better on this stress test than on the one eight years earlier. I've always worked out every morning for fifteen minutes with Mike Abrums, my trainer for the last twenty years—didn't smoke, hadn't had any alcohol at all for several months. I was rather vain about people saying, "Kirk, you don't look more than fifty." And here I was, sixty-nine years old, watching the design of my heartbeats on a TV screen and wondering what the hell had hit me.

A month before, I'd had a similar experience in New York. We were all at dinner at "21," Frank and Barbara Sinatra hosting. I was sitting between Barbara Sinatra and Greg Peck. During the meal, Barbara suddenly didn't feel well, and went home. Shortly after that, Greg disappeared. The next day he said he thought he had had too much to drink. I was feeling fine; I stayed.

People make jokes about me because I usually go to bed early. If people stay late at my house, I just put my pajamas on. Once, at a party, the guests came upstairs and carried me out of bed. One evening we had a dinner party for Henry Kissinger, back from his first secret visit to China. He had just reported to President Nixon at San Clemente. The guests were enthralled as Henry recounted the events of his trip. It was after midnight. I flicked the lights on and off. Henry said, "Yes, maybe it's getting late." The party broke up. Anne was mortified.

But that night in New York, Frank laughed when I said, "Tonight, let's stay out past ten-thirty." After dinner, we all went to Jimmy's, a night spot with drinks and lovely music, old standbys—Gershwin, Cole Porter's "Night and Day." That brought back memories. I turned to Anne. "Let's dance." She looked at me as if I were crazy; we hadn't danced in years. We got up on the floor. Just as we started to dance, I became dizzy, and developed a splitting headache. I started to crumble. Anne needed help. An alert waiter came over and helped me back to my seat. Frank assumed that I had been drinking too much, but I hadn't had anything to drink at all.

They helped me out into a waiting cab. The driver recognized me. "Oh wow! The Champion! Wait until I tell my wife who was in my cab!" I threw up into a napkin I still had in my hand from the nightclub. The driver's saying, "Boy, I loved *Spartacus!*" and I'm puking in his cab.

At the hotel, I went to bed, feeling very weak. The next day, we analyzed the whole thing as food poisoning. I felt better and went off to co-host the Liberty Weekend Central Park concert with Angela Lansbury and Zubin Mehta.

The feeling at Chasen's had been much more intense. And this time it definitely wasn't food poisoning: I hadn't had a chance to eat or drink anything. So what was it?

Lying in Intensive Care, my head tilted slightly to the left, watching the TV monitor, the heartbeats, I tried to piece it all together. Two similar experiences. What did they mean? Anne had left. The doctors had told her to go home, it was the best thing to do, I was all right and in capable hands.

Eleven-thirty at night, the door opened—Anne. At home, she was worried; she wanted to see if I was all right. She had Fifi, our maid, drive her to the hospital. Anne asked me how I felt. I said, "Hungry." She looked startled. I said, "Well, all I had was half a Cobb salad at the Beverly Hills Tennis Club for lunch, and we never did have dinner." Anne and Fifi went out to get me something to eat.

They returned with a big carton of matzoh ball soup from Greenblatt's Delicatessen. I ate most of it. Then they went home. I lay in bed, thinking about how you fool yourself. Then life catches up with you, and you're in a hospital. Anne had always said to me, "Look how lucky you are, Kirk. You've never had a serious operation. When you go to a hospital, it's to visit someone else." I dozed on and off.

In the morning, I was still bewildered by everything that had happened, still felt punk—very different from the day after my New York experience. It was reassuring to see the TV monitor going along with my heartbeats.

Anne came back early with Peter. She had called the boys the previous evening, before they found out about it some other way. It would be in the papers. You can't leave Chasen's in an ambulance on Sunday night without somebody knowing about it.

Peter stayed with me for a while, tried to cheer me up. He had meetings for A Tiger's Tale, the first picture that he was going to direct, a May-December romance starring Ann-Margret and C. Thomas Howell. He'd also written the script and was producing. He said he'd come back that afternoon.

Then Dr. Kennamer came in with Dr. Peterson, a very distinguished-looking doctor from India, a specialist in cardiac arrhythmia—irregular heartbeat. Dr. Kennamer explained that something must have happened suddenly to cut off my heartbeat or to lower it drastically. With all circulation cut off, I had no blood going to my head, which caused the dizziness and headache and numbness in my legs. Rex Kennamer confirmed that my heartbeat had plunged to thirty from the normal seventy-two, and said, "I've never seen anything lower." That scared me.

Dr. Peterson rubbed the carotid artery in my neck, the one that carries blood to the brain. He pressed it. Anne and Dr. Kennamer had their eyes glued to the monitor. He kept pressing it and I felt that unpleasant wooziness coming over me again. He said, "Cough. Cough." I coughed.

He said, "See? That's exactly what I thought."

He showed me the printout of my heartbeat, regular until he squeezed off the circulation. Then the heartbeat stopped. The jagged line on the paper was one long straight line. The problem was that when he had released the artery, my heart was slow starting to pump blood again. That was why he had asked me to cough.

Suddenly I heard the word "pacemaker." That got my blood flowing. *A PACEMAKER?!* What were they talking about? Pacemakers were for other people, old guys. Not for me. They explained again that the natural pacemaker that we all have in our hearts worked sluggishly in my case, did not respond quickly enough to get the heart pumping blood when it went down, that my pulse rate was always lower than it should be.

I said, "Now, wait a minute. You mean you want to cut my chest open and put a piece of metal inside my heart?"

They laughed. "No, no, no. It's nothing like that. A pacemaker is a wonderful technological invention. It's smaller than half a pack of cigarettes, and about as thick as three half dollars. We place it under the skin with wires going down a vein into your heart. It's just a slight bulge on top of the pectoral muscles, on either the left or right side of the chest. We can set it to any speed we want. If your pulse rate ever goes lower than that point, the pacemaker kicks in—it stimulates your heart with an electrical impulse to get it beating again."

I was really depressed.

Dr. Peterson said, "Why are you so unhappy? You should be happy?"

I looked at him as if he were crazy. *"Happy?"*

"Yes. Of all the things that could happen to you, if you're going to have something go wrong, this is the best thing that could happen to you.'"

"I thought maybe it might be something wrong with an artery, and you could just clean it out."

"That would be terrible. That would mean you have a defective heart, and you would always have that problem. But your heart is in perfect condition. All the veins that lead to it are in perfect condition."

"Are you positive this is what I need?"

"Yes, this is what you need."

I looked at my wife, and thought, Jesus. Or Jehovah. Or whoever I should be addressing. My body had failed me. What a terrible, terrible thing! I had to have a foreign metal object inside my chest, wires going through a vein into my heart. "I don't want it!"

"What is your alternative? Would you like to have that happen again?"

"Have what happen?"

"What happened when you were in Chasen's. What happened when you were in New York."

I couldn't answer.

"Mr. Douglas, suppose that happened when you were in an automobile. Your wife would be frightened to have you drive alone. Or worse yet, suppose other people are in the car and that happens? Because you never know when it could happen again."

That jolted me. "I have no alternative?"

He laughed. "That's right."

"O.K. When can we do it?"

"Whenever you'd like."

"Today."

It was now Monday afternoon. "That's not possible."

"Tomorrow?"

"Let me see what I can do."

They went off, leaving Anne and me alone in the room. I took her hand. I felt sorry for Anne. Sometimes it's easier to go through something than to be standing by seeing the person you love go through it.

A Dr. Webber came in, said he was going to perform the operation, had arranged an operating room for eleven o'clock the next morning. He seemed like a nice man.

I kept saying, "Are you sure this is what I need?"

Like everyone else, he told me what a wonderful thing it was, that I'd function much better after the operation. Another member of the Pacemaker Propaganda Society. I almost began to feel sorry for the people without them.

As he left, I said, "Doctor, please take care of yourself tonight."

He said, "Oh, I will, because tomorrow's a very important day for me."

I looked at him with gratitude.

"Yes," he said. "It's my thirtieth wedding anniversary." And off he went.

Peter came back, quite excited about the whole thing. Peter always was intrigued with computers. "Dad, this is an amazing kind of computer. It's one of the wonders of modern science. Any adjustments that have to be made to this little pacemaker computer are done from the outside with a magnet which can lower the rate of . . . "

"Goody-goody, how lucky I am! Peter, if I wanted a computer, I'd buy one and put it on my desk." But we tried to be cheerful about it, and went through the day. My wife was so wonderful. How the dividends of thirty-two years of marriage paid off! How awful it would be not to be with someone who really loved you, who really felt your pain, who was really with you. I would tell my wife not to come to the hospital early, but she'd be there. I'd tell her she didn't have to stay with me for lunch, but she'd stay. Finally, I had to kick her out by saying, "Listen, I'd like to be alone and read a little bit." I knew she had many things to do. And then she'd come back again, bringing with her from home the whole meal that Fifi and Concha had made for us. We talked; I wished that the operation was earlier than 11:00 A.M., because from midnight on I could not eat or drink anything.

Anne finally said goodnight. I tried to pretend that I was fine. But as my wife always says, I'm the worst actor in the world. Anyone can easily see how I'm feeling. So she went away feeling sad. I called her later at home, to try to reassure her. I thought how awful it is to be waiting, for her to be going through all this. I asked for a sleeping pill, tried to push everything out of my mind, dozed.

Then I heard Issur, muttering deep down inside me. "Remember what Ma said when she was dying? 'Don't be afraid. It happens to all of us.'"

I was suddenly awakened at three in the morning. Somebody came in to fill my water pitcher. Even groggy, I thought, That's odd. They woke me up to fill a water pitcher. I'm not supposed to drink any water. Of course, it was just someone curious to look at me. Several times while I was there, various hospital people would find some excuse to come into the room, to take something out or bring something in. The woman taking blood from my veins turned out to be Russian. She'd seen *Spartacus* in Leningrad, and her daughter was going to be an actress.

But morning finally came, and of course, so did Anne. This was the worst part, the waiting, waiting for the unknown. About ten-thirty they wheeled me out of the room. A friend of Peter's, Dr. Rothman, an anesthesiologist at the hospital, was there. I asked him to please take Anne to the coffee shop while I was in the operating room, because otherwise she would just sit in my room and wait. He agreed to do it; I was grateful. They walked with me to the elevator, and then they had to leave when they took me upstairs. Again, in the elevator, it was all like a movie. I can't get over how I kept thinking, "I don't like this movie. I don't like it at all."

I came to on the table. I could see the anesthesiologist behind me, equipment with dials and lights. I could feel them working on me, trying to push something into my chest, pounding it in. I thought, my God, he's having a terrible time of it. Later he told me it was just the muscles reacting to the pressure of the pacemaker.

It was over. They wheeled me into the recovery room, a large room cluttered with lots of equipment and four other people in various comatose states, recovering from operations, each assigned to a nurse. I asked my nurse if she'd do me a favor—call my room and tell my wife that I was in the Recovery Room, and that I was hungry. If Anne heard that, it would make her feel that everything was fine. Soon after that, they wheeled me down. Anne was waiting with a sandwich, which I ate gladly.

By now I felt as though I'd been in the hospital for two weeks; it had been two days. I wanted to go home right then. But they had to monitor me for a couple of days. I got up, walked a little bit. But it was as if I was paralyzed on my left side. I was afraid to move, because the doctor had said not to make any strenuous movements until everything was set and healed. Peter kept my spirits up. And of course, Anne. Anne was always there. Such a warm feeling. A wife is the person you want with you when you're in Intensive Care. I felt sorry for people who didn't have someone like that. I guess that's what love and marriage are all about—you develop, you go through many things over a period of years. I thought of all my wife had endured, always with such grace and strength. Now suddenly, here I was. And I thought, maybe this is the reason for marriage, there comes a time in your life when you *know* that you are not *alone*. Whooo, what a gratifying feeling that was.

They gave me a booklet about pacemakers. I wondered if my electric blanket would cause me to short circuit. Would I die on my annual fishing trip to Alaska if I came too close to the aurora borealis? The doctor assured me that I wouldn't. He told me he'd come by on Monday morning to take out the staples and see if it needed any alterations. Like a tailor.

I stuck it out in the hospital for one more day. They moved me from Intensive Care to another room, still with a monitoring system, but this time with a radio pack that I carried in my pocket. I started to move around more. It was like being wired for sound for a movie. Once I stood up and the wires came out. The heartbeat turned into a straight line, which would happen if somebody was dead. A herd of nurses came stampeding in, to find me standing, perfectly fine, but disconnected. They hooked me up again. Or I'd wander down the hall too far, out of range, and somebody would come running after me, because there again, nothing registered.

The next morning, my wife took me home—and my pacemaker. Somehow, I'd been hoping to leave it behind at the hospital. But this was reality—it goes where I go. For the rest of my life, I will have inside of me this little computer that sends impulses to the heart as soon as the heartbeats go lower than fifty. Then an awful thought hit me: what happens when you die? I was glad that I had decided to be cremated; I couldn't stand the idea of my corpse lying underground, this machine sending little electrical impulses to my dead heart for years, until the battery ran down.

Several weeks later, I had it checked out again. I went to the doctor's office at four o'clock. There in the waiting room sat my friend Burt Lancaster. We smiled. It was ironic—the two tough guys. Burt had had a heart operation a few years before, bypass surgery. They called us in at the same time. Burt went into one cubicle, I went into another. I saw Burt's voluminous medical file on the door, and wondered what was happening with my friend on the other side.

These feelings are all new to me. And difficult to deal with. I get angry at these reminders of mortality. Everybody else gets older. I don't. I'm the Ponce De Leon who *found* the Fountain of Youth. And suddenly you realize it isn't so. Everybody is vulnerable. You adjust. But still, it's hard. I can't even say the word "pacemaker." When I have to talk about it, I call it my music box.

Forty-one

December 9, 1986. What a terrible day. My seventieth birthday. Somehow, my sixty-ninth didn't seem so bad. But seventy . . . I felt as though I had crested the top of a high hill, and was now galloping into the setting sun. It really depressed me.

I was in London with Anne, at the Berkeley Hotel. I was shooting a miniseries, "Queenie." It seemed as if every newspaper, every TV show kept blasting, "THE BIRTH-DAY OF KIRK DOUGLAS. HE IS SEVENTY YEARS OLD." I shuddered. I couldn't even hide behind alcohol. I never drink during the making of a picture.

At the end of the day, I went straight back to the apartment. Many people had offered to have birthday parties for me. "Honey, we're going to stay in. Let's just tell all of them we're engaged. I want this birthday to pass away as quietly as it can." I got into my pajamas and robe, built a fire in the fireplace. We were just going to have a little dinner, and quietly wait for the day to end.

A knock on the door. I opened it. Nobody there. But on the carpet outside the door, a gift. A package containing a small bottle of vodka, and caviar. It had been sent by my son Eric, who was in Paris, making a movie. How thoughtful of him to remember! And how ingenious of him to arrange to get it to me.

A minute later, another knock. A message slipped under the door. I read it. It was rather cryptic. It referred to things that Eric and I had said. The last line was, "Do you plan to eat it all by yourself? Open the door."

I opened the door. Eric was standing there with a lemon in his hand. He tossed it to me and said, "You always need a little lemon with caviar."

I was elated. What a pleasant surprise. The first enjoyable thing that had happened on that unfortunate day. Eric could join us, and share our caviar, smoked salmon, in front of the fire. Oh no. Eric had made reservations at a French restaurant, Le Suguet, for nine-thirty. I couldn't very well disappoint him. I had to get out of my pajamas, into my clothes, shirt and tie. And out we went into the night.

At the restaurant a couple of Eric's friends joined us. At the end came a cake with a candle, and all the waiters singing "Happy Birthday" with French accents.

I thought, "Okay, I lived through that. How thoughtful of Eric! Now we'll go back to the apartment." Oh no. Eric had arranged a table at Tramps. No matter how much I protested, he said, "Dad, they'd be disappointed if you didn't come. I arranged a table."

Off we went to Tramps. There sat Michael Caine and his wife, Shakira, and a young couple. Michael introduced us to them—a pretty young lady and very attractive young man, who stood up. I said, "Oh please, don't get up." They seemed strangely familiar. It was Prince Andrew and his new bride, Sarah Ferguson. Tom Jones came in with his son to wish me a happy birthday. Then, out of nowhere, another cake with a candle, and the whole club singing at the top of their lungs "Happy Birthday to You."

I thought the day would never end. I was so glad to get back home into my bed, cuddle my wife, and say, "My God, it's over. It's past midnight. It's over."

But being seventy has its advantages. I was outspoken before, but now what have I got to keep quiet about? While I was in London, I made a speech to a group of American chief executive officers. This is the text:

MAKE-BELIEVE V. REALITY

I feel a little intimidated standing here before such a prestigious group. If I were hiding behind the character of Spartacus, or a Viking, with a director to guide me, it would be easy. But right now, I'm doing the most difficult thing an actor can do—just being myself. I feel naked.

Because I make my living in the world of fantasy, I have a clear awareness of the difference between make-believe and reality. The line between the two must be sharply drawn. What bothers me is that when I look around, I find a fuzziness. Everywhere, I find the world of make-believe creeping into the world of reality. Turn on your TV—the Iran-contra hearings sound like a soap opera. But in reality, we know we are watching a tragedy. Pick up the newspapers—there's more drama in the Business section than in the Entertainment section.

Make-believe in entertainment serves a useful function: it gives us respite from tension and problems. In the movie *Tough Guys* that I did with Burt Lancaster, I ran across the tops of trains, and Burt and I did all kinds of things. But it was very clear in our minds that we were creating make-believe with no aim but to entertain. A very worthwhile purpose, to allow millions and millions of people all over the world to forget their problems for a couple of hours and get wrapped up in the make-believe on the screen before going back to the world of reality.

Actors, too, have to get back to the real world. After a scene is over, I don't go around saying, "Hey, I'm a tough guy." I might say, "Oh, my back aches." We're really not so tough. Yes, we've lived physical lives. But Burt is a fellow who loves opera. I'm a fellow who loves poetry. Should I say that, or will it destroy our images?

Once, while I was driving to Palm Springs, I picked up a young sailor who was hitchhiking. He got in the car, took a look at me: "Hey! Do you know who you are?" That's a very good question. A question we all have to ask ourselves.

But when these young fellows in famous brokerage houses give themselves code names, and go to secret rendezvous exchanging bags of cash, do they know who they are? Or have they just been watching too much television? If someone handed me that script, I wouldn't do it. It's too corny.

Actors should never believe their publicity, good or bad. And we must never think we are the people we portray. After a screening of *Lust for Life*, my friend John Wayne took me aside: "How dare you play a weakling, an artist who commits suicide?"

I laughed. I thought he was kidding. Then I realized he meant it. "Come on, John. It's all make-believe."

"No," he said. "Tough guys like us have an *obligation* to keep up that image for the audience."

He really thought he was John Wayne. He could get away with it, because he worked in the world of make-believe. But when people in the *real* world start to behave like John Wayne—or Rambo—they run into problems.

Now we have movies, TV, cable, cassettes. In my childhood, books were the medium. An event was having my sister read *The Bobbsey Twins* or a Frank Merriwell book to me at bedtime. The Horatio Alger stories were important to me. If you worked well, your boss rewarded you. He might give you a gold watch. In school, I remember being impressed with the story of George Washington: "I cannot tell a lie. I cut down the cherry tree." He became President of the United States, and when he was a little kid, he felt that it was so important not to tell a lie that he risked getting spanked by his father. It made an impact on me. I remember the words ringing from Patrick Henry: "Give me liberty or give me death!" Nathan Hale—"My only regret is that I have but one life to give for my country."

Children laugh when they hear those stories now. Why not? They think it's make-believe. For them, reality is watching heroes on television in living color say, "I stand on the Fifth Amendment." Is it any wonder that our children are confused?

I advised all *my* children never to go into show business. It's such a poignant trade, the chances of success so remote. The definition of an actor—someone who loves rejection.

You see how my children listened to me. They're all in this business, doing well in spite of the fact that they never had my advantages. I was born in abject poverty. My parents came here from Russia, illiterate immigrants. I had nowhere to go but up. If *my* father had been Kirk Douglas, I don't know what I would have become. Probably a polo player. But I was brought up a poor boy in upstate New York. My sons were born in Beverly Hills. And yet, I admire how they function. It's difficult to overcome affluence.

Michael produced several blockbusters in a row—*One Flew Over the Cuckoo's Nest, The China Syndrome, Romancing the Stone, The Jewel of the Nile.* I wrote him a note. He told me it's the only note of mine that he kept. No compliment; I'd written him many times. I am not a taciturn person. But the note that he kept simply said, "Michael, I'm more proud of how you *handle* your success than I am of your success." Because that shows me that in a world of make-believe, he still has a sense of reality.

Of course, if I had known Michael was going to be so successful, I would have been much nicer to him when he was young. Be nice to your kids. You never know how they're going to grow up.

Success is hard to deal with, overpowering. All of you know that. But if you know *who* you are and *what* you are, you can deal with it. Remember Popeye? Whatever he did, his only answer was "I yam what I yam." Deep philosophy in that simple remark. Not very different from Socrates' "Know thyself."

But now, everyone is running away from himself. Everybody's going into show business. The Pope wrote a play—it's going to be a movie. Everyone realizes the power of that piece of celluloid. Only people who come across on television can get elected. To be President, you have to be slim, have a pleasant smile. Black hair helps. You can't have gray hair. Can you imagine William Howard Taft, three hundred pounds, gross, running for President of the United States today? No way.

In the 1960 election, Richard Nixon's five o'clock shadow looked very bad next to John Kennedy's fresh young face. When Nixon ran again, he had professional makeup, no shadow—and all the votes. Television presents the make-believe image as the reality. And we swallow it.

Sometimes, don't you get the feeling that newcasters are not *reporting* the news, but *creating* it? Several years ago, I was in Pakistan, visiting Afghanistan refugee camps at the invitation of the Pakistan government. I made a documentary on the plight of those refugees. I watched a very well-known American television reporter doing a broadcast. Why didn't he just sit behind a desk and tell us, clearly and rationally, what was happening? No. He has to be in show business. He has to do his broadcast from the field, crouched behind a big boulder, peering up at the camera, clutching a microphone, gunfire in the background.

Such crap. The only ones in danger were the cameraman and the soundman, out in the open, taking pictures of the newsman behind the rock.

Don't you find this insulting? Commentators all must look a certain way, use that hair drier every day. Why couldn't a bald fellow do the news? In entertainment, Telly Savalas and Yul Brynner *glorify* baldness. But on the news, bald is bad. No hair, no credibility.

In the business world, too, people can be remote from reality. Incredible amounts of money can be made with numbers on computers and voices on telephones, without creating jobs or producing a product. In a product-oriented business—even the motion picture industry—if your product, or your picture is a flop, profits go down, in response to the reality of supply and demand. It keeps you grounded.

I've met nice, bright fellows in their twenties and thirties who are worth two, three hundred million dollars. That's an unreal amount of money. But it's not enough! Gotta make more! Gotta make more! Why such greed? Why do these young people, who are making so much money, have to make more? And why do they have to cheat? It would be like a kid in school with a B+ average, who cheats to get an A. Or who has an A average, and cheats to get A+. Or maybe he has A+ and he's cheating to get . . . What? What is his goal?

I understand drive. Believe me. But I do not understand what drives these men. What made Dennis Levine or Ivan Boesky or Martin Siegel choose to do what they did? With all their intelligence, talent, personality; with all the options open to them, they chose the narrowest possible path. Tawdry little men exposed in their greed.

The lack of imagination is astounding. When they get all this money, they spend it so they can live like characters on "Dynasty" or "Dallas." And they don't even have the honor of the Mafia. The Justice Department taps Dennis Levine, he sings like a canary and fingers everybody he knows.

So now he's going to jail for two years. If he'd been caught stealing in an alley, he'd be going to jail for those two years, plus another twenty. To a *real* pen, not a *play* pen. But who is more dangerous to society? A junkie stealing to support his habit—drugs? Or a banker stealing to support his habit—thousand-dollar suits? The junkie can steal only a limited amount.

What message are we giving our children? If you're going to steal, steal a lot, because the more you steal, the smaller the penalty? If you're going to steal, wear a suit? Always dress for success?

I don't want you to think that I am condemning the field

of business and assuming that we in the entertainment world are above corruption. No. My profession possibly invented it.

I used to make three movies a year. That meant that I was constantly occupied in the world of make-believe, had very little time to deal with the reality of myself as a human being, a parent, husband, citizen. I've tried to correct that. I'm still working on it. One of my favorite quotations used to be, "How dull it is to pause, to make an end/To rust unburnished, not to shine in use." I lived by it. But now, I know, we *must* take a pause. Take inventory. Make an evaluation.

What is make-believe? What is reality? Things formerly in the realm of make-believe—television, computers, lasers— are now everyday reality. Our technology is pushing us into situations where we have not yet figured out what is right, what is wrong.

The fault lies not with our technology, but with ourselves. We have to re-examine our system of education. Children must have an understanding of the past to find a vision of the future. They have to be brought up with a clear sense of right and wrong. Corporations should include in their indoctrination programs a course in ethics. We have to revive the golden rule—"Do unto others as you would have them do unto you."

My wife shocked me not long ago by saying, "I'm glad to see, Kirk, that you're beginning to think a little bit about religion." Religion? Me? I'm a sophisticated guy, even a little cynical. God lost me years ago in Sunday school when I read the story of Abraham and Isaac. Jehovah ordered Abraham to go up in the mountain and sacrifice his only son, Isaac. God was testing him. I remember the picture in my Sunday school book—Abraham, with a long beard, in one outstretched hand holding a large knife; in the other—a frightened little boy. That kid looked an awful lot like me. A hovering angel was having a hard time restraining Abraham. How could he convince him that Jehovah was only testing him? Some test! That picture stayed in my mind for a long time.

But that little boy grew up. Now, I'm at a time in my life when I really begin to think that perhaps there *is* a *higher being*.

I'm not talking about the show business religion you get on television every Sunday night. I'm not talking about Jim and Tammy Bakker or Jimmy Swaggart—high salaries, opulent homes, and sex escapades. I'm not talking about the evangelist who got $8 million out of a gullible audience so that God wouldn't strike him dead. No, I'm not talking about greed, betrayal, and bigotry.

I'm talking about the quiet inner awareness that says there must be a higher power responsible for the perfection of the universe we live in, for this beautiful setting. Now, more than ever, there is a need to believe. Am I being dramatic? An actor? No. I'm just beginning to discover things I've never thought about.

Look around. We're all successful people. Maybe we've worked harder, had more talent. But we've also been lucky, blessed by something beyond our control. As I get older, I feel the need to give thanks to a higher power. Perhaps it's best expressed in a poem by John G. Neihardt I learned years ago.

Let me live out my years in heat of blood!
Let me die drunken with the dreamer's wine!
Let me not see this soul-house built of mud
Go toppling to the dust, a vacant shrine!

Let me go quickly like a candle light
Snuffed out just at the heydey of its glow!
Give me high noon—let it then be night!
Thus would I go.

And grant me, when I face the grisly Thing,
One haughty cry to pierce the gray Perhaps!
O let me be a tune-swept fiddlestring
That feels the Master Melody—and snaps!

Forty-two

NEW YEAR

Beverly Hills is a beautiful place. Every time I come back I'm amazed by the greenery. Palm trees soar to the clouds. Beautiful houses on either side of the street, thick well-manicured lawns, overhanging trees, exotic flowers.

The most exotic and ostentatious of these is the jacaranda. In the middle of May, the jacaranda presents the world with piercing purple bell-shaped flowers. Two weeks later—four at the most—the petals sprinkle sidewalks and roads like purple raindrops. The jacaranda is the perfect Hollywood flower: it looks spectacular, but lasts only long enough to get the shot.

As you go farther north in Beverly Hills and cross Sunset, the homes become larger. Higher walls. Higher gates patrolled by TV monitors, guards, dogs. All protecting the people who have "made it" in Hollywood. People from humble origins—little towns in the South and Midwest; the Bronx; upstate New York. People who have been catapulted into a lifestyle beyond their wildest dreams. There is no school that teaches you how to deal with this kind of success.

In these houses executives get up early in the morning, go for a quick jog, rush to the studio in the Rolls or the Jaguar, hoping to come up with a hit, the magic movie that grosses a hundred million dollars. If they're lucky, they get it. This enables them to maintain their lifestyle while they scramble for a few more years before the strain gets to them—heart attack, stroke, AIDS. The mortality rate of studio executives is about the same as second lieutenants in Vietnam.

In these houses live beautiful movie stars beginning to lose their beauty. They're having a problem with weight. The jobs are not coming as quickly. They're becoming insecure, drinking more. But you could never tell from the bougainvilleas and azaleas and gardenias blossoming in the bright California sun outside the front door.

In these homes live young actors who never imagined they would have a house so large, with Jacuzzis, terraced lawns, tennis courts. They go off to the studios, filled with hope and adulation. And perhaps the noseful of cocaine they think will give them that edge against the constant competition—until it starts eating into the income and the septum. But the house looks great to the tourists, *their* noses pressed to the tour bus window, trying to glimpse their Olympian gods.

And in these homes, amid seething tensions and insecurities, is a desperate attempt to attain normality. Children are born into an environment totally different from the one their parents grew up in. The mothers carpool in Mercedes station wagons, and take their children to the best schools. The neighborhood school and Beverly Hills High are not good enough. No. The kids must go to the Thomas Dye School, where Aunt Catherine presides over her brood. After that, the boys must attend the expensive Harvard School, the girls fancy Westlake. And yet, their parents attained success going to ordinary public schools.

In this environment, children do not thrive. These children, surfeited with every indulgence, seeing stars and limousines and Rolls-Royces coming up and down, depositing other stars and famous directors for dinners, are having miserable childhoods.

Child psychiatrists do a booming business. Parents in luxurious cars bring their offspring for treatment to help them cope with—what? The tension they feel in their home from their parents? So many of the families split up. Husbands and wives separate. Children are divided between two homes.

The daughter of a television personality jumps out a window. A movie star's son shoots himself. Another movie star's son overdoses and drowns. The son of a great producer jumps out a window. The girls have abortions. Both sexes are arrested for drunk driving. Why? To the rest of the world, it looks as if these kids were brought up with everything.

Into this environment, Anne and I brought Peter and Eric. Anne became a member of a car pool. And the wife of an agent, the wife of a producer, another actor's wife would all get together and take turns delivering their offspring to the Thomas Dye School.

There at the Thomas Dye School, Eric became a friend of Ronnie Reagan, Junior. They would take turns visiting each other on weekends. Sometimes the maid would deposit young Eric at the Reagan household, and he woud spend the weekend with Ronnie Jr. at their ranch.

Years ago, right after I arrived in Los Angeles, I had a meeting with the General Electric people. Guys in shirts and ties talked to me, pitched me on being a spokesman for General Electric, a new concept at the time. I was always interested in new concepts. I didn't think, really, that I wanted to do it, but I wanted to hear their case. They made an eloquent address about me being part of the General Electric family.

I turned it down. Ronald Reagan took on the job, became the spokesman for General Electric. Did a very good job. He spoke at meetings for them. And that led him to giving speeches in other areas. He gave one very eloquent speech in favor of Goldwater on TV. He became an eloquent communicator.

One day, Eric was dropped off at the Reagans'. As he went into the house with Nancy, he saw their station wagon in the driveway, with a Goldwater bumpersticker. Eric said, "BOOOO, Goldwater," echoing a sentiment he'd heard in our household.

Nancy was incensed. She called us immediately. "You come right up here and take this boy." Eric was crying. He didn't know what the hell he'd said. We had to send somebody to bring him back.

After that the Douglases spoke to the Reagans, but relations were strained, because it was very clear to both families how each of them thinks politically.

I was dancing with Nancy at a party at the house of David May, of the May Company department store chain. Nancy was a wonderful dancer. Still is. Somebody brought up politics. Remembering the incident with Eric, I figured I'd tread lightly. I said, "Nancy, I'm not in politics. Although I'm a registered Democrat, I vote for who I think is the best man. If I thought a Republican was the best man, I'd vote for him. For example, I would vote for Rockefeller as president." Nancy's eyes flared. She turned on her heel and walked away. I was stunned. I knew how Eric felt. Another rupture in Beverly Hills. But one tries to slide over those things. And life goes on.

The kids got older. Every year the Thomas Dye School had a fair to raise money. They had an elephant and rides. They sold prizes. And all the parents, especially the mothers, were there to help out in the different booths. Most popular was the hotdog booth, where Nancy Reagan and my wife, Anne, worked.

It was a common practice for the husbands to come later and help—a chore I did not look forward to. I came to the hotdog booth, started doling out hotdogs and mustard to the public. Soon after, Ronald Reagan came in. As we were selling hotdogs, I realized that he kept cutting in front of me to hand them out. I thought, why is he so anxious to upstage me in a hotdog booth? What does he want to do? Establish a record for selling hotdogs? I was annoyed: I had worked as a waiter, and was professionally qualified to dispense hotdogs. What experience did he have? But I stayed in the background and smeared mustard on the hotdogs, and he dealt with the public.

As we rode home from the fair, Eric and Peter in the back of the station wagon, a thought hit me. "Honey, I think Ronnie Reagan's going into politics." Soon after that, he ran for governor and won.

But when Ronald Reagan ran for President, I couldn't believe it. You just don't think that somebody you've known who was an actor is going to become President of the United States. I didn't think he could make it. But he did. He really had a quality that enabled him to communicate with people. Carter lacked that quality. In general I think Reagan exuded a spirit similar to Kennedy's: he got people inspired, excited about their country, motivated. There's no doubt about that.

When Ronald Reagan was shot, it made me think about what a tough job he has. And what a tough job the First Lady has. From that point on I began to look at both of them differently, from the human side.

There's never been a time that I went to the White House that my palms didn't get a little wet. This one building is our country, filled with history going back to its birth. And it's only been a couple of hundred years since it all happened.

I get the same feeling in the presence of the President—any President. It's a terrible job to be President of the United States. It's lonely. Even when he's no longer President, I'll never be able to call him Ronnie. He's the President of the United States. Even if he said, "Call me Ronnie," I'd say, "I'm sorry, sir. You're cursed, if you want to look at it that way, but you will always be 'Mr. President.'" The President of the United States. That's the highest office in the land, possibly in the world. Once you're there, there's no going back. You're the President.

The Nancy Reagan I knew years ago has changed. I was at the White House one day for an American Cancer Society ceremony. Nancy asked me to stay and have coffee with her, even though she knew that I had not worked for her husband in the first election, but for Jimmy Carter.

We talked. I asked her how she had felt when the President was shot. I'll never forget the look in her eyes. She said, "Oh, Kirk, it's something you live with all the time." I thought, People change. Nancy's become a much warmer person. She's sincere about her campaign to end drugs. I resent the criticisms that are made of her. My wife helps me in all situations. If there's something that she can do to help me, of course she'll do it; she's my wife. Why shouldn't the President's wife do the same? She sent us a picture and wrote on it: "We've come full circle." It was true.

Every year, there's a New Year's Eve party for President Reagan and First Lady Nancy Reagan at Sunnylands, the estate of Walter and Lee Annenberg in Palm Springs, always attended by a very small, close group of Republican friends. What a surprise when Lee Annenberg called and invited us in 1986. We accepted. We were very curious to go.

We were also invited to attend a party given by the Jorgensons and the Wilsons the night before New Year's Eve for President and Mrs. Reagan. It was at the El Dorado Country Club, far from our house. Anne doesn't like to drive at night, and she hates it when I drive. I think I'm an excellent driver. She doesn't agree. So we decided to get a driver to take us in our station wagon.

We headed out for El Dorado. Our driver, allegedly a resident of Palm Springs, made a couple of turns and suddenly we were lost somewhere in Rancho Mirage. Then I saw police cars streaking by, sirens and lights flashing. I said to the driver, "Just follow that motorcade."

He looked at me blankly.

I said, "Just follow that motorcade. Wherever it goes, you go."

Very perplexed, he followed. Of course it went directly up into the driveway of the El Dorado Country Club.

There were sixty or seventy people milling about for cocktails before dinner. Someone came up to me, very surprised.

"Kirk Douglas! What are you doing here? Have you switched?"

I said, "I always thought the President of the United States was the President of the Democrats as well as the Republicans." That confused him, and I walked on.

Nancy Reagan looked lovely. She gave me a very affectionate hello. We shook hands with the President. It is hard to believe that he's been shot at, had three cancer operations, and looks better at the end of his term than at the beginning.

President Reagan was very gracious. As we were talking, he reached into his pocket and pulled out a white envelope that had a packet of some kind inside. He said, "Who stuck this in my pocket?" He started to open it.

I said, "Mr. President, do you think you should open it?" But it didn't deter him. He went ahead and opened it. And pulled out a box of Suponeral. He looked at it, mispronounced the word. "What is this?"

I explained to him. "Mr. President, those are French suppositories used for sleeping."

He said, "I can't imagine who gave me these."

I said, "Mr. President, it reminds me of what happened to George Burns. He was having trouble sleeping. Jack Benny said, 'I've got just the thing for you,' and gave him a box of these Suponerals that you're holding in your hand now. At two o'clock in the morning, Jack Benny was suddenly awakened by the phone. It was George Burns. 'Well, Jack, what do I do now? My ass is asleep, but the rest of me is awake.' "

I don't know whether that's a proper story to tell a President, but he enjoyed it.

December 31, 1986. New Year's Eve at the Annenbergs.' We decided not to have a driver. We could get lost by ourselves. Security men stopped us at the gates of the Annenberg estate, examined our tickets. The security men said that they had to take all packages, assured us that it would be delivered. On my lap was a box of chocolates for the Annenbergs.

That beautiful estate. I'd been there several times before, once to play golf on that beautiful nine-hole golf course, the tees placed in such a way that it could be converted to an eighteen-hole course. What had impressed me then was that they had a four-hundred-yard driving range. They asked if I wanted to hit some balls before I played, and I said yes. They put me in a beautiful, brand-new golf cart, and gave me a large bucket of brand-new golf balls. A whole bucket of new golf balls. Never had any of them been used. I was quite impressed by that. On the fairway, I hit the ball, then started to replace the divot. The ambassador said, "Please don't do that. The boys will take care of it." I looked behind us. Discreetly following us were gardeners who replaced all the divots and kept the fairway in immaculate order.

We drove up the long, winding driveway, lit up by lights in the shrubbery, to the beautiful house on an elevated piece of land—a rarity in mostly flat Palm Springs—with a wonderful view of the Coachella Valley.

The foyer is very large and spacious, the walls covered with magnificent Impressionist paintings. Wherever you look, a masterpiece—a beautiful Van Gogh painting, a stunning Gauguin. A Renoir. A gorgeous Monet of water lilies in the pond. And Walter and Lee enjoy them.

The party turned out to be much looser than I had expected. With all the problems of Iranscam, I expected to find much more tension. Secretary of State Shultz was there. Weinberger was there. Chief of Staff Donald Regan was conspicuous by his absence.

In general, everyone was very pleasant, in good spirits. Nancy looked ravishing, wearing her favorite color, red, a Galanos gown. Tony Rose's orchestra supplied the music. Everyone was dancing. The President danced almost every dance. He looked good for a man who was undergoing one of the biggest setbacks in his entire career, and, in addition to that, faced admittance to the hospital for a serious operation in four days.

The First Lady was dancing with our host, Walter Annenberg. When he danced with her for the second or third time, I walked over and grabbed him firmly by the arm, "You're not sharing the wealth." He was taken aback for a moment, but graciously relinquished his dancing partner. And Nancy and I danced together.

Years ago at parties Nancy was one of my favorite dancing partners. She's an amazingly graceful woman.

I took Nancy back to her seat, kissed her, and said that I wanted to make sure I had a chance to kiss her in the last moments of the year.

Then Walter Annenberg made a toast to the New Year. "Hail to the Chief" was played, and the President got up and made a gracious opening remark. "I've been in this office for six years, and yet every time I hear that music, I turn around wondering who they're playing it for." He made another toast to 1987, there were kisses all around, and the dancing resumed.

Shortly after that, Anne and I left. On the way home, we passed Frank Sinatra's house. He had invited us to stop by. But it was almost one o'clock in the morning, a little too late —for us, not for him. Besides, Anne and Eric and I would be there for New Year's Day dinner.

Anne said, "Maybe Frank will prepare one of his marvelous pasta dinners."

I said, "Did I ever tell you about the time Frank got into a fight in Las Vegas?"

"You mean the trial?"

"No, a fist fight."

"Never."

"It was when Frank was young and rambunctious. He was performing in Las Vegas, and after his act was over, he gambled, exceeded his limit. They told him he couldn't gamble any more without permission from the owner of the casino, Carl Cohen. Frank said, 'So get him.' They wouldn't; it was the middle of the night, Mr. Cohen was asleep. Frank insisted, started making a scene. So they woke up Carl Cohen. He came downstairs. Frank started yelling at him. Cohen punched him in the face, knocked out a couple of teeth."

Anne said, "Don't ever mention that story to him."

"I already did."

Anne glared at me.

"You know what Frank said—'I learned something, Kirk, never fight a Jew in the desert.' "

Forty-three

THANKSGIVING

Today, Thanksgiving Day, I'm thankful to just rest. I've spent most of 1987 working on my autobiography. It's early in the morning, six o'clock. Everything is quiet. My wife is asleep. I lie in bed, look at the bookshelves surrounding me, each book autographed by the writer to me. I read every book. My mother and father never learned to read. How sad! Oh, they learned to read the Hebrew prayers phonetically, but never understood the words. Ma, you're right, "America, such a wonderful land." Here, you have a chance. On this day I give thanks to both of you for not missing the boat.

I look up at three shelves of hardbound black volumes, the scripts of my movies, the titles in gold. They overflow onto a fourth shelf—every movie I've done, good and bad, in chronological order. Each one a piece of my guts, spilling out something from deep down inside. How many will last? The movies I liked the best were never the financial successes: *Lonely Are the Brave, Paths of Glory, Lust for Life.*

I look at those scripts. How many millions of people around the world have seen those movies? How many did they enjoy? Did they really help someone forget their problems for a while? Did they get lost in what was happening on the screen? Is it important? Has the world been altered? Is the world a better place to live in because of it? But there it is, my life's work.

Why is it that looking at those black volumes doesn't fill me with much happiness? They made me a millionaire. They made much, much more for the studios. Where is the happiness? Where was the joy that I felt when I first had a job at the Tamarack Playhouse and I played a little part, and we all worked together?

Black volumes, all neatly placed in a row, the titles in gold, and below, the year in which they were made. How much of my life did I pour into them? Was it worth it? Be careful of what you dream. It might come true. But then, you do what you have to do. I wonder how much there is within us that controls what we do in life, and how much is there beyond us that guides our destiny?

So many of the characters in those black books seem to be more real than I am. Midge Kelly in *Champion*, fighting so desperately: *"I don't want to be a 'Hey, you!' all my life. I want people to call me 'Mister.'"*

Van Gogh pouring out his guts to Gauguin: *"Paul, when you look back, so much of our life is wasted in loneliness. There's not one of us who doesn't need friends."* Poor Van Gogh—not knowing whether he was man or woman, just being driven, painting constantly in the blazing sun, producing one masterpiece after another. Where were the critics then? Not one critic during his lifetime to say, "You have talent, you are a master." Nothing. So, finally, poor little Vincent, standing in the field of ripening grain, haunted by the crows flying around him, which became demons in his mind. And then, the gunshot. He didn't succeed at suicide and was brought back to a lingering death.

In the dim light I see that very first volume on the shelf. That must be *The Strange Love of Martha Ivers*. I remember the line I said to Barbara Stanwyck at the end of the picture before I shot her and then shot myself. We were standing in the window; she was crying. The man she preferred to me was walking down the driveway. I tried to reassure her: "It's not your fault; it's not anybody's fault. It's just the way things are. It's just how much you want out of life and how hard it is to get it."

I keep staring at those volumes. One of them must be labeled *Gunfight at the O.K. Corral,* and inside must be pictures of Burt Lancaster and me valiantly walking down the street to the O.K. Corral. "If I'm going to die, let me do it with the only friend I ever had."

And then "Jack for short," in *Lonely Are the Brave.* Out of all the characters, I love John W. Burns the most. He's the one that's closest to Issur. "I'm a loner clear down deep to my very guts." Poor misfit. How hard it is to be an individual. He just wanted to help his friend. He just wanted to be himself. It's very difficult. You have to conform or the forces of society come down on you like a truckload of toilets.

I see Spartacus fighting the Romans; Einar slashing away with the Vikings; so many westerns, shooting it out, bullets flying, swords clashing. My God! How many people I've killed in movies! Rivers of blood! Is that what people want to see? I used to watch the TV reports on Vietnam and be appalled by some of the scenes. *That* was for real, not make-believe. I guess violence is a very strong part of the human animal.

Years from now, maybe my grandson, Cameron, will look at those movies. What will he think? Will he laugh? Might he enjoy my antics in *20,000 Leagues Under the Sea?* Will he be touched by the poor detective in *Detective Story,* who couldn't cope with his problems? Maybe he turns on the film for a while, gets bored, flicks a switch, and the image will fade to blackness.

Will this book be up on that shelf some day? Maybe this book will put the pieces together and present a complete picture.

I have so much to be thankful for—Fifi and Concha.

Fifi has been with us for twenty-eight years. She arrived, a young farm girl from Germany named Elfriede. Eric couldn't say her name and called her something that sounded like "Fifi." That became her name.

She's now part of the family. Often, I wake up in the morning looking for a certain pair of pants.

"Fifi, where's my brown pants?"

"I threw them away."

"What do you mean—'threw them away'! Those are my favorite pants."

"Mr. Douglas, you can't wear old pants like that."

And, of course, Anne agrees with her.

Concha is the newcomer—a Mexican woman who has been with us for almost twenty years.

I wake up on a cold morning and walk into the living room.

"Concha, *mucho frio.* Put on the heat!"

"Mr. Douglas, it's not cold. The heat kill plants."

It stays cold. She guards the plants and flowers as if they were her children.

I love both of these members of our family.

I'm grateful for my house in Palm Springs. The kitchen was the last room that we remodeled. It became an obsession with me. I was after the plumbers, carpenters, painters, cabinet makers—pushing, pushing, pushing. Now, it's finished.

Early this Thanksgiving morning, I went into the kitchen, sat at the counter alone. My wife was asleep. Peter, visiting for Thanksgiving, was also sleeping. Eric was in Los Angeles, rehearsing a play. Joel was in Nice with his wife. Michael was in New York, shooting a picture. Our yellow Labrador, Banshee, lay in the corner, looking up at me, his tail thumping the floor. I sat quietly, drinking coffee, looking out the window.

In the garden, I have a collection of statues made out of scrap metal. Fitting for the son of a junkman. They were made on a kibbutz in Israel. There's little David with a slingshot, facing the giant Goliath, who has a bicycle chain, like a bandoleer, across his chest. Don Quixote is on a rearing horse. My favorite is a stork perched on one leg, wings outstretched. I put him on top of the tennis house. I always say that when I die, that bird will fly off the roof.

Yesterday, we brought in a bronze horse with legs folded up that we placed under the tree, and he's peacefully lying on the grass. I named him Bill, after my father's horse. I feel good.

The feeling goes back more than sixty years, to when I was a little kid in the first circle of my life, the kitchen on 46 Eagle Street, when my older sisters were off at school, my youngest sister, Ruth, wasn't born yet, and the twins, Ida and Frieda were still asleep. And I was all alone in the kitchen with my mother. I felt so secure, so happy. Through that window, she saw the gold box I was born in. I want to go back. That's why I was so anxious to finish the work on the kitchen—my womb of contentment.

I remember other Thanksgiving Days—the Salvation Army delivering a basket of food to "Harry Denton," instead of "Harry Demsky," at 46 Eagle Street, so we lost out to our upstairs neighbors; the Salvation Army running out of food in the Bowery the day the Greenwich House was closed; the sumptuous dinner the next year at Guthrie McClintic and Katharine Cornell's house with Tallulah Bankhead, my first season on Broadway; the exotic meal years later, sitting on the ground in Pakistan with refugees from Afghanistan, where every day is a day of thanksgiving.

Thanksgiving is my favorite holiday, because it has nothing to do with the color of your skin, or your religion. It's just a day of trying to give thanks for what you have.

I am thankful for all my friends. How few of them one really has. How much more important they become as you get older. When I was a kid with six sisters, one of the things that I used to gnaw on at night before I went to bed was the fantasy of having a big brother. Sometimes he would give me a little money, or advice. Or a pat on the back. How wonderful to have a brother. Thank you, Jack V. and Jack T., Noel B. and Gary H. and Ray S.

I heard a chuckle deep inside of me.
"Well, Issur, what is it now?" I groaned.
"Kirk baby, as they say in Hollywood—you've come a long way."

"Yeah. Eagle Street seems as far away as the moon."

"And yet, as close as your heartbeat."

"You're always there to remind me of that."

"Come on, don't feel so sad, Kirk baby."

"Stop calling me that."

"Okay. I'll call you what you are—the Ragman's Son—who never got a pat on the back from Pa."

I thought a long time about what Issur said.

"Yeah. I guess you're right. I needed that pat on the back. It's like being denied your birthright."

"So what," said Issur. "You've done a lot in life. You gave all your kids a pat on the back. Give yourself a pat on the back."

"What are you talking about?"

"Don't you remember that song we sang in the second grade?"

I remembered.

Issur began to hum softly. "Give yourself a pat on the back, a pat on the back . . ."

He chuckled, "All together now . . ."

And both of us sang softly, "Give yourself a pat on the back, a pat on the back . . . a pat on the back."

I felt it was going to be a good Thanksgiving Day.

I am seventy years old, walking briskly to my Beverly Hills office on a beautiful day, feeling alive after my early morning work-out with Mike Abrums, who has just told me that I look better now than I did in *Champion*, forty years ago. The California sun is warm on my skin, the purple trumpets of the jacarandas are music to my eyes. I am eager to hear the response of yet another studio executive to a script I own, a picture I have tried to make for years, a role I want to play very much.

I dash across Wilshire Boulevard, wave back to some hard-hat construction workers. I answer the call of a passing taxi driver—"Hi, Spartacus!" I think I hear a timid voice say "Mr. Douglas," but keep on walking. The timid voice becomes a little stronger—"MR. DOUGLAS." I stop and turn and see a very pretty, tall, young blond girl wearing shorts.

I can spare a minute of my time for her, a fan hoping for my autograph; perhaps an aspiring actress who wants the benefit of my expertise. After all, I have lasted more than forty years in Hollywood, where stars come and go. Not bad for the ragman's son. All my life, I always knew I would be somebody. Wasn't I born in a gold box? And now, the rest of the world knows who I am, too.

She looks up at me adoringly with eyes the color of jacaranda blossoms.

I suck in my gut, puff out my chest, slap a bicep.

In a velvet voice, she says, "Wow! Michael Douglas's father!"

INDEX

Photo Credits